For Laura,
with whom I
share the joy and
value of inquiry.
warmest regards,
George

Agent-centered Morality

Agent-centered Morality

An Aristotelian Alternative to Kantian Internalism

GEORGE W. HARRIS

University of California Press

BERKELEY   LOS ANGELES   LONDON

University of California Press
Berkeley and Los Angeles, California

University of California Press, Ltd.
London, England

© 1999 by the Regents of the University of California

Library of Congress Cataloging-in-Publication Data

Harris, George W.
    Agent-centered morality : an Aristotelian alternative to Kantian
internalism / George W. Harris.
        p.   cm.
    Includes bibliographical references and index.
    ISBN 0-520-21690-3 (alk. paper)
    1. Ethics.   2. Agent (Philosophy)   3. Kant, Immanuel.
1724–1804—Ethics.   4. Aristotle—Ethics.   I. Title.
BJ1012.H318   1999
171'.3—dc21   98-44176
                                                                    CIP

Manufactured in the United States of America

08 07 06 05 04 03 02 01 00 99   10 9 8 7 6 5
4 3 2 1

The paper used in this publication meets the minimum requirements of
ANSI/NISO Z39.48-1992 (R 1997) (*Permanence of Paper*).♾

For Rachel and Jenny and Patty

Contents

Preface

My project in this book is to argue for what, subject to some important departures, I will call an "Aristotelian" perspective against various "Kantian" views. Though there will be plenty of detailed argument in the text, here I would like to provide some autobiographical thoughts that might help the reader to understand something of the soul of this book. When I was an adolescent in the late 1950s and early 1960s growing up in the cotton mill villages of South Carolina, I somehow came across Harper Lee's *To Kill a Mockingbird*. I can't really remember what possessed me to read the book, but I did; and I have not been the same person since. Anyone familiar with the Deep South at that time and with that book should know why. The experience began a process that continues to this day, a process in search of moral coherence where innocence has been lost. Much later in my life, with much less innocence and a great deal more complexity, I discovered Kant, who for a long time seemed to restore equilibrium. But innocence lost is never regained and coherence restored is always only partial and often temporary. One of the events (there were several) that crystallized my disaffection with Kant was the discovery of another work of fiction, William Styron's *Sophie's Choice*. This book has left an indelible impression on me, much of which is expressed in my book *Dignity and Vulnerability*. Reading Styron led me to think more deeply about moral luck, to the current philosophical literature on that topic, and to read Aristotle again. This led me even farther away from Kant and to the views expressed here in *Agent-centered Morality*. What does not get fully expressed in this book is how my discovery and appreciation of the work of Isaiah Berlin, especially his objective pluralism, require me to reject some central theses of Aristotle. The implications of my analysis clearly show that there are plural and conflicting values that can come into conflict in irreconcilable and tragic ways,

ways that I do not believe Aristotle fully appreciated. But I do not here show or attempt to show that there might be persons whose quality of character is both different from and incommensurable with the kind of character I think many of us want most to be like. I do think there are such persons. Nor do I discuss the Aristotelian doctrine of the unity of the virtues, a doctrine that I believe is incompatible both with the facts regarding the plurality of human valuing and with the facts regarding the neurological possibilities for members of our species. I say all this because I have come to Berlin late but can already tell that reading him at this much later point in my life is like having read *To Kill a Mockingbird* so many years ago. I just do not yet know how much Berlin's thought will affect my adjustments to a fundamentally Aristotelian way of seeing things. Perhaps in the future I will write a book that will reveal that I can reconcile what I think is right about Berlin's pluralism with what I think is right about Aristotle's ethics. Or perhaps, though far less likely, I will write a book that will reveal yet another transition of a deeper kind that leaves both Kant and Aristotle behind. Though it might seem odd to preface a book ten years in the writing with a cautionary note of this sort, I hope it reflects some honesty and some reassurance to those who find themselves involved in similar struggles to understand and appreciate the complexities of life. *Agent-centered Morality* is, I believe, a mature book, but it does not represent the end of the process or a final coherence. Under Berlin's influence, I have come to doubt that there is such a thing.

One of the special difficulties involved in writing a book is the task of defining its parameters. This is motivated in part by the simple desire to finish. But if this were the only motivational current at work, the task would be easy. One could just quit with the desire to move on. The agony begins, however, at the confluence of the desire for closure and myriad other concerns. Among them are the desires for rigorous argumentation, thoroughness of analysis, felicitous presentation, and fairness to one's rivals. Any good writer or thinker is deeply committed to all these things, and being committed to all is what makes being a writer so very difficult. Nevertheless, the one feature of a book that is not contingent, if it is to find its way to readers, is that it must come to an end. On the other hand, a book can lack some rigor of argumentation; it can lack completeness of analysis; it can tolerate a good deal of infelicitous expression; and, as we all know, it can be very unfair to its rivals. The various motivational factors involved in the desire to finish are diverse, and some are more pressing than others. Death approaches, your children want and need your affection, papers require grading, the joys and duties of citizenship beckon, and there are fish yet to be caught. So if one is to do these other things and finish the book, one must do the best one can under the circumstances. I have tried to be true to these commitments, especially regarding fairness to my rivals. Doubtless my depiction of the opposition could in some cases be more detailed. But at some point more detail regarding the thoughts of others runs against the current of the desire to state one's own. My apologies, then, where I have not dealt with others as I might were we not all walled in by space and time.

I am extremely grateful to Ed Dimendberg, the philosophy editor at the University of California Press, for his interest in my work. The production of my previous book, *Dignity and Vulnerability*, was simply superb. An author could not ask for more professional treatment than I have received from Ed and the people at California. I am especially grateful to Cindy Fulton, production editor, and to Sheila Berg, copy editor, for their excellent work.

Many others have contributed in both direct and indirect ways to the manuscript. Paul Davies, more than anyone else, has been a constant sounding board and reliable critic. Greg Baier, Larry Becker, E. J. "Ted" Bond, Douglas Browning, Keith Butler, Tony Cunningham, Dwight Furrow, Brie Gertler, James Harris, Robert Kane, James Klagge, Mark Katz, Steven Leighton, Noah Lemos, and John Sisko are all due special thanks, as are the referees for the Press. I wish also to thank Marcia Baron and Christine Korsgaard for answering some questions by email regarding their work. To my students at the College of William and Mary who have made many valuable contributions to my work, I am enormously grateful, as I am to Debbie Wilson, the department secretary, who has been an utterly reliable resource. I wish also to thank the College of William and Mary for two research leaves to complete this project. And to many others I have failed to mention, I express my heartfelt gratitude.

During the period in which this book was written, three of the most important events of my life transpired. I married my wife, Patty, and my two daughters, Rachel and Jenny, were born. It is to the three of them that this book is dedicated.

Part 1

BEGINNINGS

I think you're right, Lysis, to say that if we were looking at things the right way, we wouldn't be so far off course. Let's not go in that direction any longer.

Socrates—from Plato's Lysis

This book is about human agency, practical reason, and morality, in this order. The order is important, because the results of inquiry are often dictated by where it begins. I start then with a brief explanation of why I proceed in the way that I do and where I think it leads. I distinguish my approach from two others, one that begins with morality and proceeds to agency and practical reason and another that begins, as I do, with agency. The latter view has gained much currency among contemporary moral philosophers with the revived interest in the ethics of Immanuel Kant. I refer to a school of thought called Kantian internalism. Among the proponents of this version of Kantianism are Barbara Herman, Marcia Baron, Alan Donagan, Thomas Hill, Jr., Onora O'Neill, Henry Allison, David Cummiskey, and Christine Korsgaard.[1] The project of this school is to provide a rational defense of an agent-centered conception of morality that can be

1. See Barbara Herman, *The Practice of Moral Judgment* (Cambridge, Mass.: Harvard University Press, 1993); Marcia Baron, *Kantian Ethics Almost Without Apology* (Ithaca: Cornell University Press, 1995); Alan Donagan, *The Theory of Morality* (Chicago: University of Chicago Press, 1977); Thomas Hill, *Dignity and Practical Reason in Kant's Moral Theory* (Ithaca: Cornell University Press, 1992); Onora O'Neill, *Constructions of Reason: Explorations of Kant's Practical Philosophy* (Cambridge: Cambridge University Press, 1989), and *Towards Justice and Virtue: A Constructive Account of Practical Reason* (Cambridge: Cambridge University Press, 1996); Henry E. Allison, *Kant's Theory of Freedom* (Cambridge: Cambridge University Press, 1990); David Cummiskey, *Kantian Consequentialism* (New York: Oxford University Press, 1996); and Christine M. Korsgaard, *Creating the Kingdom of Ends* (Cambridge: Cambridge University Press, 1996), and *The Sources of Normativity* (Cambridge: Cambridge University Press, 1996).

constructed from Kant's ethics. My primary goal here is to construct an agent-centered conception that is largely Aristotelian in its structure and to argue that it is superior to the alternative of Kantian internalism.

I.

According to a long and venerable philosophical tradition dating back to the Enlightenment, morality is a normative perspective that has three essential features. It is impartial in its evaluations and demands; it universally applies to all human beings who can properly be called agents; and it is one that is rational for all rational human agents to take against alternative perspectives. A major reason that the order that begins with human agency is important is that if we proceed in this way we find that all three Enlightenment claims regarding morality are false, or so I will argue. An even more important reason is that we can discover a better alternative.

The reverse order of the one suggested here is the approach historically associated with one interpretation of the Enlightenment tradition. Because the Enlightenment tradition, on this interpretation, begins with an analysis of the morality of actions and obligations and proceeds to the morality of agents and character, it is act-centered rather than agent-centered. A major puzzle of this approach is that it quickly generates the problem of why we should be moral: Somehow we are first to understand what morality requires of us and then to worry over whether those requirements are rational. But if we are concerned with rationality, why begin with morality at all? Why not begin with an account of practical reason and see if anything resembling morality shows up within the account? The danger of the traditional methodology is that distortions of practical reason will be imposed to save the conception of morality.

This explains, then, why I think that practical reason comes before morality. But why think that a prior conception of agency is necessary for a conception of practical reason? I defend the claim that practical rationality is character-relative in the sense that what is practically rational for an agent turns on the kind of person the agent is. In this regard, we sometimes describe others as courageous, temperate, or long-suffering. When we do, we employ aretaic concepts involving self-control. On other occasions, we describe others as respectful, sympathetic, loving, or devoted. When we do, we employ concepts involving virtues that I call virtues of caring. It is in terms of the latter, the virtues of caring, that I claim practical reason is character-relative. That there is no standpoint outside character that is the foundation for practical reason I take to be a central Aristotelian point. Thus I begin not with an account of morality in terms of moral agency but with an account of practical reason in terms of human character, in terms of the integrity of human agency. I then provide a conception of morality within that conception of practical reason.

Finally, the claim that practical reason is character-relative (a point to which I will return at the end of this introduction) does not in itself deny the universality of morality, for character might be shared among human beings in a way that establishes a substantial universal form of practical reason and therefore of morality. Very reluctantly, I have come to the conclusion that there is no such form. Nevertheless, there is a conception of morality, I will argue, that is practically rational for a surprisingly large portion of humanity. Things are relative but not as relative as some relativists would have us believe. Constructing this conception of morality is by far the main task of this book.

I argue for a conception of human agency that begins with the concept of human integrity. In the process, I argue that criteria for practical rationality are character-relative. I then argue that normative beliefs, including beliefs about obligation, have rational foundation in terms of their providing solutions to what I call integration problems. Moreover, it is the notion of integrity that provides us with a test for adjudicating philosophical disputes about the nature of rational agency. This test I call the integration test. It will turn out that the dispute between the view presented here and the view of Kantian internalism turns on a dispute about the nature of rational agency. If such a dispute can be rationally adjudicated and one of the views is correct, there must be some test that selects for the better theory. It is the integration test that plays this adjudicating role. Later, we will see what this test is.

A reason for suspecting that integrity is the clue to providing an adequate conception of practical reason involves a central issue of this book: the issue of regulative norms and their relationships within practical reason. Less technically and more generally, the idea is something like the following. People care about a variety of things in a variety of ways. They love their friends, their families, and their communities; they respect, sympathize with, and esteem strangers; they are dedicated to their work and enjoy their play, and they are committed to causes, practices, and principles. All these things factor into practical reason being what it is for at least most human beings. As factors within practical reason, these various concerns take on the status of norms that regulate our thinking about how to live and what to do. Some of these norms are "partial" because they involve personal connectedness in a sense that others do not. Loving a child is a good example of a partial norm. Other norms lack this personal element and are best understood as "impartial." Respect and sympathy for strangers are usually good examples. One of the central questions of this book is, How are we are to understand these norms and their interrelationships such that they are the norms *of a person* as a practical reasoner? A very general answer is that they must be integrated as a roughly coherent set of norms. To be a set of norms that reflect personhood and practical reason they must achieve a certain kind of integrity as a whole. As such, they must constitute a *psychology*.

Another, more specific answer, of course, is to be found among the various Enlightenment conceptions of practical reason and morality, the most developed of which is the Kantian branch of that tradition. In chapter 2, I argue that to achieve the necessary kind of wholeness or integrity and to account for the right psychology, the relationships among these regulative norms cannot be hierarchical in the way required by the Enlightenment tradition. More precisely, I argue that this is true on the assumptions of our considered moral judgments.

Against some of the most recent attempts to defend an Enlightenment view, I argue that human agents must integrate the kinds of concerns they have into a manageably coherent life in order to be agents at all and that there is no way of achieving such integration through a dominant norm that regulates other norms without being regulated in any way by them. That is, the regulative relationships among norms must be symmetrical rather than asymmetrical in order to achieve integration of the sort necessary for at least most humans. If this is true, I argue, then neither impartial respect nor impartial sympathy can do the work required of them by Kantians and utilitarians. Moreover, I argue that no norm can be asymmetrically dominant over other norms within practical reason, no matter whether it is partial or impartial. The reader might think of this as a hypothesis and the remainder of the book as a test of it. On this view, the role any norm plays in an agent's life will be recognized by how it regulates and is regulated by other norms in an agent's psychology in a way that preserves the integrity of that psychology. It is from this perspective that I develop a specific answer to our question that is an alternative to the Enlightenment tradition.

The methodology I find distorting, then, is one that begins with a conception of moral agency according to which an agent is a moral agent only to the extent to which he or she deliberates on normative criteria that are in principle entirely independent of considerations of the agent's own good or particular personal commitments. Call this an agent-neutral theory, since it employs an asymmetrical regulative norm that is neutral regarding the more personal concerns of an agent's life. To be sure, any agent-neutral theory may either allow or require an agent under appropriate circumstances to pursue his or her own good, but this occurs in only two ways. One involves moral coincidence: The permission to pursue one's own good is the coincidental result of applying moral criteria in a completely agent-neutral way; as moral luck would have it, happiness coincides with duty. The other involves an instrumental necessity to the ends of an agent-neutral conception of morality: The pursuit of one's own good is instrumentally necessary to an overall agent-neutral good; duties to oneself flow from the necessity for moral preparedness in one's duties to others.

Increasingly, many contemporary philosophers share the view that human agents are surely not the kinds of agents required by agent-neutral theories of morality. They also share the view that it is a good thing they are not.[2] Some even have the view that human agents are not moral agents. Lacking in this literature, however, is any developed conception of practical reason and morality that represents an alternative to the Enlightenment tradition. What is needed is an alternative moral psychology that will supply the account of regulative norms that the Enlightenment tradition has failed to provide. Moreover, that account must accommodate what is valid in recent Kantian defenses against contemporary philosophical attacks.

While I share the view that it is a good thing we are not the kinds of agents required by agent-neutral conceptions of morality, I do not reject the moral status of our agency. What allows me to do this is a reversal of methodology, which is Aristotelian in spirit. I begin by asking what human agents are like. Is there an essential connection between the agency of any

---

2. See Michael Stocker, "The Schizophrenia of Modern Ethical Theories," and Susan Wolf, "Moral Saints," both in *The Virtues: Contemporary Essays on Moral Character*, ed. Robert B. Kruschwitz and Robert C. Roberts (Belmont, Calif.: Wadsworth, 1986), 36–45 and 137–52, respectively; Michael Slote, *Goods and Virtues* (Oxford: Clarendon Press, 1983); Lawrence Blum, *Friendship, Altruism, and Morality* (London: Routledge and Kegan Paul, 1980); John Cottingham, "Ethics and Impartiality," *Philosophical Studies* 43 (1983): 83–99, and "Partiality, Favouritism and Morality," *Philosophical Quarterly* 36 (July 1984): 357–73; Julia Annas, "Personal Love and Kantian Ethics in Effi Briest," *Philosophy and Literature* 8 (April 1984): 15–31; Bernard Williams, *Moral Luck* (Cambridge: Cambridge University Press, 1981).

particular human and the good of that human? Only after coming to a somewhat affirmative and informative answer to this question do I proceed. I then ask if there is any importance in retaining a moral/nonmoral distinction regarding human agents. I believe that there is.

If I am right about this, then all morality must be agent-centered in one very important sense: There can be no acceptable theory of moral obligation that is entirely agent-neutral. Moral obligation cannot be entirely independent of what is good for the agent who has the obligations of morality. Nor can it be completely without connection to the agent's particular personal commitments.

The connection for which I argue is this: To be an ongoing agent is not to be the agent of a principle that comes into play willy-nilly as dictated by events external to the agent's reasons for living; rather, it is to be an agent whose actions have their coherence and meaning within the agent's way of life with its own constitutive good. Being an ongoing agent, therefore, essentially involves finding life worthwhile and having reasons for living. It also involves having reasons for living one way rather than another. No way of life, then, is morally obligatory that is entirely independent of a human agent's own good. If this is true, then no individual act that is destructive to the most fundamental goods of that life can be morally obligatory for an agent.

My methodology, therefore, commits me first to come to terms with the connection between the concept of human agency and the concept of a particular human agent's own good. Only then does it allow me to proceed to questions of obligation. Moreover, it commits me to giving an account of an agent's sense of obligation in terms of how an agent's reasons for action emerge in the context of those things in virtue of which the agent finds life meaningful.

II.

If we are to think of morality as a function of practical reason and understand practical reason in terms of the integrative functions of human consciousness, we need a general account of an integrative function. For this we need a general account of integrity. I call this general account the thin conception of integrity.

The thin conception of integrity focuses on the person to whom we are willing to attribute at least four features. Here I will simply state these features, leaving developed discussion and argument for them for the remainder of part 1, beginning especially in chapter 3. The first of these features is a sense of self that is sufficiently unified to allow us to say that the person has at least one and no more than one basic "self." The second is a level of self-knowledge inconsistent with a life of pervasive self-deception (or insanity) regarding that person's basic sense of self. The third is the strength of character to meet significant challenges to that which makes this sense of self possible. And the fourth is a sense of self as intrinsically important to some degree as a separate and numerically distinct person. A human lacks integrity in this sense, then, by lacking sufficient unity of self to be at least one and no more than one person, by being unable to live with a level of self-knowledge that reveals who and what the person basically is, by lacking the capacity to meet challenges natural to a human environment, and/or by being unable to assign any intrinsic importance to the fact that he or she is a separate and numerically distinct person.

I say much more about the concept of integrity and motivate its elements in chapter 3, but it seems important for purposes of clarity to comment briefly here on the first two elements. To say that a person of integrity has at least one and no more than one basic "self" is not to endorse any strongly Cartesian views on the unity of consciousness. It may very well be true that the best explanation of certain forms of irrationality is in the notion of "partitioned" systems of consciousness.[3] Self-deception is a possible example. But if partitioning is the best explanation for such phenomena, certain conditions must hold. Foremost is that each of these systems must achieve a certain level of integration or unity within its own domain to constitute a personality system. This system then must be segregated in significant ways from other personality systems that somehow functionally relate to the same human organism. Each such system must have an identity of its own. If these identifiable personality systems are sufficiently conflicting and separate, no overall unity of personality is possible for the human to which they functionally relate. If this is true, then the human lacks the substantial unity of personality required for personal integrity. Similar comments apply if the personality system that represents a particular human's "true self" is partitioned from explicit consciousness. Such a person lacks integrity despite having a very unified personality on any particular occasion.

3. See Donald Davidson, "Deception and Division," and David Pears, "The Goals and Strategies of Self-Deception," both in *The Multiple Self*, ed. Jon Elster (Cambridge: Cambridge University Press, 1985), 79–92 and 59–78, respectively; and David Pears, *Motivated Irrationality* (Oxford: Clarendon Press, 1984).

It is important, then, to keep in mind two points regarding the first two elements of integrity. First, there must be some overall substantial unity or integration of personality for a human to be a person with integrity. This is in contrast to being a human with several partitioned personality systems with their own self-contained integration. Second, the human who suffers from serious cases of fragmented personality is not a person to whom integrity is attributable, and the same is true of the human whose sense of unity of personality is partitioned from conscious recognition.

From these observations, we can now say in general what an integrative function is. The general conception of an integrative function as it applies to practical reason is that it is a function of one's psychology that makes the basic elements of integrity in the thin sense possible. Later, it will become clear that one major difference between the view advocated here and Kantian internalism is the account of what makes such a function in the general sense possible.

Any specific, as opposed to general, conception of an integrative function would require a substantive conception of integrity. If there are different substantive conceptions of integrity that realize the basic elements of the thin conception and they yield integrative functions significantly different in their configurations, practical relativism is the result.[4] The conception of morality defended here is a function of one specific conception of integrity. I call it the thick conception of integrity.

The thick conception of integrity includes the features of the thin conception but adds others as well. More accurately, the thick conception is only one version of how the thin conception might have substance rather than mere form. This is to say that there might be many different thick conceptions that realize the thin conception other than the one I consider; hence the possibility of relativism.

The agent I have in mind is one who has self-respect and self-esteem, as well as impartial respect, sympathy, and esteem for others. These attitudes regarding others, then, express the relevant impartial norms of the agent of integrity in the thick sense. But in addition to these concerns, this agent also has a number of other concerns that express his or her partial norms.

---

4. I must hedge here. I am now only beginning to take seriously Isaiah Berlin's claim that moral pluralism is neither relativistic nor universalistic. So while I will continue to use the term "relativism," it should be understood here simply as the denial of universalism, leaving open the possibility that there are at least two ways of denying universalism, by appeal to relativism proper or to moral pluralism. For Berlin's discussion, see his book, *The Crooked Timber of Humanity* (Princeton: Princeton University Press, 1990), esp. 1–20.

Some of these involve personal love for others, including being a loving parent, a loving friend, and a loving neighbor. Finally, this agent leads a life containing a great deal of intrinsically meaningful activity, much of which is aesthetic in value and is dedicated to excellence, that is, to doing what he or she does well, where these concerns are among his or her partial norms. So described, it is important to note that there is nothing about this agent that Kantians should find objectionable. In fact, Kant is plausibly interpreted as claiming that we have duties to cultivate personal capacities in regard to all the features of the thick conception of integrity. The issue is whether he and his advocates can account for this in an acceptable way. More generally, the question is, How can an agent who has these concerns, partial and impartial, integrate them in a way that makes the basic elements of integrity in the thin sense possible? Most of this book is given to answering this question.

I argue for a specific conception of the integrative function of practical reason as it applies to the agent of integrity in the thick sense and consider alternative conceptions. In this regard, it is important to distinguish three major competitors, one of which is associated with Aristotle and two of which are associated primarily with Kant.

The first I call simply the Aristotelian conception of the integrative function as it applies to the thick conception of integrity, with the understanding that the conception is Aristotelian in spirit and not in historical detail. The conception defended here is clearly revisionary in regard to its Aristotelian origins, as is much of Kantian internalism in regard to its Kantian origins. It reflects an inclusive-ends view of eudaimonia (the good for a human) and includes the following two claims:

a. The rational grounds for practical judgments are those multiple goods in terms of which the agent finds life meaningful from his or her own point of view. (This does not mean that practical reason aims at eudaimonia, but at the goods that make up the life of eudaimonia for the particular agent.) [5]

5. Eudaimonism, like Kantianism, is very easy to caricature. It is also subject to different contending forms. If we think of hedonistic eudaimonism as the paradigm, we are bound both to be misled and to overlook the most promising forms. Most important, we are likely to misunderstand the best eudaimonistic account of practical reason. Korsgaard has attempted to show that Aristotle and Kant have very similar views on the role of reason and reflectiveness in practical reason. The eudaimonistic account offered here is meant to be plausibly Aristotelian in both form and content and different in significant ways from Kant. For Korsgaard's account, see Christine M. Korsgaard, "From Duty and for the Sake of the Noble," in *Aris-*

b. None of the regulative norms of such a conception are asymmetrical in their regulative functions.

Several comments on (a) are in order. First, although scholars debate whether Aristotle endorsed an inclusive-ends conception of eudaimonia or a dominant-end conception (which emphasizes the highest value of contemplation),[6] I do not pursue this issue here: first because this is not a scholarly book on Aristotle and second because the implications of my argument clearly rule out the dominant-end conception.[7] Hereafter, then, when I refer to the Aristotelian conception I am referring to the inclusive-ends view.

Second, some clarification is necessary of how considerations of eudaimonia enter into the deliberations of a practically rational agent. On what is to my mind a rather crass view, Aristotle's agent simply asks what is conducive to his or her happiness, and means-ends reasoning ensues. Interpreted narrowly, a passage from book 1 of the *Nicomachean Ethics* might seem to support this. There Aristotle says:

---

totle, Kant, and the Stoics: Rethinking Happiness and Duty, ed. Stephen Engstrom and Jennifer Whiting (New York: Cambridge University Press, 1996), 203–36.

6. W. F. R. Hardie was the first to make the distinction between the inclusive ends and the dominant end interpretations of Aristotle, in W. F. R. Hardie, "The Final Good in Aristotle's Ethics," in *Aristotle: A Collection of Critical Essays*, ed. J. M. E. Moravcsik (Garden City: N.Y.: Anchor Books, 1967), 297–322. Leading defenders of the dominant end view are David Keyt, "Intellectualism in Aristotle," in *Essays in Ancient Greek Philosophy*, ed. John P. Anton and Anthony Preus (Albany: State University of New York Press, 1983), 364–87; and Richard Kraut, *Aristotle on the Human Good* (Princeton: Princeton University Press, 1989). Advocates of the inclusive ends interpretation are J. L. Ackrill, "Aristotle on Eudaimonia," in *Essays on Aristotle's Ethics*, ed. Amelie Oksenberg Rorty (Berkeley: University of California Press, 1980), 15–34; Sarah Broadie, *Ethics with Aristotle* (London: Oxford University Press, 1991); and Anthony Kenny, *The Aristotelian Ethics* (London: Oxford University Press, 1978) and *Aristotle on the Perfect Life* (London: Oxford University Press, 1992).

7. The Aristotelian conception interpreted as involving a dominant end would include the following two claims:

a. The grounds for practical judgments are those multiple goods in terms of which the agent finds life meaningful from his or her point of view, and among these goods is one that functions as a dominant end. (Again, this does not mean that practical reason aims at eudaimonia, but at the goods that make up the life of eudaimonia for the particular agent.)

b. Though the norms grounded in subdominant ends might be symmetrical in their regulative functions vis-à-vis each other, the norms grounded in the dominant end are asymmetrical in their regulative functions vis-à-vis the norms of the subdominant ends.

> For our present purposes, we may draw the conclusion from the pre-
> ceding argument that happiness is one of the goods that are worthy
> of honor and are final. This again seems to be due to the fact that
> it is a starting point or fundamental principle, since for its sake all
> of us do everything else. (*NE* 1101b:351102a:4)[8]

However, I think if we consider book 1 more carefully, we need not get the
crass view.

One of the primary functions of book 1, I believe, is to get clear on the
sense of good relevant to ethical inquiry. When we find clarity on this issue, we get a much more plausible view of how eudaimonia enters into an
agent's practical deliberations, and this is important to how I am interpret-
ing the Aristotelian scheme.

The first thing Aristotle wants to establish is that the sense of good rele-
vant to the study of ethics is one that must be relevant to practical reason.
Consider in this regard the following passage that begins at *Nicomachean
Ethics*, 1096b:53. He says:

> Perhaps one may think that the recognition of an absolute good will be
> advantageous for the purpose of attaining and realizing in action the
> goods which can be attained and realized. By treating the absolute good
> as a pattern, [they might argue,] we shall gain a better knowledge of
> what things are good for us, and once we know that, we can achieve
> them. This argument has, no doubt, some plausibility; however, it does
> not tally with the procedure for the sciences. For while all the sciences
> aim at some good and seek to fulfill it, they leave the knowledge of the
> absolute good out of consideration. Yet if this knowledge were such a
> great help, it would make no sense that all the craftsmen are ignorant
> of it and do not even attempt to seek it. One might also wonder what
> benefit a weaver or a carpenter might derive in the practice of his own
> art from a knowledge of the absolute Good, or in what way a physician
> who has contemplated the Form of the Good will become more of a
> physician or a general more of a general. For actually, a physician does
> not even examine health in this fashion, he examines the health of
> man, or perhaps better, the health of a particular man, for he practices
> his medicine on particular cases.

The central point here is that even if there is a good in the absolute sense
in which Plato asserted, its relevance to ethics is questionable in the same

---

8. Aristotle, *Nicomachean Ethics*, trans. Martin Ostwald (Indianapolis: Library
of Liberal Arts, Bobbs-Merrill, 1962). Hereafter, all quotes from the *Nicomachean
Ethics* are from the Ostwald translation.

way that its relevance is questionable to the weaver, the carpenter, the general, and the physician. Why? Because the crafts and ethics are concerned with how to live and act, rather than with what is true in the Platonic sense. Thus the relevant sense of good must be one that guides or is capable of guiding practical reason. This is to say, in Barbara Herman's terms, that the sense of good relevant to the study of ethics is the one that applies to things that appear within our deliberative field, that present themselves to us as things to be pursued, cherished, nurtured, maintained, respected, loved, and so on.[9] Being clear on this, however, only tells us something about what we are looking for in the relevant sense of good. We need to know much more.

The comments on the physician are especially important. Aristotle seems to express some ambivalence about whether the sense of good should be relativized to the individual, as in the physician's case, or should be taken as good for "man" in the sense of the good for humanity. Actually, I do not believe that it is either of these, for there is another possibility. Consider the difference between the good for humanity, the good for this particular human, and the good for this particular kind of human, for example, the ideal Athenian. Taking the latter as a guide to interpretation, we can read Aristotle as rejecting as too broad (and thin) the conception of humanity as the proper subject of inquiry and as too narrow the study of some particular human. The question is how to specify the subject matter in a way that is neither too broad and thin for substance nor too narrow and particular for purposes of generalization.[10]

I take it that the ideal Athenian, for us, fails on the latter grounds. Still, we can take the reference to the ideal Athenian in another way. We can take it to mean that any study of ethics that yields any substantive results will always be relative to a way of life and to the character of those for whom that way of life is in some sense a natural expression of who they are at the core. In this sense, the person with integrity on the thick conception is the subject of the current study, rather than the ideal Athenian. And by taking the thick conception as the subject, we both leave behind some objectionable features of Aristotle's view and remedy some deficiencies. The views

9. Herman, *The Practice of Moral Judgment*, 152, 166, 168, 172, 179, 180, 181, 182–83, 191, 193–94, 196–202.

10. Aristotle shows some sensitivity to this concern at *NE* 1097B–6. There he says, "We do not mean a man who lives in isolation, but a man who also lives with parents, children, a wife, and friends and fellow citizens generally, since man is by nature a social and political being. But some limit must be set to these relationships, for if they are extended to include ancestors, descendants, and friends of friends, they will go on to infinity."

on slavery and gender are left behind, and added are the concerns of respect and sympathy for those who are not in any important sense closely connected to us. The Aristotelianism I defend here, therefore, is clearly a revised version. Unlike neo-Kantians, I am more inclined to revise Aristotle to accommodate impartial norms than I am to think that Kant can be understood or revised in a way to accommodate partial norms. The project of Kantian internalism is not, as I understand it, to be perfectly true to Kant's own project but to construct from some understanding of the categorical imperative a conception of the personal life that is rich and robust but also appropriately demanding in terms of impartial respect for self and others as rational agents.[11]

Similarly, the current project of Aristotelian internalism is not to be perfectly true to Aristotle. Aristotle was wrong about all sorts of things, as was Kant. So I will not be defending Aristotle as a disciple of some sort, devoted to showing that the master had things right. Rather, I will be constructing a conception of what it is to be a person of integrity in the thick sense that runs in the opposite direction of the Kantian analysis. Rather than fit the analysis of partial norms within the context of the categorical imperative with its perfect and imperfect duties, I argue that it is best to fit the concerns for those who are not closely related to us within a conception of our own good in the sense that their well-being is central to the meaningfulness of our own lives when we are persons of integrity in the thick sense. Much more will be said as I proceed.

The relevant sense of good, then, is one that can guide practical reason and is relative to a character of a certain sort and to the way of life expressive of that character. But we need to know more about how this sense of good enters into the deliberations of the agent in the form of eudaimonia. Here we must see how the criteria of finality and self-sufficiency function and in what sense the Aristotelian agent (as constructed here) aims at eudaimonia. I think the best way of understanding Aristotle is that practical reason aims at eudaimonia only in the sense that practical reason is guided by a sense of good that raises the issues of finality and self-sufficiency in its evaluation of how to act and to live. About finality, Aristotle says:

> What is never chosen as a means to something else we call more final than that which is chosen both as an end in itself and as a means to something else. What is always chosen as an end in itself and never

11. The most developed account of this sort is by Nancy Sherman in her book, *Making a Necessity of Virtue: Aristotle and Kant on Virtue* (Cambridge: Cambridge University Press, 1997).

as a means to something else is called final in an unqualified sense. (*NE* 1097a:30–35)

And about self-sufficiency, he says:

For the present we define as "self-sufficient" that which taken by itself makes life something desirable and deficient in nothing. (*NE* 1097b–15)

I construct Aristotle's scheme to mean that one aims at eudaimonia in the sense that one evaluates actions and their place in life in terms of the criteria of finality and self-sufficiency and that this is not to aim at some mental state (or any other state) called "happiness."[12] On this construction, finality and self-sufficiency are criteria to be employed in practical reasoning itself; they are not simply criteria employed in philosophical debate about the ultimate goal of life. Whether Aristotle actually meant the criteria to be employed in this way is a matter of unimportance to my project.

What does all this come to in regard to the agent of integrity in the thick sense? In terms of finality, it means that the agent experiences life in a way that many things appear within his or her deliberative field as good. That is, they are goods that are relevant to practical reason, things to be pursued, cherished, nurtured, maintained, respected, and loved, and they are, as such, valued as ends. However, they are final only as they appear as ordered within a life as a whole, for it is only from the viewpoint of life as a whole that the issue of finality can arise. In this regard, to aim at eudaimonia is nothing more than to attempt to see the various goods of life as ordered in a way that the choice of the life in which they appear is chosen for itself and for no further end. To the extent to which a life with its goods is ordered in a way that meets the criterion of finality it is practically rational. Why? Because it is to that extent guided by the relevant sense of good. The other criterion is self-sufficiency, which operates a bit differently than finality. Whereas finality requires that the goods be ordered in a way that makes them the proper object of final choice, self-sufficiency requires that all the goods get into the ordering, if at all possible. Nothing of importance can avoidably be left out. In this regard, to aim at eudaimonia is nothing

---

12. Aristotle seems to mean one thing by self-sufficiency in book 1 of the *Nicomachean Ethics* and another thing in book 10. In book 10, he emphasizes the notion of independence rather than the notion of completeness when he provides the divinity argument for the highest value of contemplation. The idea is that the gods, who spend their time in contemplation, are invulnerable to supporting conditions for their way of life in a way that other creatures are not. Since appeals to divinity will play no positive role in my argument or the Aristotelianism I construct, I will not employ this notion of self-sufficiency.

more than the reflective concern that every good thing or as many kinds of the most important good things as possible get a place in life. Again, it is not to aim at some state called "happiness." To aim at eudaimonia, then, is simply to employ as reflective criteria the criteria of finality and self-sufficiency in the evaluation of how to live and to act, given that we value some things as ends.

As I employ these concepts, however, I want to make four clarifications: one having to do with the concept of eudaimonism itself; one, with the criterion of finality; one, with the concept of evaluating from the perspective of a life as a whole; and one, with self-sufficiency.

Beginning with eudaimonism, I want to distinguish between what I call subjective eudaimonism, on the one hand, and objective eudaimonism, on the other. The distinction between the two can best be made out in terms of Aristotle's definition of eudaimonia, that is, activity of the soul in accordance with virtue, and how he understands the status of external goods in the life well lived. According to what I call the subjectivist interpretation, external goods are not a part of one's well-being but are the equipment one needs for living the life of virtue. Perhaps the best expression of this view is found in Richard Kraut's book, *Aristotle on the Human Good.* His interpretation of Aristotle is that external goods are not a part of one's well-being but are the equipment for acting virtuously. In some cases, this makes sense. Wealth is the mere equipment whereby the generous person can act magnanimously. But what about the people who benefit from such generosity? Are they merely equipment needed for virtuous activity? Kraut's answer is that they are not, but insofar as they are valued for themselves, they do not reflect on the well-being of the generous person. Rather, concern for them reflects an altruistic attitude toward others. A similar analysis is given of the virtues of friendship and justice. On this view, that things go badly for other people is not something that makes life go badly for the agent, except insofar as things going badly for others lessens the occasions for one's virtuous activities. Thus to say that eudaimonia is activity of the soul in accordance with virtue is to assert that there is an *identity* relationship between eudaimonia and some exercise of the self. Since external goods are not parts of the self or its activities, they are not components of eudaimonia, the life well lived.

According to the objectivist construction of eudaimonia that I want to defend, some external goods, most notably friends, family, fellow citizens, and others, are intrinsic constituents of eudaimonia itself for creatures like us. On this understanding, the definition of eudaimonia is best understood as activity of a psychology (soul) in accordance with virtue and the goods to which that virtue is attached. The virtue of justice attaches us to persons worthy of respect; the virtue of sympathy, to persons in need; and the virtues of friendship and parental love, to our friends and children. Our character, on this Aristotelian construction, attaches us to items in the world and to the intrinsic well-being of those items. If this is true, then when things go badly for those items, things go badly for us. When asked how his life is going, the virtuous person's answer will often be couched in terms solely related to the well-being of others. Contrast in this regard these responses: Things are going badly because I have a headache, I have nothing virtuous to do, my child is ill, my friend's home was destroyed in a fire, workers are being cheated out of their pay, people are starving in Africa. Notice that many of the responses on the list do not mention the self but others, but they are mentioned in the context of why life is not what it could be. Also contrast these positive responses to the same question: Things are going really well because I feel great, my child just had her first recital, my friends and I played bridge last night, the workers strike has been settled in a way that is fair to all sides, and the drought has ended in Africa. These responses, both negative and positive, are intrinsic to what it is to thrive as a social being. Now, when eudaimonia is understood in this way, the self does not dominate the understanding of how well life is going in the way that it does on Kraut's understanding of Aristotle. And it should be noted that eudaimonia on this view involves vulnerability because of the way in which one's character attaches one's well-being to items in the world that are external goods. When Aristotle says that we do not deliberate about external goods, part of what that means on this interpretation is that social beings bring certain values to the task of practical reason and with these values in place, they ask, How am I to live in a way that best accommodates these goods?[13]

The criteria of finality and self-sufficiency are brought to the task of answering this question understood on the objectivist reading of eudaimonia. Regarding finality, it is important to keep in mind that it can come in degrees. Among alternative ways of life open to an agent, none of them might satisfy the criterion perfectly. In such cases, we can speak of the way of life that is most final, the one that is most chosen for itself as an end and not as a means to anything else. This clarification accommodates the fact that

---

13. Aristotle is usually taken to be a perfectionist, but the Aristotelianism I construct here is pluralistic in that there are goods other than perfection. For a contrasting, perfectionist construction of Aristotle, see Thomas Hurka, *Perfectionism* (New York: Oxford University Press, 1993).

none of us has among his or her alternatives the perfect way of life. Also, I will understand the criterion of finality as having two aspects: the first applies to a life as a whole, that it be chosen for itself and for no further end; the second applies to the goods within the life that is chosen for itself. This second aspect of finality requires that if something appears within one's deliberative field as good as an end, then it is rational, if at all possible, to order one's priorities within a way of life to accommodate that good as the kind of end it is taken to be within that deliberative field. The second aspect of the finality criterion is not met, then, if one's priorities do not properly recognize a good for the kind of good it is within one's deliberative field. This can occur in a variety of ways: by misconstruing the value of a good as not good at all, by misconstruing the value of a good that is an end as a means only, or by misconstruing the kind of end a good is. This aspect of the finality requirement is such that a failure to meet it means a failure to meet the self-sufficiency requirement as well. The difference between the second aspect of finality and self-sufficiency is that in the former case the value of some good is misconstrued; whereas in the latter a good is missing, either because its value has been misconstrued or because it simply is not there. To take a friend for granted is one thing; not to have a friend is another. But in neither case is there a life that is chosen for itself and self-sufficient.

Regarding the evaluation from the perspective of a life as a whole, it needs to be recognized that we do not have the kind of access to our lives that allows us in any literal way to evaluate from this perspective. We have only a relatively vague notion of what our lives will turn out to be as a whole. This is why we should understand this perspective as simply requiring us to place our choices, at least the most fundamental ones, within the context of how our priorities fit within a way of life, and we do have some idea of what this is. The contrast is a decision model the rationality of which is defined independently of a concern for how things fit within a way of life at all.

Finally, there are two concepts of self-sufficiency that should not be confused. The first, which is the one employed here, is the idea that all the goods for a meaningful life are included. The second is that the kind of life that includes all the goods in the first sense is free of the contingencies of moral luck. Both the Stoics and Aristotle thought it rational to pursue a life that was self-sufficient in the first sense, but they differed on whether the life of eudaimonia was self-sufficient in the latter sense.[14] Because he thought ex-

14. There is a dispute about this among Aristotelians. Kraut takes Aristotle to put a great deal of emphasis on invulnerability on his intellectualist interpretation

ternals were intrinsic goods of the best life, Aristotle thought that we need a modicum of good luck for good living. Because they identified the best life with untroubledness (ataraxia), the Stoics rejected the value of externals and identified the best life with the life of virtue and hence immune to the forces of luck. For the Stoics, the goods of virtue are all under our control, immune to luck, and are all the goods there are in a life well lived. As will become clear, I side with Aristotle. It is only in understanding the fact that many of us are creatures with a character full of caring about externals that practical reason is made what it is for us.

To sum up, then: The Aristotelian conception first involves the appearance of things that are good (in the relevant sense) within an agent's deliberative field. The agent then considers different sets of priorities as candidates for accommodating those goods. Each set of priorities is considered as the basis for the imaginative projection of a way of life and how the things thought of as good by the agent appear within that way of life. Finally, the criteria of finality and self-sufficiency are employed to evaluate which set of priorities is rational. To the extent to which a set of priorities meets the criteria of finality and self-sufficiency it solves the integration problems of the agent. All this assumes that it is the appearance of things that are meaningful within the agent's deliberative field that generates the need for an integrative function in the first place. It makes no assumption about happiness as the goal of one's deliberations.

In contrast with the Aristotelian conception of the integrative function of practical reason are two impartial conceptions. The first I call externalist impartialism, which includes the following two claims:

a. There is a dominant impartial norm that is asymmetrically regulative of any other norms within consciousness, though there are other subdominant norms that are symmetrical in their regulative functions vis-à-vis each other.
b. The rational grounds for the dominant, asymmetrical norm are independent of those goods that make life meaningful from an agent's own point of view.

On this conception of impartialism, the demands of practical reason are pure in the sense that they are in no way dependent on the psychological

---

and takes himself to be disagreeing with Martha Nussbaum. See Kraut, *Aristotle on the Human Good,* and Martha Nussbaum, *The Fragility of Goodness* (Cambridge: Cambridge University Press, 1986). For a philosophical defense of the notion of vulnerability as it applies to human dignity, see my *Dignity and Vulnerability: Strength and Quality of Character* (Berkeley: University of California Press, 1997).

attachments of the agent. Shelly Kagan endorses a view of this sort.[15] But also there is a plausible interpretation of Kant that takes this line, for there are passages from Kant, as I note later, that suggest we have the duty not to commit suicide, even if we do not find life meaningful at all. On any view of practical reason, whether Kantian or non-Kantian, that takes this form, there is a radical distinction between the demands of practical reason and a particular agent's own good. The Kantian version of externalist impartialism I call traditional Kantianism.

The second conception of impartialism I call internalist impartialism, and it includes the following two claims:

a.   There is a dominant impartial norm that is asymmetrically regulative of any other norms within consciousness, though there are other subdominant norms that are symmetrical in their regulative functions vis-à-vis each other.

b.   The rational grounds for the agent's norms, including the dominant, asymmetrical norm, are the goods that make life meaningful from an agent's own point of view.

In contrast to traditional Kantianism, Barbara Herman, Marcia Baron, Christine Korsgaard, Henry Allison, Nancy Sherman, and David Cummiskey (all of whom I discuss later) defend versions of internalist impartialism. It is important to note that internalist Kantianism is a conception of practical reason that bridges some of the gap between the Aristotelian conception and traditional Kantianism. On this view, impartial respect for persons and their rational nature is still a dominant impartial norm, but it functions within consciousness as a dominant good apart from which no rational agent would find life meaningful from his or her own point of view with the basic elements of integrity in the thin sense intact. Later, I point out advantages of internalist Kantianism over the traditional variety. But it is the central thesis of the book that the thick conception of integrity requires the Aristotelian (inclusive-ends) conception of an integrative function of consciousness. The negative (as opposed to the positive) thesis of the book can be stated as follows: Against traditional Kantianism, I argue that all norms have their foundation in the goods that make life meaningful from the agent's own point of view. The argument for this occurs primarily in part 2, where I show that the goods of respect, as Kantian internalists insist, must be given an internalist account. If traditional, externalist Kantianism cannot account for the role of respect in our lives, it stands no chance of ac-

15. See Shelly Kagan, *The Limits of Morality* (Oxford: Clarendon Press, 1989).

counting for other goods. The remainder of the book is given to an argument against internalist Kantianism, where I argue that no conception of practical reason that employs an asymmetrical regulative norm can solve the integration problems of the agent of integrity in the thick sense.

III.

The basic contrast of this book, then, is between two conceptions of practical reason. As best I can, I want here to provide a brief sketch of the contrast. Herman has argued that one requirement of an adequate conception of morality is that the rightness of an action must be the nonaccidental result of its motive. This she (rightly) takes to be one of Kant's most fundamental points. If we combine this requirement with the claim that morality is based on practical reason, then the rightness of an action is both (i) the nonaccidental result of its motive and (ii) practically rational, all things considered. All Kantians, I think, would agree. Moreover, on the interpretation given here, the Aristotelian would as well. The difference between the Kantian and the Aristotelian conceptions of practical reason is in how they account for these two requirements and in what Korsgaard has called reflective endorsement.[16]

Consider first the Kantian account. Here some comments by Herman are helpful. She makes an illuminating distinction between the end or object of an action and the motive for an action. The end or object of an action, she says, "is that state of affairs the agent intends his action to bring about."[17] About motives, she says, "The motive of an action, what moves the agent to act for a certain object, is the way he takes the object of his action to be good, and hence reason-giving."[18] Now consider how this distinction might shed light on how the rightness of an action could be the nonaccidental result of its motive and rational, all things considered.

Imagine a case in which three people—A, B, and C—all do the right thing from different motives—A from narrow self-interest, B from natural sympathy, and C from the Kantian sense of duty. Let us assume that the right thing to do in the context is to render aid to someone in distress. A takes the object of his action to be good as a means of promoting his own narrowly self-interested goals, and it is in this sense that he sees the object as giving him a reason for action. Perhaps the person in distress is someone

16. See Korsgaard, *The Sources of Normativity*, 49–89.
17. Herman, *The Practice of Moral Judgment*, 25.
18. Ibid.

likely to benefit him in some way. Though his action is right, its rightness is not the nonaccidental result of his motive. B takes the object of his action to be good simply because it relieves the distress of someone in need, and it is in this sense that it gives him a reason for action. There is no further motive of self-interest. However, the rightness of B's action is not the non-accidental result of its motive. This is because B takes the fact that his action relieves the distress of someone in need as a sufficient condition for its goodness. But surely this is not a sufficient justification. For in some circumstances relieving the distress of someone might be wrong because of other considerations. If this is true, then B's action, while right, is not the result of full rationality, that is, rational, all things considered. It is this failure that shows that B's action is not the nonaccidental result of its motive. C, on the other hand, takes the object of his action as good because he believes that relieving distress in the circumstances is the right thing to do. This is because he believes that doing so is required by the categorical imperative, that is, rational, all things considered from an impartial point of view. Unlike A and B, the rightness of C's action, Herman claims, is both the nonaccidental result of his motive and rational, all things considered.

No doubt, the Kantian view is a very powerful one, one not to be taken lightly or dismissed with caricature. How does the Aristotelian view, as I construe it here, differ? The major differences are these. First, full rationality, on the Aristotelian view, is not achieved by an impartial decision procedure, and second, there are no norms, on the Aristotelian view, that are asymmetrical in their regulative functions. On the Kantian view, the dominant norm of practical reason is the concern that one's deliberations take a certain form, namely, the impartial employment of the CI procedure (categorical imperative decision procedure). It is the fact that deliberations take this form that guarantees that the rightness of an act is the nonaccidental result of its motive. But on the Aristotelian view there is no such procedure. Rather, norms are the various ways an agent has of caring about himself or herself and others and other things in the natural and social environment. Hence, on this view, norms are at once both psychological and ethical. How, then, does the Aristotelian view guarantee that the rightness of action is the nonaccidental result of its motive? Here the concept of integrity plays a crucial role. The most general answer is that the character of an agent of integrity is such that any form of caring is influenced and balanced by the need to make a place for the other forms of caring indicative of the agent's character. Different things appear as good within the agent's deliberative field because the agent cares about a variety of things in a variety of ways. Practical reason, then, is not the capacity to employ an impartial decision procedure. Rather, it is a complex capacity that assists a psychology in its move-ment toward the equilibrium of integrity. This involves not only means-end reasoning but other things as well. Among them is the capacity for merio-logical analysis (the ability to relate parts to wholes) and the exercise of imagination. In order to gain an intuitive understanding of this, consider the agent of integrity in the thick sense.

The agent of integrity in the thick sense is one who cares in a variety of ways, including those of self-interest, natural sympathy, and impartial re-spect for others. It is the fact that such an agent is both sympathetic and re-spectful that he is not narrowly self-interested. Hence, A (above) reasons badly because his sense of self-interest is not regulated by other concerns. The Aristotelian self-interested agent could not see rendering aid as good simply because it serves some narrow self-interest. Why? Because his char-acter is such that he cares about things other than himself, and his practi-cal reason is guided by a sense of good that employs the criterion of self-sufficiency. Remember that self-sufficiency is the concern that all goods that appear within an agent's deliberative field be included within a way of life. Moreover, this concern is at once both psychological and ethical. Thus, his concerns, guided by the criterion of self-sufficiency, do not allow him to reason egoistically, because the objects of his actions are not seen by him to be good in a way that allows for such practical reasoning. Not only is it false that actions that render aid have only instrumental value for him; they are intrinsically valued as parts of the life most worth living. This con-sideration reflects the criterion of finality. The Aristotelian agent's practi-cal reasoning, then, is one in which he is moved by the imaginative projec-tion of a life of a certain sort. Why is it that he is moved by such a thought? Because of his character, the kind of person he is, one who is caring in a va-riety of ways and whose evaluations are guided by a certain sense of good. Thus he does not act for the goal of eudaimonia in the sense of pursuing happiness but for those goods envisioned within a way of life in which they are most meaningfully secured and balanced. It is his character that makes the vision both intrinsically alluring and rational. It is not the thought that these goods are means to the life most worth living.

Now consider the Aristotelian conception of a naturally sympathetic agent. The Aristotelian agent would not see the case of relieving distress as good simply because it serves some narrow self-interest. Nor would the Aristotelian sympathetic agent see rendering aid as good simply because it relieves distress. He would be concerned that it also be consistent with all the other things with which he is concerned. That is, he would see it as good because it relieves distress and it is consistent with the respect, love, and other concerns he has. Again, this concern reflects practical reason guided by a certain conception of good. But the concern would not be a concern that the agent's deliberations take a certain form, as on the Kantian view.[19] Rather, it would be entirely because of the substance of what the agent is concerned about, guided by the criteria of finality and self-sufficiency. In both the case of self-interest and the case of natural sympathy, the rightness of the Aristotelian's action would be the nonaccidental result of its motive. This is because the Aristotelian's normative conception of self-interest and sympathy are regulated by the other norms of the agent's psychology. By this I mean that what such an agent sees as in his or her interest or as sympathetic is shaped by other considerations. Thus, on the Aristotelian view as understood here, it is substance, not form, that regulates substance. Moreover, the norms of this psychology are such that they are all symmetrical in their regulative functions—impartial respect notwithstanding.

The contrast between the Kantian and Aristotelian views should now stand out in greater relief in the way that they account for both the requirement that an act be the nonaccidental result of its motive and the requirement that a right act is rational, all things considered. On the Kantian view, agents reason from an impartial perspective and the CI procedure, and the capacity for such reasoning governs their natural inclinations, which might otherwise lead them to do the wrong thing. This perspective employs an asymmetrical regulative norm and informs agents of how their characters are to be formed. On the Aristotelian view, the reasoning of an agent is shaped by the fact that an agent has a certain core character, one that cares in a variety of ways about himself or herself and other things in the natural and social environment and is guided by a certain sense of good. This is what it means to assert that practical reason is character-relative. It is the imaginative projection of a life shaped by a set of priorities that ultimately determines how the agent sees the object of his or her action as good and reason-giving, and it is the fit between vision and character that ultimately constitutes full rationality. If we apply these thoughts to the agent of in-

19. Later I will consider a distinction between procedural constructions of Kant and nonprocedural, or substantive, constructions. I take Sherman to suggest a non-procedural understanding of the categorical imperative, whereas Korsgaard endorses a procedural view. Allen Wood also defends a procedural understanding in "The Final Form of Kant's Practical Philosophy," *Kant's "Metaphysics of Morals,"* Spindel Conference 1997, *Southern Journal of Philosophy* 36, supplement (1998): 1–20.

tegrity in the thick sense, we will get, or so I argue, a better account of the rightness of actions. Nothing about such projection, however, requires an impartial decision procedure, and I take it as a requirement of the Aristotelian view to show how this is possible.

I also argue that the Aristotelian view gives us a better account of reflective endorsement than does the Kantian account recently defended by Korsgaard in her Tanner Lectures. There she says:

> "Reason" means reflective success. So if I decide that my desire is a reason to act, I must decide that on reflection I endorse that desire. And here we run into the problem. For how do I decide that? Is the claim that I look at the desire, and see that it is intrinsically normative, or that its object is? . . . Does the desire or its object inherit its normativity from something else? Then we must ask what makes that other thing normative, what makes it the source of a reason. And now of course the usual regress threatens. What brings such a course of reflection to a successful end?[20]

The Kantian solution to the regress problem entails a view of what full practical rationality is in terms of a conception of what, on its view, is the widest possible reflective endorsement. Complete reflective endorsement is reached on this view by the employment of the CI procedure. This means that the widest possible reflective endorsement is from the impartial point of view of respect for self and others. On the Aristotelian view, the widest reflective endorsement is from the point of view of a life as a whole and how that life accommodates all the goods found by the agent to be intrinsically important (finality and self-sufficiency). This means that one cannot accept the results of the CI procedure until one can see how those results factor into a life as a whole, a way of life. It also means that should those results fail to integrate within a way of life the goods that appear as ends within the agent's own deliberative field, then acting from the point of view of the CI procedure is neither fully reflective nor fully rational. I say more about this notion of reflective endorsement in the following chapters.

IV.

Part 1 is concerned with the thin conception of integrity and the general conception of practical reason appropriate to it. Chapter 1 is concerned with methodology, especially as it bears on the dispute between the Aristotelian conception of practical reason and Kantian internalism. There I consider

20. Korsgaard, *The Sources of Normativity*, 97.

views by Henry Allison, Barbara Herman, Christine Korsgaard, and John Rawls. My goal is to show that contrary to Allison and Korsgaard, the deepest division between the Aristotelian alternative and Kantian internalism is not that of differing conceptions of rational agency (though these differences are certainly there). Rather, the deepest differences are methodological. I argue that how we understand the internalism requirement regarding practical reason turns on our beliefs about rational inquiry. This in turn leads to a different general conception of rational agency. Chapter 2 provides a sustained argument that an adequate conception of practical reason for agents like us, or at least most of us, must consist of norms that are symmetrical in their regulative functions if it is to capture our considered moral judgments. Chapters 3 and 4 provide the general conceptions of integrity and practical reason that accommodate these functions. Parts 2 through 4, the bulk of the book, are given to a substantive account of integrity (the thick conception) and practical reason that I claim applies to a large portion of humanity. Part 2 gives a preliminary analysis of the role of impartial respect within the psychology of the agent of integrity in the thick sense and is designed to put traditional Kantianism aside and to prepare the way for the debate between Aristotelian and Kantian internalism. Part 3 addresses various partial norms involving different forms of personal love. The issue at each point is how to understand the regulative functions among the agent's norms in a way that solves the integration problems of an agent who is not only impartially respectful of others but also personally loving in a variety of ways. Finally, part 4 addresses further integration problems involving intrinsically valued activities and our concern with excellence. There I consider the role of the aesthetic dimensions of life in practical reason. In each of the parts devoted to the various goods, the analysis is intended to show two things: first, the ways in which these goods function as the grounds for both practical reason and the meaning of the agent's life from his or her point of view; and second, that the integration of these goods is achieved without norms that are asymmetrical in their regulative functions. This is to say that the analysis in parts 3 and 4 is intended to show that a thorough implementation of the integration test will reveal that the Aristotelian conception of practical reason is true regarding a large portion of humanity and that Kantian internalism is false.

I turn now to a discussion of the internalism requirement and a defense of the methodological significance of the integration test for rational inquiry concerning the nature of practical reason.

1. The Internalism Requirement and the Integration Test

My concern in this chapter is with the terms of debate with Kantian internalism. Consequently, I will say little in argument against the externalist view. As I construe them here, Kantian internalism and Aristotelianism have several things in common. They both seek to provide a foundation for morality in practical reason, and they are both forms of internalism. As forms of internalism they seek to provide a foundation for morality within those goods that make life meaningful from a rational agent's own point of view. They are united, then, in their opposition to externalism, the view that an agent can have reasons for action that are not founded in the goods that give life meaning. A significant difference between them, however, is in their conceptions of regulative functions. The Kantian view has it that impartial respect has an asymmetrical regulative function within practical reason, and the Aristotelian view has it that the norms of practical reason are all symmetrical in their regulative functions.

Another crucial difference is in their conceptions of rational agency. Henry Allison and Christine Korsgaard, both Kantians, have argued that the most fundamental difference between contemporary thinkers such as Bernard Williams, who belong to an Aristotelian/Humean tradition, and themselves is that they have rival conceptions of rational agency. I argue in this chapter that although there are fundamental differences about rational agency, we should attempt to find as much common ground as possible between the two traditions, including common methodological commitments that will allow us to adjudicate disputes about rival conceptions of rational agency. A great deal turns on what one considers a rational method of inquiry in this regard. I show that there are differences on this issue that affect how one sees internalism as a requirement for any adequate conception of practical reason and that differences about rational agency are often underwritten by these differences of method.

On the Kantian view, as understood by Allison and Korsgaard and by what I call the Kantian metaphysical school, rational inquiry about human agency proceeds a priori, but on the Aristotelian approach, it proceeds empirically. In turn, this difference in method leads to a different understanding of the internalism requirement. I argue that Korsgaard's claim that almost any moral theory passes the internalism requirement is a function of methodological commitments that we should reject. However, if we accept an empirical approach, the internalism requirement will lead to the integration test as the appropriate method of adjudicating disputes about human agency, and it is questionable that any current theory meets the internalism requirement on such a reading. The central thrust of the argument is that any conception of practical reason must assign a functional role to practical reason within an overall psychology and that these functional claims are best construed in a way that render them empirically falsifiable.

This might seem to rule out a priori the possibility of Kantian internalism, but it does not. It does not because there is a difference among Kantian internalists about methodology. In addition to the metaphysical school of Kantian methodology, there is an internalist school of thought called Kantian constructivism. Members of the constructivist school want to distance themselves from Kant's methodology insofar as it is tied to his metaphysics. I argue that Kantian constructivists must accept an understanding of the internalism requirement that, when combined with their understanding of the function of practical reason, requires the integration test for adjudicating disputes about rational agency. This method, however, leaves open whether it is some constructivist version of Kantian internalism or Aristotelian internalism that passes the integration test. Thus the issue over the internalism requirement and the integration test turns not so much on different conceptions of rational agency as on different conceptions of rational inquiry about that topic.

1.

In *Kant's Theory of Freedom*, Henry Allison attempts to defend Kant against an attack by Bernard Williams, whose views have influenced the conception of practical reason defended here. One line of Allison's defense is to argue that Williams starts from a different conception of rational agency than Kant and that from this conception his criticisms logically follow. Allison then asserts that Kant's view "may be mistaken, perhaps even deeply mistaken . . .; but Williams has done nothing to show that it is."[1] I take this as a valid request for an argument and to imply the assumption that there is some test that can rationally adjudicate the dispute between these rival conceptions of rational agency.

This assumption naturally raises the issue of what the test might be, and it might be thought that one's conception of the test will turn on how one understands the internalism requirement. In a way this is true, but I will argue that how one understands the internalism requirement turns on one's methodological commitments.

A fundamental commitment of the Aristotelian/Humean tradition is that we should understand the capacities for practical reason as psychological capacities. Whatever else they are, they are features of our psychologies. Why have such a commitment, other than its inherent plausibility? One very plausible understanding of this tradition and its reason for thinking in this way is that it is only by thinking in this way that practical reason can be adequately studied. The thought is that the only way to gain any objectivity to claims about practical reason is to construe what practical reason is in such a way that disputes about it are rationally resolvable. This means that there is a fundamental tension between this tradition and divine command theories of morality and with intuitionist views that require special moral facts. The tradition also looks skeptically on any methodology that attempts to settle claims about rational agency without appeal to the empirical facts regarding human psychology. And it is this, rather than some dogmatic commitment to a conception of rational agency, that leads to skepticism about Kant's a priori conception of practical reason.

At another level, there is skepticism from this tradition about theories of practical reason that speak of rational agency per se rather than of human agency. How one is to study rational agency per se is not at all clear. One possibility is to gather all the known species of animals that we are inclined to call rational and conceptualize a notion of practical reason in light of the empirical facts of their psychologies. From the currently known facts, that would probably leave us with a study of human psychology. Most surely, that study would not include reference to psychologies that could not be empirically investigated, especially the psychology of God. This is why for Aristotle, considerations of neither beasts nor gods were of much influence

---

1. Henry E. Allison, *Kant's Theory of Freedom* (Cambridge: Cambridge University Press, 1990), 196.

in his conception of rational agency.[2] Of course, we would need a conceptual scheme, a philosophical psychology, that would allow us to map those facts onto a conception of practical reason and rational agency. The point of this tradition, however, is that the arguments for the categories of the philosophical psychology must be such that they show that those categories are both empirically accommodating and rather tightly connected to the study of humans. By "empirically accommodating," I mean that an argument for the categories of a philosophical psychology must be carried out in terms of how those categories allow us to comprehend the facts of our experience. It is this, I suggest, that motivates Hume's insistence on the necessity of desire for rational agency, and this is a methodological motivation.

My major points here about skepticism are three. First, the tradition of skepticism about pure practical reason is founded on a methodological skepticism that insists that claims about the essentials of human agency be in principle empirically testable. Second, the categories of any adequate philosophical psychology must be empirically accommodating. Whether we insist that motives include desires is one thing, but whether claims about motives include claims about our psychologies that are subject to empirical testing is another. And third, the kind of test that adjudicates between competing conceptions of rational agency must be carried out in regard to humans, rather than gods, beasts, or imaginary creatures far removed from human experience. Thus, skepticism about the Kantian claim that reason alone can motivate is skepticism about two things: (i) whether that issue has been conceptualized in a way that empirically accommodates the facts of our psychology and (ii) whether inquiry about that issue takes the right point of departure, namely, the study of ourselves.

This method leads quite naturally to the issue of what function practical reason is to serve within a psychology, which in turn leads to the thought that the appropriate test for a conception of practical reason can be carried out in terms of its functional claims. In what follows, I will consider in this

---

2. See *Politics*, 1253a. There is some room for debate on this point. For one view, see Martha Nussbaum, "Aristotle on Human Nature and the Foundations of Ethics," in *World, Mind, and Ethics: Essays on the Ethical Philosophy of Bernard Williams*, ed. J. E. J. Altham and Ross Harrison (Cambridge: Cambridge University Press, 1995), 86–131. For a somewhat different view of the role of god in Aristotle's ethics, see Christine M. Korsgaard, "From Duty and for the Sake of the Noble," in *Aristotle, Kant, and the Stoics: Rethinking Happiness and Duty*, ed. Stephen Engstrom and Jennifer Whiting (New York: Cambridge University Press, 1996), 203–36.

regard methodological implications of views of three prominent Kantians: Barbara Herman, Christine Korsgaard, and John Rawls.

2.

Consider first Herman's understanding of Kant and the nature of practical reason.[3] A brief analysis of the structure of her version of Kantian internalism as developed in *The Practice of Moral Judgment* will help in articulating the aforementioned integration test and its importance.

The key difference between Herman's understanding of Kant and the traditional understanding is that she thinks that the concept of value is more basic to Kantian theory than the concept of right action. Kant, on her view, gives priority to the "good" over the "right" within his conception of morality. It is this fact, when properly understood, that allows us to see that Kantian morality is not an alien force threatening to disrupt our lives and intrude on our integrity in the way that many claim it does on the traditional interpretation of Kant that begins with obligation.

The theory of value, however, does not function the way it does in a consequentialist theory. It does not serve as a means of ranking states of affairs from best to worst on impartial criteria. What, then, is its function within the theory as a whole? Traditionally, the other way in which value has played a central role in a conception of morality is as a measure of human well-being, of human flourishing, of human good. I have in mind the kind of agent-centered morality found in Aristotle, where the most fundamental issue is not what one ought to do but what is the kind of life most worth living. In this vein, Herman interprets Kant's treatment of the unqualified value of the good will as the most fundamental element in his conception of the well-being of any rational being as such. This being the case, respect for human beings as agents of pure practical reason is a regulative norm that shapes and limits the other projects within an agent's life. So construed, respect for others is not a factor external to the meaningfulness of an agent's life from his or her own point of view but the most fundamental value of a meaningful life for a rational being. Thus when our respect for others puts limits on what we can do for our loved ones, this respect is not an alien force external to what gives our lives meaning but something central to the meaning we assign to love and its place in life. Therefore, to

3. Allison's views are greatly influenced by Herman. See Allison, *Kant's Theory of Freedom*, 278 n. 49.

live a good life, a life of flourishing, for a rational being involves regulating the other values in one's life by respect for ourselves and others as agents of pure practical reason.

To be an agent of pure practical reason is both to deliberate in a certain way about the components of one's life and to have one's will determined by this type of deliberation rather than by the affective and conative capacities of our empirical nature. Our sentiments, interests, wants, and desires stand on a different level than the willings of pure practical reason. Indeed, our natural affective and conative capacities provide only incentives to action, never motives; only pure practical reason, which is a purely cognitive capacity, can provide reasons by what it does with the incentives of inclination. It is the decision procedure involved in the various formulations of the categorical imperative that constitutes the pattern of deliberation indicative of a person of good will. Following Herman, we can call this the CI procedure.

The subtleties of Herman's interpretation of the CI procedure are rich and worthy of detailed examination, an examination that is beyond anything I can attempt here. What I want to focus on is the general function of the CI procedure within the kind of moral theory she construes Kant's to be. If the CI procedure is to do the work she thinks it is designed to do, it will provide a solution to any of the integration problems of any rational being. It will organize all the elements that factor into the meaning of a person's life from his or her own point of view in a way that is consistent with respect for persons as agents of pure practical reason. Without this, it cannot accommodate the integrity of human beings and the complexity of that which gives their lives meaning. As applied to this complexity, the CI procedure governs the deliberations of an agent, since that agent is respectful of self and others. Moreover, the patterns of deliberation captured in the CI procedure are the rational standard for the integration of the other elements of a person's life: sympathy for others, personal love, the value of intrinsically meaningful activities, and so on. That is, it is the standard if the person is rational. This, I believe, is the guiding principle in how to interpret the demand of the procedure and how it works. And on this view, Kantianism is not as far from Aristotelianism in terms of the structure of moral theory as has been thought, even though, on Herman's view, deliberations about one's own good are regulated by an impartial decision procedure.[4] On

4. For further development of her views in regard to Aristotle, see Barbara Herman, "Making Room for Character," in *Aristotle, Kant, and the Stoics,* ed. Stephen

this view, practical reason is an integrative function of consciousness that relates to other features of consciousness somewhat as output function to input, where the output function is a purely cognitive faculty and our wants, needs, desires, and sentiments are inputs.[5]

Herman's view suggests that what shows that the Kantian conception of rational agency is correct is that it, and only it, will pass the integration test. That is, it is the only conception of rational agency that includes a conception of an integrative function that will actually integrate the various concerns of rational human agents in a way that preserves integrity. On this view, practical reason, interpreted as the capacity for employing the CI procedure, plays a certain functional role within the psychology of any rational agent: It regulates all the concerns embedded in the psychology of a rational being in a way that preserves integrity.

Now this seems to provide an excellent test. So construed, this conception of the function of practical reason has the very desirable feature that substantive claims about its content are falsifiable. Alternatives to the capacity for employing the CI procedure can be constructed and tested against each other in terms of their integrative success as applied to the psychology of actual human beings. Among these alternatives is the Aristotelian conception defended here. If the Aristotelian alternative makes more sense of the integrative capacities of actual human beings than the CI procedure on its most favorable Kantian interpretation, then Herman is wrong about the CI procedure. If, however, the best Kantian interpretation of the CI procedure achieves superior integrative success than all other candidates, she is right, and those of us who have opposed Kant can now embrace him without the need for faith or his metaphysics.

There are some deep questions, however, that must be raised about the CI procedure on this view. Herman wants to interpret the procedure in a way that steers a course between an interpretation of Kant that places moral demands on a foundation outside the factors that go into the meaningfulness of one's life from one's own point of view and a clearly Aristotelian view that does not involve an impartial decision procedure. The issue, then, is whether she can construct the procedure in a way that does not collapse either into the traditional conception of the procedure or into a form of

---

Engstrom and Jennifer Whiting (New York: Cambridge University Press, 1996), 33–62.

5. For the Kantian, of course, it is important that this output function is a feature of agency that can be combined with freedom of the will.

Aristotelianism that is not, for her, appropriately impartial. It is here that the concept of pure practical reason comes into potential conflict with the requirement that the procedure solve the integration problems of human agents.

I cannot see that it is a purely conceptual issue whether a pattern of deliberation will provide a solution to such problems for humans. This is surely in part an empirical issue, which illustrates the necessity of the integration test. Whether a certain way of attempting to integrate the kinds of concerns an agent has will in fact integrate them is in part an issue to be settled by empirical observation. Later, in chapter 3, we will see what behavioral responses will count as evidence that integration has failed to occur. The point here is that if Herman simply defines the procedure as whatever pattern will pass the integration test, she runs the risk of collapsing Kantianism into a more robust Aristotelianism than she desires. This would be true if impartiality and respect do not have the kind of role in the procedure one would expect on a Kantian view. On the other hand, if she defines the procedure independent of its ability to pass such a test and then it fails the test for large numbers of apparently rational humans, she has to say that they are not rational beings, which would reveal that the test is superfluous. And she would have to say this regarding any form of practical consciousness in which impartial respect is regulated by some other norm, partial or impartial. However, denying the status of rationality to such a form of practical reason reverts to the traditional, externalist view of Kant, for it imposes a conception of the meaningfulness of life on an agent from a source independent of that agent's own point of view. As long as she retains the notion of pure practical reason and the a priori cognitive psychology that goes along with it, I do not believe that she can avoid the dilemma. Moreover, I believe this applies to any version of Kantian internalism.

3.

My reasons for thinking that this dilemma applies to any Kantian internalism with strong a priori commitments arise in response to Korsgaard's influential arguments regarding internalism.[6] I show that Korsgaard must ei-

6. See Christine M. Korsgaard, "Skepticism about Practical Reason," *Journal of Philosophy* 83, no. 1 (January 1986): 5–25.

ther revise her understanding of the internalism requirement in a way that entails the integration test as a means of adjudicating disputes about rational agency or run the risk, as Herman does, of becoming an externalist. I will again show that the commitment to the integration test need not prejudice a priori the case for or against either Kantian or Aristotelian internalism. This, I believe, makes a good case for considering the integration test as a part of a methodology that provides common ground between Kantians and Aristotelians for adjudicating disputes about rational agency.

Kantian internalism includes the claim that reason alone can motivate, and according to Korsgaard, to be skeptical about this is to be skeptical about pure practical reason. The reason Kantians, whether internalist or externalist, feel compelled to claim that reason alone can motivate is that they see no other way of ensuring that morality is universally binding on all rational beings. Their reasoning is that as long as it is possible that a kind of motive is one that a rational being might not have, then it is not the kind of motive that can bind all rational beings. Moreover, there is, on their view, no necessary feature of rational agency attached to desires and sentiments. Their point is not only that there are no particular desires and sentiments that all rational agents have; it is also that not all rational agents even have desires and sentiments. It is not difficult, then, to see what drives the Kantian to a conception of practical reason in which reason alone can motivate. Nor, I take it, is it difficult to see why someone might be skeptical about this claim. After all, much of Kant's writings in moral philosophy are intended to remove such skepticism.

Korsgaard's argument is a defense of only one particular kind of basis for skepticism about pure practical reason or the view that reason alone can motivate. Specifically, her argument is a defense against the view that skepticism about pure practical reason follows from internalism itself.

The target of Korsgaard's argument is her understanding of a skeptical argument by David Hume and Bernard Williams. She distinguishes between content skepticism, which questions that reason alone can provide us with a mechanism for deciding what to do, and motivational skepticism, which questions that reason alone can function as a motive. She then claims that the latter has no independent force, which is to say that if it could be shown that reason alone can provide a decision mechanism, the claim that it could not motivate would itself have no philosophical motivation. Thus any rational skepticism can only take the form of content skepticism. The following is my formulation of the argument that her argument is designed to attack.

1. *The internalism requirement:* Practical claims, if they are really to present us with reasons for action, must be capable of motivating rational persons.[7]

2. For any rational person, P, P has a motive to do x only if P has a desire to do x or x is a means to satisfying some of P's desires.

3. Therefore, for any practical claim, R, that P do x, R gives P a reason to do x only if P has a desire to do x or x is a means to satisfying some of P's desires.

Korsgaard wants to assert that since the second premise is necessary to get to the conclusion, which constitutes the denial that reason alone can motivate, it is not the internalism requirement itself that leads to skepticism of pure practical reason. From this, she wants to assert that Williams's insistence on internalism itself does no work against Kant. It is only the additional claim involved in the second premise—that desire is necessary for motivation—that we get the skeptical conclusion, and this premise needs an independent argument.

My purpose here is not to defend Williams but to consider Korsgaard's argument that internalism itself does not entail skepticism about the issue of the motivational force of pure practical reason.[8] I believe that she is right that the internalism requirement itself does not preclude the truth of the claim that reason alone can motivate. But when the internalism requirement is understood from the perspective of a methodological commitment to the integration test, it requires that any functional claims about the role of practical reason within an overall psychology are falsifiable in terms of that test. To deny this, is to endorse a methodology that is not tightly connected to the study of ourselves. Hence how one understands the implications of the internalism requirement turns on one's methodological commitments. Thus both the claim that reason alone can motivate and its denial must be understood in a way that they can be put to the integration test. Moreover, I will argue that we should be committed to the integration test

7. This is Korsgaard's exact wording. See "Skepticism about Practical Reason," 11.

8. Williams's view is more complex than represented here. He has never meant by a desire a mere animal urge, as Allison puts it. And Williams has recently said that Kantian internalism is a limiting case of internalism. See Bernard Williams, "Replies," in *World, Mind, and Ethics: Essays on The Ethical Philosophy of Bernard Williams*, ed. J. E. J. Altham and Ross Harrison (Cambridge: Cambridge University Press, 1995), 186–94.

as the appropriate method of adjudicating between rival conceptions of rational agency.

To see this, we have to recast the argument in a manner that reframes the issue to allow for the possibility of rationally resolving the question of whether reason alone can motivate.

Consider the following argument.

1. *The internalism requirement:* Practical claims, if they are really to present us with reasons for action, must be capable of motivating rational persons.
2. For any rational person, P, P has a motive to do x only if the consideration of x by P has some psychological pull with P for doing x.
3. Therefore, for any practical claim, R, that P do x, R gives P a reason to do x only if the consideration of x by P has some psychological pull with P for doing x.

Now it might seem that this is just a superficial attempt to evade the issue of desire versus reason as motivators, that "psychological pull" is just a synonym for "desire." But whether this is true depends on the conditions placed on assigning a truth value to the claim that a certain consideration has psychological pull with a rational agent. If Korsgaard is right that motivational skepticism turns on content skepticism, we should interpret the second premise in light of alternative conceptions of the content of practical reason. I propose that we understand the claim that reason can motivate with the claim that the CI procedure can have psychological pull with a human being. This defines practical reason in terms of a content, assuming that the CI procedure generates content, and a function, namely, an integrative function. But what about the second premise? We must understand this premise in a way that its meaning leaves open the possibility that the CI procedure can have psychological pull. This is to say that one way of understanding the meaning of (2) is in terms of what might make (2) true, and we understand this in terms of a certain content practical reason might have, that provided by the CI procedure, and the function it is to serve.

Of course, we must also understand the second premise in a way that leaves open the possibility that it is false that reason can motivate. How shall we understand, then, the denial of the thesis that reason alone motivates? Instead of formulating the most general logical denial, I propose we contrast the thesis with one among several ways in which that thesis might be denied. Since our concern is with a dispute between Kantian and Aristotelian versions of internalism, we can say that the Kantian thesis is false if the regulative norms of practical reason are all symmetrical in their regulative functions. We can say this because the CI procedure requires that impartial respect is a norm within practical reason that functions asymmetrically in relationship to all other norms. This will be required of any content it generates. On the other hand, the Aristotelian alternative will be true just in case the norms of practical reason are all symmetrical in their regulative functions and the goods that give rise to those norms are those one would expect on an inclusive reading of an Aristotelian view, which is reflected in the thick conception of integrity.

Both alternatives, that reason alone motivates and that it does not, are defined in terms of content and function. Thus, in this sense, the issue of motivational skepticism turns on content skepticism, just as Korsgaard requires. But to be skeptical of content in regard to the CI procedure is to be skeptical that the content of the CI procedure can carry the burden of the integrative function of consciousness with regard to human beings. This is to be skeptical that the CI procedure will pass the integration test, that the CI procedure can provide an integrative function that preserves the elements of integrity for admirable human beings. Thus content skepticism is based on methodological skepticism.

How is the integration test to be administered? Kantian internalism is committed to the thesis that the CI procedure can motivate, which means that the CI procedure has a content and a function. To test this claim we need first some idea of what that content is, and then we need to put that content to a test to see if it can serve its designed function. That test is the integration test: Can the CI procedure serve the role of the integrative function of human consciousness in a way that preserves the elements of integrity for human beings of the sort reflected in the thick conception of integrity? I shall argue in parts 2 through 4 that it cannot.

I will construe the Kantian internalist claim that reason can motivate as the claim that the CI procedure cannot only have psychological pull for human beings but considerable pull. If the Kantian asserts that the CI procedure has no psychological pull for a rational being but nonetheless provides a reason for action, I will understand that to be a denial of internalism and an endorsement of externalism. Otherwise, it is difficult to see what would count as externalism. The considerable pull that the CI procedure must have is that it must play a certain role within the psychology of a rational being. Its pull must be the central integrative force of the psychology of a rational human being. This does not mean that the agent cannot act against that force. It does mean, however, that if the agent does act against that force there are repercussions for the structure of the agent's psychology. I will say more about this when I come to chapter 3, the thin conception of integrity, and categorical interests. But it is important here to recognize that these observations underscore the threat of the previous dilemma facing Kantian internalism: If the integration test is rejected, externalism is waiting in the wings. It is waiting in the wings because the rejection of the integration test imposes a conception of practical reason on humans from a source external to their psychology, which includes their motivational set.

It is not, however, only the CI procedure that will be put to the integration test but the Aristotelian conception of practical reason as well. According to the Aristotelian conception, there is a clear path from the goods that make life meaningful for most human agents to the thick conception of integrity in which a network of practical norms are all symmetrical in their regulative functions. Thus applying the integration test will involve a detailed elaboration of the content of the Aristotelian model as it applies to the agent of integrity in the thick sense.

My argument, therefore, in no way depends on the claim that internalism itself settles the issue of whether reason can motivate. Moreover, it accepts the claim that motivational skepticism turns on content skepticism. The issue of content skepticism, however, turns on an empirical issue of whether the CI procedure on its best interpretation can play a certain role in human psychology: Can it integrate the various concerns a human agent has in a way that preserves the elements of integrity? If the relevant concepts can be made clear enough, the rest is a matter of empirical testing. I want to formulate the Kantian and Aristotelian theses so that they can be tested and to argue that the evidence tells against the Kantian conception and for the Aristotelian conception of practical reason for a rather large portion of humanity.

4.

Here it is important to consider Kantian alternatives. One possibility is for the Kantian to reject the methodology that leads to the integration test. I have no doubt that Kant himself would have taken this course and that it must be the course of the metaphysical school of Kantian methodology. According to the metaphysical school, as I understand it, we can derive a conception of rational agency from the concept of what it is to act for a reason.

This will include considerations of universalizability, consistency, impartiality, and the like. The point is that the rational method of formulating a concept of rational agency is an a priori method that relies in no way for its essentials on the facts of human psychology. Indeed, according to this methodology, we can learn psychology from moral theory. Korsgaard herself distinguishes between two types of internalism: "one that takes the psychological facts as given and supposes that we must somehow derive ethics from them in order to achieve an internalist theory, and one that supposes that metaphysical investigations—investigations into what it is to be a rational person—will have psychological conclusions."[9] On her view, Kant's thought is an example of the second, and I take it that hers is as well. When she says, then, that "the internalism requirement is correct, but there is probably no moral theory that excludes it,"[10] she is presupposing internalism that is tied to a certain methodological interpretation, and it is just that interpretation that is a stake in the dispute between the two traditions.

Thus the denial of the relevance of the integration test might rest on the Kantian doctrine that the rationality of pure practical reason is established a priori, the so-called fact of reason argument presented in *The Critique of Practical Reason*.[11] For metaphysical Kantians, this will mean that we can know that reason alone can motivate because we can know a priori that rational beings have certain obligations. This doctrine implies that the procedure determines a priori what our obligations are independent of whether we can as a matter of fact perform the actions they require. And since *ought* implies *can*, we can perform these actions. The syllogism is something like the following:

1. Necessarily, P ought to do x.
2. Necessarily, if P ought to do x, P can do x.
3. Therefore, P can do x.

It is the fact that the first premise is necessarily true on the Kantian view that prevents its falsification by showing that the consequent of (2) is false. This argument can then be employed to show that reason motivates by add-

9. Korsgaard, "Skepticism about Practical Reason," 23 n. 17.

10. Ibid., 23.

11. See Immanuel Kant, *Critique of Practical Reason*, trans. Lewis White Beck (Indianapolis: Bobbs-Merrill, 1956), 5:30–31; Marcia Baron, *Kantian Ethics Almost Without Apology* (Ithaca: Cornell University Press, 1995), 44–45; Allison, *Kant's Theory of Freedom*, 230–49.

ing the premise that necessarily P can do x only if P has a motive to do x. Thus we can learn psychology from moral theory.[12]

It is difficult to see how to accept this argument as it stands without endorsing conclusions that I am sure neither Kant nor Korsgaard would accept. For example, the CI procedure is supposed to put some rather severe restrictions on breaking one's promises, perhaps not as absolute as Kant himself thought, but nonetheless severe. But surely the fact that keeping my promise would require violating the laws of logic or mathematics provides a good reason both for thinking that I cannot keep my promise and for thinking that I do not have the obligation to do so. If I promised you yesterday that I would today square the circle, surely I do not have the obligation to square the circle just because that is something I cannot do. The CI procedure on its best interpretation, then, will assume that we cannot get to the truths of logic and mathematics through moral theory. Similarly, if keeping my promise would require violating the laws of physics, a similar conclusion would follow. If I promised you yesterday that I would today jump over the moon, surely I do not have the obligation to jump over the moon just because that is something I cannot do. The CI procedure on its best interpretation will assume that moral theory cannot get us to the truths of physics. Moreover, that interpretation of the procedure will construe the truths of physics in such a way that they are accessible to us only through a methodology that is a posteriori in nature. Thus the best interpretation of the procedure in this regard imposes limits on the metaphysics, and this is the central point. Our metaphysical understanding of agency is structured not only by what we know about the formal truths of logic and mathematics but also by what we know about the laws of nature. Good metaphysics and good metaphysical methodology recognize this.

But, then, this is to admit that some considerations of fact a posteriori can falsify the "claims of reason," on a fully a priori understanding of the claims of reason. Now, however, comes the slippery slope. What is to stop some of these facts from being the facts of our psychology? Once the Kantian has construed the best interpretation of the CI procedure to accommodate the a posteriori truths of physics, it is difficult to see what principled *methodological* reason there can be for exempting the truths of psychology from their independent status. And, of course, if the truths of psychology are independent of moral theory and to be discovered by an independent methodology *and* if internalism is correct, then the correct version of internalism is not the one Korsgaard has in mind. It is one that leads to a de-

12. Korsgaard, "Skepticism about Practical Reason," 23–25.

nial of the independent status of moral theory. Whatever role metaphysics plays in our formulation of a concept of rational agency, it is not one that is a priori in the way that Korsgaard and Kant require. The best conception of metaphysics is one according to which metaphysics begins with and is restricted by a large body of empirical knowledge. Good metaphysics, then, is never entirely a priori, perhaps not even largely so. The best conception of rational agency will recognize this, as will the best interpretation of the CI procedure, neither of which will yield the result that the facts of psychology are accessible through an independent moral theory. And, according to the methodology that requires the integration test, it is irrational to accept a methodology that requires us to ignore a vast body of knowledge we already have in the formulation of our metaphysics. This is no less true of psychology than it is of logic, mathematics, physics, or biology. That Kant would reject this was in part a function of his belief that psychology is not a science, but our increasing understanding of both cognitive and clinical psychology will not allow us this belief.

I cannot, then, see how it can be rational to insist that the facts of psychology do not have the kind of standing that can invalidate a normative claim or a conception of practical reason. To do so would be to endorse an irrational methodology that requires that we ignore knowledge that we might already have or that we might come to have by a reliable method. To advance a claim about a person having the capacity for a certain motive is to advance a claim about that person's psychology (which, on the most plausible view, includes a claim about the capacities of a certain neurology). It is to advance a claim that a certain kind of consideration has psychological pull. To advance a conception of practical reason, then, is to advance a claim about the functional capacities of a certain psychology. This is an issue concerning a claim the truth of which can be determined independent of moral theory by means of the integration test and the best methods of social science.[13] To conceptualize the issue of rational agency in such a way

13. Finally, there is a possible coherence problem with such a denial for an internalist, especially for Korsgaard. According to her, intuitionism is a version of externalism, and "intuitionists do not believe in practical reason" ("Skepticism about Practical Reason," 10). Korsgaard is right to insist that there is no essential connection between the truth of a moral claim and its practical rationality according to intuitionism. This is directly due to the fact of intuitionism's externalism. Yet Korsgaard seems to deny that we should understand what it is to have a motive in terms of what Williams calls an agent's subjective motivational set. I am not sure what motivational set is to replace it, but if she is suggesting that we should understand having a motive independent of the fact that a certain consideration has psychologi-

that it is not subject to such testing seems motivated less by a concern for inquiry than by the desire to protect a favored conception against any possible incriminating evidence. And, in this regard, it is difficult not to notice that Kant's metaphysics maps very neatly onto his Christian heritage. For it is crucial to his argument that it is possible to be a rational agent and not have desires and sentiments because God is such a being. How one is to evaluate claims about God's psychology, however, is beyond empirical testing. In fact, how one is to evaluate such claims is mysterious by any means, and this is a worry about a conception of agency that arises from a worry about method.[14]

It is difficult to know what to say if deep disagreement over methodology persists past these observations. I can point to the kind of illumination philosophy might be capable of when structured within a larger body of knowledge that is achieved through the reliable methods of science. If a philosopher does not accept the requirement that philosophical knowledge must be not only consistent with scientific knowledge but also continuous with it, I simply do not know what else to say. That metaphysical Kantians do not accept the continuity requirement seems evident in the fact that they conceptualize the issue of rational agency in a way that the conditions for the possibility of rational agency might be discontinuous with the facts of human psychology. With this in mind, I can point to the dangers of conceptual schemes that have allowed themselves to reject the continuity requirement. The history of theology is full of examples. At any rate, I should have said enough by now to make clear the reasons for my methodological commitments, even for those who will not accept them. Perhaps this is all that can be done.

---

cal pull, then it is not clear that she is even talking about motives. Indeed, it seems that she is an externalist after all. Ironically, however, this means that she has given up on founding morality on practical reason, which is a requirement of her own theory.

14. Kant's distinction between an impurely rational being and a purely rational being corresponds to a distinction between human beings, who have desires and inclinations, and God, who does not. Since we need a distinction between purely rational and impurely rational agents, how is a conception of agency that is tightly connected to the study of human beings to accommodate the distinction? Rather easily, I think. A purely rational being is not one who does not have desires, sentiments, and inclinations but one who deliberates in the light of the relevant facts, is fully competent in the formal requirements of logical reasoning, and does not suffer from psychological encumbrance. Whether such an agent employs the CI procedure is an open question. And it is the integration test that provides the means of answering it.

5.

Unlike the metaphysical school, however, Kantian constructivists can accept much, perhaps all, of what has been said so far regarding methodology. I will argue in what follows that if Kantian constructivists want both to base morality on practical reason and to do so in a way that is independent of metaphysics, then they must accept the integration test rather than what they call reflective equilibrium as the ultimate arbiter of rival conceptual schemes. Moreover, I will argue that the integration test does not rule out Kantian internalism a priori.

In his Dewey Lectures, John Rawls claimed that there is a kind of moral theory that has yet been unnoticed, which contrasts markedly with the Kantian metaphysical tradition.[15] This kind of theory Rawls calls a constructivist theory. As I understand the structure of such a theory, any instance of it has three features: a decision model spelled out in terms of an original position, a conception of reflective equilibrium that provides an explanation of our moral sentiments and values, and a conception of the justification for moral principles.

The construction of a decision model employs Rawls's now-famous notion of an original position. One aim of the decision model is to describe the original position in a way that will allow anyone in that position to make a rational choice regarding alternative principles to govern behavior, policy, or the development of character. Of course, the decision model can be set up in a variety of ways, depending on how the original position is described. John Harsanyi, for example, has long ago constructed an original position that leads to the choice of average utilitarianism.[16] No doubt different models could be constructed to yield a wide variety of other possibilities. How, then, is one to choose between these possibilities, and what does the choice reveal?

It is the notion of reflective equilibrium that allows the choice between the alternative ways of setting up the original position. Reflective equilibrium is gained when the original position has been set up in a way that not only allows a choice of principles that are rational from that position but also where the results of the choice model yield maximal coherence be-

15. John Rawls, *Political Liberalism* (New York: Columbia University Press, 1993), 89–130.
16. John Harsanyi, "Morality and the Theory of Rational Behavior," in *Utilitarianism and Beyond,* ed. Amartya Sen and Bernard Williams (Cambridge: Cambridge University Press, 1982), 39–62.

tween one's judgments regarding particular cases and general moral principles.[17] Thus the argument for one conception of the original position over another is that one yields a greater coherence within our moral experience. And the claim is that the reflective equilibrium resulting from the model succeeds in providing us with a certain kind of explanation. What is explained is something about our moral psychology, namely, what our deepest moral sentiments and values are. So construed, a constructivist theory is, according to Rawls, "a theory of moral sentiments (to recall an eighteenth century title) setting out the principles governing our moral powers."[18] On this view, the rationality of the choice of one set of principles over another by those in the original position is explained by the fact of the sentiments of a certain psychology, the ones built into the assumptions of the original position. That the characterization of the original position yields a result that achieves reflective equilibrium reveals that these assumptions are features of *our* psychology, not the psychology of those in the original position.

Rawls's own attempt is to construct a model that is "Kantian" in content and that applies to issues of distributive justice regarding the basic institutions of society. The claim is that if we set up a decision model in a certain way—a way that provides a clear rationale for basic principles of justice— and if this way of setting up the model achieves the desired reflective equilibrium, then we have a good argument that the model captures our notion of moral rationality. Were we to set up the model in a different way that yielded different principles but nevertheless achieved the desired reflective equilibrium, this would provide an argument for another conception of moral rationality. Rawls's claim about distributive justice is that when we set up the decision procedure with Kantian assumptions about rational agency we are able to test different substantive conceptions of distributive justice in a way that allows us to get reflective equilibrium. The reasonable assumption is that though there is a kind of predictability that if you start with a procedure built on Kantian assumptions you will get substantive Kantian results, there is no advance reason for thinking that this will result in reflective equilibrium. Hence the achievement of equilibrium adds something to the argument: It constitutes evidence that Kantian assumptions are behind our considered judgments.

The methodological point is that we should understand moral rational-

17. John Rawls, *A Theory of Justice* (Cambridge, Mass.: Harvard University Press, 1971), 20 ff., 48–51, 120, 432, 434, 579.
18. Ibid., 51.

ity as proceeding from our deepest moral sentiments and in terms of that decision model that allows us to achieve reflective equilibrium regarding our considered moral judgments. The task of moral theory is to provide such a model, and Rawls claims that, in this sense, moral theory is an independent philosophical discipline, one that is independent of metaphysics, as well as theory of meaning, epistemology, and the philosophy of mind.[19] Whether moral theory is independent of psychology and social science is another matter, one that we will come to later.

The third feature of a constructivist model is a conception of what justifies moral principles. Not only does reflective equilibrium explain our moral sentiments by revealing how they structure our judgments; the principles yielded by the decision model that achieves reflective equilibrium are justified by that very fact. The reason they are justified is that they are the rational result of our deepest moral sentiments and values. As Rawls says, "I have not proceeded then as if first principles . . . have special features that permit them a peculiar place in justifying moral doctrine. They are central elements and devices of theory, but justification rests upon the entire conception and how it fits in with and organizes our considered judgments in reflective equilibrium."[20] Kantian constructivism, then, is the claim that if we set up a decision model on Kantian normative (but not metaphysical) assumptions, we will get reflective equilibrium in a way that we will not on any non-Kantian model. By so doing, we gain both an explanation of what our deepest sentiments are and a justification for the resultant moral principles.

This conception of justification reveals a methodological commitment regarding the study of rational agency that is decidedly different from that of the metaphysical school. At the most general level, constructivist method is committed to the view that what morally justifies a set of principles is that

19. I cannot see that this is a good argument for the independence of moral theory from psychology, if what is meant is that moral obligations have a nonpsychological foundation. On this view, the method of reflective equilibrium is a method of psychological inquiry, one that is designed to reveal features of our psychology. Perhaps the claim is that *methodologically* constructivism is not among the disciplines of psychology as a social science. Fair enough. But this is a fairly weak claim about the independence of moral theory from psychology, one that metaphysical Kantians would not allow as strong enough. Constructivism does not yield a priori truths about our moral sentiments. It takes the data of what we report as our considered moral judgments and makes explicit the values behind such judgments. This is the study of the norms embedded in a psychology. See John Rawls, "The Independence of Moral Theory," in *Proceedings of the American Philosophical Association* (New York: American Philosophical Association, 1974), 5–22.

20. Rawls, *A Theory of Justice*, 579.

it expresses the deepest moral sentiments and values of a certain psychology, namely, ours. Moreover, it is committed to an a posteriori method of discovering what those values are. To be sure, there is the philosophical construction of the decision model and the original position. But the test for this model is whether it achieves reflective equilibrium. And it is a contingent fact whether any particular model achieves this result, a fact that rests on the contingencies of our psychology. What we must understand through reflective equilibrium is what moral rationality comes to for humanity or some subsection thereof. There is no a priori argument that only the CI procedure will result in the desired reflective equilibrium. Understood in this way, constructivists are committed to the empirical tradition: Moral rationality serves the moral values most deeply embedded in our psychology. Hume and Aristotle would most heartily agree. For constructivists, what those values are can be discovered through constructivist methodology, which is at once a kind of moral theory and a kind of psychological study. It is not a branch of metaphysics, and it proceeds independently of metaphysics.

This methodological difference between constructivist and metaphysical Kantians requires a difference in a general conception of rational agency. For constructivists, the fact that is explained by reflective equilibrium is that the principles yielded by the decision model rationally express our deepest moral sentiments. Moreover, it is this very fact that rationally justifies these principles. No metaphysical deduction of the CI procedure is appealed to, nor could it be and reflective equilibrium be the justification for the principles. For the metaphysical Kantians, on the other hand, reflective equilibrium could never play this justificatory role. The reason that the metaphysical school persists is that they see that Kant was right that the only kind of moral theory that will yield the rational necessity of moral principles that bind all rational agents is one that employs a metaphysical deduction of the moral law. If this is true, then the most reflective equilibrium can do is elucidate our deepest moral values; it can do nothing to justify them. The justification must come through pure practical reason. For this reason, one cannot be both a constructivist and a metaphysical Kantian, where constructivism includes the claim that reflective equilibrium justifies the acceptance of moral principles.[21] Thus on the Kantian constructivist

21. It is possible to endorse something called constructivism and delete the third feature, the claim that reflective equilibrium justifies the selection of moral principles. The cost of the deletion, however, is that the theory loses any claim to being normative.

view, moral rationality comes to acting on our deepest values, and the evidence that we have so acted is in principle provided by a moral theory that achieves maximal coherence in explaining what our deepest values are. And methodologically, even if the CI procedure were to result in reflective equilibrium, there would be no necessity in this fact. It would simply be a function of a contingent fact about our psychology. Hence the constructivist methodology is committed to a conception of rational agency that can be empirically studied.

There is, however, a problem. The problem is that it follows that acting on our deepest moral sentiments and values is practically rational only if we assume that the conception of moral rationality constructed in the original position is practically rational. But reflective equilibrium of our moral judgments could never assure this. Only a reflective equilibrium of all our considered practical judgments could yield this result. What is needed, then, is some further test that supports the claim that our deepest moral sentiments and values, on some interpretation of what they are, are in fact fundamental to our overall psychology. Since the method of reflective equilibrium reveals that the foundation for the rationality of our moral judgments is to be found within our psychology, namely, within our deepest moral sentiments, consistency requires that the foundation for the rationality of our practical judgments is to be found in the deepest values of our psychology. This follows from the psychological basis for the explanation of rationality appealed to vis-à-vis the notion of reflective equilibrium. And it should be noted that this model for rationality is squarely within the Aristotelian/Humean tradition. Thus to assert that the Kantian constructivist view of the CI procedure is rational is to assert that it and it alone can serve a certain psychological function, the one discovered in the discussion of Herman. Therefore, if we are to accept constructivism as a method that bases morality on practical reason, as Kantian internalism does, then either the notion of reflective equilibrium will have to include the integration test or the integration test should be understood as the arbiter of whether our deepest moral sentiments are rational. Without the integration test, constructivism will not have yielded the claim that our deepest moral sentiments and values have a rational foundation in practical reason. And thus constructivism will have reverted either to externalism or to the metaphysical school, in which case the notion of reflective equilibrium is justificatorily inert.

If a constructivist model is to be independent of metaphysics and it is to be defensible as practically rational, it will have to show that our deepest moral sentiments provide a basis for practical reason that can sustain the elements of integrity in the thin sense over time. I do not see how the method of reflective equilibrium can achieve this, as long as the equilibrium, however "wide," includes only our moral sentiments and judgments.[22] For it seems that from the perspective of practical reason, it is always an open question whether independently specifiable moral concerns are among the deepest concerns of our psychology. That they are (on some interpretation of what "moral" concerns are) could be revealed by the integration test. For if it is true that moral concerns on some interpretation are among the deepest concerns of our psychology, then the frustration of those concerns rising from the attempt to live apart from them or contrary to them will result in the inability to sustain the elements of integrity in the thin sense.

It is instructive in this regard to think of how equilibrium might be achieved and lost. At one point in the not too distant past, reflective equilibrium regarding the morality of gender and race relations would have yielded much different results than today. What explains this? A glib answer is that we have different expectations of ourselves and others today because we now live in a different culture. A more plausible answer is that we tried to live with certain expectations of ourselves and others and found that we could not sustain those values over time and maintain the elements of integrity. The burden of self-deception imposed by those expectations and the stress incurred by the attempt to find meaning in them simply would not allow them to retain a central place in our psychology. And this is why they are not and were never practically rational. This is not to say that reflective equilibrium is not an important device of inquiry. But it is to say that what explains reflective equilibrium is the belief that we have found the values that are at the core of our psychology and that they can sustain integrity over time. Thus if it is the belief that the integration test reveals that any particular reflective equilibrium is trustworthy, then it is the integration test that is the ultimate arbiter of rival conceptual schemes. I see no reason why constructivists could not accept this point as a necessary stage of constructivist inquiry.

If, however, constructivists reject the necessity of this stage of inquiry, they are doing one of two things: either they are covertly endorsing Kant-

22. For discussion of a conception of wide reflective equilibrium different from that of Rawls, see Norman Daniels, "Wide Reflective Equilibrium and Theory Acceptance in Ethics," *Journal of Philosophy* 76 (1979): 256–82, and "Reflective Equilibrium and Archimedean Points," *Canadian Journal of Philosophy* 10, no. 1 (March 1980): 83–103.

ian metaphysics, or they are suspending judgment about whether Kantian morality is practically rational. If they are doing the latter, it is hard to see in what sense they are defending a conception of morality founded on practical reason.

The best interpretation of constructivism, then, is one that accepts the integration test and is willing to put the CI procedure and the conception of practical reason associated with it to this test. In chapter 3 we will see more of what the integration test involves in terms of human behavior. But here the important thing is that there is nothing a priori that rules out the possibility that Kantian internalism, understood as the claim that the CI procedure must serve a functional role within our psychology, might pass the test. In what follows, then, I will proceed with the methodological commitment of applying the integration test to both the CI procedure and the Aristotelian conception of practical reason.

The argument against Kant, however, must be against the best interpretation of the CI procedure and its results. This task is made more difficult by the fact that there are both consequentialist and deontological interpretations of the procedure, as well as various deontological interpretations. These are disputes over the content of the CI procedure. Rather than define and address these issues here, I will address them as they become relevant to the myriad contexts in which the CI procedure, on any interpretation, must exercise its function. I bring up this issue now for two reasons. The first is to reassure the reader that I will make a good faith attempt to evaluate the most plausible and developed views of the CI procedure rather than implausible caricatures. The second is to insist on two features that must accommodate any employment of the integration test. The test must be administered in a way that is both context-sensitive and contextually thorough. To be context-sensitive it must be applied to contexts in terms of all and only the relevant features of the context, and to be contextually thorough it must be applied to a substantial range of contexts to which the conception of rational agency might plausibly apply. My argument will be that the deliberative strategies available to Kantians through the CI procedure are not rational across the range of contexts an agent must face in living a life. This means that any contextually thorough implementation of the integration test will reveal that the CI procedure fails in significant contexts and that the Aristotelian alternative does not. It also means that implementing the test requires very careful and detailed work. Showing that a conception of rational agency is plausible in some contexts is not sufficient for rational acceptance of that conception. This is why the analysis in parts 2 through 4 is so detailed. As in science, there is no shortcut to testing a theory, and, as in art, glossed blemishes eventually penetrate the veneer designed to conceal them. Philosophy involves hard, detailed work.

6.

The result, then, is that I accept Allison's requirement for an argument for the conception of rational agency employed here and explicated in general in the remainder of part 1. The test is the one implied in Herman's arguments for the CI procedure. If Kantians believe that this is not the appropriate test, they must give us philosophical reasons for rejecting the integration test as the appropriate test and then provide the appropriate test with an argument for it. Without this, the claim that I have not given an argument for rejecting the Kantian conception of rational agency will seem mysterious.

2. Impartiality, Regulative Norms, and Practical Reason

This chapter aims at establishing a point about our considered moral judgments, namely, that they reflect a conceptual scheme in which the relationships between regulative norms are all symmetrical in their regulative functions. None of these norms function asymmetrically. If this is true, then our considered moral judgments reflect a central feature of the Aristotelian conception of practical reason rather than either of the Kantian conceptions. Establishing this will provide prima facie evidence that no Kantian constructivist model can achieve reflective equilibrium. Of course, we might discover after philosophical reflection that our considered moral judgments lack a rational foundation. Nevertheless, if it can be shown that the Aristotelian scheme has a home in our judgments, this constitutes an important first step in an argument for that scheme. It will remain to be shown, then, that there is a rational foundation for this scheme. This can be provided if the scheme can be developed sufficiently and, once developed, can be shown to pass the integration test.

Before I begin with the argument, however, I wish to engage in a little diplomacy, which is sometimes called for in philosophy when argument breaks down due to mistrust. Both sides of a dispute feel that their arguments have been treated unfairly; so they withdraw and accuse. This is somewhat true of the current debate between Kantians and non-Kantians concerning the role of impartiality in ethics. Kantians often complain, sometimes bitterly, that objections to Kantian ethics are based on caricature and that if more careful attention were paid to the role of regulative norms in practical reason the objections would lose their force. Non-Kantians express frustration about the cursory treatment by Kantians of alternative positions, accusing them either of providing only a gesture in the direction of a response to serious alternatives or of an unwillingness to specify criteria that might show that they are wrong. The evidence suggests, I believe, that there are good grounds for complaint on both sides: the tendency to see everything that is said against one's views as caricature can be as pernicious a form of dismissal as the tendency to caricature itself.

The only way to combat both tendencies is with hard philosophical analysis. What I intend to do here is to construct an inquiry regarding the role of regulative norms in practical reason in a way that studiously avoids caricature and argue that recent Kantian defenses fail to consider a very important conceptual alternative to their view. What they have said thus far in the debate does not address the alternative I will present. If I succeed, the only appropriate response is a philosophical argument that shows where I fail. On the principle, then, that a careful argument requires a careful reply, I accept the Kantian challenge to avoid caricature in understanding the Kantian project, but I lay down the challenge of a non-Kantian view that requires an equally serious and detailed reply rather than a gesture in the direction of a response. One final diplomatic point. Kantian ethics has for some time now enjoyed a favored status, especially in the United States. This is due in no small way to the contributions of some very talented thinkers. But if wide consensus among philosophers establishes the presumption that the view held should be taken seriously and not oversimplified by its opponents, then the dangers of consensus require that the prestige of opinions plays no argumentative role in inquiry.

So much, then, for diplomacy; now for argument.

1.

Recent defenses of Kantian impartiality have employed the concept of regulative norms.[1] My purpose here is to clarify this concept, to show how it defuses some criticisms of Kant, and finally to argue that a clear understanding of regulative norms undermines Kantian claims about the role of

---

1. "Principles" is preferred among Kantians instead of "norms," but there are philosophical reasons for the latter. It might turn out that the regulatory work thought to be done by principles is actually done by other kinds of norms. "Norms," then, allows us to employ a philosophically neutral vocabulary. See especially, BarTbara Herman, *The Practice of Moral Judgment* (Cambridge, Mass.: Harvard University Press, 1993), 222–23. Others might have other sources of discomfort with the term, but I have been unable to find another term that is as neutral between philosophical conceptions.

impartiality in practical reason. I argue that impartial norms play a very important role in the practical reason of an admirable agent but not the one attributed to them by Kant and his defenders. Moreover, the position I defend is not one that has yet been considered on either side of the debate regarding the role of impartiality in ethics. So it is important not to read what follows as a defense of some standard objection to Kantian impartiality.

I define a regulative norm in terms of what I call its regulative effect on other norms. Two definitions will be given: one in the language of practical reason and one in the language of morality. For the sake of simplicity, the definitions assume contexts in which only two norms are relevant.

> For any two norms, A and B, A is regulated by B just in case there is some practical context in which (i) acting on A is irrational because it violates B and (ii) were it not for B it would be rational to act on A.

The second condition should be understood as "(ii) were it not for B it would be either (iia) not irrational to act on A or (iib) irrational not to act on A." That (i) and (iia) are sufficient for regulative effect is reflected in the fact that in a context in which were it not irrational to act on A condition (i) could not obtain. Since (iib) entails (iia), (i) and (iib) also reflect regulative effect, but (iib) is not a necessary condition. A third feature of regulative effect is that when A is regulated by B in the previous sense, not acting on A in such contexts is not contrary to A. For example, where, say, acting for the sake of a friend is regulated by the concern for respect for others, not acting for the sake of a friend is not contrary to friendship. (I will say more about this third feature shortly.)

The same concept can be formulated in moral terms.

> For any two norms, A and B, A is regulated by B just in case there is some practical context in which (i) acting on A is wrong because it violates B and (ii) were it not for B it would be permissible to act on A.

The second condition should be understood as "were it not for B it would be either (iia) not wrong to act on A or (iib) wrong not to act on A." (i) and (iia) are sufficient for regulative effect, since any context in which acting on A is not wrong is a context in which condition (i) does not obtain. Of course, if not acting on A is wrong in a context, it is not wrong to act on A in that context, though acting on A might not be wrong without its being obligatory. Finally, the third feature of regulative effect expressed in moral terms is that when A is regulated by B in the previous sense, not acting on A in such contexts is not wrong in terms of A itself. For example, where acting for the sake of a friend is regulated by the concern for respect for others, not acting for the sake of a friend is not an act of betrayal or disloyalty. This third feature of regulative effect contrasts with a way of talking about competing duties overriding each other. In contexts of the sort just mentioned, the language of regulative effect allows us to avoid saying that the duty of respect for others overrides the duty of friendship. This latter way of talking implies that in the context friendship requires acting in one way and respect for others in another. But the language of regulative effect for such contexts would not have us say that friendship requires us to do one thing and respect requires that we do another but that since favoring the friend would be disrespectful of others, friendship does not require what it otherwise would permit. This turns out to be a very powerful conceptual feature of regulative effect.[2]

I will assume without argument that any acceptable conceptual scheme that employs regulative norms in moral terms inherits the burden of mapping that conceptual scheme onto a defensible conception of practical reason. In other words, the language of morals must be translated into the language of practical reason, where it is shown that the obligations of morality are practically rational. This does not rule out uniquely moral obligations, but it does require that if there are such obligations, they must be practically rational for agents like us.

2.

To understand how this conception of regulative norms aids in a defense of Kant, it is first necessary to understand the kind of objection to which it is a response. The kind of objection I have in mind applies to the impartiality requirement as a necessary feature of any rational morality. Those who defend such a requirement have come to be known as "impartialists" and those who deny such a requirement as "partialists." Both terms are distorting, I will argue, for they are misleading as characterizations of either morality or practical reason. Among the leading partialists is Michael Stocker, and one of his examples has become a touchstone in the debate. I quote his example from his now-famous article, "The Schizophrenia of Modern Ethical Theories." He says:

> Suppose you are in the hospital, recovering from a long illness. You are very bored and restless and at loose ends when Smith comes in once again. You are now convinced more than ever that he is a fine fellow and a real friend—taking so much time to cheer you up, traveling

2. I would like to thank A. M. MacLeod for comments on this point.

all the way across town, and so on. You are so effusive with your praise and thanks that he protests that he always tries to do what he thinks is his duty, what he thinks will be best. You at first think he is engaging in a polite form of self-deprecation, relieving the moral burden. But the more you two speak, the more clear it becomes that he was telling the literal truth: that it is not essentially because of you that he came to see you, not because you are friends, but because he thought it his duty, perhaps as a fellow Christian or Communist or whatever, or simply because he knows of no one more in need of cheering up and no one easier to cheer up.

Surely there is something lacking here—and lacking in moral merit or value. The lack can be sheeted home to two related points: . . . the wrong sort of thing is said to be the proper motive; and, in this case at least, the wrong sort of thing is . . . essentially external.[3]

According to these observations, loving, partial acts must be motivated directly by love, and when apparently loving acts are done from nonloving, impartial motives, they cease to be loving acts. This is surely correct. But Stocker seems to suggest that if an act is done from a sense of obligation it cannot be done from love, and it is here that some impartialists think he has misunderstood the role of regulative norms in practical reason.

3.

The point against Stocker has been made most explicitly by Marcia Baron whose view is very similar to Herman's.[4] They agree that there is something objectionable about the moral psychology of the person in Stocker's example, but they disagree with him that what is objectionable is due to any inherent problem with a fully impartialist conception of morality. We can see this when we understand how a Kantian conception of morality employs regulative norms. I will make what I take to be their point in my own terms.

3. See Michael Stocker, "The Schizophrenia of Modern Ethical Theories," in The Virtues: Contemporary Essays on Moral Character, ed. Robert C. Kruschwitz and Robert C. Roberts (Belmont, Calif.: Wadsworth, 1986), 41, 42.

4. See Marcia Baron, "The Alleged Repugnance of Acting from Duty," Journal of Philosophy 81 (1984): 197–220. See also her Kantian Ethics Almost Without Apology (Ithaca: Cornell University Press, 1995) for a developed discussion of the role of imperfect duties and their regulatory role in Kant's moral theory. For Herman's views, see The Practice of Moral Judgment. Add to this Allison's Kant's Theory of Freedom (Cambridge: Cambridge University Press, 1990) and the result is a trilogy of books that presents a powerful picture of Kantian morality that relies heavily on the notion of regulative norms.

A norm can function either regulatively or determinately. It functions determinately when it is act-specific in its action-guiding role: when (with ample background conditions) it is sufficient for determining the act from among those available to the agent that is practically rational for the agent to perform in the circumstances. On the other hand, a norm functions merely regulatively in a context when though it is sufficient (given ample background conditions) for determining that some actions are practically *irrational* for an agent in the circumstances, it is not act-specific in its action-guiding role: it is not sufficient to determine which specific act is rational. Note that this way of making the distinction does not ascribe the functional features of norms to norms *simpliciter* but to their function in a context. So described, the distinction involves the concept of rational justification.

Also important, however, is the concept of motivation. In contexts in which a norm functions determinately as a justifier, it is also the determinate motive, as affection is to a hug.[5] Similarly, where a norm functions regulatively, it is only the regulative motive, as the desire for good health is to the avoidance of fatty foods.[6] What impartialists like Baron and Herman want to claim is that for any moral act there must be either a determinate or a regulative justifying norm that is completely impartial. Moreover, this does not prevent there being contexts in which the determinate norm is partial in both its justificatory and motivating aspects. Such contexts are those in which no impartial norm functions as a determinate justifier. Thus friends are free to visit each other in the hospital out of love where the love is determinate both as justifier and motivator and where such visits do not contradict the practical requirements of any relevant impartial norm. Most important, being motivated by a concern not to violate such impartial requirements does not intrude on our psychology in the way that Stocker imagines.

If Baron and Herman are right, and I think they are, we should be able to see in our own conceptual scheme the features of the regulative effect of impartial norms on partial norms, like the various forms of personal love. If we stay with the hospital situation and friendship, we should be able to see the following:

> Friendship is regulated by Impartial Respect just because there is some practical context in which (i) acting on Friendship is irrational (wrong)

---

5. Influenced by Herman, Baron calls this a primary motive. See "The Alleged Repugnance of Acting from Duty," 207.

6. Again following Herman, Baron calls this a secondary motive. "The Alleged Repugnance of Acting from Duty," 207.

because it violates Impartial Respect and (ii) were it not for Impartial Respect it would be rational (permissible) to act on Friendship.

Now consider two contexts, one in which an impartial norm is regulative and another in which it is determinate, both of which illustrate that we do in fact accept the truth of the above claim of the regulative effect of impartial respect on friendship.

In the first context, Smith's visiting you in the hospital does not involve his doing so at the cost of his failing to show proper impartial respect for others. He visits you as a loving friend who is also respectful of others. Here respect for others functions regulatively both as justifier and as motive, but friendship functions determinately in both regards. The regulative motive is revealed by some counterfactual statement to the effect that Smith would not have felt free to visit you had he thought it contrary to respect for others. Where the counterfactual condition is satisfied, Smith's sentiments of personal affection are free to express themselves directly rather than "externally," as Stocker would have it. The test, then, for whether some determinate norm is regulated by some other norm is whether there is some counterfactual condition at work in our approval of the determinate norm. The test is that when a norm is regulatively influenced by another norm yet is determinate in the context there is some counterfactual statement to the effect that there is some other context in which conditions (i) and (ii) hold regarding some other norm's regulative effect on that norm.

We need only imagine a second context to see that we do indeed recognize such a counterfactual in the background of our approval of Smith's visit in the first context. In the second context, Smith believes that his visiting you in the hospital would come at too great a cost to others and would not be consistent with impartial respect for them. Perhaps you are only slightly ill and Smith is scheduled to testify in court concerning the innocence of someone falsely accused. Here one would expect any fully admirable agent to have his or her course of action determined by the impartial consideration of respect for others. That is, one would expect that friendship should be regulated in such a way that it is respect that is the determinate justifier as well as motive in practical conflicts of this sort. Thus, on this view of friendship and impartial respect, impartial respect does not allow Smith to visit you in the second context, and friendship does not require it. It is this last feature—what I have previously referred to as the third feature of regulative effect—that shows that we accept a regulated conception of friendship as a partial norm. Surely, anyone alienated by such a conception of friendship suffers from bad character.

The point of both examples is that determinate justifiers and motives match up in just the way one would expect for a practical reasoner with good character. As far as this goes, Baron and Herman are right that Stocker's example does not pay due attention to the role of regulative norms and how they can function on an impartialist theory. On this analysis, however, the claim that morality is impartial comes to the claim that for any fully admirable moral agent there are no partial norms that are not subject to the regulating functions of impartial norms. In what remains, I will argue that such a claim is not sufficient reason to endorse fully impartialist conceptions of morality, and it is here that I will present an alternative not yet considered in the debate over impartiality in ethics. I will limit my comments to Kantianism.

4.

Kantians are right to insist that our view of partial norms and sentiments, like friendship and parental love, involves their being "filtered" through other considerations. Consider a conception of friendship not filtered by the regulative effects of other norms, partial or impartial. On this view, friendship requires one always to give priority to friends no matter what other considerations are at stake. No matter whether it involves love of family, sympathy for those in need, or respect for the dignity of others, friends always come first. On this view, any failure to give priority to friends in cases of conflict is an act of betrayal, for when the counterfactual test is applied to this conception of friendship, it reveals that there is no possible world in which others take priority over one's friends. The counterfactual test shows, then, that friendship on this conception is *asymmetrical* in its regulative effect on all other norms within this conception of practical reason. Other kinds of norms on other conceptions of practical reason can have this same property. Abraham's willingness to sacrifice Isaac seems to give religious faith this kind of status in Kierkegaard's understanding of the teleological suspension of the ethical.[7] Also, many moral theories afford some norms this status. What should be clear at this point is that attributing such a property to partial norms is counterintuitive, to say the least.

For now, however, it is important to see that some regulative norms can and do have another property, namely, the property of symmetrical regula-

7. Søren Kierkegaard, *Fear and Trembling,* trans. Walter Lowrie (New York: Anchor Books, 1954).

tive effect or function.[8] Consider in this regard friendship and parental love. For most of us, conceptions of these norms ascribe to them the property of having symmetrical regulative effect on each other. That is, not only do we believe that

> Friendship is regulated by Parental Love just because there is some practical context in which (i) acting on Friendship is irrational (wrong) because it violates Parental Love and (ii) were it not for Parental Love it would be rational (permissible) to act on Friendship

we also believe that

> Parental Love is regulated by Friendship just because there is some practical context in which (i) acting on Parental Love is irrational (wrong) because it violates Friendship and (ii) were it not for Friendship it would be rational (permissible) to act on Parental Love.

Within a conception of practical reason where the only regulative influences on these norms come from each other, considerations of family sometime override considerations of friendship but there are no other exceptions for the priority given to friends. On this view, some cases of favoring family over friends are not acts of betrayal and should not be so viewed by the friends. Think here of what you would expect of a friend if you had to cancel an appointment because your child was ill. A conception of friendship that makes exceptions in this way only for family is a conception of friendship involving a minimal regulating influence, which is revealed by the scope of the counterfactual conditions regarding other norms. A maximally regulated conception of friendship would be one the normative dimensions of which were influenced by the entire range of considerations a fully admirable agent would have, including impartial sympathy and respect for others. So it is implausible that any acceptable conception of friendship or any other partial sentiment will reflect the concept of asymmetrical regulative effect on other norms. Moreover, it will reflect the regulative effect of other norms on it, including the regulative effect of im-

---

8. The concept of symmetrical regulative function or symmetrical regulative effect is similar to the concept of bidirectionality found in the work of Henry Richardson. I discovered and read Richardson's excellent book, *Practical Reasoning about Final Ends*, only after the manuscript of *Agent-centered Morality* was sent to the copy editor. For his discussion of bidirectionality, see Henry S. Richardson, *Practical Reasoning about Final Ends* (Cambridge: Cambridge University Press, 1994), 141, 143, 176–77, 182.

partial respect. This can be captured in a rather complex statement of the counterfactual conditions included as a test of the extent to which the partial norm is regulated by other norms. Partial norms, then, are regulated both by other partial norms and by impartial norms, and at least some of the regulative functions between partial norms are symmetrical.

If my conception of friendship includes within it a reflection of a regulating influence of parental love, then I will *not* think of some cases of my giving priority to my children over my friends as cases of betrayal of my friends; and I will expect my friends to see this as such. Similarly, if my conception of parental love includes within it a reflection of a regulating influence of friendship, then I will *not* think of some cases of my giving priority to my friends over my children as cases of betrayal of my children; and I will expect my children to see this as such. It is only through conceptions of sentiments or norms that display such symmetry of regulating influence that we can integrate various kinds of partial sentiments and norms into our lives and avoid devastating alienation. Think what it would be like for friends and children to lack an intuitive understanding of the symmetry of norms alluded to here.

5.

Now consider how impartial norms might be regulatively influenced by other norms. First, impartial norms can reflect the regulative influence of other impartial norms. Consider the Kantian point about sympathy, for example. According to Kant, the following is true of the regulative function of impartial respect in regard to impartial sympathy.

> Impartial Sympathy is regulated by Impartial Respect just because there is some practical context in which (i) acting on Impartial Sympathy is irrational (wrong) because it violates Impartial Respect and (ii) were it not for Impartial Respect it would be rational (permissible) to act on Impartial Sympathy.

We do not think, as Kant rightly insists, of sympathy unregulated by other considerations in its conception as being mature sympathy.[9] Suppose I have a conception of sympathy such that it acts as justifier and motive for me regardless of other considerations. I will then think of anyone not giving pri-

9. Immanuel Kant, *Groundwork of the Metaphysic of Morals*, trans. H. J. Paton (New York: Harper Torchbooks, 1964), 66.

ority to considerations of sympathy regardless of other considerations as lacking in sympathy. But we do not think this. We do not think of a person who sometimes places respect for autonomy over the concern to alleviate distress as necessarily being unsympathetic. What this shows is that our concept of sympathy does not require that we always give priority to those with whom we are sympathetic on pain of being guilty of being unsympathetic, just as our concept of friendship does not require that we always give priority to friends on pain of being disloyal or guilty of betrayal.

Here, however, begins the problem with Kantianism. Respect is a norm that is a regulating influence on all other norms and sentiments, even including other impartial sentiments. This seems right. But what seems deeply wrong is that respect is not regulated by other norms, as is the case on a Kantian view. Two points are crucial here to seeing that, according to Kant, impartial respect is asymmetrical in its regulative features. First, to respect self and others on the Kantian view just is to be willing to deliberate in a certain way regarding how one should act. It is to submit one's deliberations regarding self and others to the categorical imperative decision procedure. Second, the CI procedure is an all things considered form of rationality according to Kant; therefore, there cannot be anything more that can regulate such rationality or such respect. Moreover, it would be odd to say from a Kantian perspective that there is a symmetrical regulative relationship between sympathy and impartial respect. This would mean that a natural inclination has a regulating influence over rationality.

Now consider, in contrast to Kant, how the regulative relationship between impartial sympathy and impartial respect might be symmetrical. Let us admit with Kant that the regulative influence of impartial respect is found in our conception of impartial sympathy. Thus the previous claim regarding the regulative effect of impartial respect on impartial sympathy is true. But where symmetry rather than asymmetry exists between these two impartial norms, the following will also be true.

> Impartial Respect is regulated by Impartial Sympathy just because there is some practical context in which (i) acting on Impartial Respect is irrational (wrong) because it violates Impartial Sympathy and (ii) were it not for Impartial Sympathy it would be rational (permissible) to act on Impartial Respect.

Why would anyone think that this is true, especially as applied to our considered moral judgments? A striking case, I believe, involves our feelings toward animals. According to Kant, respect is an attitude appropriate only toward rational agents, but sympathy can be had toward so-called lower animals (animals that lack some human cognitive capacities) that are not rational agents. Since moral concern, on Kant's view, is motivated directly only by impartial respect and concern for agents *per se*, this means that we have no direct moral concern for animals. (I will come to the point of indirection shortly). But consider a person who is both respectful of agents and sympathetic toward lower animals. He leaves his home one day to meet you for a luncheon appointment he promised to keep. If he misses the appointment, you will be a bit disappointed but nowhere near devastated. Between home and the restaurant he comes upon a man cruelly beating a dog. It is clear that the beating is a case of cruelty rather than something somehow necessary for a greater good. Moved by his sympathy for the dog, he stops and intervenes to prevent any further cruelty or harm to the animal. As a consequence, he is unable to make the appointment and only afterward is he able to call and explain the circumstances that prevented his meeting you.

The first thing to note is that these actions, given the circumstances, were surely both the right thing to do and perfectly rational for someone who both respects people and has sympathy for animals.[10] The second thing to note is that the actions on behalf of the dog affected the autonomy of two people—the dog beater and yourself—and were done for the sake of an animal that has no Kantian autonomy. Moreover, it is clear, I believe, that, contrary to Kant, we admire such actions because they show *direct* concern for animals.[11] Some advocates for animal rights prefer the language of "respect" for lower animals. With Kant, I believe that this is a mistake. Respect is an attitude appropriate toward rational agents, and dogs are not rational agents. They are nonetheless sentient creatures that can be cruelly treated and harmed. For this reason, we can sympathize with them. This is just what our exemplar did. Our exemplar, then, displays a conception of practical reason in which impartial respect for the autonomy of rational agents is regulated by something other than respect for the autonomy of rational agents. Moreover, I do not think any of us would say that the actions

10. The details might need filling in a bit to make this obvious, but no doubt it can be done.

11. We should be careful to distinguish direct concern from unreflective concern. When one has direct concern for another, one's concern is not the function of some other concern. This does not mean that the concern cannot be reflective and take into account other concerns.

of our exemplar were disrespectful of either you or the dog beater. Still, it remains true that were it not for his sympathy for the dog it would have been disrespectful to you for him simply not to have shown up for the appointment. Yet, because of the dog, it was not disrespectful. Conditions (i) and (ii) are clearly satisfied, as they were in the previous claim regarding the effect of respect on sympathy, which illustrates the symmetrical regulative functions of impartial respect and impartial sympathy.

Kantians, as far as I can see, have only one line of defense here, and it is an embarrassing one. They can argue that neither condition (i) nor (ii) is satisfied because it would have been wrong on the Kantian view itself to keep the appointment under the circumstances. The only way they can argue for this, however, is by appeal to the indirect connection between lack of concern for animals and concern for respecting rational agents. What one is morally concerned about, on this view, is not the welfare of the animal but either (a) the effect on one's own capacity for respecting rational agents if one allows oneself to be indifferent to the plight of animals or (b) the fact that the animal somehow belongs to a rational agent and hence harming it would be disrespectful to the owner. This seems to run directly into Stocker's problem in another context: there is a clear mismatch between reason and motive for action. Not preventing the cruelty would have been a wrong done *to the dog,* even at the expense of your slight disappointment and the sadistic interests of the dog beater. The Stocker problem is that Kantians cannot get the dog properly into the picture, as long as they treat impartial respect as asymmetrically regulative within practical reason.

If the Kantian does not allow that this is a counterexample to the asymmetry of impartial respect as a regulative norm, it is difficult to see why. If we should accept Kant's appeals to ordinary moral experience to establish that sympathy is regulated by respect in our understanding of a respectful agent of good character, then why should the above example not establish the same point regarding the regulative effect of sympathy on respect? Of course, if it is a counterexample, it implies that we are not pure practical reasoners. That we are not and that we do not aspire to be is evident in these very sentiments. One thing is certain: The argument from this example relies in no way on a caricature of Kant. It is appropriate, then, to expect a reasoned reply. And in the context of working out a theory of regulative norms, a familiar objection to Kant takes on added significance; it cannot be shrugged off as a minor flaw in his theory. More important, I will argue that the analysis of sympathy for lower animals generalizes in a very important sense (which is to be made clear) to the analysis of other norms.

6.

Indeed, the consideration of our sympathy for lower animals should open the way for a wholesale challenge to a conception of practical reason in which impartial respect for the autonomy of rational beings as such is asymmetrical in its regulative effect on our other concerns. In this section, I will argue that within our concern for persons, where lower animals are not an issue, impartial respect and impartial sympathy are symmetrical in their regulative functions, which is contrary to either the Kantian or the utilitarian view of these norms. I will focus on Kant's account of a duty to render aid, or what is sometimes called the Duty of Beneficence, and argue that the appeal of the Kantian analysis is not what Kantians take it to be. To illustrate the point, I will consider the constructivist model and argue that a distinction crucial to the Kantian project is not preserved.

The crucial distinction is between norms that have been "filtered," on the one hand, and norms that are the result of the "special application" of the CI procedure to the circumstances of human beings, on the other. These are not the same thing, and collapsing the distinction leads to serious errors about practical reason. Moreover, when we understand the distinction, we can see that the Kantian view must argue for the special application interpretation of the CI procedure over the filtering view, and I will argue that what actually occurs in Kantian universalizability tests, when they are successful, is filtering, not a special application of a decision procedure.

A stark way of seeing the filtering view is to consider how one can adjust two desires or sentiments to make room for both. Reflection on one's desires for both intrinsically meaningful work and the intimacy of a family life reveals various possibilities, one of which is a smaller family and a less demanding career. Becoming aware of this possibility appears as the solution to your problem when it adjusts each desire to the other within your psychology by being projectable into the future as your life. If the adjustment does not take place on reflection, filtering in this way has not yet solved the problem. The function of reflection in this case is simply to bring to consciousness different ways of living in which the intimacy of family life and a meaningful career can be conjoined or disjoined so that the psychological adjustment of desire can have its effect. And, of course, sometimes filtering does not adjust desires to each other; it sometimes removes a desire. For example, reflection on the marketing conditions involving young calves might extinguish one's desire for veal. Here one's tastes have been filtered through one's sentiments. Finally, filtering can sometimes fail to resolve conflicts simply because desires and sentiments reach a point of incommensurability: choosing which of your children to surrender to the Nazis might simply render you paralyzed regarding the future.

Filtering cannot be what is happening on the special application view, and it is the latter that is required by Kant. The worry that generates the special application view is ultimately traced to the notion that moral imperatives must be categorical and necessary rather than hypothetical and contingent. To secure categorical necessity, practical reason must be pure, which means, among other things, that the content of one's judgment is rational in virtue of its form alone, namely, the form of reasoning of a rational being as such. Thus the Kantian thought is that form is applied to content, but it is the form that is crucial; content is only the special occasion for judgment. Otherwise, contingency enters to vitiate the purity of practical reason and to undermine the categorical demands of morality. It does this when sentiment and desire—contingent features of a psychology—are not merely the occasion for judgment but the ultimate determinants of action and rational choice. Not only are particular desires and sentiments contingencies of rational agency on Kant's view, but the mere having of desires and sentiments is also a contingency of rational agency. For Kant, God, who is a rational agent, does not have desires and sentiments; yet God can employ the CI procedure. In some of its applications, the CI procedure adjusts to the special circumstances of human beings who are rational agents and who do have desires and sentiments. This is not because God *desires* that human beings do well or because God has sympathy or some other sentiment for human beings. God is completely unsentimental. He is, however, rational. He can apply the CI procedure to the special circumstances of human beings and is allegedly motivated without desire or sentiment to do so. This means that the CI procedure must be such that it can yield a rational choice independent of the kind of filtering alluded to earlier; hence the special application interpretation of the CI procedure cannot involve filtering for God. Nor can it for us, for filtering cannot ensure the categorical necessity sought for in the universalizability tests. Whatever, then, is distinctively moral about moral reflection is purely intellectual and must be so if the requirements of morality are to be categorical. It is crucial here to keep in mind that to make sense of the special application view, Kant must take recourse to the notion of God as a rational being who does not have desires and sentiments.

With this distinction between the filtering view and the special application view of moral reflection in mind, consider Kant's analysis of the duty to render aid, or the Duty of Beneficence.

Kant himself believes that our duties to others involve more than mere noninterference. He believes that it is rational for a respectful person to be concerned about more than mere noninterference with the autonomy of others and that it is sometimes irrational for a respectful person to be concerned only with noninterference. He endorses a version of the Duty of Beneficence, that we should help others where doing so would come at little cost to ourselves or others and would benefit others significantly.[12] But why is one conception of respect that sometimes requires more than mere noninterference rational and the other conception that never requires more than noninterference irrational? The reason, I believe, for our thinking this is parallel to the case of animals. In the case of animals, sympathy for them regulates our conception of respect for persons because we care, in different ways, for both lower animals and for human agents. Were we to accept respect for persons as an asymmetrical regulative norm, our conceptual scheme would be different from what it in fact is. In the case of human agents, our sympathy regarding the limits of human self-sufficiency regulates our concern for noninterference, the overall effect of which is a regulated conception of respect for human autonomy. Again, the regulative effect is brought about by the fact that we care in different ways for human beings. Were we to accept concern for noninterference as an asymmetrical regulative norm, our conceptual scheme would be different from what it in fact is. Thus our concept of respect for autonomy includes sympathy for humans as limited in autonomy, which, to my mind, clearly reveals that our conception of respect for persons has undergone its own filtering process.

But it is not enough simply to assert this. To do so would be simply to assume the truth of the very thing at issue, namely, that our sense of respect for persons is filtered through our sympathy for persons. I must give some principled reasons for thinking that the animal case generalizes in an important sense to the case of persons.

In this regard, consider an example very similar to Kant's own example in *The Groundwork for the Metaphysics of Morals*. Imagine a person walking along the shore of a lake, when suddenly she hears someone crying for help. Immediately it is clear both that if she does not help the person will drown and that the only cost to her if she does help will be the minor inconvenience of getting her clothes dirty. There is no risk to her at all, and there are no other pressing considerations. Now most of us surely believe that the person not willing to help in such circumstances lacks something of

12. Kant, *Groundwork*, 90.

moral importance. Yet let us assume that though she would not be willing to help, she would nonetheless take great risks to avoid interfering with the rights of people to express their political views. What is lacking here?

One might say that she has respect for people but no sympathy for them. This cannot be the Kantian response, because Kant believes that the categorical imperative, and thus impartial respect for the drowning victim, requires the actions of the Duty of Beneficence in such a case. She cannot, then, have Kantian impartial respect for persons in such a case and feel free to stand on the excuse that she is not interfering, though she is not rendering aid either. Another possibility is that she has neither respect nor sympathy for people. But if this were true, how could we explain that she is quite willing to take on significant risks not to interfere with free political speech? What we should say here, I believe, is that she has a distorted conception of impartial respect; moreover, I believe that Kant would say this as well. If this is correct, then she is acting irrationally due to a distortion. The question now becomes, What undistorted form of practical consciousness is there that would make acting in accordance with the Duty of Beneficence practically rational for her?

We have already given one reason, namely, that she has a conception of impartial respect that is regulated by a conception of impartial sympathy. The effect of this is that her respect for human autonomy is filtered through her sympathy for the limits of self-sufficiency, a very straightforward, utterly familiar sentiment. Kantians, however, must give a different account. They must distinguish between "filtering," on the one hand, and "taking account of the special circumstances of human agents," on the other, and argue for the latter to secure the purity of practical reason and the categorical status of moral demands.

Kantians can take this line, of course, only on the condition that there is a universalizability test that yields the right results and that the test does not involve the filtering of impartial respect. Here they might appeal to Kantian constructivism, or to the constructivist model of impartial respect.

The constructivist model can be understood as like the one found in John Rawls's *A Theory of Justice*.[13] Though Rawls himself did not intend the model to be applied to morality in general, it is instructive to consider how it might be applied in the current context. On the proposed application, we

13. See John Rawls, *A Theory of Justice* (Cambridge, Mass.: Harvard University Press, 1971), esp. pt. 3, 118–94; Stephen L. Darwall, *Impartial Reason* (Ithaca: Cornell University Press, 1983), 220, 230–31, 240–49. Darwall believes that the Kant-

can imagine self-interested practical reasoners operating with limited knowledge behind a veil of ignorance faced with a choice between the Duty of Beneficence and a simple Duty of Noninterference. The reasoners in the original position have general knowledge but no specific knowledge regarding their special circumstances. The general knowledge includes all the general facts of human psychology, especially those related to the limits of human self-sufficiency, but no specific knowledge of their own psychological characteristics. Finally, the reasoners are risk averse, making it rational for them to adopt strategies that avoid worst possible outcomes. Would it be rational for them to choose the Duty of Beneficence over the simple Duty of Noninterference? Given the choice situation and the assumptions regarding the reasoners, I believe that it would.

Kantians will think that this proves that there is a purely rational derivation of the Duty of Beneficence from the concept of rational agency per se and the special circumstances of human agents. Thus one need not appeal to sympathy as a basis for the practical rationale for the Duty of Beneficence. Since the principle is established merely by appeal to the results of an intellectual procedure—an interpretation of the CI procedure—there is no need to ascribe regulative effect to impartial sympathy on our conception of impartial respect, and the asymmetrical regulative function of impartial respect is preserved for our conception of practical reason. Kant is then vindicated, and pure practical reason prevails.[14]

There is, I believe, a decisive response to this. It is that whether one comes out with the rationality of the Duty of Beneficence or the Duty of Noninterference turns on how the decision procedure is set up in the first place. By making the reasoners rationally self-interested, by excluding special knowledge, and by assuming certain attitudes toward risk, we assured the result we wanted. Yet in doing so, we made the reasoners deliberate in ways that assured sympathy, just as we made them deliberate in ways that assured respect. Notice that God, who has neither inclinations nor interests, is not a party to the contract. We are only able to get the desired result by appealing to a conception of agency that includes *as an essential part of agency itself* the having of interests. When we control for special self-knowledge by implementing the veil of ignorance, we transform self-

---

ian interpretation of Rawls provides the basis for a general conception of practical reason.

14. I believe something like this is the import of the view suggested by Stephen Darwall regarding sympathy in *Impartial Reason;* see esp. 173 ff.

interest into generalized sympathy. The assumption of aversive attitudes toward risk ensures the separateness of persons and impartial respect. The conception of agency we have instantiated in the model, then, is not the reasoning of a pure practical reasoner, a God who does not have desires and sentiments, but that of a sympathetically respectful and a respectfully sympathetic agent, a being whose psychological apparatus includes both sympathy and respect as sentiments essential to its capacities of practical reason.[15] But this is filtering; it is not the application of a purely intellectual universalizability test to the special circumstances of human agents. That it is filtering is made clear by two facts: we could not have set up the model to get *any* results had we not made the persons in the original position interested behind the veil of ignorance, and we could have gotten *different* results by setting up the model with other constraints. The first point shows that we do not have a conception of rational agency without desires and sentiments, and the second point shows that only some forms of rational agency yield the desired results. These two facts give us principled, sufficient reasons for thinking of the regulative functions between sympathy and respect for persons as being analogous to the relationship between sympathy for lower animals and respect for persons. For the only way we could set up a constructivist model to cover the case of lower animals would be to make the persons in the original position care about lower animals, and this would clearly be filtering, not the application of a purely intellectual procedure to the special circumstances of lower animals. It is in this very important sense that the analysis of the case of lower animals generalizes to the case of sympathy and respect for persons.

Could we have staged a decision context in which the reasoners were concerned with noninterference but not with rendering aid? Perhaps we could have by employing some notion of risk. The reason we do not set up the procedure in that way is because we want our agents to be sympathetic in their understanding of the limits of self-sufficiency. That we can set up the procedure to secure this result only reinforces the fact of the regulative

15. Kantians might assert that God is both sympathetic and loving as well as respectful but that sympathy and love are purely cognitive capacities in God's case; they carry no affective or conative functions. They are simply epistemic capacities that allow God to employ the CI procedure in its application to the special circumstances of human agents. But surely this is implausible? We have no awareness of what it would be like to love or sympathize with another person where affective and conative capacities are not in play. It is hard, then, to see this kind of response as anything other than ad hoc.

influence of impartial sympathy on our conception of impartial respect. It does not confirm the Kantian notion of impartial respect as an asymmetrical regulative norm, and this should be reinforced in retrospect by our thoughts about sympathy for lower animals. Lower animals do not have even instrumental rationality, or at least many of them do not, let alone the capacity for the autonomy of pure practical reason. How are they to be parties to the contractual model envisioned by Kantian constructivism? Yet we are firm in our beliefs about the importance of lower animals, which is a clear instance of our impartial respect being filtered through our sympathy for animals.

Kantians, of course, worry that if we make a place for sympathy like this in our conception of practical reason, then we will lose not only the concept of the purity of practical reason but also the guarantee that morality is universal.[16] Those who lack sympathy will lack this conception of impartial respect.

So they will, and there is no way to weasel out of this. In the end, one has to choose between the concept of guaranteed universality[17] and some other concepts. Among these are a conceptual scheme that is true to our actual values—think here again of our sympathy for lower animals—and a plausible philosophy of mind. Kant's views on human volition and action and his general philosophy of mind are controversial even among Kantians.[18] On the other hand, that sympathy and respect, understood as sentiments, have a mutual influence on each other as psychological norms within human behavior is plausible on its face. We understand what it is like to be agents and to a degree self-sufficient, and we understand what it is like to be vulnerable and limited in our capacities. That we care about both is enough to make plausible the symmetry of these two impartial norms, without appealing to the concept of God, to a questionable metaphysics, or to a hypo-

16. For the general point about contingencies of human agency and universality, see Onora O'Neill, *Constructions of Reason: Explorations of Kant's Practical Philosophy* (Cambridge: Cambridge University Press, 1989), 52–55. For more specific discussion of sympathy and universality, see Darwall, *Impartial Reason*, 162–63, 173–74.

17. For Kant, universality must be secured by necessity rather than by empirical fact: intersubjectively shared norms cannot provide practical laws, no matter what their content or the scope of their sharedness among humans.

18. John Rawls, *Political Liberalism* (New York: Columbia University Press, 1993), 89–130; Thomas Hill, *Dignity and Practical Reason in Kant's Moral Theory* (Ithaca: Cornell University Press, 1992), 226–50.

thetical decision procedure. This is not to deny that some hypothetical decision procedure might help us clarify what is rational for us to do, given that it captures the symmetrical relationship between sympathy and respect. What it cannot do is establish a purely intellectual reason for this rationality, for it will be rational for us to accept the artificial procedure only if we are in fact respectfully sympathetic and sympathetically respectful in the way that the procedure assures.

The crucial point of this section, then, is that the Kantian must construe the constructivist model to establish that there is a purely intellectual reason for the Duty of Beneficence because the choice of duties or principles is merely an application of the categorical imperative to the special circumstances of human agents. That this is not the case is reinforced by our discussion of sympathy for lower animals, because the CI procedure, even in its constructivist form, cannot be construed to include lower animals as parties to the social contract and hence as a special application to their circumstances. Just as our sympathy for lower animals sometimes regulates our concern for the autonomy of human beings, our sympathy for human beings sometimes regulates our respect for the autonomy of other human beings. And I can see no reason that a similar analysis does not apply to the test for imperfect duties sketched by Kant in the *Groundwork*, out of which the constructivist model is built.[19]

Kant's universalizability test for imperfect duties, which is the test that would apply to the kind of context we are considering, is this: as a rational being who has respect for self and others one must be able to will that *any* rational being live in a system of nature in which one's maxim is a natural law. The imaginative thought project here cannot be carried out by someone who is not sympathetic in his or her respectful response to the plight of others. At least, this must be true if the duty to render aid is to be the rational result. To secure the result we want regarding the plight of lower animals, we would have to extend the imperfect duties test to cover nonrational, lower animals in our concern for the environment in which creatures have to live. We have, then, the same reasons for thinking of the imperfect duties test as filtering as we do for the constructivist model. Hence the argument regarding the constructivist model applies without dissimilarity to the imperfect duties test. Whatever plausibility these tests have is due to the fact that they filter our sentiments, including impartial respect; it is not due to the purely intellectual application of a procedure to the spe-

19. Kant, *Groundwork*, 89–92.

cial circumstances of human agents. To a large extent, this explains why there is sometimes disagreement about what the results of the procedure are for particular cases among people of similar intelligence but different sentiments. It also explains why the purely formal aspects of the procedure provide little in the way of guidance to someone who has no sentiments, which is to say that such a procedure would provide Kant's God with little direction. We should be very suspicious of theories of practical reason that rely on appeals to God, and as we see here, when we eliminate God from the picture we see that filtering is what is secured by the tests.

7.

Thus far we have seen that impartial norms regulate partial norms and that impartial norms regulate each other in our conception of practical reason. Regarding the latter, we have seen that impartial norms are symmetrical in their regulative functions, both as they apply to relationships between persons and lower animals and as they apply to relationships among persons themselves. I turn now to the issue of whether our conception of practical reason reflects symmetrical regulative functions between partial norms and impartial norms regarding relationships among persons. If it does, then our conception of practical reason does not give a place to impartial norms that are asymmetrical in the way required by both Kantianism and other modern moral theories.

I will consider impartial respect and the partial norm of parental love and argue that they are symmetrical in their regulative functions. Once again, I will argue that there is something very important about the analysis of sympathy for lower animals and respect for persons that generalizes to the analysis of parental love and impartial respect. I leave it to the reader to extend the analysis to other partial norms. My goal in this section, then, is to clarify the problem facing the Kantian view. The goal of the next section is to provide an argument against a Kantian solution.

That impartial respect regulates parental love is not difficult to establish. There are many contexts in which if we favor our own children over others we will be acting disrespectfully. Moreover, in those very same contexts, our favoring others over our own children is not betrayal, though it would be were it not for our respect for others. My serving jury duty might come at some cost to my child, though my exacting that same cost for other reasons might constitute betrayal. In some contexts, then, refusing to serve jury duty is disrespectful and is not required by parental love, though it otherwise would be.

The more controversial issue is whether impartial respect exhibits the regulative effect of parental love. I believe that it does, and if I am right, we accept the truth of the following claim.

Impartial Respect is regulated by Parental Love just because there is some practical context in which (i) acting on Impartial Respect is irrational (wrong) because it violates Parental Love and (ii) were it not for Parental Love it would be rational (permissible) to act on Impartial Respect.

Consider the following case. I can either send my daughter to college where she can get the best education consistent with her abilities or use that same amount of money to send several other youths to college. An important difference is that my child has been accepted to several of the best private and public schools in the country. The problem for the other students is that they cannot afford to go to the more expensive superior schools, though these students have also been accepted. There are other schools to which these other students might go, however, that are quite good and less expensive, but the students and their families cannot afford them. Moreover, these other students are as deserving or maybe even slightly more deserving than my daughter and there are more of them than there are scholarships and loans to support. There are even other very deserving students, a greater number of them, who were unable to get into the very top first- and second-rung schools but who have been admitted to some very good to decent schools, none of which they can afford. Now I can either send my daughter to the best school I can afford that is consistent with her talents or I can support a greater number of students at the second-rung schools or even a greater number at the third-rung but still decent schools. Now assume that the talents of my daughter are such that there would be a significant difference in the results of her education at the very best schools than at the second-best schools and that this is also true of some of the other students. Assume, also, that everything else is equal. That this is a realistic case in terms of costs can be confirmed by checking the widely different costs of higher education, depending on the institution involved. The example is selected because many of us in higher education have talented children who put us in the position of making just such a choice.[20]

What would it be rational for me to do if I am both a respectful person

20. I thank James Klagge for suggesting this kind of example.

and a loving parent? Would my sending the other students to college be a betrayal of my daughter's love? Would my sending my child to the best college consistent with her abilities be disrespectful to the other children? Surely the answer to the second question is yes and to the third question no, both of which provide an answer to the first question. A conceptual scheme that cannot allow for the fact that an impartially respectful but loving parent is significantly more committed (but not to an unlimited degree) to his or her own children than to others condemns itself to irrelevance to loving parents. I take it, then, that this example is firm in its result regarding what would be the rational and right thing to do, given the circumstances.

Now we must see if this example presents any problems for the Kantian view of impartial respect as a regulative norm that is asymmetrical in its regulative effect on the partial norm of parental love. A clear rationale for the priorities is available on a conception of practical reason within which impartial respect and parental love are symmetrical in their regulative functions vis-à-vis each other. The jury duty example illustrates the regulative influence of impartial respect on parental love, and the education example illustrates the regulative influence of parental love on impartial respect. Conditions (i) and (ii) of the counterfactual condition are met in both directions, which is the mark of symmetrical regulative function.

Kantians, however, might, in an attempt to preserve our values, argue for the rationality and rightness of sending one's own child to college in such circumstances. This would seem to defuse the example. And indeed it would if the argument to this effect were to meet certain conditions. To do so, the argument must first establish precisely how impartial respect expressed in the CI procedure as applied to the context would require sending one's own child to school and not using one's money for the other children. This is not a case of it being merely permissible to favor one's own. The Kantian position seems plausible as long as the focus is on contexts involving merely permissible actions. We are thinking here of parental obligations, not mere permissions. Moreover, the argument must be constructed in a way that does not employ a conception of respect that has already been filtered through considerations of parental love. Just as Kantians can rightly insist that a conception of parental love that has already been filtered though considerations of impartial respect cannot pose a threat to the moral status of impartial respect, non-Kantians can insist that a conception of impartial respect that has already been filtered through considerations of parental love cannot pose a threat to the moral status of parental love. How, then, can Kantians ensure against such filtering? There are only a few possibilities, which represent different conceptual models for understanding impartial respect as an asymmetrical regulative norm.

The Simple Noninterference Model

One strategy mentioned before involves a minimalist view of impartial respect. It depends on an understanding of respect that requires only noninterference and nothing in the way of positive aid, where failing to promote is not counted as interference. On this view, as long as my sending my child to college did not interfere with the other children and their education, I would not be showing disrespect for them by not coming to their aid. This being true in the present case, I would be free to send my own daughter to college.

There are several problems with such a view, two of which are most relevant here. First, it is clearly not Kant's view, which should be evident from previous discussion. Only a caricature could saddle Kant with this model. Second, it fails, as Kant saw, because it is not, in some respects, demanding enough. Kant's worry was that it does not demand enough in terms of positive duties to render aid, and he was surely right about that. Therefore, it is enough to reject this view that it is not demanding enough in terms of impartiality alone.[21] Moreover, there are few Kantians or other impartialists who want to defend anything like this model. I include it only to indicate the counterintuitiveness of minimalist moralities.

The Strict Egalitarian Model

A more complicated model is more demanding and has an initially intuitive appeal. On this view, impartial respect would have us treat everyone on a strictly equal basis, which, though strictly egalitarian, would not guarantee sameness of outcome. Anticipating differential outcomes, I might rationally favor one person over another while treating them equally from the perspective of impartial respect. The idea is something like the following. Persons are respected equally when the relative importance of their interests from their own points of view are given equal weight in practical deliberation from the moral point of view. Suppose we distinguish interests lexically and roughly as first order, second order, and third order interests.

---

21. There is another sense in which such a morality would be too demanding. If we could never justify interfering with the autonomy of others, we simply could not get on with much of anything. On any plausible view of noninterference, we can interfere even if it is only to minimize noninterference. It is notoriously difficult, however, to specify a rationale for mere noninterference that does not lead to positive duties.

The idea is that first order interests are those that are the most important from a particular person's point of view (their ground projects, what life is most about for them); second order interests are the second most important from that person's point of view (very important but not absolutely central interests); and third order interests are the least important from the personal point of view (comparatively minor interests). The idea, as suggested by Korsgaard's Tanner Lectures, is that a person's autonomy is gauged best in terms of the concerns that factor most centrally in his or her identity.[22] For present purposes, further fine tuning of these distinctions regarding kinds of interests is unimportant, though doing so will be crucial to elaborating the theory of practical reason presented in following chapters. All we need to note here is the general conception of equality on such a view. It is this: To treat two persons equally and with respect is to give equal weight to their interests as long as the interests are of the same category on the lexical scale. Otherwise, disputes are resolved by giving first priority to first order interests over second order interests and to second order interests over third order interests. This allows strict equality of consideration but differential outcome, a plausible view in many deliberative contexts.

Moreover, it is consistent, in many contexts, with being both a loving parent and an impartially respectful person. For example, suppose I can satisfy some minor interest of my daughter but only at the cost of some vital, first order interest of some innocent third party. I am faced, say, with taking her to the circus or rescuing another child from a burning building. How can it be impartially respectful to give priority to my child's interest in the circus over the vital interests of the other child, and on what conception of parental love is this required? The point is that no plausible conception of impartial respect would allow such inequality, and no plausible conception of parental love would require it. What we see in this conception of respect that we did not in the previous conception is a more plausibly demanding impartial norm.

The problem is that though this conception of impartial respect has rational results in many cases, it does not in others. Most notably, it has irrational results for the loving and respectful parent in our education example. Strict equality would require a loving parent to send the other children to school instead of his or her own. This is a direct result of this conception of

---

22. See Christine M. Korsgaard, *The Sources of Normativity* (Cambridge: Cambridge University Press, 1996), 17, 18, 102–3, 73. Korsgaard does not endorse anything like Strict Egalitarianism. Such a view is closer to David Cummiskey's view in *Kantian Consequentialism* (New York: Oxford University Press, 1996).

strict equality, even construed as not requiring sameness of outcome: to send one's own child on these assumptions would afford a disproportionate weight to the fact that it is the interests of one's own child that are at stake. Once we make this conception of impartial respect an asymmetrical regulative norm, there seems little place for the most commonplace priorities of partial sentiments. That this is not our conception of impartial respect is evident in the sentiments of people who love their children and yet do a good deal for other people. Although their priorities do not reflect such strict egalitarianism, we admire them for loving their children in the way they do. We cannot think, then, that our education example satisfies conditions (i) and (ii) of our claim *and* accept the strict egalitarian conception of impartial respect.

Of course, these observations refute Kantian ethics only if this is the only sense in which impartial respect could be asymmetrical in its regulative function vis-à-vis other norms. To conclude this at this point, however, would be premature. What, then, are the other possibilities?

The Indirect Model

Someone might object that our rejection of the strict egalitarian model has been hasty, for there might be an indirect route to the priorities reflected in our example within the strict egalitarian model itself. It should be noted that the strict egalitarian model accommodates a consequentialist framework very well, though not utilitarian in nature. When problems can be solved simply by appeal to the lexical ordering of interests, maximizing is not at issue. But when conflicts are within one category of interests on the lexical scale, resolving disputes by a maximizing strategy is, from an impartial viewpoint, quite rational, everything else being equal. Recognizing this, one might argue that, given human variables, the maximal degree of equality achievable among persons is best brought about when loving parents act on the priorities reflected in our example and in our claim regarding regulative effect than when they act directly on the strict egalitarian conception of impartial respect.

This is an old story originally employed by utilitarians and still with much currency among many moral philosophers today.[23] I will not pursue it very far, except to point out that it runs directly into Stocker's problem.

23. See Peter Railton, "Alienation, Consequentialism, and the Demands of Morality," in *Friendship: A Philosophical Reader*, ed. Neera Kapur Badhwar (Ithaca: Cornell University Press, 1993), 211–44; and Cummiskey, *Kantian Consequentialism*.

Herman seems to want to avoid such a strategy just because she recognizes that it would result in an objectionable moral psychology.[24] Just as people who care about animals in ways that we respect do not care for them indirectly but directly, loving parents care for their children directly and their reasons for acting on their behalf are direct. To endorse indirection here is to revise or abandon our conceptual scheme, and recognizing this was part of the original motivation Kantians had for bringing attention to regulative norms in the first place. Resorting to indirection, therefore, seems to admit the defeat of the original strategy and to sacrifice its original insight, which is considerable.

At this point, then, we can say that whatever the Kantian reply is it must satisfy the following conditions: it must (i) secure the results of our example, (ii) reflect a more substantial conception of respect than found in the Noninterference Model, (iii) avoid the results of the direct application of Strict Egalitarianism, (iv) avoid the distorting effects of Indirect Egalitarianism, and (v) achieve all this without filtering the concept of impartial respect through considerations of parental love.

8.

How to construct the constructivist model is problematic in itself. The reasons are that Rawls himself did not intend the model to cover the entire scope of morality and other attempts have either been found inadequate or incomplete. There was an early attempt by David A. J. Richards in *A Theory of Reasons for Action*, which has received little support, and a later sketch by Thomas Hill, Jr., which by his own admission is incomplete.[25] Neither has been taken up by recent writers in defense of Kantian impartiality against partialist attacks. Rawls's model is designed for the choice of principles governing basic social institutions. The problem here involves norms that govern one's personal life, in many ways a much messier affair, and capturing these complex nuances is the major part of the difficulty. The best that I can do here is to construct the model in a way that avoids caricature and is sufficient to provide guidance in regard to evaluating the current issue.

24. Herman, *The Practice of Moral Judgment*, 161–62, 173.

25. Thomas Hill sketches an attempt at expanding Rawls's constructivist model, but I do not see how to employ it in the current context. What I do in what follows is an attempt to alter the model in reasonable ways to accommodate the issue. See David A. J. Richards, *A Theory of Reasons for Action* (Oxford: Clarendon Press, 1971); Hill, *Dignity and Practical Reason in Kant's Moral Theory*, 243–50.

I will be guided by two crucial thoughts. First, not only should the model yield a result that is rational given the constraints of the choice situation; it must yield the result that it is rational for persons to act on the norms that would be chosen in the hypothetical situation in actual situations with all the known facts. The model is simply a means of elucidating our deepest values. This, I believe, is a feature of Rawls's view as well. Otherwise, the norms are not rational for agents like us but for some other kind of agents. Second, the model must not obviously filter for parental love.

We must characterize the choice situation in terms of an original position in which rational agents must choose from among a list of principles to govern cases. The original position will include a veil that filters out all irrelevant specific knowledge and allows only relevant general knowledge. Much of the problem is in understanding what is to count as irrelevant specific knowledge and relevant general knowledge. I will consider three different characterizations in this regard and evaluate each, arguing that none is successful.

I will assume aversive attitudes toward risk for those in the original position, for without them we are not likely to get anything like a Kantian result. For similar reasons, I will assume the Rawlsian maximin strategy of avoiding worst outcomes, which assumes that worst outcomes are most probable. If we assume equiprobability of alternative outcomes under conditions of uncertainty, we will end up with something like utilitarianism and be far from anything Kantian, as John Harsanyi has already shown.[26]

Now imagine that these reasoners are presented with a choice of norms to govern their lives once the veil is lifted. Here we are concerned with the rationality of a choice of those in the original position between the following alternatives.

a. Simple Noninterference with autonomy;
b. Direct, Strict Egalitarianism;
c. Indirect Egalitarianism; or
d. Limited Partialism (the priorities involved in our education example).

A necessary condition for the Kantian rejection of our example as establishing the symmetry of regulative functions between impartial respect and

26. John Harsanyi, "Morality and the Theory of Rational Behavior," in *Utilitarianism and Beyond,* ed. Amartya Sen and Bernard Williams (Cambridge: Cambridge University Press, 1982), 39–62.

parental love is that the reasoners would choose (a) Limited Partialism. It is necessary because Noninterference is not robust enough, Direct, Strict Egalitarianism does not establish the results of our example, and Indirect Egalitarianism runs afoul of Stocker's problem. Allegedly, it would be sufficient, baring other difficulties, because it would establish those priorities through a procedure that did not build the partial norm of parental love into the decision procedure itself.

First Construction

The first way of constructing the model employs all the above conditions and assumes that all the parties in the original position are parentally loving and that the veil of ignorance does not filter out this specific knowledge. Now it does not take much imagination to see that constructing the model in this way will lead to the desired result of their selecting Limited Partialism over the other principles. But, then, it is equally easy to see that the first construction filters for parental love in a way that does not serve the Kantian view.

We should not think that, relative to the current issue of partial norms, the constructivist model can be treated the way it was relative to the issue of the symmetrical functions of sympathy and respect. The reason is that we must distinguish between being self-interested, which all the parties to the choice are, and different psychologies that embed different partial norms. When we make the reasoners self- interested behind the veil of ignorance, we effectively make them sympathetic reasoners. Thus we get conceptions of respect and sympathy that are symmetrical in their regulative functions relative to each other. For the moment, I propose that we bracket this philosophical conclusion about the symmetrical function of respect and sympathy and consider other results of the model. Relevant here is the fact that the reasoners in the current case will only know that among the different psychologies they might have after the veil is lifted is one that includes parental love. It might also exclude it, rather drastically. If we are to capture what it is to respect people with different ways of life autonomously chosen, we cannot favor one way of life over another in the way that the choice situation is set up. Thus there are many ways of life with many attendant psychologies, and the model must honor this if it is to remain Kantian. Accordingly, the reasoners in the original position are sympathetic, but they are not parentally loving. Of utmost importance is that the original position be set up in a way that makes the reasoners sympathetic and respectful but neutral between conceptions of ways of life that include parental aspirations versus conceptions that make little or no place for such relations. Behind the veil, the reasoners are not psychologically constituted in any way specific to a way of life. They know only that when the veil is lifted they will have some specific psychology fitted to some particular way of life, ranging from highly communal ways of life to highly individualistic ones that include no love for children. For this reason, the first construction is to be rejected: though it will yield the right decision, it is set up in a way that it filters for parental love.

Second Construction

Now consider a second construction in which the veil of ignorance filters out all specific knowledge of individual psychology and that all the other features of the first construction remain.

Enough has been said, I believe, to rule out Noninterference as a rational choice, but I believe that Limited Partialism is irrational as well, given the choice assumptions. The reason is quite simple in the end: Direct Strict Egalitarianism ensures best against worst outcomes. To be sure, there are many contexts in which Limited Partialism and Strict Egalitarianism will yield consistent results. Since Limited Partialism has been filtered through the regulatory functions of a conception of respect, it will be consistent with those contexts in which the interests of strangers take priority over the interests of loved ones, namely, those contexts in which the stranger's interests are higher up the lexical scale than those of the loved one. Moreover, impartial respect will require that priority in these contexts is given to the interests of strangers. Yet if the order is reversed, if the interests of loved ones are higher up the scale than the strangers, loved ones will get priority. This is true on both Limited Partialism, as I intend it here, and Strict Egalitarianism.

They will differ where the conflicts involve interests within the same category on the lexical scale, most poignantly, when the conflicts involve first order interests. Strict Egalitarianism will maximize here. It will require acting in a way that brings about the greatest overall equality, which means giving priority to that option that will accommodate the most persons with their first order interests satisfied. Limited Egalitarianism will not maximize, though it will be sensitive to avoiding what we can call catastrophic outcomes, outcomes where extremely large numbers of people have their first order interests and hopes destroyed. To test this last point, merely think of what it would be like to reject the counterfactual that one would sacrifice one's self and loved ones in order to save the world. This is different from rejecting the counterfactual that one would sacrifice one's own first order interests and those of one's loved ones in order to marginally increase overall equality. Strict Egalitarianism and Limited Partialism are different in this important regard. What remains is the issue of worst outcomes.

If the reasoners are risk averse and maximin strategists, they will choose that option that is most probable to minimize worst outcomes for themselves once the veil is lifted. Strict Egalitarianism is preferable to Limited Partialism in this regard, for it will minimize the number of people who have their first order interests unsatisfied where the conflict is between first order interests alone. Thus, barring other considerations, the parties can know through purely general knowledge that it is less probable on the Strict Egalitarian view than on Limited Partialism that they will be victims of social inequalities.

But what about these other considerations? Might they not be such as to turn things in favor of Limited Partialism from the point of view of the reasoners in the original position? Now it might be argued that from purely general knowledge the reasoners can know a fact of developmental psychology, namely, that it is highly unlikely that anyone deprived of the benefits of some degree of parental favoritism of the sort reflected in our example (though not necessarily involving the issue of education) will develop in a way that will make him or her an autonomous chooser of a way of life. If this is true, then the autonomous choice of even a highly individualistic way of life requires the benefits of Limited Partialism. Thus from general knowledge from behind the veil of ignorance the reasoners would choose Limited Partialism and reject Strict Egalitarianism.[27]

The response to this is that even assuming that the reasoners in the original position would make such a choice with such general knowledge, this construal of the rationality of Limited Partialism is the result of indirection. It is, in fact, Indirect Egalitarianism. From the point of view of the original position, the concern for parental interests is, on this argument, an indirect concern for equality. But, once again, this way of arguing defeats the very purpose of introducing the concept of regulative norms in the first place. It was, after all, the original purpose of introducing the concept of regulative norms to allow for the rationality of direct partial concerns. To resort to indirection is to admit that the notion of regulative norms cannot deliver on what was originally promising about it.

27. I would like to thank Dwight Furrow for discussion on this point.

Third Construction

The third construction alters the second without admitting that it is a general fact of developmental psychology that to become autonomous choosers requires parental favoritism in children's upbringing of the sort displayed in our example. It only admits that it might be in certain cultures and that the reasoners can know this. Moreover, the reasoners are allowed to know this specific fact of social psychology that theirs is such a culture. Now, some might object that the construction cannot include this and remain Kantian. But this will not be my objection. I see no problem at all with allowing this within the Kantian framework. And with this assumption, there is a way of arguing directly to Limited Partialism. It is this: The reasoners in the original position reason disjunctively that *either* they will have parental interests of the sort involved in parental love *or* they will need the benefits of parental favoritism to develop into autonomous choosers of a way of life. Either way, Limited Partialism is preferable to the other principles on the list. What this construction captures, I believe, is that we respect people who are loving parents and people who have no interest in having children. The disjunctive reasoning captures this, in my opinion; hence there is nothing objectionable in the indirect reasoning of the second disjunct.

What, then, could possibly be wrong with the third construction? The only answer could be that it involves filtering. The Kantian must argue that the model is designed to take into account the special circumstances of human agents, and the non-Kantian must argue that the model filters in the first disjunct for parental love. If we confine ourselves to the current issue and ignore the issue of the regulative influence of impartial sympathy in the previous discussion in the case of both lower animals and the Duty of Beneficence, it might seem that there is a standoff, that there is no way to choose between these accounts. I believe, however, that the observations about sympathy for lower animals and the argument for the regulating effect of sympathy on our conception of respect for human beings themselves should lead us to see that the model filters rather than applies to the special circumstances of human beings. The philosophical account in all these cases is, on such a construal, the same. There is no philosophical motive to change the structure of the account. The way in which we generalize from the previous accounts of sympathy (first, for lower animals and respect for persons and, second, for sympathy for persons and respect for persons) to the account of parental love and respect for persons is that there is no philosophical motive to change the structure of the accounts. Once we recognize that the symmetrical nature of the regulative functions between sympathy and respect is the result of filtering, we have no philosophical motive for not thinking of the regulative relations between parental love and respect for persons in the same way.

Thus we have not discovered in our three versions of the constructivist model one that will both provide the right decision and avoid the other pitfalls. Now, it might be that there is some other construction that will do the work, but it can hardly be said that the argument here has relied on caricature, unless it can be shown that there is a clear model that will provide the desired result and that I should have seen rather clearly what it is. Baron has a view of imperfect duties that, I believe, is intended to cover such cases, but she has not explained the casuistry necessary to get from the general notion of imperfect duties to a solution to cases like the one presented here.[28] Until she addresses these issues, her view of imperfect duties is as yet only a gesture of a response to the current argument, however adequate it is to Stocker.

Nor will it do to say that problems of this sort would not occur in an ideally just world, that in a just world loving parents would not have to make such decisions. First, I am not at all sure that this is true, but I am sure that the ethics we need is for a world in which such decisions have to be made. One might object that ethics needs to deal with nonideal circumstances, but this does not show that we can argue straightforwardly from what it seems right to do in nonideal circumstances to the principles that justify norms. Nothing in this area, it might be said, is as simple as I make out. My response is that I am not the one who is assuming that things are simple. Along with Isaiah Berlin, I do not believe that there is any coherent notion of an ideally just world. I might be wrong about that (as Berlin might have been) but it is just simpleminded to assume that such a world is coherent without giving an account of its coherence, and Kantians have not given such an account. To allude to an ideally just world to avoid the present difficulty, then, is merely to gesture in the direction of a response, and it is this sort of gesturing that non-Kantians want Kantians to avoid as much as Kantians want their critics to avoid caricature. Moreover, even if an ideally just world is possible (which, again, I doubt), what is its relevance to nonideal circumstances? We do not live in that world, and even if it is possible it is not clear in what sense it is normatively relevant. In any event, to ap-

28. Baron, *Kantian Ethics Almost Without Apology.*

peal to an ideal world either without an account of its possibility or without an account of the path from its possibility (routed through current circumstances) to its actuality is to refuse to consider other alternatives.

9.

Finally, someone might object that my argument only shows that impartial respect is not a norm that is asymmetrical in its regulative effects, but it does not follow from my argument that there is no impartial norm that has such a function. Here the thought is that the Kantians have erred simply in locating the wrong impartial norm.

My response in this regard is brief and to the point. First, this objection is not open to the Kantian. Thus even if I have not established the larger point, I have nevertheless made an important one. Second, the objection itself might arise from two sources, both of which are questionable. One source might be an a priori commitment to the notion that the unity of practical reason requires a norm that is asymmetrical in its regulative effects. But, of course, the veridicality of such a commitment is anything but self-evident, nor can I see that it is even plausible. Nevertheless, if it can be shown that the very notion of the unity of practical reason requires a norm that is asymmetrical in its regulative functions, I will, of course, retract my larger claim. The burden, however, is on those who are committed to the a priori view. The other source of the objection might be some concrete suggestion about a particular norm that is claimed to have the relevant asymmetrical function. If so, then it will have to be demonstrated that the suggested norm meets the requirements of the criteria set out here. I have found no such norm, but I will gladly accept that there is one if an argument can be presented that demonstrates its presence within the practical reason of those most admirable. However, once again, the burden is on those who would claim that there is such a norm.

10.

What are we to make of these arguments? First, we should note that they strongly suggest that central features of our normative framework do not fit well within the Enlightenment tradition as it is tied to asymmetrically dominant, impartial norms, especially the Kantian version of that tradition. Second, we should note that our considered moral judgments as they are reflected here support the second condition of the Aristotelian conception of practical reason: All norms within practical reason are symmetrical in their regulative functions. However, this is not enough to establish the

Aristotelian conception of the integrative function of consciousness. For this, we need to be able to show how the features of our normative framework have a rational basis in the goods that make life meaningful for us from our own points of view and how reflective endorsement by means of the criteria of finality and self-sufficiency leads to these norms. We will then be in a position to employ the integration test. Before we can do this, we need to understand how the thin conception of integrity illuminates the relationships between the goods of an agent's life and his or her reasons for action.

3. The Thin Conception of Integrity and the Integration Test

Any conception of morality that begins with practical reason, whether Kantian or Aristotelian, inherits several burdens. One is the assignment of a functional role to practical reason within an overall psychology. As we have seen, that role for both the Kantian and the Aristotelian models must be understood in terms of the norms of practical reason and their regulative functions. Another burden is to provide the relevant test for whether the function assigned to practical reason is actually instantiated within the psychology of human beings. I have claimed that the integration test is the appropriate test for determining whether any candidate for meeting the first burden is successful. I have also claimed that in order to run the test, we need an adequate philosophical psychology. It is the purpose of this chapter and the next to provide such a psychology and to show how it is responsive to the integration test. The basic categories of the psychology are set out in this chapter and related to how they facilitate the integration test. In the next chapter, the categories are put to use in a general conception of practical deliberation.

The guiding thought here is that an adequate philosophical psychology is one that allows us to have an understanding of practical reason in human beings who are agents of integrity in the thin sense. The overall function of practical reason, then, is to be spelled out in these terms. The categories of the philosophical psychology are to be accepted only to the extent to which they illuminate how practical reason could have a regulative function within the psychology of a rational human agent who has integrity in the thin sense.

On any plausible view, there can be many different kinds of persons with many different kinds of character who are agents of integrity. Mother Teresa and Eleanor Roosevelt, Martin Luther King, Jr., and Malcolm X, Mahatma Gandhi and Field Marshal Rommel, Voltaire and Sir Thomas More—all have been noted for their integrity, and all are very different sorts of people. But to qualify as agents of integrity at all, they must satisfy the minimum criteria of the thin conception: They must have a sufficiently unified personality to have at least one and no more than one basic "self," a level of self-knowledge inconsistent with a life of self-deception regarding their basic sense of self, the strength of character to meet significant challenges to that which makes their sense of self possible, and a sense of self-worth as separate and numerically distinct persons. And, as ongoing agents, they must have positive reasons for living. The goal here is to provide a general way of understanding how the basic elements of the thin conception of integrity are possible. For it is only within the conditions for the possibility of integrity in this sense that a functional role for practical reason can be assigned. It is because that role is an integrative task that the appropriate test for competing conceptions of practical reason is the integration test.

Finally, we should expect an adequate philosophical psychology to include categories that empirically accommodate facts about both cognitive and clinical dimensions of human psychology. What is needed is a philosophical psychology that reflects the psychology of a *personality* in which practical rationality has a definitive role. No psychology that included only cognitive categories could yield a conception of a human person. For this, we need a philosophical psychology that can yield a notion of practical reason with *pathos*. We need categories that illuminate how a psychology can have energy and a core, how it can flourish and how it can break down. And it is ultimately by empirical observations of how a personality so conceived is successfully integrated that we can apply the integration test to adjudicate between rival conceptions of rational agency.

2.

Among the most fundamental things to understand about a human agent of integrity is that such an agent has interests and has a way of setting priorities among them. Without a strong sense of priorities, the basic elements would be impossible, and, without interests, the basic elements, even if possible, would have no point. Thus it is in terms of interests that a psychology has pathos, and, as we will see, it is in terms of distinctions among interests that a psychology has the structure of a personality.

Elementary among these interests are vital interests and the hedonic interest in avoiding unnecessary pain. Vital interests are the interests in biological life and the necessary means to it. A bare interest in biological life would be an interest in being alive in the biological sense without any consideration for the quality of that life. But it is doubtful that anyone has such an interest. If we distinguish between a person's "taking an interest in" something and something "being in the interest of" a person, it is plausible to say that a person has vital interests—in the sense of "taking an interest in" biological life and the necessary means to it—only if a person has other kinds of interests. Also, it seems plausible to say that a potential person (such as a fetus) has vital interests—in the sense of something "being in the interest of" that potential person—only if it potentially has other nonbiological kinds of interests.

If we were to imagine a human fetus developing into an insect rather than a person under drastic environmental changes, we would hardly maintain under these conditions that its genetic endowment suffered no loss of importance. Also, if we were to discover some new biological species, we would conclude that its life was of intrinsic rather than mere instrumental value only if we held some beliefs about the quality of the life it could live. If it could live only a life of excruciating pain, there would be little sense of intrinsic loss and a great sense of relief on its extinction.

The life of mere excruciating pain, then, is reason enough for not taking an interest in biological life. Perhaps this is why burning in an eternal fire is the most vivid picture of hell. On the other hand, freedom from pain alone does not generate vitality. Schopenhauer seems to have thought that many people will to go on living in the most dire circumstances, even when they have given up hope.[1] But if it is not hope that keeps them going but mere habit, then it is not for something, let alone for a reason, that they go on living. Yet a person of integrity is a person who, under normal circumstances, has reasons for living—reasons founded in interests other than the interest in avoiding unnecessary pain.

Having positive reasons for living, however, is not sufficient to explain the basic elements of integrity. What we need is a way of understanding the psychological structure among an agent's interests before we can see how the elements of integrity can emerge. For this we need to understand the

---

1. See Arthur Schopenhauer, *The Will to Live: Selected Writings*, ed. Richard Taylor (New York: F. Ungar, 1967), and *The World as Will and Representation*, trans. E. F. G. Payne (Indian Hills, Colo.: Falcon's Wing Press, 1958).

relationship between the agent's interests and the agent's sense of priorities as they relate to his or her reasons for living.

3.

The interests of the person of integrity associated with his or her reasons for living can be called categorical interests. They are interests apart from which there is a serious loss in the unity and meaning of one's life from one's own point of view. Sometimes this loss of meaning results in a loss of the will to live at all.

Aristotle shows a keen awareness of these kinds of interests in the *Eudemian Ethics*, book 1:5, where he says:

> About many things it is not easy to judge correctly, but it is especially difficult to do so in regard to that which everyone thinks is most easy and within anyone's capacity to know; namely, which of the things in life is worth choosing, and such that one who obtains it will have his desire fulfilled. After all, many things that happen are such as to induce people to abandon life—disease, extremes of pain, storms, for example; so that it is evident that, on account of those things at any rate, it would, given the choice, have been worth choosing not to be born in the first place. Again, [there is] the life which men lead while they are still children. For no one in his right mind would tolerate a return to that sort of existence. Moreover, many of the things that involve neither pleasure nor pain, or involve pleasure, but of a reprehensible sort, are enough to make not existing at all preferable to being alive. In general, if we put together all the things that everyone does or undergoes, but not voluntarily (because they are not done or undergone for their own sake), and an infinite stretch of time were provided in addition, no one would choose in order to have *them* to be alive, rather than not. Nor again would anyone who was not a complete slave prefer to live solely for the pleasure associated with nutrition and sex, if all the pleasures were removed that knowing or seeing or any of the other senses bestow upon human beings; for it is evident that, for a man who made such a choice as *this* for himself, it would make no difference whether he were born a beast or a man. Certainly the ox in Egypt, which they honor as the god Apis, has a greater abundance of several of such things than many sovereigns. Similarly, no one would prefer life for the pleasure of sleep; for what difference is there between sleeping without ever waking from one's first day to one's last, over a period of ten thousand years—or however many one likes—and living the life of a plant? . . .
>
> They say that Anaxagoras, when someone raised just these puzzles

and asked him what it was for which a person would choose to be born rather than not, answered that it would be "in order to apprehend the heavens and the order in the whole universe." (*EE* 1215b:15– 1216a:15)[2]

Notice that the concern in this passage is not with what makes one kind of life more worth living than another but with what makes living preferable to death. Aristotle is here concerned with the most fundamental interests that make the prospects of life at all alluring. To be sure, we would not all give Anaxagoras's answer, but the person of integrity has some such answer.

Following Bernard Williams, we may call the objects of categorical interests ground projects.[3] They are ground projects because they serve to ground the unity and meaning of one's life from one's own point of view. In fact, they are the grounding necessary for a person's having a point of view at all such that we can attribute one basic, significantly integrated self to that person. This is in contrast to attributing no or many selves to a human. And the person of integrity is the human to whom we attribute at least one, and no more than one, basic, significantly integrated self.

Of course, people do not, in any self-conscious way, usually think of those things that play the role of ground projects as being the means to unity and meaning in their lives. They simply care about things in a way that brings focus and meaning. Something is valued categorically in this sense, then, when it is what life is most centrally about for a person and is such that its loss brings with it, at minimum, a serious loss in the coherence of life or, at maximum, a loss in the allure of life itself. The objects of categorical interests, then, appear within one's deliberative field in a very fundamental way (and depending on one's character they attach one to items in the world, a defining mark of objective eudaimonism).

Imagine a woman dedicated to being an excellent surgeon to the exclusion of all else. As far back as she can remember, she has always pursued

2. Aristotle, *Eudemian Ethics: Books I, II, and VIII*, trans. Michael Woods, Clarendon Aristotle Series (Oxford: Oxford University Press, 1992), 4–5.

3. See Bernard Williams, *Problems of the Self* (Cambridge: Cambridge University Press, 1973), *Moral Luck* (Cambridge: Cambridge University Press, 1981), and *Ethics and the Limits of Philosophy* (Cambridge, Mass.: Harvard University Press, 1985). See also Williams's use of the concept of categorical desires in "Persons, Character, and Morality," in *Moral Luck*, esp. p. 11. I attempt to develop the notion of categorical interests in a way that is more closely tied both to psychological phenomena and to different kinds of reasons for action than I find in Williams and to show that we can say more about our normative concepts and how we think about resolving disputes than Williams does.

this goal, sacrificing many other valuable aspects of life along the way. After several years of medical practice and at the pinnacle of her success, she discovers that within a short time she will be permanently blind.

The trauma of her discovery is easy to imagine. Her life is in shambles because she has lost her ground project and with it her point of view toward her life and its future. A guiding perspective is impossible because she lacks a point of view from which to assess her life, except in terms of what has been lost. The thought, "I am the person who has lost that which is most important to me, my surgical practice," is what we may call her identifying thought, a thought that need not be self-conscious but implicit within a person's overall psychology. It is the kind of thought that allows a person to express identification with his or her life and its components. In this sense, an identifying thought is an answer to the question, Who am I?

Of course, the question, Who am I? is not unambiguous. It is important, then, to be as clear as possible on what it does and does not mean. It is not a question regarding the identification and reidentification of particulars, as applied to persons. The person who suffers puzzlement regarding the question as intended here is not confused about whether she is Sue or Sarah or Jane or Jill. She might know very well that she is Sue and nonetheless be puzzled in a way that raises the question, Who am I?

Rather than reflect puzzlement over the reidentification of particulars in this sense, the question reflects a different quandary. It is the quandary over how to identify with one's life so that it provides a sense of who one is in terms of which one's past, present, and future are comprehensible as a significantly integrated whole. The puzzlement arises in contexts in which an agent faces the future without adequate direction. The need is to bring to bear thoughts of oneself and what one values to resolve the issue of direction, where there is an absence of the relevant sorts of thoughts that will provide this guidance into the future. The thoughts that do provide this sense of self and that prevent or resolve such puzzlement I am calling the agent's identifying thoughts.

Further clarification of what is meant by an agent's identifying thoughts is revealed in the experience of emotions of self-assessment.[4] A positive example is that of pride. It is in terms of the thought that one has exceeded some minimally acceptable standard of expectations that one experiences the emotion of pride. As such, it is a thought that identifies the agent as one worthy of special self-affirmation. A negative example is that of self-

4. See Gabriele Taylor, *Pride, Shame, and Guilt: Emotions of Self-Assessment* (Oxford: Clarendon Press, 1985).

contempt, where the thought that one is a person of a certain sort identifies one as unworthy of respect.

As with emotions of self-assessment, certain interests are possible only with identifying thoughts that reflect a conception of oneself as a significantly unified personality over time. The interest in being a good parent is an excellent example. Absent other concerns, a person having the interests and character of a good parent would be puzzled regarding the direction of life at the unexpected loss of his or her child. Other interests, however, cannot play this role in a person's identifying thoughts. Under normal conditions, the thought that one has not had quite enough sleep does not raise the puzzlement over who one is and the direction of life, even where there is some interest in a bit more sleep.

Note that a person, such as the woman in our example, who has completely lost her ground project has only a backward-looking identifying thought. As such, it gives her no direction for her life. It gives her no identity in terms of her future. It tells her who she was rather than who she is and who she is to be. Such disarray in terms of her identifying thoughts reveals that her loss was that of a ground project, rather than something of less importance.

To have reasons for living, then, she needs an identifying thought that directs her toward the future. In this sense, her identifying thoughts must be motivating ones, the kinds of thoughts generated by a positive interest in life. Unless motivating thoughts emerge, there will soon be no identifying ones. For the emergence of new identifying thoughts requires the appearance in her life of a new ground project in which she has a categorical interest.

Not all identifying thoughts, however, are either backward looking or based on motivating categorical interests. Some such thoughts express categorical aversions. These are aversions to actions or ways of life that have serious consequences for the agent. The consequences are that if the person performed such actions or participated in these ways of life serious disunity of the self and loss of meaning in the person's life would result. This might extend to a loss of a will to live at all. The cliché, "I would rather be dead than red," is putatively an identifying thought that expresses a categorical aversion. But like purely backward-looking identifying thoughts, these thoughts do not express reasons for living. Only motivating categorical interests in ground projects can provide this. A person of integrity, as we will see in later chapters, has both categorical interests and categorical aversions. Yet one's life has categorical value from one's own point of view only if one has a categorical motivating interest in a ground project. Within such a project and among such interests might be the interest in being an agent of pure practical reason and governing one's life in accordance with the CI procedure. If so, then such an interest serves the most fundamental integrative task of that psychology. There is nothing, then, about the concepts of categorical interests and categorical aversions as employed here that rules out Kantian internalism in advance of the application of the integration test.

4.

It would be a mistake, however, to think that since ground projects are the objects of categorical interests, they are permanently fixed in the life of the agent. Ground projects can and do evolve and change over time. Such evolution, however, is never a matter of simple choice by the agent. Views of human agency that treat human choice as though everything about the agent is under the power of the human will are simply flights of fantasy. Nevertheless, the agent's choices, as well as other factors influencing the agent's life, can bring about fundamental changes in what life is most about for the agent. In this sense, ground projects can be malleable, but, even in exceptional cases, only to a degree.

Nor should we think that ground projects are so rigidly placed within the priorities of any agent that recovery from the loss of such a project is simply out of the question. It might be that for some agents recovery is possible and for others it is not. Here it is important to distinguish different descriptions of a loss a person might suffer. To describe a loss as irretrievable is to say that the agent cannot get the thing that is lost back. Immortality aside, the loss of life is irretrievable, as is the loss of innocence, virginity, youth, and some forms of ignorance. On the other hand, some descriptions apply more to the effect of the loss on the agent than to the thing that is lost. To say that a loss is irretrievable is not in itself to say anything about the effects of the loss on the agent. People, for example, might respond differently to the loss of virginity—some with joy, some with guilt, and others with indifference. But, to describe a loss as "debilitating," for instance, is to say something about the agent, and, of course, some irretrievable losses can be debilitating—and to different degrees. Some such losses are ones from which an agent can never recover, while others are those from which an agent can recover, though with difficulty. The gauge of debility is the loss of integrity in one of the ways in which that is possible, some of which are permanent and thus mortal losses of integrity. Here we are clearly dealing with the possibilities of pathos.

Imagine that through support from loved ones, or through therapy, or something of that sort, the fictional surgeon recovers. What she lost was irretrievable, yet she recovers by taking on some other interest that is motivating in that it gives her reasons for living and provides her with unity and meaning in her life. She is able to "put her life back together again," which is a necessary condition for her being an ongoing agent of integrity.

If she is able to do this, the loss of her original ground project proved to be a debilitating loss but not a mortal one. If the loss of the original project was such that the woman was psychologically unable to put her life back together in a coherent way, the loss of the ground project was a mortal loss. If it resulted in the loss of the will to live or left her with a permanently and seriously disfigured sense of self, it was likewise a mortal loss of her integrity.

There are many ways in which an agent can suffer a mortal loss of integrity, and it is one of the goals of this book to explore the significance of this. I will argue that personal integrity is far more social and far less individualistic than one might think from the original surgeon's example. But this argument will come only with the analysis of the thick conception of integrity. The point here is that it is only in terms of categories of pathos that we are able to make sense of a psychology in which integrity resides.

5.

An important distinction for understanding degrees of loss concerns the relative simplicity or complexity of ground projects. So far, I have been speaking as though ground projects were simple and that loss of a ground project was necessarily complete. But this is misleading. Such projects can vary greatly in complexity. The surgeon's project, for example, was a simple one. A more complex and more normal project would include several components. Imagine an altered version of the surgeon example in which the surgeon has children. If on the discovery of her impending blindness the surgeon's interest in life is unaffected by any interest she might have in her children, then her children do not figure into her ground project. Suppose, however, that her love for her children were to aid her in surviving her sense of loss. This does not mean that her surgical practice was not a component of her ground project. It was as long as its loss resulted in a serious, though perhaps not a complete, loss of unity and meaning in her life. A project is a component in a larger ground project if its loss affects the identifying thoughts of the person and this result is viewed with severe regret from that person's point of view. In this way, we can clearly speak of distinguishable components of a complex ground project and the loss of a ground project as partial or complete. We also may clearly speak of either a component or the entire project in terms of whether its loss is mortally threatening to the agent.

6.

An understanding of categorical interests and aversions, then, is central to an understanding of the psychological structure of the person of integrity as a rational agent. But to further clarify the concept of integrity, we need to understand how noncategorical interests shape the priorities of a human agent. For our purposes, we may distinguish two types. If an interest is such that its frustration has no effect on the identifying thoughts of the agent but does lead to serious disappointment, it is an important noncategorical interest. Frustrations of these kinds of interests, though painful, do not seriously threaten the unity and meaning of a person's life. If an interest is such that its frustration leads to little disappointment to the agent, it is a minor noncategorical interest.

Reflection on the difference between many cases of embarrassment and severe guilt is revealing in regard to the distinction between important noncategorical interests and those that are categorical. The emotional response of severe guilt strikes deep at the structure of a personality, reflecting the workings of an interest fundamental to the psychology in which it is embedded. Indeed, often such guilt results in debilitating depression. On the other hand, embarrassment does not usually have this feature. True, embarrassment is structurally revealing, but it is not usually associated with serious depression or something of that psychological depth. Yet none of us likes to be embarrassed, and in most cases we think it important to avoid. Typically, embarrassment of the more severe sort temporarily disorients us at most; it does not threaten the very unity and meaning of our lives, even if an embarrassing episode causes some short-term depression. The difference between a categorical interest and an important noncategorical interest then is a structural one.

An additional comment on the experience of pain will perhaps further clarify the distinction. Unless intense physical pain is prolonged, it does not in itself typically affect the view one has of oneself and of one's life prospects. It does not typically affect a person's identifying thoughts. Pain of this sort differs, then, from emotional pain that does affect the view one has of oneself and one's life. To feel the pain of guilt or of humiliation is structurally different from mere physical pain, even when the former is far less intense than the latter. This is not simply because the emotional pains are more likely to be of greater duration, for the pain of even temporary embarrassment is also different from physical pain in that the former involves the self in a different way than does the latter.[5] Categorical interests function at the core of a psychology in a way that noncategorical interests do not, and important noncategorical interests play a structural role that minor interests do not. Without awareness of these differences, there is a failure to understand how priorities function in the life of an agent. Thus it is through interests that goods are presented as ends within an agent's deliberative field, but the sense of how important those goods are to an agent depends on the kinds of interests through which they enter the field.

7.

Perhaps it would be wise here to consolidate the previous observations regarding the thin conception of integrity within a psychological setting and then to relate these observations to both Aristotle's "function argument" and the integration test. To consolidate we need to index both the kinds of interests that might be affected within an agent's life and the kinds of effects on the agent when those interests are frustrated. I will describe the latter in terms of agent states, states the agent might be in as a result of the frustration of the interests in the other part of the index. Consider, then, the following chart:

1. Vital interests	death
2. Hedonic interest in avoiding pain	wide range, from mild discomfort to complete insanity
3. Categorical interests	suicidal despair, extreme depression, hysteria, dysfunctional lethargy, pervasive self-deception, denial, disposition to violence toward others, self-destructiveness, etc.
4. Categorical aversions	same as with (3)
5. Noncategorical interests	
a. Important	moderate to mild depression, temporary lethargy, moderate and temporary self-absorption, anger, embarrassment, etc.
b. Minor	mild irritation or discomfort

---

5. Of course, if intense enough, physical pain can be the object of a categorical aversion, in which case it does have structural significance.

What I am aiming for is a conception of human interests as those interests are structured within a personality. Without the distinctions in the left column, we are unable to understand the interests as those of a person, especially those of a person of integrity. Notice that neither Bentham's categories of intensity and duration nor cardinal measurements of individual utility reveal anything resembling a personality. Without the list of the agent states in the right column, we are unable to fully understand the distinctions in the left column as they apply to human personalities. Agent breakdown, then, can be viewed as involving changes in agent states that occur sometimes as a result of the frustration of different kinds of interests the agent has.[6] (Other times, of course, such breakdown occurs as a result of nonintentional states of the human body.) When these breakdowns occur at the core, they reflect the disintegration of personality.

Now, how does all this relate to Aristotle's function argument and to the integration test? In the *Nicomachean Ethics*, book 1:7:1097b:21–24, Aristotle says, "To call happiness the highest good is perhaps a little trite, and a clearer account of what it is, is still required. Perhaps this is best done by first ascertaining the proper function of man." The word translated as "function" is *ergon*, which means "activity." Reflecting his biological bent, Aristotle claims that every natural kind has an activity that is natural to it, that expresses its most fundamental nature, and the good for any natural kind is to be able to express its nature by engaging in those activities that allow it to survive and flourish in its natural environment. He comes to the conclusion that the good for man is "activity of the soul in accordance with virtue" (*NE* 1098:a15). If we demythologize "soul" to mean "psychology," we get the notion that eudaimonia is an active life that is expressive of a psychology that is most natural to humans. Though we should be cautious about Aristotle's assumptions about the species-wide good, especially in regard to humans, demythologizing the soul in this way in our understanding of human well-being opens the way to empirical tests for whether some way of life is as a matter of fact good for a person of a certain kind. Just as an arid environment is not good for an acorn because it will not be conducive to the kind of flourishing that we observe in healthy oaks, some ways of life characterized by their activities are not good for most humans. The function argument in Aristotle is supposed to ground some sort of empirical testing for whether a way of life is one that fits the nature of humans

6. I discuss what I call integral breakdown in considerable detail in my *Dignity and Vulnerability: Strength and Quality of Character* (Berkeley: University of California Press, 1997).

and hence is good for them. I suggest that we understand the function argument in terms of the integration test and the latter in terms of how a psychology can break down.

The consolidation of our philosophical psychology, then, provides us not only with an understanding of how a psychology can have pathos and structure but also with an understanding of how we can test for claims about the integrative function of practical reason. One thing we see is that the unity of a personality is made possible by the fact that some interests regulate other interests in their demands on the overall psychology. In this sense, there is a hierarchy within a personality: Categorical interests and aversions are dominant relative to noncategorical interests and aversions. It might seem to follow from this that if norms are, in part, a function of interests, then necessarily there will be regulative norms that are asymmetrical in their regulative functions. But this thought is based on conceptual confusion. True, categorical interests asymmetrically regulate noncategorical interests, but it does not follow from this that there are any categorical interests that are not regulated by other categorical interests. This means that it is possible that there are no partial or impartial interests that are unregulated by other partial and impartial interests. Looking back at chapter 2, this is what we would expect. Moreover, by viewing our experience from these categories, we begin to understand how practical reason can have an integrative function within a psychology by construing practical reason as essentially connected to what gives a psychology its pathos. And most important, we can see how to test for whether integration has been achieved. Do the occurrent interests of the agent allow for the agent's flourishing, or do they lead to agent breakdown? These are empirical questions answerable by sophisticated social science in terms of the integration test guided by an adequate philosophical psychology. It is in terms of such a test that we can determine whether the value of rational agency in Kant's sense or Aristotle's sense is among our deepest values.

We should, however, be careful to distinguish on the one hand between the integration test and the function argument, which take place from the third-person point of view, and practical deliberation on the other, which takes place from the first-person point of view. Neither the function argument nor the integration test is an explanation or model for *how* to deliberate or to reason practically: Deliberative models have justificatory functions. Rather both are naturalistic accounts of *why* we deliberate and reason in the practical way that we do, and hence they have explanatory functions. When we confuse the latter with the former, as Aristotle himself sometimes does, our understanding of practical reason itself becomes confused. That we are social animals is on both Aristotle's and my view an explanation for why we sometimes reason in the way that we do. This does not mean that it is a factual premise in our deliberations that we are social animals. We do not derive values from facts in that or any other way. It is one thing, then, to give a naturalistic account of why the most admirable persons reason in the way they do; it is quite another to give an account of how they deliberate from the first-person point of view. All that is required philosophically is that the explanatory account match in a coherent way the justificatory account. It does this by being explanatorily accurate in regard to persons of character we admire. But admiration comes from the first-person point of view. If we do not admire and desire to emulate persons of a certain character, there are no merely factual beliefs that will lead us to a normative guide. Still it remains true that there is some naturalistic explanation for why we admire some kinds of persons and not others.

In its most sophisticated form, the integration test is administered by the most developed social science, which was not available to Aristotle. It is for this reason that I suggest we understand the function argument in terms of the integration test. If we do, I think we arrive at a more fine grained account of practical reason than Aristotle himself did, simply because we have a more sophisticated test. Here the best clinical psychology can both diagnose agent breakdown and, in those cases in which it is true, trace its causes to the values influencing the agent's life. For example, clinical depression might be diagnosed and traced to the misplaced values of adolescence; it might also be traced to tragic losses that are nearly impossible for anyone to handle. But as Korsgaard rightly points out, the practical point of view for any agent is the first-person point of view, not the point of view of social science. How, then, does failure to pass the integration test appear from the point of view of the first person? A brief answer is that, under the appropriate conditions, the agent experiences deliberative difficulties with the relevant clinical consequences. Much more will be said about the kind of difficulties I have in mind in chapter 4.

Here, however, several things need to be explained, and to do so I will appeal to some thoughts of Charles Sanders Peirce. In "The Fixation of Belief," Peirce gave a sketch of how we should think about belief naturalistically.[7] On his account, our beliefs serve us in the task of integrating our lives in relationship to our environment. The moment of doubt arises when we face a problematic situation, a situation in which the network of our be-

7. See Charles Sanders Peirce, "The Fixation of Belief," in *Philosophical Writings of Peirce*, ed. Justus Buchler (New York: Dover Publications, 1955), 5–22.

liefs is no longer sufficient for unifying our experience in a way that can provide cognitive guidance. We become baffled in our attempts to accommodate the problems of experience, due to the poverty of our concepts. We regain confidence when we form concepts that can project us into the future in a way that gets us past the problems that we can foresee on the horizon. Inquiry is a way of fixating belief, relative to whatever cognitive problems have emerged for us. As I understand his view, we are justified in a reflective endorsement of a way of conceptualizing things to the extent to which we can imaginatively project a cognitive understanding of our experience in which problematic situations, occasions for doubt, do not occur. Now I want to think of practical deliberation in an analogous way. Our practical reflective lives begin with a pattern of normative beliefs. Eventually, life presents us with a problematic situation, a situation in which the network of our normative beliefs, a network of beliefs about how to live, is no longer capable of organizing our practical experience. Instead of cognitive bafflement, what we experience is puzzlement over the direction of life. It is the concern over the direction of life that gives rise to the problem of reflective endorsement in the first place. And here I am talking about the first-person point of view. What will count as a solution to this problem, therefore, must fit the problem itself, namely, how to get from here into the future within a life. Thus the revision of one's values must be such that those values are placed within a conception of a life in which the problematic situation no longer appears. The very nature of the problem of reflective endorsement from the practical point of view dictates that the widest reflective standpoint is the point of view of one's life as a whole. For it is a problem about life that requires a solution, and the solution is adequate only insofar as it gives coherent meaning and guidance to a life. A set of values, then, fails from the first-person point of view when it presents the agent with a deliberative field the agent cannot integrate in terms of its implications for a way of life.

But what are the appropriate conditions under which a set of values fails to provide a basis for integration from the first-person point of view? One condition is that reflective consideration of the problematic situation is not unduly hindered by self-deception or prevented by the lack of character to face the facts. These are conditions imposed by the thin conception of integrity. Another condition is that the agent takes the point of view that allows for the imaginative projection of a way of life in which all the relevant values are given their chance to appear as the ends they are taken to be within the agent's deliberative field. It is for this reason that the Aristotelian criteria of finality and self-sufficiency are relevant; they fit the kind of problematic situations that give rise to the tasks of practical reason. The final condition is that the agent cannot project a way of life in which all the values of the agent can find a place in a set of priorities the agent can endorse. Thus the failure of a set of values to pass the integration test from the personal point of view takes the form of deliberative difficulties in the face of the alternative ways of life available to the agent from his or her own point of view. And, of course, such difficulties come with the attendant clinical implications for his or her psychology. I will say more in the next chapter on these deliberative difficulties, but here the main point is that the task of practical reason is a problem the nature of which requires the point of view of a life as a whole as the widest possible reflective position an agent can take in regard to it. This should reinforce the view that if the CI procedure is to be reflectively endorsed, it must be endorsed from the point of view of a life as a whole, from the viewpoint of a *way* of life, thus making the criteria of finality and self-sufficiency central to the tasks of practical reason.

8.

Before concluding my comments on the interests and priorities of the person of integrity, I must say something about the essential concept of commitment. I must say what it is and why the concepts of human agency, human character, and personal integrity, whether moral or nonmoral, require it.

Perhaps there could be an environment where there were no possible challenges to human interests, where frustrated interest would not be possible. But it is not possible that human beings could be agents in such an environment, and it is the concept of agency that is our subject. The reason that humans could not be agents in such an environment is because they could only be passive regarding their interests. That is, they could not pursue their interests. Nothing they could possibly do would count as not satisfying their interests, and in this sense there would be no alternatives. Without the possibility of challenge, the frustration of interest does not make sense, and without the possibility of the frustration of interest, the concept of agency does not make sense.

Yet it might be thought that there can be agency in an environment in which frustrated interest is possible but never actual. In heaven, that is, things are arranged in a way that renders the anticipation of such frustration practically nil. In such a heaven the likelihood of frustration attached to any alternative available to an agent is improbable beyond the point of psychological significance. But if this is true, all available alternatives stand on a par; so in what sense are they alternatives? How are they alternatives if they in no way constitute a greater or lesser threat to the objects of the agent's interests? Or more positively, how are they alternatives if they are all equally satisfactory. Among other things, such an environment (like the environment in which frustrated interest is not possible) would render the formation of intentions—a concept crucial to the notion of agency—problematic. The concept of agency, then, does not make sense in an environment in which challenges to interests are not possible. Nor does it make sense in an environment in which such challenges are practically remote beyond the point of psychological significance. Therefore, the concept of agency requires the concept of an environment in which challenge to interests is to some significant degree likely.

This, of course, is true of the natural environment in which humans live. Thus the analysis of human agency and human integrity is in this sense naturalistic: It is an analysis of human agency in terms of a human being (i) as an inhabitant of a native environment, (ii) as having different kinds of interests in itself and that environment, and (iii) as having different capacities for responding and adapting to that environment.

Commitment is the human capacity that enables us, as agents, to meet the challenges to our interests.[8] Whether as a moral or as a nonmoral agent, to be an agent of integrity one must be able to meet these challenges with some degree of success. The scale that gauges the success required for agent-integrity is one that by now should be familiar. It is the ability to retain the degree of coherence in one's life to qualify as having one rather than no or several selves and to have reasons for living. This is why agents must be committed to categorical interests in a way that they are not to other interests if they are to survive as agents of integrity.

If human agents are to survive with their integrity, then, they must be committed to their ground projects categorically. This is the foundation for their identifying thoughts. Thus, given the human condition, there are no stable identifying thoughts without categorical commitments.[9] And it is through the capacity for categorical commitment that categorical interests can have the standing of norms. For it is the mark of an interest that it expresses a norm that it is held with some degree of commitment; otherwise,

8. I avoid here the dispute between deterministic and libertarian accounts of commitment and human volition.
9. See John Kekes's reference to identity conferring commitments in "Constancy and Purity," *Mind*, no. 92 (1983): 499–518.

it is only an interest. Moreover, it is the mark of a commitment that it functions as a norm in an agent's practical reasoning. Thus we can speak of categorical and noncategorical norms.

The concept of categorical commitments and norms helps to explain two important features of agent-integrity. The first is the unity of the self necessary for an ongoing agent. The second is the strength of character required for the survival of that unified self as an agent meeting challenges to its interests in its environment. It does not follow, of course, that if an agent has integrity in this sense he or she is thereby wholly admirable. For it is possible that the person is categorically committed to the despicable. Admirable integrity is a subject for consideration in later chapters. But here it is important that unless a human being has integrity in at least this sense he or she cannot be an admirable agent simply because there is not an agent with a character. It is only by seeing how norms are expressed in the structure of a character that we can assign them a functional role within agency. For this, we need the distinctions regarding categorical and noncategorical interests and how they function as norms as expressed in the commitments of a structured psychology. In parts 2 through 4 the inquiry involves the structure of this psychology as it is revealed in the agent whose character expresses the thick conception of integrity.

9.

It has been argued by some that to be an agent of integrity is to have a sense of self such that one sees one's commitments as one's own. To be an agent of integrity I must be conscious at some level of awareness of a distinction between the categorical worthiness of some project and my commitment to that project. If this is true, it would offer some explanation for the importance of the "separateness" or the "distinctness" of persons taken as a foundational moral value by Kantians.

The claim seems correct for two reasons. First, it is necessary for any concept one might have of oneself as a human agent. If Sue's awareness of her behavior lacks a sense of "herself-as-bringing-it-about-that" such and such happens, then she is not aware of herself as an agent to whom we can ascribe responsibility. Also, if she is unaware of "herself-as-being-affected" by events, it is difficult to see how she could see herself as having any interests.

The second reason that awareness of one's interests and actions as one's own is a fundamental feature of integrity is this: It is necessary to make coherent many of the interests that are of categorical value to human beings. If I am committed to a shared relationship with someone, I am not only aware of myself in a certain role; I am acutely aware of its being my role and of the importance of my fulfilling that role.[10] What would it be to see myself as a parent, to be very concerned that the needs of my children are met, but be indifferent to who meets those needs as long as they are met? Nor is my commitment to my own work reducible to the concern that the work gets done; it includes the thought that I do it. I simply cannot have these interests if I do not have an awareness of myself as a separate and distinct person and assign some importance to the fact of this distinctness. This sense of distinctness, then, is crucial to the identifying thoughts of the agent whose self is at risk in a challenging environment, for without a personal attachment to one's own life such survival is not an issue.

Moreover, it is categorical value that gives survival a point. Since humans do not have a bare interest in living, survival becomes an issue only when a person is within an environment of a certain sort: one in which there are things one can take a categorical interest in and to which one can make a categorical commitment. The first challenge to the possibility of integrity, then, is the challenge of nihilism, the view that life is not worth living, that suicide is—to answer Camus's question—the only course of action.[11] Since it is ludicrous to think of nihilism as an a priori doctrine, meeting its challenge requires an understanding of the things that can provide categorical value for humans, things that can appear within one's deliberative field that give one reasons for living. We can meet this challenge if we can satisfy two conditions: first, specifying what things must be within an environment to make survival an issue for humans, and second, showing that these things are at least sometimes within our environment.

If nihilism can be refuted and survival has a point, there remain other challenges to integrity, challenges regarding human capacities. Failure of these capacities is perhaps the most illuminating way to think about them. The first is the failure in the capacity to make any commitments at all. In such cases, the agent has interests—perhaps even categorical ones—but is completely unable to meet any challenges to those interests. Thus the agent

10. Acute awareness, here, should not be construed too strongly. As James Harris has pointed out to me, there must be some room for thoughts to the effect that "I didn't realize that I was in love with you, or how much you meant to me." Still it would be more than just odd to live a life in which one could say at the end, "I didn't realize that any of you mattered to me."

11. See Albert Camus, *The Myth of Sisyphus and Other Essays*, trans. Justin O'Brien (New York: Vintage Books, 1991).

is constantly abandoning and changing his or her interests the moment a challenge arises. Self-awareness is merely that of various episodes connected at best only in memory. In these cases, the failure is a failure of character, an inability to live with any priorities at all. It is the failure of having a psychology in which there are interests but no norms. Also, there are failures related to commitment to too many things, to the lack of capacity for self-denial, and to commitment to conflicting projects. Finally, there are failures that are the result not of the lack of normal capacities but of bad luck.

10.

Whether, then, one is Socrates or Galileo, Richard Nixon or Winston Churchill, van Gogh or Gauguin, or Uncle Ralph or Aunt Clara, one must have a sense of the categorical and the noncategorical to have the basic elements of integrity in the thin sense. For without such a sense of the categorical and the commitments that attend it, there is no way for a sense of priorities to emerge that explains the emergence of the basic elements of integrity. The thin conception of integrity, therefore, is essential to an adequate moral psychology. For it is within a sense of priorities psychologically conceived that we are able to understand human agency and any place that morality and an agent's norms might have within it. These thoughts should provide a guide for thought about practical deliberation, the subject to which I now turn.

4. An Integrity-Sensitive Conception of Human Agency, Practical Reason, and Morality

Understanding the place of morality within the life of a human agent requires an integrity-sensitive conception of both human agency and morality. This, in turn, requires an understanding of how, as an agent, one's reasons for action emerge from the meaning of one's life from one's own point of view. This follows from the fact that one's categorical interests are both those in terms of which an agent finds life meaningful and those in terms of which the structure of one's psychology is built. And, as we have seen, this requirement does not in itself rule out the Kantian CI procedure from being defensible in terms of our categorical values. Thus an adequate philosophical conception of morality must be true to whatever the relationship is between an agent's reasons for action and the agent's own perceived good. In this chapter, I discuss a thin conception of the good for an agent of integrity, the implications of this thin conception for an account of an agent's reasons for action, and what this conception of the good requires of a moral conception regarding its sensitivity to the integrity issue.

1.

Just as nihilism is absurd as an a priori view of the human condition, so is an a priori answer to the question of what things are of categorical value to humans. The answer to such a question must be found in what humans actually find under reasonably favorable conditions to make life worth living. In this sense, though perhaps not in others, categorical value is not an issue of justification but of explanation.

Consider in this regard how we are both like and unlike other animals. It is natural for a dog to bark, but the dog's bark can be eliminated without eliminating the dog. This might be done for reasons of social utility, human rights, or the will of God. But to eliminate the dog's bark is to disfigure the dog, even if such disfigurement is justified by other considerations. It is, of course, one thing to justify disfiguring the dog but quite another to require of the dog that it should justify its bark. Dogs are just the kinds of natural organisms that find barking natural. They also find copulating and fighting rather natural. Still these things too can be eliminated and perhaps on justifiable grounds. But if the dog's bark and its sexual and predatory instincts are eliminated, the disfigurement borders on eliminating that which makes a dog a dog. There are just some interests, then, a dog has because it is a dog. No sense is to be made of a dog's having and pursuing these interests for a reason or being justified in it.

Of course, a dog is not a reason-giving animal and hence does not live in terms of justifications. We, on the other hand, are reason giving and do live in terms of justifications. But however reason giving we are, we are still animals. Taking offense at this is simply taking offense at the truth. To be sure, the forms of meaningful life of which humans are capable are diverse in ways that the good for dogs is rather uniform for the entire species. But the central point remains that our reason giving proceeds outward from our categorical interests, which have their substance in whatever source of human meaning it is that has its deepest grip on us.

The call for justification, then, is at least unclear when it comes to reasons for living and to Camus's worries about the worth of life. It is at least worth asking what one is wondering about regarding the meaning of human lives where humans have self-respect, are involved in good personal relations, have some intrinsically meaningful work to do, have a healthy amount of play and leisure, are not suffering from serious physical or psychological abnormalities, and seem to take up their activities with vigor. These things do not justify their lives but are the values in terms of which human justifications normally proceed, at least for the overwhelming majority. Remove these things and most humans simply struggle to take any interest in life at all. Thus it is only from the things that add meaning that practical justifications emanate.

Someone might object, however, that what I have just said is simply false, that there are people who have all the things I have just mentioned in their lives but still wonder if their lives are meaningful. According to one version of this objection, these people, on looking out over their deliberative fields, are asking the question, Is this all there is? Such a question expresses a dissatisfaction with life because it lacks something; something is missing. In Aristotelian terms, the goods of life are not self-sufficient; in fact, they are not minimally sufficient to make life worthy of being chosen for itself.

What this "something" might be that could be added to life in addition to the things already mentioned to make life worthy of choice is unclear in most cases. Still it is possible. Since I have not mentioned a relationship with God, this is certainly one possibility. Other possibilities might present themselves, though it is difficult to think of clear cases. Not enough security or not enough excitement come to mind. Yet it is difficult to see that these things would not be included within good personal relations and intrinsically meaningful activities of work and play. But whatever this something that is lacking might be it must be something of categorical value if the question about the meaning of life is deep enough to seriously disturb the person who asks the question. So understood, this version of the objection turns out to be no objection at all to the general point about justification: Justification proceeds from what is most meaningful for us; it does not precede it. For most people, I believe, meaning derives from the elements I have mentioned and are included within the thick conception of integrity. I will argue this in more detail in parts 2 through 4.

Another version of the objection construes the wonder about the meaning of life differently. According to this objection, some people who have all that I have mentioned in their lives still wonder whether the substantive focus of their lives is *justified* from some objective point of view. In yearning for a meaningful life, they seek not only the things above but these *plus* an objective justification for living this kind of life. Without the belief that such a life is justified, they do not find life meaningful.

One theoretical way of construing this line of thought about the meaningfulness of one's life is in terms of some conception of what value is. Consider how we might think of questions about the meaningfulness of our lives from the perspective of a certain view of intrinsic value. I have in mind the view of intrinsic value begun by the intuitionists (Brentano, Moore, Ross, Ewing, etc.) and developed by Noah Lemos in his book, *Intrinsic Value*.[1] According to this view, there is a kind of intrinsic value that attaches to states of affairs that is nonrelational which contrasts with both instrumental value and relational intrinsic value. Some things are instru-

1. Noah Lemos, *Intrinsic Value: Concept and Warrant* (New York: Cambridge University Press, 1994). Also, see my review of Lemos's book in *Mind* 105, no. 418 (April 1996): 496–503.

mentally good for something; others are intrinsically good for someone; and others are intrinsically good period. Hammers are instrumentally good for driving nails; playing the piano is intrinsically good for the music lover; and (perhaps) the flourishing of a tropical forest is intrinsically good period, regardless of whether there is anyone around to appreciate it. Of course, it is controversial that there is any such value as being intrinsically good period, but this is not something I am concerned to challenge here. The point here is to assume there is such value for the moment to see what relevance it might have to the question of the meaningfulness of one's life from one's own point of view and the issue of justification. In this regard, the point here is similar to the one we considered in the introduction that Aristotle made against Plato concerning the relevant sense of good: What sense of value is relevant to how we live our lives?

According to Lemos, intrinsic value is not only nonrelational, its existence is independent of any psychological attitude. This is true despite the fact that Lemos explicates the concept of intrinsic value in terms of a state of affair's being intrinsically worthy of love. He says,

> (P2) p is intrinsically worthy of love if and only if p is necessarily such that, for any x, the contemplation of just p by x requires that x love p and not hate p.[2]

Bringing in love in this way to explicate the concept of intrinsic value would seem to contradict both the claim that such value is independent of any psychological attitude and the claim that it is nonrelational. When properly understood, however, the concept of being intrinsically worthy of love deepens our understanding of the nonrelational, psychological independence of intrinsic value. Lemos insists that the word *requires* in (P2) cannot be read causally but normatively. Thus (P2) is logically consistent with "x hates p even when contemplating just p." When x contemplates just p what x sees is that loving p is fitting. This does not mean that contemplating just p causes x to love p. Indeed, to see that love is fitting is to perceive a state of affairs, a fact, namely, that p is intrinsically good. Intrinsic value, on this view, then, is another fact about the world, and judgments about intrinsic value are about such facts. Not only is the fact "the tropical forest is flourishing" intrinsically valuable, but "the flourishing of the tropical forest is intrinsically valuable" is a fact. Moreover, it is a fact that obtains in-

2. Lemos, *Intrinsic Value*, 12.

dependent of anyone's believing it to obtain, and our belief that it obtains is true only if it obtains.

Though Lemos does not raise the question of the meaningfulness of life, we might understand what it is to justify one's life in terms of this concept of intrinsic value. Suppose one has one's self-respect, sympathy and concern for others, and love in a variety of forms for others and is committed to excellence at what one does. Assume also that one is in reasonably good physical and psychological health and that things are going well for those about whom one cares where one cares in the ways described. Further, assume that one is able to achieve some level of excellence acceptable from one's own point of view. Finally, assume that one has all this with the basic elements of integrity intact. Now, on the view under consideration, one might still wonder about the meaningfulness of one's life by wondering if it is justified. One would be wondering about whether the sentence "My life so described is intrinsically good" is true, that is, whether this sentence reports a fact. One would not, on this view, necessarily be wondering if one could on reflection endorse or approve of one's life.

So construed, if this is my worry, the wonder about justification is decidedly not about how to live my life but about the epistemic justification for believing that a certain fact obtains, namely, that my life is intrinsically valuable. Suppose this fact obtains and I justifiably believe that it does. There remains the question of how to live my life, unless I am psychologically constituted in a way that I find life meaningful only if I believe that I am justified in believing as fact that my life is intrinsically valuable in this sense. Therefore, even if we accept this ontology of value, there remains the issue of how such value bears on practical reason. There is a gap, on this view, between believing that something is intrinsically valuable and taking such a fact as even remotely of practical significance. For it is a contingent matter, on this view, that I assert that p is valuable and that I endorse or approve of or value p.[3] I might on this view care deeply that my beliefs about intrinsic value be justified but care not at all that my life is intrinsically valuable in this sense. Indeed, believing, on this view, that my

---

3. In this regard, Lemos says, "Even if it were true that whoever accepts that a thing is intrinsically good also approves or desires that thing, it is possible that he could conceive or entertain that thing's being intrinsically good without conceiving of his approving or desiring that thing." *Intrinsic Value*, 115. There is then no essential connection, on this view, between x's believing that p is intrinsically valuable and x's valuing p. Indeed, one could *believe* that p is intrinsically valuable and not *value* p at all.

life is not intrinsically valuable in this sense gives me no reason whatever for changing my life. For on this view, to be aware that something is good and of intrinsic value is not to be aware of something as appearing within one's deliberative field.

I cannot see that when most people are wondering about the meaning fulness of their lives they are worrying about whether it is a fact that their lives are intrinsically valuable in this sense. But if there are those who are and if their worry in this regard is at the center of their lives, then they have categorical values regarding epistemic justification that others lack. When their beliefs about intrinsic value affect their lives, it is not simply because they *believe* certain propositions concerning value to be true but because certain values are categorically instantiated in their affective (not merely cognitive) psychologies. What intuitionism lacks, then, is a conception of value that is relevant to practical reason. I believe the same applies to any externalist account of morality or what it is to have reasons for action, including traditional Kantianism. And this is one argument in favor of Kantian internalism.[4]

There is a difference between a moral epistemology, a theory of which is included in the second part of *Intrinsic Value*, and a theory of practical reason. At least, there is a difference on the intuitionist's view. Judgments of intrinsic value are on Lemos's view like axioms except that they have only modest a priori justification,[5] which is to say that they are defeasible judgments about necessary truths regarding value. As axiom-like, however, they are not practical norms. They cannot be, given that the assertion by a speaker that p is intrinsically valuable is not an endorsement or expression of approval of p; prescriptivity is thus external to the judgment that something is intrinsically good. To accept an axiom as a practical norm, however, is to see it as prescriptive, and it is only so that an axiom has a place in practical reason.

Why we should care about intrinsic value is, according to the intuitionist view, a separate issue from whether our value beliefs are epistemically justified. It is this separate issue that is both about practical reason and

4. Christine Korsgaard also faults intuitionism along these lines in *Creating the Kingdom of Ends* (Cambridge: Cambridge University Press, 1996), 52, 66, 228, 246–47. She similarly rejects realism in *The Sources of Normativity* (Cambridge: Cambridge University Press, 1996), and, I believe, decisively wins the argument against Thomas Nagel there. For the exchange between Korsgaard and Nagel, see *The Sources of Normativity*, 200–9, 219–58.

5. They are not axioms in the strong sense of having strong a priori justification.

about the meaningfulness of our lives. And what can be said in this regard about intuitionism can be said for any conception of "objective" value that is independent of the facts about human psychology.

It is one thing, then, to wonder if one is living according to one's deepest values or to wonder what one's deepest values are, or even whether one's life is anchored in some deep set of values at all. It is quite another to wonder *with any sense of urgency* if one's life is justified after careful reflection on one's deepest values where one finds that one's life is going well in terms of those values. What could one be wondering about? Here it is crucial to note that this is anything but a rhetorical question. It is rather a request for the hard philosophical work of providing a clear understanding of what the question of meaning is calling for and what its connection is with the issue of justification. Without the fruit of such work, the question of meaning seems itself rhetorical, even superficial. So when I say that ultimately categorical values are not in need of justification, I am not simply trying to circumvent a difficult philosophical problem. I am asserting that there is a clear understanding of practical justification that proceeds *from* categorical values rather than *to* them and that it is unclear what the issue of meaning is that motivates the denial of this conception. As we will see, there is some limited room for deliberation about one's categorical values, but these facts do not deny what has been said about practical justification and its structure. Contra Aristotle, we can deliberate about ends but only in a limited and special way.[6]

There is, of course, a sense in which categorical values are justified. They are justified from the agent's most reflective point of view, namely, the point of view of life as a whole. For this to be the case, those values must be such that they provide the basis for an agent's perceiving a way of life in which those values have a coherent place and that way of life is chosen for itself. But this does not mean that there is some point of view outside of any particular agent's own point of view from which the agent derives a justification for his or her deepest values. In this sense, explanation and justification converge. From the third-person point of view, what explains the rationality of one's actions are the very same factors that justify it from the first-

---

6. The best discussion I have seen in the literature on the possibility of revising final ends through deliberation is by Henry Richardson. There may be some difference between Richardson and me on what counts as a matter of deliberation, but on the view I defend there can be a change in one's final ends. How much change and how such change is effected by deliberation turns somewhat on what one counts as a matter of deliberation. See Henry S. Richardson, *Practical Reasoning about Final Ends* (Cambridge: Cambridge University Press, 1994).

person point of view, namely, a coherent set of values instantiated within a psychology with integrity. Hence the kind of naturalism suggested here does not commit the naturalistic fallacy: Practical judgments are normative through and through, but the explanation for why we value what we do is to be found in a naturalistic explanation of our psychologies.

2.

If what I have just said is true, that practical deliberation proceeds from our categorical values rather than to them, we are in a position to say something more about the notion of an action being rational, all things considered. The "all things considered" clause must always be understood as relative to a point of view, namely, the point of view of whatever the deepest values are of a particular agent. If Kantian internalism is correct, then the integration test should reveal that for agents who pass the test, their deepest concern is that their actions conform to the requirements of the categorical imperative. If the Aristotelian model is correct, then the integration test will reveal that for large numbers of people who pass the test, they will be agents of integrity in the thick sense whose practical norms are symmetrical in their regulative functions. Moreover, we should make sense of their practical reasoning in terms of their actions and their reasons for them as proceeding from their character. This means that they will see an action as rational, all things considered, because of its place in a way of life. And this life they will see as a whole in which none of its parts provide a basis for their taking as good, in Herman's sense, something that could provide a reason that is asymmetrically regulative of their other concerns. In either case, we must understand the notion of rationality, all things considered, as proceeding from those goods apart from which an agent could not find life at least minimally meaningful from his or her own point of view. And, of course, this means that the point of view of reflective endorsement is the point of view of life as a whole.

Now there is some irony in this for Kantians. To be committed to the view that practical reason proceeds from the bases of meaning in an agent's life from his or her own point of view already leans in the direction of the Aristotelian model. This is because on the view that practical deliberation proceeds from rather than to categorical values, it could never be rational, all things considered, to act in a way that is contrary to the most fundamental goods of a way of life valued categorically by an agent, where that agent had a clear view of that way of life in which his or her actions are seen as parts. Thus there is a connection between the insistence on meaning and having reasons and that part of the Aristotelian model that insists on a certain notion of rationality, all things considered. It is this: An act could never be rational, all things considered, if the act were contrary to a way of life consistent with the deepest values of an agent's psychology. Rational rejection of a deliberative alternative would occur where the agent's imaginative projection of the place of an act within an overall way of life was an accurate projection and the agent would in the light of this projection reject that way of life and the actions it involves. It is only Kantian externalism that can reject this notion of rationality, all things considered, since it is only this brand of Kantianism that rejects the connection between meaning and having reasons. Kantian internalism, then, cannot maintain that the results of the CI procedure are *necessarily* rational, all things considered, and accept the integration test with its connection between meaning and reason. Proponents of that view can only maintain that *as a matter of fact* the CI procedure will result in full rationality, all things considered. I will argue that CI rationality is not even contingently rational, all things considered, and in so doing I will employ the only notion of full rationality consistent with an essential connection between meaning and reason, namely, reflective endorsement from the point of view of life as a whole. Thus pressure is brought on the Kantian internalists either to defend externalism or to accept the Aristotelian model with its emphasis on the meaningfulness of an agent's life from his or her own point of view. The latter leads directly to the criteria of finality and self-sufficiency in its conception of reflective endorsement.

3.

It is, of course, another issue whether all ways of life worth living for humans are moral ways of life. Nonetheless, one point cannot be overlooked: Just as other animals cannot have obligations to be nonanimal-like in their living, humans cannot have obligations to be nonhuman in theirs. Why? Because on the most plausible view of what it is for agents to have reasons in their living they could not possibly have reasons for this. Our reasons for action emerge from the sources that make human life meaningful from a human point of view. More specifically, a particular human cannot have an obligation to be nonhuman on whatever particular form of human good it is that gives his or her life its deepest meaning. A way of life, then, cannot be morally obligatory for a human unless it is a life that is at least minimally worth living for a human. In other terms: Without categorical value there are no categorical imperatives. Thus the meaning of morality finds itself within the meaning of human life, within the meaning of individual human lives.

Thus the point of any theory of human agency is not to reflect a conception of morality but to be as true as possible to the facts of human agency. Among those facts are those concerning the structural features of the interests and priorities of the person of integrity in the thin sense elaborated in the previous chapter. A test of any moral theory is that it must be true to these facts. Accordingly, I will argue for what I call an integrity-sensitive theory of human agency and place a conception of morality within it.[7] On this conception of morality, a way of life cannot be obligatory unless it is minimally worthwhile. This does not mean that one will believe that actions may never be required that will end one's life. Rather, it means that when death is required it is because there is no alternative that preserves a way of life that is minimally worthwhile from the agent's own point of view. There will be no alternative way of life that makes even a minimal place for the agent's ends so that life is worthy of choice in terms of finality and self-sufficiency.

Therefore, an integrity-sensitive theory places an agent's reasons for action within a conception of the agent's own good. Yet the primary emphasis is not on human flourishing, as in Aristotle, but on those goods that make life minimally worth living and the elements of integrity possible.[8] It is not that I believe that Aristotle was wrong about practical reason and considerations of the *best* way to live but that there is much to be learned about practical reason from thinking about a life that is minimally worth living. Accordingly, an integrity-sensitive theory, as I conceive it, places an emphasis on the survival of the agent of integrity. This has implications for the integration test and for conceptions of justification and obligation.

First, it means that the integration test will test for whether a particular

7. Some will object that what I suggest is not a conception of morality at all. Certainly, what I suggest is not a form of what Bernard Williams calls "the peculiar institution." *Ethics and the Limits of Philosophy* (Cambridge, Mass.: Harvard University Press, 1985). I cannot see, however, why the tradition being attacked by Williams there has any copyright on the term "morality." So I refuse to yield the term while recognizing that I am rejecting that tradition. The question is whether I give good enough reasons for this. See also Charles Taylor's discussion of Williams's views on "the peculiar institution": "A Most Peculiar Institution," in *World, Mind, and Ethics*, ed. J. E. J. Altham and Ross Harrison (Cambridge: Cambridge University Press, 1995), 132–55.

8. This is not to deny the Aristotelian conception of the integrative function of practical reason. It is merely to pay attention to those features of human well-being that give the pursuit of flourishing a point.

good has foundation in the agent's categorical values. The behavioral manifestations that a good is a categorical good will be exhibited in personality disintegration should that good be denied the agent. Or such disintegration will occur, as we will see, as a result of what I call categorical evils. The kinds of disintegration will be those alluded to in chapter 3.

Second, the emphasis on survival puts limits on issues of justification. A human does not need justification for being a human. Nor does a human need justification for surviving *as a human*, even where justification for surviving might be in order. Indeed, it is hard to see what such justification would come to. Since having reasons to survive involve the pursuit of a minimally worthwhile life, an integrity-sensitive theory of human agency must reject the view that a human needs a justification for pursuing a minimally worthwhile life. It must also reject the view that an agent needs a justification for not pursuing a life that is not minimally worthwhile from the agent's own point of view. It is this fact that leads to the Aristotelian interpretation of the "all things considered" clause of practical rationality. For it could never be practically rational to act contrary to that way of life that one believes is essential to those things one values most.

This leaves open, of course, the possibility of radical relativism regarding practical reason. So it does. It does not, however, either ensure such relativism or rule out a strong form of universalism. In this regard, one should view with suspicion any antirelativistic conception of practical reason that declares itself the only logical possibility. Similarly, one should view with suspicion any relativistic conception of practical reason that declares radical relativism true without appeal to the facts of actual human reasoning. When we look at those facts, I believe we discover that while relativism is true it is seldom radical, and when it is radical, it is not nearly so extensive as many declare it to be. Nevertheless, the recognition that one's reasons for action proceed from one's categorical interests does not rule out that Kantian internalism accurately accounts for the values of any agent who possesses the qualities of an agent of integrity in the thin sense.

The third implication of the emphasis on survival by these theories is that they place limits on an agent's obligations. According to some moral theories, that a way of life is not minimally worthwhile for a person is consistent with that person having the obligation to adopt it. Many consequentialist moral theories and traditional Kantianism are like this. But this cannot be true for any theory that is integrity sensitive. That a way of life is not minimally worthwhile for a person is inconsistent with that person having the obligation to adopt it. To deny this would be to assert that as an agent one feels obligated to take on a life on criteria independent of any meaning it has from one's own point of view. To some, this denial will not sound so strange. But I hope to show that to deny this is to misconstrue the actual place of impartial norms in our lives and in the lives of those we admire most.

As with other animals, then, the issue of justifying certain interests is miscast when applied to humans. As is the issue of whether a human life is worth living when a human is able to live a life that is at least minimally worthwhile in a natural and social environment. Moreover, there are limits to how much disfigurement can take place from curtailing human interests without eliminating the human element altogether. This is the issue of the survival of human agency, which is central to an integrity-sensitive theory. It can be put in this way: What goods are there that if eliminated from a human life or if not available to a human in its environment would make life not worth living for that human?

4.

Clearly the answer to this question concerning survival should be expressed in categorical terms. Here I want to clarify what it is for a particular human to *find* that the object of a human interest is a categorical good.

To survive as persons of integrity agents must have practical wisdom, which includes a sense of their own good. They must recognize their good when it is available to them. In part, this consists in having a clear picture of what appears within their deliberative field in a way that they see everything that is there (self-sufficiency) and do not misconstrue the value of what is there (finality). But also in part, a person's own good consists in having a set of interests with the structure of the person of integrity in the thin sense. It consists in having the objects of those interests in the agent's life in the way set by the priorities of that structure embedded within their psychology as norms. Thus the recognition of one's own good comes with practical wisdom. This consists (in part) in having a clearheaded set of priorities that reflect the structural features of the interests of the person of integrity in the thin sense. It does not consist in every instance or even in most instances of thoughts of a meaningful life and the means to such a life. The thought of a meaningful life does not usually enter the recognition of one's own good in this way in everyday deliberations.

Nevertheless, the person of practical wisdom has the ability to envision different ways of life and to see that some actions and character traits are consistent with some ways of life and not others. Indeed, it is this capacity that allows the agent to make judgments of full rationality. Were the agent either unable to place things within some overall way of life or unable to place more meaning on some ways of life than others, the agent would lack the capacity essential for rational agency. For the lack of such a capacity is a failure in the ability to relate meaning to action. To be sure, the person of practical wisdom is not constantly engaged in assessing the overall meaning of every action; just as the Kantian agent is not always thinking through the CI procedure. Nevertheless, the kind of reflectiveness that requires seeing meaning in the context of life is required for practical wisdom and rational agency itself. Thus without the ability to employ, even if only intuitively, the criteria of finality and self-sufficiency, the capacity for practical reason is compromised.

Practical wisdom, then, includes the ability to recognize the importance of things within a set of priorities that are one's own. Without this wisdom, persons may think they find that something has a certain degree of importance when it does not. That is, humans can be mistaken about matters of categorical and noncategorical value. Such mistakes are reflected in the degree to which humans can flourish and maintain the elements of integrity in their lives. Mistakes of this sort we may call mistaken findings.

One kind of mistaken finding regarding categorical value concerns mistakes to the effect that some things would make life worth living for a particular human agent under favorable conditions when in fact they would not. John, for example, might think that a life confined to drugs and casual sex is of categorical value, that it is worthy of choice for itself and is deficient in nothing. Yet within a lifestyle of this sort he might discover that life tends to lose its allure for him, that confusion results regarding his self-identity. He may, in fact, find that these things are categorical evils because of their threat to other things that are the most meaningful in his life. Here the process of living must refine his capacities for seeing his life as a whole and how things fit into a way of life. If it does not or if he discovers his mistaken finding too late, his prospects for a worthwhile life are bleak at best.

Similarly, John might have a worthwhile life and be mistaken about which of its elements are actually of categorical value and which of its elements are not. Failure of discernment in this regard is a lack of practical wisdom due to the inability to employ the finality criterion, and the security of the categorical goods of such a person's life is tenuous. The problem is that an agent of this sort lacks the capacity for seeing which things actually are a part of a way of life and which things are not. This is one kind of failure in the capacity for reflective endorsement, and, as such, it is a failure in practical reason.

John also might be mistaken about whether his life is worthwhile at all.

It may not include the things that he thinks it does, and he may be unable to face this fact. For example, he may think his wife loves him, unmistakenly find life not worth living without her love, and yet simply be mistaken about her affections for him. Moreover, he may not be able to see the truth of the matter because his fear of the loss of her love threatens his reasons for living. Mistaken findings of this sort undoubtedly involve more than a failure in practical wisdom. Here the agent can envision a worthwhile life, but because he does not satisfy the conditions of integrity, he cannot see that his way of life is not the way of life he envisions.

John might also be mistaken about the value of a way of life simply because he is too inexperienced to see what things he would value were he only to experience them. Acquired tastes are one kind of example, but there are others. Contrast acquiring a taste for wine, a taste for classical music, and coming to love a child. Some values once acquired might lead to an overall reordering of one's values and to rejecting one's previous way of life in favor of another. Acquiring a taste for wine does not usually lead to such overall reordering. On the other hand, if one is a dedicated music lover, acquiring a taste for classical music over a previous affinity, say, for at least some forms of popular music, might lead to some reordering. But surely coming to love a child where one had previously been indifferent to such love might lead one to change one's way of life in an extensive way. Indeed, it might lead one to see one's previous way of life as rather shallow, even where it previously had some depth.[9]

From this, we can see that the issue regarding the categorical value of any human good can be put in terms of whether judgments about it are based on mistaken findings. What is it, then, for a particular human good to be categorical for a particular agent? It is one that under adequately informed conditions of choice a particular human agent of integrity and practical wisdom would not unmistakenly find life worth living without and be able to maintain the basic elements of integrity. What is it for a particular human good to be a universal categorical good? It is one that under favorable conditions of choice no human agent of integrity and practical wisdom would unmistakenly find life worth living without it and be able to

9. Any plausible form of internalism must accommodate these facts, and I can see no reason why it cannot. Whether Williams's view can accommodate them is debated in the literature. See especially John McDowell, "Might There Be External Reasons," in *Mind, World, and Ethics*, 68–85; and E. J. Bond, *Reason and Value* (Cambridge: Cambridge University Press, 1983). Richardson's discussion of deliberation and final ends is also relevant. See Richardson, *Practical Reasoning about Final Ends*.

maintain the basic elements of integrity. It is a relative categorical good if some but not all adequately informed human agents of integrity and practical wisdom would make a similar finding regarding it. At this point, I leave open whether there are any universal categorical goods, and I consider this a requirement of inquiry concerning an integrity-sensitive conception of human agency and morality.

Also important in this context is an understanding of what it is to discover a mistaken finding. From the third-person point of view, it is to discover the source of the loss of unity, meaning, and reasons for living in an agent's life in the agent's commitments and norms. These are commitments and norms that cannot establish and sustain the agent's integrity. To make such a discovery is to discover that some goods or a constellation of goods are not ones that will provide a conception of rational agency that will pass the integration test for that person. From the first-person point of view, to discover a mistaken finding is to discover that one's priorities are such that they do not structure a way of life that is self-sufficient and final, that is inclusive enough regarding what one values and is worthy of choice for itself.

Thus the categorical value of any human good is solely determined by its status in a worthwhile human life. No otherworldly, nonhuman conception of value is being imported to determine the worthwhileness of any human life. Nor—and this is of the greatest importance—is there reason to worry on a related front: No conception of the human good is being imposed independent of the kind of life a particular person of integrity actually would find worthwhile under favorable conditions. The only restrictions besides those regarding unmistaken findings and favorable conditions are those regarding the thin elements of integrity. Nothing I say about that concept gives any a priori bias against any conception of the good life for humans, except those that revere alienation, insanity, and self-deception. For all I have argued to this point, as opposed to what I have suggested or asserted, there is no a priori reason for ruling out many possibilities, especially Kantian internalism. At any rate, there is a test for whether any particular set of priorities for any actual agent is based on mistaken findings. It is whether those priorities can be sustained with the elements of integrity intact in a way of life in actual historical circumstances over time. This is the integration test. But it should be emphasized that the integration test when employed from the third-person point of view is a device of theory. The agent discovers a mistaken finding from the first-person point of view by getting a full picture of the place of some consideration within an overall way of life and finding that that way of life has no meaning for him or her. It is the philosophical account of agency that employs the integration test from the third-person perspective.

5.

I move now to some comments on what it is for a way of life to be an available alternative for the person of integrity and practical wisdom. The most fundamental condition is that the way of life must make possible the elements of integrity. Again, these are substantial unity of self, self-preserving character, awareness and importance of one's distinctness as an individual, and sufficient perspicuity of self-perception. It also must be a deliberative alternative for the agent in question. This means that the alternative must be one that can be considered as a practical possibility for the agent through the agent's own deliberations.

Doubtless, some important sense can be made of a way of life being "available" to an agent in a nondeliberative sense. But the current issue leads us to focus on contexts involving an agent's deliberations. It centers on how we are to give an account of how an agent's reasons for action emerge in the context of living a life. That is, we are focusing on that aspect of an agent's behavior that is deliberative. For this, we want an account of the agent's normative thoughts, how they are prescriptive for the agent, and how they emerge in the agent's life. These issues lead to the current focus on deliberative contexts and therefore on deliberative alternatives. It is to these contexts that an integrity-sensitive theory must be responsive in a way that other theories are not.

The contexts for a particular human agent's deliberating about alternative ways of life are many. But the most fundamental are those in which the agent is deliberating about whether to change his or her way of life. Of similar importance are those in which the agent is deliberating about the way of life to which he or she is to introduce others. The latter typically occur within parenthood, but I will focus on the first sort of deliberation. I choose this focus because it applies directly to decisions involving an agent's considering whether his or her way of life or a particular moral demand is justified.

Sarah is deliberating about changing her life because she is anxious about its moral standing in terms of the lives of others. Can she deliberate about a change in her categorical values and in what she sees as categorically good? If she can, we can make sense of the notion of deliberative contexts involving categorical change.

There are such contexts, but it is important to understand their limitations. Sarah can deliberate about a change in her categorical values but only to the degree to which she can entertain the possibility of retaining some stability to her identifying thoughts through the transition. Otherwise, *she* cannot entertain the change as a change in *her* life. This means that Sarah cannot deliberate about a complete change in her ground projects and her categorical values. Such deliberation is simply incoherent. One could never deliberate about a complete change in one's categorical values, because there would be no substantive basis for the deliberation.[10] Since one's categorical values function as the foundation for deliberation about changes in one's way of life, a change in these values precedes a change in categorical deliberations.

Incomplete categorical changes that result from deliberation are possible but only for people with complex ground projects. A deliberative incomplete categorical change occurs, then, from deliberations that reveal conflicts or shortcomings within one's categorical values. Also, the agent's deliberations about the resolution of such conflicts must be consistent with the agent maintaining his or her identifying thoughts through the transition. This is possible only if some categorical goods function as the basis for giving up or adjusting one's commitment to other perceived goods. In this

10. The difference between moral imagination and moral deliberation is an important one here. It is quite possible for a person who *knows* that Kennedy and Churchill are dead to *imagine* that they are still alive. But in an important sense it is not possible for such a person to *believe* that they are still alive. Why? Because imagination contrary to knowledge requires the playful suspension of belief. And suspending belief in this way is not the same as not believing. Similarly, it is possible to imagine oneself being an ax murderer, but it is quite another to enter into practical deliberations in the direction of the actions of such a person. In fact, such deliberations are simply psychologically impossible—however imaginable they might be—for the overwhelming majority of us.

Perhaps, then, I can imagine myself as a completely different person, though even this is fraught with difficulties. But even if I could imagine myself as a completely different person, this would not establish the fact that I can deliberate about becoming a completely different person. Often moral theory fails to take seriously the distinction between moral imagination and moral deliberation. The latter does not allow for the kind of abstraction from the concrete circumstances in the way that the former does. Moral imagination allows us a degree of abstract distance from our own conative and affective dispositions that is not possible in our practical deliberations, at least in regard to our most central dispositions. And though moral imagination has its own importance in the moral life, it can, if not tempered with real deliberation, lead to a life of mere fantasy.

See also Michael Sandel, *Liberalism and the Limits of Justice* (Cambridge: Cambridge University Press, 1982), the last chapter.

way, contrary to what Aristotle says, it is possible to deliberate about ends without turning them into means. In these contexts, the agent is moved to envision different ways of life, each of which excludes something treasured categorically by the agent. The agent will see one of these ways of life as the deliberative choice only if the agent has one categorical value that is more fundamental to the agent's psychology than the other. Envisioning different ways of life allows the agent to filter some values through other values and in some cases allows the agent to bring resolution to a problematic situation by projecting one alternative way of life as the agent's own. This occurs only when the envisioned way of life brings about a change in the agent's values and interests by adjusting them to each other within a way of life. And it is in this way that the agent's character determines the rational choice among ways of life, which is the most fundamental way in which practical reason is character-relative. Though there is significant room for an agent shaping his or her own character, these observations mark the most fundamental limit on such an ability.

I am not asserting here that there cannot be complete categorical changes in a person's way of life and consequently in one's identifying thoughts. Rather I am saying that complete categorical change is at best only partially deliberative. It is more fundamentally the result of nondeliberative evolutionary changes in one's categorical values.[11] Sarah's doubts about the moral standing of her way of life may very well indicate an evolutionary transition in her categorical values. This would explain why they are unsettling to but are not totally disruptive of her identifying thoughts.

Some categorical goods, however, are, if lost, irretrievable goods of a ground project, even where the project is complex rather than simple. If an agent rightly regards a particular good to be irretrievable and its loss a mortal one, no way of life that excludes that good is an alternative way of life for that agent. Nor is it a way of life the agent can consider in practical deliberation, and therefore it is not available to the agent in this subjective sense. No human agent, then, can deliberate to the normative thought of the obligation to adopt a way of life that threatens the irretrievable goods valued categorically by that agent. When there are conflicts between irretrievable categorical goods, there is deliberative impasse, and for problem-

11. John McDowell seems to have nondeliberative change in mind in "Deliberation and Moral Development in Aristotle's Ethics," in *Aristotle, Kant, and the Stoics,* ed. Stephen Engstrom and Jennifer Whiting (New York: Cambridge University Press, 1996), 19–35, as well as in "Might There Be External Reasons?"

atic situations of this sort there is no point of reflection from which rational endorsement of an alternative is possible.

Considerations, therefore, that require categorical changes in a way of life can have important but limited room in the deliberations of a human agent. But these considerations do not exhaust the field, for some changes are noncategorical changes. There is much more room for deliberative alternatives here, where we can begin to make sense of deliberations that require adopting one worthwhile way of life rather than another.

There is nothing about the concept of integrity and its elements that is threatened by a change in life that does not affect a person's core categorical values. Thus there is nothing about a person's integrity that precludes an agent's deliberating to the conclusion that another way of life requires noncategorical changes. In this sense, there are many ways of life that are deliberative alternatives for the person of integrity. Some of these might involve significant and important changes in one's life.

Later, I will argue for a thick conception of integrity that includes what can reasonably be called moral values among an admirable agent's categorical values and norms. Some are partial, and others are impartial. Yet a person's impartial values and norms are not among his or her reasons for living. But they are among the reasons for living one way rather than another. That is, there can be no sense made of practical deliberation in which an agent deliberates to the worthwhileness of his or her life on impartial norms alone. Still there is much in an agent's deliberating to the conclusion that one worthwhile way of life is preferable to another on impartial grounds. Finally, there is also the possibility of an agent's deliberating on impartial grounds to the conclusion that none of the alternative lives available are either worthwhile or permissible. Later, we will see how this is especially true of respectful people. What we will see is that their respectfulness involves categorical aversions to some ways of life and that these aversions give rise to norms that are strongly regulative of an agent's ability to see a way of life as even minimally meaningful. In themselves, these arguments will do a great deal of work against traditional Kantianism but little against Kantian internalism. The work against Kantian internalism will be done by arguments in parts 3 and 4 that the norms of practical reason are all symmetrical in their regulative functions.

6.

Thus far, I have tried to do several things regarding the claims of the introduction. In chapter 1, I made clear my methodological commitments and argued that these commitments have a clear rationale that leads to an understanding of the internalism requirement in a way that entails the integration test as a means for rationally adjudicating between rival conceptions of rational agency. In chapter 2, I tried to establish that our actual employment of normative concepts reflects a conceptual scheme in which asymmetrically dominant norms are absent. Impartial norms like sympathy and respect regulate each other as well as partial norms like friendship and parental love. But, similarly, partial norms like friendship and parental love regulate each other as well as impartial norms like respect and sympathy. This suggests that if our conceptual scheme has any kind of rational foundation, then a central feature of both externalist and internalist impartialism (whether Kantian or non-Kantian) is to be rejected, namely, that the integrative function of practical reason is achieved by an impartial norm that is asymmetrical in its regulative function. It also suggests that the first part of the Aristotelian, inclusive-ends conception of practical reason is true, that all norms are symmetrical in their regulative functions. In chapter 3 and in this chapter, I have tried to introduce a conceptual apparatus for showing how in general the rational foundation for practical judgments is to be found in the goods that make life meaningful from an agent's own point of view. Categorical and noncategorical goods provide both the meaning of an agent's life from his or her own point of view and the foundation for practical judgments. Moreover, understanding the distinctions between categorical and noncategorical goods provides us with an account of how the thin conception of integrity is possible. Before I can conclude, however, that we should accept the Aristotelian conception of practical reason, I must show in some detail how the agent of integrity in the thick sense, with the goods that make his or her life meaningful, comes to have the kind of conceptual scheme found in chapter 2. This is the task of parts 2 through 4.

Part 2

THE GOODS OF RESPECT

To live without self-respect is to lie awake some night, beyond
the reach of warm milk, phenobarbital, and the sleeping hand on
the coverlet, counting up the sins of commission and omission, the
trusts betrayed, the promises subtly broken, the gifts irrevocably
wasted through sloth or cowardice or carelessness. However long
we postpone it, we eventually lie down alone in that notoriously
uncomfortable bed, the one we make ourselves. Whether or not
we sleep in it depends, of course, on whether or not we respect
ourselves.

Joan Didion, Slouching Towards Bethlehem

In part 1, I addressed the issue of the thin conception of integrity. More
specifically, the previous two chapters developed in general terms the concept of the good for the person of integrity in the thin sense and a conception of practical deliberation. Gleaning from those comments, I will say
that the good for any agent of integrity includes all that contributes to the
agent's flourishing. This includes whatever is necessary for that person's
survival where survival finds its point in the categorical values of the agent.
Here I begin to take up the thick conception of integrity, specifically, that
component of the thick conception that involves the agent's respectfulness
of self and others. Part 2, then, has two aims: one critical and one preparatory. The critical aim is to provide the primary argument against traditional, externalist Kantianism. By showing how the respectful agent's reasons for action, including the agent's respectful actions, emerge from those
goods that are related to the meaningfulness of the agent's life from his or
her own point of view, I take sides with Kantian internalists against their
traditional counterparts. I take it that if I can show that traditional Kantianism cannot account for the role of respect in the moral life, then I will not
need to address its inadequacies in regard to the goods of love and the goods
of activity. I will then be free in the remainder of the book to focus my

attack exclusively on Kantian internalism. The preparatory aim is to provide a phenomenology of respect that must be accommodated by any adequate internalism, whether Kantian or Aristotelian. Therefore, part 2 contains limited argument against Kantian internalism because the argument against that view requires an argument that respect does not function as an asymmetrically dominant norm within the practical reason of the agent of integrity in the thick sense. This argument cannot be provided in full until goods other than respect have been considered. Consequently, that argument will come in parts 3 and 4.

I.

I will say that a person acts for the sake of his or her own good only if the person acts for partial or agent-centered reasons. This is a delicate point. Philosophers often speak as though a person's own good is always separable in principle from the good of others. This leads almost imperceptibly to the thought that if an agent is acting intrinsically for the sake of another's good, then it cannot be for the sake of his or her own good that the agent is acting. But this is surely a mistake.

To see that it is a mistake, consider the distinction between two different kinds of interests. The first are interests that are satisfiable from the perspective of the person having them without any intrinsic interest in the satisfaction of anyone else's interests. Call these individual interests. Clear examples are the interest in having an itch soothed or the preference for a favorite flavor of ice cream. There are others, and they are important, as we will see. But these are very clear examples, and they serve to clarify a distinction between these kinds of interests and others. The others I have in mind are social interests. Social interests, as I mean to refer to them, are those interests that reflect an intrinsic interest in the satisfaction of the interests of others. Among these are the interests we have in our loved ones. Now the mistake in thinking of a person's own good as in principle always separable from the good of another is in equating a person's own good with the satisfaction of individual interests. Surely this is a strange way to understand a person's good.

If I act intrinsically for the sake of my friend, I am also acting for the sake of my own good. This is true despite the fact that the motive is nonegoistic. To act for the sake of one's own good is to act for the sake of the things that make life most worth living and to which one is most personally committed. If it is not, it is difficult to tell what would be short of the crassest form of hedonism. Hence the truth of objective as opposed to subjective eudaimonism. As social beings, we come to the question of what is the best life to live with social ends, with ends that are independent of ourselves. In part, we identify our well-being with the well-being of others, which takes one of its forms in our identification with our friends. Thus one can act nonegoistically—for the sake of one's friend—and yet be acting for the sake of one's own good. In this way, there can be partial but nonetheless nonegoistic reasons for action. But unless there is some agent-centered connection of this sort between the intended beneficiary and the agent conferring the benefit, the agent is not acting for the sake of his or her own good.

One contrast, then, with partial but nonegoistic reasons for action are actions done for the sake of another but not for the sake of oneself. To have such reasons is to have agent-neutral or impartial reasons for action. I will try to show how the agent of integrity has such reasons and how they are sometimes overriding from the agent's point of view. That is, I will try to show how such reasons function as determinate norms for such an agent. Also, I will argue that to act contrary to such reasons when the agent perceives them as overriding is contrary to the good for any remotely normal human agent. Therefore, I argue, such overriding reasons are always in accordance with the good of such an agent. But it is one thing to act in accordance with one's own good; it is another to act for the sake of it. Acting on impartial nonegoistic reasons is not acting for the sake of one's own good. This is true even if acting contrary to such reasons is acting contrary to one's own good. In part 2, I argue that to act out of respect for others is often like this and that respect for others is a categorical good for the person of integrity.

Thus, in part 2, I begin to address the issue of the goods that figure into the good for the human agent of integrity as represented in the thick conception. This is the person who satisfies the criteria of the thin conception and who is also respectful, sympathetic, and esteeming of others, who is embedded in loving relationships in a variety of ways, who is involved in many intrinsically meaningful activities, and who is dedicated to excellence, to doing whatever he or she does well. The emphasis is on those goods that are crucial to survival, to life's having any point or meaning. In this sense, these are goods that when lost can be mortal losses for the agent. Of special importance are the roles these goods play in the agent's reasons for action.

I begin with some comments on human goods as the objects of the intentional dispositional states of human agents. On the view that I will defend here, human goods just are objects of intentional dispositional states, and it is in virtue of this fact that human goods can play the roles they do in practical reason. For it is as the objects of these states that various goods make their appearance within the agent's deliberative field. This is true whether the goods in question are the goods of respect (part 2), the goods of love (part 3), or the goods of activity (part 4). Consequently, a thorough understanding of the structure of intentional dispositional states in their variety is crucial to understanding how reasons for action emerge from the source of life's meaning. For this reason, the analysis of these states requires great care.

The components of the states of particular interest here are attitudes (especially those expressed in emotions), evaluations, interests, and beliefs. More specifically, the concern in part 2 is to give an analysis of the goods of respect in terms of such states and their behavioral manifestations with an aim to showing how the objects of respect appear within the respectful agent's deliberative field. Chapter 5 gives a conceptual analysis of the dispositions of the respectful person. Chapters 6 and 7 provide an analysis of the importance of respect in the life of a respectful agent of integrity. Chapter 6 argues that a clear understanding of the place of respect in the psychology of a respectful person clearly rules out any externalist account. Chapter 7 adds to this argument against traditional Kantianism but also includes an argument against Kantian internalism. The argument is that Kantian internalism has difficulties accounting for the symmetrical regulative functions between different forms of respect, some of which are impartial and some of which are partial. Thus the argument of chapter 7 involves a limited application of the integration test and is designed to show that the goods of respect have a very central role in personality integration for most human beings. Without these goods, most personalities disintegrate in serious ways, and it is this fact that tells against any externalist account of respect. Yet even among goods of respect and the norms associated with them, regulative functions are symmetrical across impartial and partial forms of respect, and this fact tells against Kantian internalism.

II.

States are dispositional in terms of their behavioral manifestations and are usually intentional in four senses: They have an "object," and they involve interests, evaluations, and beliefs. Fear is a dispositional state of a person with the behavioral inclination to take a defensive or protective posture and is intentional in the four above senses: (i) the person experiencing fear is afraid of someone or some thing; (ii) the fearful person is interested (in the typical cases) in his or her own welfare; (iii) the person experiencing fear evaluates the object of fear negatively as dangerous or threatening, as something to be avoided; and (iv) the fearful person interprets the object of fear as dangerous through certain beliefs the agent has about the object. In one way or the other, the agent believes the object to be harmful.

It would be a mistake, however, to think that all dispositional states are intentional. General boredom is a good example of a disposition that is not intentional; so too are some forms of depression. Despite manifesting themselves in various forms of floundering, these states do not have objects. Because of this, they can be of little direct relevance to a discussion of goods that can be pursued, protected, cherished, and the like, by human agents. This is not to deny that they (or their absence) figure into the good for a human being in other ways. For example, they are factors in mental health, which, of course, is an object of human interest. Nevertheless, their direct relevance to a discussion of categorical and noncategorical goods is limited.

Nor is it clear that all dispositional states that are intentional display all the intentional features of fear, though many of them do. This may mean that some attitudes and emotions are more subject to criteria of rationality than others. In any event, if the concern is to distinguish various human goods, we may find here a way of doing this. It is in terms of distinguishing the various kinds of intentional dispositional states common to human beings as they respond to themselves and items in their environment. Such states, then, might differ either in terms of their behavioral manifestations or in terms of their intentional features. Since all intentional dispositional states have at least the first feature of having an object, they might differ in several ways regarding their intentionality. They might

i. lack one or more of the other intentional features,
ii. take different kinds of objects,
iii. involve different kinds of interests in the object,
iv. involve different kinds of evaluations, or
v. involve different kinds of beliefs in different ways.

As a dispositional state, respect is only one among many sentiments a human agent can have regarding itself and other items in its environment. Moreover, understanding the place of respect in the psychology of a human agent is one, but only one, step in understanding the social dimensions of personal integrity. For a complete understanding, we need an account of all the goods that factor into the thick conception of integrity. Again, the reason that such states are crucial to practical reason is that it is as the objects of these states that various goods make their appearance within the agent's deliberative field, and it is this sense of good that is relevant to both practical reason and ethics. With these points in mind, I turn to a discussion of the goods of respect as the objects of a particular type of intentional dispositional state with an eye ultimately to showing how these goods factor into practical reason. I hope to show that, ironically, the Aristotelian model better accommodates respect for self and others than the Kantian model.

5. General Features and Varieties of Respect

The purpose of this chapter is to isolate the general features of respect as an intentional dispositional state, to show how the respected person appears within the deliberative field of the respectful agent, and to provide a taxonomy in terms of which later analysis will be carried out. In the course of the chapter, I distinguish six different kinds of respect in terms of their intentional features. Ultimately, the work done here will provide the basis for argument against traditional Kantianism. It will also set a task for either the Kantian internalist model of practical reason or the Aristotelian model, namely, that if either theory is to attach rationality to being respectful of self and others, it must account for the general features of respect as they are delineated here.

1.

In order to survive with one's integrity intact, one must be able to tolerate oneself. To find oneself intolerable is to believe oneself deficient in terms of some minimal standards for self-affirmation. The attitude one has toward oneself as having met such standards is the attitude of self-respect. That one meets these standards, that one is worthy of self-respect, is a categorical good for any person of integrity.

The attitude one has toward oneself as having exceeded what one believes to be the minimal conditions of self-tolerance is the attitude of self-esteem.[1] To hold oneself in esteem, then, requires an evaluative response to oneself beyond that of mere tolerance. Thus self-esteem is related to the

1. See David Sachs, "How to Distinguish Self-Respect from Self-Esteem," *Philosophy and Public Affairs* 10 (1981): 346–60.

survival of the person of integrity in a different way than is self-respect. If the only attitude one could take toward oneself were that of mere tolerance, then life would hardly seem worthwhile. Self-esteem, on the other hand, seems, everything else being equal, to indicate a level of well-being sufficient to make life worth living. Therefore, self-esteem is also a human good that stakes a significant claim to being one of universal categorical value. But more on self-esteem later.

2.

Perhaps the most illuminating way of understanding self-respect as a human good is in relationship to what I call simple respect for others. Simple respect is a disposition that relates to its intentional object as falling under a certain description. A person is an object of simple respect insofar as the person appears within the respectful agent's deliberative field as meeting certain standards. It is as meeting these standards that the agent sees the person as good in the sense of being worthy of respect. To have this attitude toward one person is to be disposed to have this attitude toward anyone believed to be relevantly similar.

This is not to say that the evaluative standards for basic tolerance are the same for all respectful persons. It is merely to say something about our willingness to describe someone as "respectful." We call a person "respectful" only when we can tell a causal story of a certain sort about the relationships between the person's attitude and his or her dispositions, evaluations, interests, and beliefs. That the story is a causal story, a story about the causal relationships between these factors, is very important.

The contrast is a merely logical story. A purely rationalistic account of respect puts the emphasis on showing how logical contradictions emerge when one fails to act with respect. On this view, reason requires respect and leads inexorably to it. Both Kant and Alan Gewirth have defended views of this sort,[2] and both, I believe, failed, largely for the methodological reasons given in chapter 1. In contrast, I am not offering such a rationalistic account of the place of respect in the lives of persons but providing an analysis of how the sentiment of respect functions causally in the life of a respectful agent. The details of that story regarding the concept of simple respect are important here.

In this regard, it is possible for the intentional objects of respect to be

2. For Gewirth's view, see *Reason and Morality* (Chicago: University of Chicago Press, 1978).

among a wide variety of things. One can respect, in some sense, the skill of a thief, the power of God, the destructive force of the weather, the rights of animals, or persons in general. Yet I suspect that the concept of respect varies in important regards with the variety of its objects. For a boxer to have respect for his opponent's right cross is not for him to value his opponent intrinsically. It is rather to recognize and heed him in a certain way as a source of peril. The respect shown to a person of great courage, on the other hand, is clearly of a different sort. In regard to simple respect, my concern is with a form of respect that takes persons and only persons as intentional objects. The reason is that there is a form of respect that one takes toward oneself as a person for whom simple respect is the analogous attitude taken toward other persons as persons.

The evaluative judgment expressed in the attitude of simple respect for persons as intentional objects is that a person worthy of respect is of intrinsic value to some degree. If a person's attitude toward another does not express and recognize some intrinsic value in the other person, then the attitude is not that of respect. This contrasts with attitudes of indifference, aversion, or of mere instrumental interest. Thus the respected person appears within the deliberative field of the respectful person as an end. Of course, this can be said of attitudes other than respect as well, but it is nonetheless an essential feature of simple respect.

Also, the person who is in a dispositional state of respect toward another person takes an interest in the other person as a being of intrinsic value. This is to recognize that the other person deserves to be treated as an end, for that is how the other appears within the deliberative field as an end.

From the evaluation of another as an end, respect generates its own normative thoughts about obligation. Without some sense of obligation to others, without some sense that others can be mistreated, there is no sense of respect for others. An agent, therefore, cannot truly claim to have respect for another and fail to recognize at least some obligations to that person in some contexts. These obligations the agent perceives as restrictions on how the respected person may permissibly be treated by the agent and others for mere instrumental purposes. Thus the recognition of these obligations is internal to the interest in a person evaluated as a being of intrinsic value and worthy of respectful treatment. In this sense, respect is a norm within a certain psychology, and it will be our concern in what remains to see how respect functions within that psychology when other norms are present.

The behavioral manifestations of simple respect have their origins in the normative thoughts of the respectful person, some of which involve obligations. As including only prohibitions against interference, the obligations may be felt as minimal, reflecting one sense of the intrinsic value of the re-spected person. On the other hand, they might be experienced as extensive, including the promotion of the respected person's welfare, reflecting an-other.[3] But if an agent lacks any disposition felt as a restraint on his or her other interests for the sake of the intrinsic worth of others, then that agent does not have simple respect for others. What is missing is a regulative function of the required sort within the agent's psychology.

The role of beliefs in relationship to the other features of simple respect is crucial in two ways. The first concerns the relationship between beliefs and evaluations and the general qualities of persons. To have simple respect for another is to evaluate the other as a person of intrinsic value in terms of some quality or set of qualities one believes the other to have. Call these R-qualities. Theoretically, R-qualities might include all and only whatever the agent takes to be the essential qualities of personhood or some other set of qualities. Different conceptions of respect vary with different conceptions of R-qualities. Conceptions that only emphasize noninterference are mini-malist, designating as R-qualities features of agency distinct from welfare and character with the notion of autonomous choice playing a large role. Other more extensive conceptions involve either more substantial no-tions of autonomy or other qualities of the agent, usually involving both welfare and character. But any conception of respect includes the require-ment that the respectful agent has at least implicitly the factual belief that the respected person has some set of R-qualities. It also requires that the respectful agent makes the evaluative judgment that the respected person is intrinsically valuable *because* he or she has these qualities. Moreover, assuming no countervening cognitive, affective, or conative influences, the respectful agent's factual belief that another person has the relevant R-qualities will *cause* the agent to be respectfully disposed toward the other person. Thus factual beliefs concerning the general qualities of persons play this triggering role in the dispositions of the respectful agent, which is one feature of how respect functions as a norm within the relevant psychology.

This brings us to the second point regarding the role of beliefs and the other elements of the dispositional attitude of simple respect for others. It concerns identity beliefs, beliefs about the identities of persons. It is this: The dispositional attitude of simple respect for others is dispositionally in-

3. Compare the role of respect for rights in John Rawls, *A Theory of Justice* (Cambridge, Mass.: Harvard University Press, 1971), in Ronald Dworkin, *Taking Rights Seriously* (Cambridge, Mass.: Harvard University Press, 1977), and in Robert Nozick, *Anarchy, State, and Utopia* (New York: Basic Books, 1974).

different to beliefs about (i) the identity of its object and (ii) the identity of the agent of normative responsibility. What does this mean?

As a way of making the features of respect and subsequent dispositional states vivid to the reader from the first-person point of view, I will formulate the points in the second person. Consider, then, the indifference of simple respect to identity beliefs of the first sort. Beliefs about the identity of the object of respect play no causal role in triggering the attitude in a specific case. Suppose that, as a respectful person, you mistake one person, A, for another person, B, that is, that you misidentify them, and that you are cognitively, affectively, and conatively normal. Assuming that you have simple respect for A whom you have misidentified as B but whom you clearly believe to have the relevant R-qualities, your discovering that you have simply misidentified A will not affect your respectful disposition toward him.

This fact illustrates a central feature of our concept of simple respect. It is that there is no essential causal relationship between respect (of this sort) and beliefs about the identity of its object. The belief that a person has the relevant R-qualities is sufficient to trigger the disposition in a specific case in any truly respectful agent. Beliefs regarding identity are notwithstanding, assuming, of course, normal cognitive, affective, and conative conditions. This fact also illustrates that simple respect involves an impartial interest in persons as intrinsically valuable, because the object of simple respect is generalizable: Identity does not matter. I have tried to show here how simple respect with its generalizability has causal repercussions exemplified in both its dispositional sensitivity and its dispositional indifference regarding its object. Qualities matter; identity does not.

Now consider the indifference of simple respect to identity beliefs of the second sort. To be indifferent to beliefs about the identity of the agent of responsibility is to see someone as having an obligation only in virtue of falling under a certain description. To have simple respect for another is to have the normative thought that the other person ought to be treated with respect. This much we have seen. But by whom? The answer is by any respectful person in a position to act in the ways required by respect. Thus the respectful agent will believe that the obligations of respect are his or her responsibility only when the agent believes that he or she rather than someone else fills the description of the person in the best position to act in the ways required by respect.

Imagine believing that respect requires helping another with some difficulty. Your belief regarding *who* has the obligation to assist the person plays a causal role in triggering your disposition to help only when you believe that you are the person in the best position to do so. If you discover that someone else rather than yourself is in that position, then the thought that the person needs help will not trigger your disposition to offer assistance. If anything, you will be disposed to admonish the other person to help. Also, if you believe that you and several others are in an equal position to help and everything else is equal, you will be indifferent to the identity of who is to help. The person's being helped is the main thought. Who is to help is solely a function of who is in the best position to do so. This fact of how an element in one's deliberative field generates a normative belief is reflected in the dispositional indifference of the respectful agent's attitude to identity beliefs in his or her sense of self-reproach. If you are motivated solely by simple respect, you will not be disposed to self-reproach if another person respectfully helps the person in need. This is true if you believe that you would have helped if you had been the only one who could help or had no one else been willing. Thus identity beliefs play an indirect role in triggering the behavioral manifestations of respect only through general descriptive beliefs about agents. Again, qualities matter; identity does not.

The fact that identity beliefs play no direct causal role in the interests associated with these dispositions makes them impartial or impersonal interests. They are impartial because beliefs about personal identity are not essential to them. Simple respect, then, involves an impartial or impersonal social interest and an impartial social norm. As such, simple respect shapes how a certain kind of good appears as an end within the respectful agent's deliberative field.

3.

I have not yet argued that simple respect is a universal and categorical human good for the person of integrity, but there are good reasons for thinking this to be true. For self-respect, which is such a good relative to the class of agents of integrity, is simply an impersonal good become personal. To be dispositionally sensitive to beliefs about R-qualities and dispositionally indifferent to beliefs about the identity of the object of respect is an impersonal interest, as I have shown. To be concerned about how one stands in terms of the possession of these qualities is a personal interest. It is to be dispositionally sensitive both to beliefs about R-qualities and to beliefs about self-identity as the object one believes to possess those qualities.

The only difference in kind, then, between self-respect and simple respect is that self-respect is dispositionally sensitive to beliefs about the identity of its object in a way that simple respect is not. This difference in kind makes self-respect a disposition involving a personal or partial, as opposed to an impersonal or impartial, interest. Thus the ability to tolerate oneself in terms of valued R-qualities matters more to a person of integrity than does the ability to tolerate others, especially regarding thoughts about responsibility for the kind of person one is.

Yet this does not mean that one can have the attitude of self-respect without having the attitude of simple respect for those believed to be relevantly similar. Suppose you claim to have self-respect by having the R-qualities and that others have the same qualities. Then suppose you claim that these other persons are contemptible and unworthy of respect with no intrinsic value of their own. We would simply have to deny that you have the concept of self-respect. One of the difficulties in viewing the "pride" of racists as self-respect is in seeing how poorly they exhibit the qualities they extol and how indifferent they are to these qualities in those they hold in contempt.

Nor can one have the attitude of simple respect toward others and be indifferently disposed toward one's own standing in terms of R-qualities. Even the concepts of simple respect and self-respect are lacking in someone who claims to respect others because they have the R-qualities yet claims to lack such qualities but does not care at all about these deficiencies. One of the masks of flattery is the feigning of praise for qualities a person does not have. Another is the feigning of praise for the qualities a person does have. The former reveals itself when the flatterer scorns the person's true qualities. The latter reveals itself in the indifference of the flatterer to such qualities in himself or herself.

Also, to think of oneself as worthy of respect is to think of oneself as worthy of being treated in a way that recognizes one's value. It is to have oneself appear within one's own deliberative field as an end worthy of the respect of others. When one is a person of self-respect, then, one is dispositionally sensitive not only to beliefs about R-qualities and to beliefs about the identity of the object of respect but also to the attitudes and behavior of others toward oneself as having those qualities. Here I am not thinking so much about the person who relentlessly insists on his or her rights. Rather, I am thinking about the fact that self-respect and servility are incompatible dispositions.[4]

The sensitivity of self-respect toward the respectful attitudes of others

4. Thomas Hill, "Servility and Self-Respect," *Monist* 57, no. 1 (1973): 87–104.

is that one desires to be respected by those one respects. To be held in contempt by those whom one respects is an aversion to a person of integrity and if extreme can be a categorical aversion. It is possible, of course, to have self-respect and not have the simple respect of one's respected peers. But it is not possible to have self-respect and to be indifferent to such a fact. Also, to be sensitive to the simple respect of one's respected peers is to be sensitive to the other elements of respect as well, which includes the behavioral manifestations of the obligations of respect. Thus if one has self-respect, then one will find it intolerable to be treated in ways that do not recognize one's intrinsic worth, at least regarding one's R-qualities. This intolerance will extend to all those whom one believes to be capable of respect and by whom one is mistreated.

"Who cares what they think?" is often little more than disingenuous rhetoric. It might express sincere indifference on occasions where "they" are held in low regard. But it is an evasive thought at best when "they" are clearly respectable people. Think of what it would be like for those for whom you have even minimal tolerance to believe that you are a child molester. To be thought guilty of something contemptible like that by respectable people is a horror to a self-respecting person. The disposition to have them know of one's innocence is clearly not reducible to the desire to avoid punishment, though it might include this. What one wants with the belief that one is innocent is the return of their respect.

Established in the fact that self-respect is dispositionally sensitive to the simple respect of one's respected peers are other important facts. Simple respect is an impersonal social good, and the personal good of self-respect entails the recognition, at least implicitly, of this impersonal good. This might seem in tension with the feeling that self-respect is an individual good. For is it not possible to care about one's own standing in terms of R-qualities even if one believes that no one else either has such qualities or cares if they have such qualities? Is it not possible to have self-respect even if one believes that one has no respectable peers?

An affirmative answer to these questions is certainly correct. In this important sense, self-respect is an individual rather than a social good. But it is not an individual good in the strong sense that involves an interest that is essentially satisfiable without any intrinsic interest in the satisfaction of the interests of others. Here these are the interests of those whom one would respect if one believed them to have the relevant R-qualities. Besides, insofar as we are social beings, we are intrinsically interested in there being persons other than ourselves with the relevant R-qualities. For our social interests are limited by our ability to find other human beings at least minimally tolerable. The solitude of self-respect, then, is necessarily bittersweet for the person of integrity isolated from any respectable peers and surrounded by those worthy only of contempt. Goods that are individual in the strong sense need not include this element of bitterness.[5]

4.

Until now I have spoken of the goods of respect as though they neatly divide into those of simple respect for others and those of self-respect. But if we recognize important distinctions regarding respect for others and self-respect, this division is too simplistic. It fails to distinguish adequately the kinds of goods of respect that are agent-neutral from those that are agent-centered. It fails to distinguish adequately forms of respect that are sensitive to identity beliefs and those that are not. It also fails to distinguish adequately among kinds of R-qualities.

In distinguishing among forms of respect, we must be careful to distinguish six kinds of cases, reflecting six kinds of respect. The first two are kinds of simple respect.

If you act from simple respect for another (as the subject of your action), your attitude is sensitive to beliefs both about your own R-qualities and the person's for whom you act. This is true in any case of respect for others. For if, as a respectful person, you knowingly treat another with disrespect, you will feel that you have not only wronged the other person but have also negatively affected your own intrinsic worth. In the case of simple respect, the respectful agent is indifferent not only to beliefs about the identity of the beneficiary (the subject) of his or her action but also, as we have seen, to beliefs about the identity of the agent of the action. It is this kind of indifference that marks the first two kinds of respect for others as forms of simple respect.

Yet there are two kinds of simple respect. One is respect for persons for their agent-neutral qualities, their capacities for being impartial. Think here of respecting someone for being fair, kind, benevolent, or generous to strangers. The respect is for the qualities of persons independent of their

5. Think of the difference in these goods: (i) respecting oneself for doing the right thing when everyone else is doing the wrong thing, (ii) drinking fine wine *alone*, and (iii) getting a good night's sleep. All are goods of much worth, but the first two have a melancholy hue the other does not.

special roles or relationships. The other is respect for persons for their agent-centered qualities, their qualities for having personal or partial commitments. Think of respecting a stranger as a good parent, as an authentic artist, or as a reliable friend to someone else. In these cases, the respect is for the qualities of persons in their special roles, circumstances, and relationships.

The mark of simple respect, then, is that it involves an agent-neutral or impartial reason for action. It features a dispositional indifference to beliefs regarding the identity of the agent of the action for the agent who has this sort of reason. In Herman's terms, it presents the object or end of action as good within the agent's deliberative field simply in terms of the object's general qualitites. The difference in the first kind of agent-neutral respect and the second is that the first includes no sensitivity to special roles and circumstances and the second does. The second form of respect shows respect for someone's agent-centered qualities, where he or she is not specially related to the agent. Thus both forms of simple respect for others are agent-neutral. One recognizes impartial R-qualities of the respected person; the other, partial R-qualities.

Conceptions of simple respect might include either or both of these kinds of respect. Yet a conception of R-qualities might include qualities central to being a person whose good includes relationships that involve personal love. If so, it is not possible to restrict the respect of others only to that of the first sort. For it is not possible that an agent could be a loving person without having agent-centered reasons for action.

Agent-centered reasons for action are dispositionally sensitive to beliefs about the identity of the agent of the action. This feature of agent-centered reasons serves to distinguish the third kind of respect for others from the first and second. The third kind of respect is that due to a person regarding the person's special role or circumstance. Call it special respect for others. In this case, it is where the agent stands in a special relationship to the respected person regarding that role or circumstance. One might, for example, have respect for one's parents, which is not the same as showing respect for parenthood anywhere one finds it. If you are motivated by respect of the third sort, you are sensitive not only to beliefs about your R-qualities and those your actions are designed to serve but also to beliefs about your and their identities. Suppose you believe that a good parent is due a certain kind of respect from his or her children. You cannot be indifferently disposed to beliefs regarding the identity of the particular agent who owes this respect, if you believe that a certain person is both a good parent and your parent. Thus you can have this sort of respect regarding the parental qualities of a certain person only if you believe that this person is in fact your parent. It is the dispositional sensitivity to beliefs about the identity of the agent that marks the agent-centeredness of this form of respect for others. Here there is room for a disposition to self-reproach lacking in simple respect. For you might feel that you yourself have failed your parent by not helping, even where others have provided adequate help. Accordingly, special respect is agent-centered respect for others. This contrasts with the two kinds of simple respect for others, on the one hand, and with self-respect, on the other. In Herman's terms, special respect for others takes the end or object of action to be good both in terms of general qualities and as a numerically specific individual. This is a crucial fact about how a good can appear as an end within an agent's deliberative field in a way that is different from how other goods can appear there as ends.

From this, we should see that there is another kind of special agent-centered respect for loved ones, namely, respect for their impartial R-qualities. This is a fourth kind of respect. I have in mind respecting loved ones because they have simple respect for others. That our loved ones are good people in this sense is of utmost importance to us, as I will argue in a later chapter.

Self-respect, then, comes in two kinds as well, which are the fifth and sixth kinds of respect. There is self-respect for one's impartial qualities, on the one hand, and self-respect for one's partial qualities, on the other. But in both cases, self-respect is agent-centered. If you have the disposition of simple respect in all its forms and all else is equal, you will feel self-contempt if you believe that you have become a certain kind of person, namely, one who treats others without regard to their status as having R-qualities. This might include disrespect for others regarding their impartial R-qualities. It also might include disrespect for partial R-qualities, either where there is no special relationship between the respected person and the agent or where there is. That is, you could feel self-contempt for a perceived lack of minimal concern for respectable people whoever they are, and you could feel self-contempt for being, say, a bad parent, a bad friend, or a bad neighbor. You will also feel self-contempt if you believe that you have become someone who allows yourself to be treated by others without regard to your R-qualities—without regard to the kind of person you are.

In summary: the forms of respect for others are (1) simple respect for others for their impartial R-qualities, (2) simple respect for others for their partial R-qualities, (3) special or agent-centered respect for loved ones for their partial R-qualities, and (4) special respect for loved ones for their impartial R-qualities. The forms of self-respect are (5) special respect for oneself for one's impartial R-qualities and (6) special respect for oneself for one's partial R-qualities. These are ways, then, that oneself and others can appear within one's deliberative field as good in the sense of an end worthy of respect. With these distinctions in mind, we can turn to the issue of where the goods of respect fit into the life of an agent of integrity and begin to understand how these forms of respect function as regulative and determinate norms within a psychology.

5.

Before turning to that task, however, I must say something about respect and human dignity and how human dignity appears within a respectful agent's deliberative field as a value. One way of construing Kantian deliberation is as a pure procedure; whatever substance is involved regarding the contingencies of the human condition are shaped by a procedure that is a priori in nature. Specifically, the procedure just is the universalizability tests contained in the first two formulations of the categorical imperative found in the *Groundwork* as applied to the special circumstances of human agency. From this perspective, *The Metaphysics of Morals* is taken to imply that its conclusions can be reached by some casuistry generated by the universalizability tests, despite the fact that those tests are seldom alluded to there and even less are they employed. On the procedural view, the objects of respect enter the respectful agent's deliberative field as due the kind of concern that the universalizability tests are designed to accommodate. The kind of concern in question is the concern for human dignity, and on the procedural view of respect, human dignity accrues to our higher-order capacities to set our ends in conformity with the requirements of the universalizability tests.[6]

In contrast with the procedural interpretation of Kant is what we might call the substantive interpretation. On this view, Kantian deliberation is not simply a matter of applying the universalizability tests, and human dignity is not simply a matter of having the capacities for applying those tests and conforming our actions to them. Rather, though the universalizability tests

---

6. I take it that this is the view of procedural realism alluded to by Christine Korsgaard in *The Sources of Normativity* (Cambridge: Cambridge University Press, 1996); see esp. 35–37, 44–48, 112, 205–8, 245–46.

do some of the work of practical deliberation, a great deal of deliberation is left to judgment guided by the thought that we are always to respect ourselves and others for our rational nature. On this interpretation, the Formula of Humanity as one of the formulations of the categorical imperative plays a large role in the account of Kantian practical reason. The thought is that the universalizability tests do a limited amount of work in practical reason and that much is left to be done by the thought that judgment is to be guided by thinking of humanity as an end. So on the substantive view, the objects of respect in regard to their human dignity appear within the respectful agent's deliberative field, not simply as agents who are bound by and who are potential beneficiaries of the universalizability tests, but as having a certain kind of value that is to guide practical reason beyond what can be yielded by the universalizability tests alone.[7]

On either view, the objects of respect enter the respectful agent's deliberative field as having dignity, and dignity has a certain kind of value within that field. A major and perhaps the central difference between the Kantian and the Aristotelian view presented here concerns how human dignity appears within the respectful agent's deliberative field. About dignity and its value, Herman says, "As rational agents, we each have the capacity to bring our wills in conformity with the principle of good willing, and so each has all the dignity there is to have." She continues on the same page, "As the final end of rational willing, rational nature as value is both absolute and nonscalar. It is absolute in the sense that there is no other kind of value or goodness for whose sake rational nature can count as a means. It is nonscalar in the sense that (1) it is not the highest value on a single inclusive scale of value, and (2) it is not additive: more instantiations of rational nature do not enhance the value content of the world, and more instances of respect for rational nature do not move anything or anyone along a scale of dignity. There is no such scale."[8] In a similar vein, Hill says, "Dignity cannot morally or reasonably be exchanged for anything of greater value,

---

7. I take Allen Wood and Nancy Sherman to be the clearest advocates of this view, but I think Barbara Herman and Marcia Baron are also best understood in this way. For Wood, see "The Final Form of Kant's Practical Philosophy," in *Kant's Metaphysics of Morals,* ed. Nelson Potter and Mark Timmons, Spindel Conference 1997, *Southern Journal of Philosophy* 36, supplement (1998): 1–20; and for Sherman, see *Making a Necessity of Virtue: Aristotle and Kant on Virtue* (Cambridge: Cambridge University Press, 1997).

8. Barbara Herman, *The Practice of Moral Judgment* (Cambridge, Mass.: Harvard University Press, 1993), 238.

whether the value is dignity or price. One cannot, then, trade off dignity of humanity in one person in order to honor a greater dignity in two, ten, or a thousand persons."[9]

Needless to say, for anything to have value of this sort is for it to have a very special kind of value. I will argue that the best account of respect for persons will show that this account of the importance of human dignity is not one that on reflection we accept. While it is important to see that respect for human dignity does preclude some kinds of consequentialist reasoning, it does not preclude others. Moreover, even if we think of human dignity as a higher value than other values, this does not commit us to the view that there are no trade-offs between human dignity and other values. We certainly do not think that there is no trade-off between respect for human autonomy and other concerns. Our previous observations regarding our sympathy for lower animals is sufficient to show this. We are willing to limit the choices and autonomy of human beings for the sake of the well-being of lower animals, and our regulated conception of respect for persons shows this, which also shows that we do not accept the notion that the objects of respect enter a respectful person's deliberative field in the way that Herman and Hill claim. Later, I will argue that this puts severe limits on the substantive interpretation of Kantian practical deliberation and the role of impartial respect within practical reason. On the substantive interpretation, practical reason (whether in the employment of the universalizability tests or in the latitude allowed for judgment) cannot ever reveal a pattern of deliberation that does not treat human dignity as absolute, nonscalar, nonadditive, and immune to trade-offs in terms of other values in the way indicated by Herman and Hill. In fact, it is a consequence of the argument that the norms of practical reason are symmetrical in their regulative functions that we do not accept this Kantian notion of the value of human dignity. The objects of respect simply do not enter a respectful agent's deliberative field shrouded with *this* kind of value.

9. Thomas Hill, *Dignity and Practical Reason in Kant's Moral Theory* (Ithaca: Cornell University Press, 1992), 49.

6. Respect, Egoism, and Self-Assessment

In this chapter, I begin to consider how respect is a human good for the respectful agent, how respect relates to the meaningfulness of life from the agent's own point of view, and how respect provides an agent with reasons for action. The arguments here should provide a basis for rejecting traditional Kantianism's account of the role of respect within practical reason. They should do this by showing how respect is related to the meaningfulness of the respectful agent's life from his or her own point of view.

1.

Perhaps the most illuminating way to begin to understand the relationship between the goods of respect and a person's integrity is by focusing on a question: What attitude would one have toward oneself if one failed to have the attitude of self-respect?

The first way someone could fail to have self-respect is simply by lacking the attitude of respect at all. People of this sort do not judge themselves deficient for not having R-qualities; they just do not make the evaluative judgments constitutive of the dispositional state of respect. This might be true of some people who are perfectly able to make the factual judgments that a person either has or lacks the relevant R-qualities. Hearing the talk of personal assessment, they pick up on the criteria used by others but are evaluatively disengaged from those criteria. They might even display behavior normally characteristic of respect, but when they do, that behavior has its origins in some source other than a respectful disposition. Such people are in an important sense evaluatively indifferent to R-qualities in themselves and others.

The difficulty, however, is that anyone lacking the good of self-respect because of evaluative indifference to it cannot be an agent of integrity. This is because of the relationships between self-worth and self-tolerance, on the one hand, and integrity, on the other. Self-worth is crucial to the concept of integrity because it is central to the concept of the distinctness or separateness of persons. I made this clear earlier, and it is difficult, if not impossible, to understand self-worth in a way that excludes the notion of self-tolerance.

It might be thought, however, that egoism denies the conceptual ties between the notions of integrity, self-worth, and self-tolerance. On one construal of egoism, the egoist has a sense of self but lacks any sense of self-worth or self-tolerance. Here the sense of self does not generate judgments of self-assessment. On another construal of egoism, judgments of self-assessment are not forthcoming because the egoist simply lacks a sense of self. But as arguments against a connection between the goods of respect and integrity, these alternatives fall on the horns of a dilemma.

Consider the first construal of egoism where the egoist has a sense of self but lacks any sense of self-worth or self-tolerance. Who is this creature? What kinds of interests does it have? And how are we to describe it? A being with only appetitive interests would perhaps lack a sense of self-worth, but it would not be recognizably human in any nongenetic sense. Nor would it be "egoistic." The popular view of pigs sees them as purely appetitive creatures, but they are not thought to be egoistic for that reason. To be egoistic with a sense of self is to care about oneself intrinsically and about others only instrumentally, if at all. A purely appetitive being has no sense of self to be concerned about. Who, then, is the egoist, according to the first construal of egoism, and how is the egoist concerned about his or her sense of self?

The problem is that the egoist must have nonappetitive interests but lack any interests that carry with them any concern for self-tolerance. But what could they be? Neither social nor individual interests seem plausible. Social interests are ruled out on two counts: They are not egoistic, and they carry with them a strong sense of self-evaluation. That they are not egoistic is clear from the fact that they include intrinsic interests in the interests of others. That they require self-tolerance is manifested in the fact that one cannot experience one's sense of self as a loving parent, friend, or neighbor and be indifferently disposed toward beliefs about the R-qualities associated with those relationships. On the other hand, individual, nonappetitive interests that do not require a sense of self-tolerance are elusive. One cannot experience one's fundamental sense of self as, for example, an artist, an athlete, or a scientist and be indifferently disposed toward beliefs about the R-qualities associated with those roles.[1] This is not because the interests in these roles need be nonegoistic but because there are success criteria attached to these roles and the interests in them. Assuming, then, that no sense is to be made of a bare interest in the self, it is difficult to see what nonappetitive individual interest could support this construal of egoism. If this is true, then the first construal of egoism must be rejected. It cannot offer a sense of self that does not carry with it the notions of self-worth and self-tolerance.

On the second construal of egoism, the cut between integrity and the concepts of self-worth and self-tolerance is between the concept of the egoist and the concept of having a sense of self. The egoist, on this view, has no substantial sense of self but only interests and an awareness of them, none of which expresses an intrinsic interest in the interests of others. Such a person, to be sure, can have the thought "my interests over the interests of others." Yet the only self-awareness such a person has is an interest, plus the thought that the interest can be threatened by the interests of others. But if this is to have a sense of self, it would seem to be one of which a dog is aware when it defends a bone. Someone like this might have, for example, aesthetic interests without "having a sense-of-self-as-artist" or as filling any role related to aesthetic activity. Indeed, she might even be an artist without "seeing" herself at all in terms of "myself-as-artist." She might simply have an intrinsic interest in aesthetic experience and artistic activity but not an interest in others or their interests. Thus the egoist can have interests that are not in the self without having an intrinsic concern for others.

If there are such persons, they are rare. But rare or not, this kind of egoist has no sense of self, let alone a sense of self-worth, and without a sense of self, there can be no question of self-tolerance. But for the person of integrity there is a sense of self that carries with it a sense of self-worth and thereby a sense of self-tolerance. Without this sense, there could be no sense of oneself as a separate and numerically distinct person, one of the basic elements of integrity in the thin sense. For this person, the evaluative

---

1. Of course, we are often self-deceived about these things, and it is possible that someone could be completely self-deceived about them. We might even call some such self-deceived persons egoists. But if this is the egoist, then the egoist *is* dispositionally sensitive to his or her beliefs about R-qualities, is very much concerned about self-worth, and achieves self-tolerance only at the expense of the loss of integrity that comes with self-deception. Moreover, such an egoist is *not* an egoist from his or her point of view.

indifference to beliefs about R-qualities is impossible. Therefore, we cannot sever integrity from self-worth and self-tolerance, which is one of the reasons that Aristotle persistently insisted that the beastly life with its lack of concern for others is not for humans.

Also, the egoist's lack of a sense of self that includes self-evaluation is the lack of something any person of integrity can see as nothing other than a human disfigurement, which is why we see beastly indifference to self-evaluation as natural only to something very distant from us in kind. For whatever else the relative factors are in the concept of self-respect, the respected person's perceived sensitivity to how he or she stands in terms of R-qualities is not among them. What follows, then, if self-respect is a categorical human good and if sensitivity to it is a universal R-quality for persons of integrity? It follows that the person of integrity cannot unmistakenly find the egoistic life worth living or the incorrigible egoist worthy of respect. Thus respectfulness is a regulative norm for any agent of integrity, and its regulative status is a function of those values that give life meaning from the agent's own point of view.

This in itself is revealing regarding traditional, externalist Kantianism. According to traditional Kantianism, a respectful agent might have to make a choice between two ways of life. One of these might be the egoistic, self-interested life, which might be meaningful from the agent's own point of view. The other might be the respectful life, which might not be meaningful from the agent's perspective. Moreover, should such a choice arise, it would be practically rational on this view to decide for the meaningless but respectful life. The advantage of internalist Kantianism is that it does not construe the role of respect within practical reason in this way. It recognizes, with the Aristotelian conception, that the egoistic life is ruled out as meaningful from the respectful agent's own point of view. Any serious deliberation about whether to live the egoistic life or the respectful life would show, on either the internalist Kantian view or the Aristotelian view, that the agent simply was not a respectfully sensitive person. Thus, for both internalist Kantianism and the Aristotelian conception, respect functions as a regulative norm in the form of a categorical aversion: Lives devoid of respectability are not worth living.

There are, however, differences between the Kantian (internalist) view and the Aristotelian view. First, for a Kantian internalist of the metaphysical school, the egoist would necessarily be irrational, a nonrational human being. On the Aristotelian view, the egoist might very well be rational from his own point of view. But since the respectful person has certain categorical values embedded within the foundation of his or her character and psychology, the egoistic way of life could only be the object of a categorical aversion. For this reason, the egoistic way of life would be irrational for a respectful person because of the person's character. I take it that the constructivist Kantian would agree. But there is a difference between the Aristotelian view and the constructivist school. On the constructivist view, the irrationality is traced to the result of an impartial decision procedure, but on the Aristotelian view, the irrationality is a function of the fact that a set of priorities indicative of the egoistic way of life is not true to the agent's deliberative field and the goods that appear there, one of which is oneself as an end worthy of respect. Thus the priorities of the egoistic way of life fail both the finality and the self-sufficiency criteria. That way of life is neither to be chosen for itself nor does it include the goods that are fundamental to a life worth living for a respectful person.

2.

Having rejected, then, the egoist as an agent of integrity, but not necessarily as irrational, we can refine the statement of the current issue: What is the effect on the integrity of a nonegoistic agent who is disposed to simple respect of having the belief that he or she lacks the relevant R-qualities?[2] The answer to this question further reveals the relationship between considerations of respect and the meaning of an agent's life from his or her own point of view.

Respecting another person involves the person appearing within one's deliberative field as an end, as someone with a degree of intrinsic worth. Without this sense of another's worth, there is either aversion, in the form of contempt, to the other person or indifference. But whether there is contempt or indifference, failure to respect another person is directly linked to one's attitude toward the other person's integrity. It is to evaluate the other as lacking the qualities that make a person worthy of respect as a separate and distinct person.

To have self-respect is to appear within one's own deliberative field as an end, as someone with a degree of intrinsic worth. Without this sense of one's own worth, there is either self-aversion, in the form of self-contempt, or indifference to allowing others to treat oneself as a mere means to any of their ends, which is itself a less active form of self-contempt. To lose one's

2. Lynne McFall finds other reasons associated with the concept of commitment for rejecting the egoist as an agent of integrity. See her article, "Integrity," *Ethics* 98 (October 1987): 5–20.

self-respect, then, is to lose one's sense of oneself as important as a separate and distinct person. It is to lose one's integrity. Thus it is not possible to have the attitude of simple respect and fail to care about one's own standing in terms of the relevant R-qualities. Therefore, the response of the person who has the attitude of simple respect and believes himself or herself to lack the relevant R-qualities can only be that of self-contempt.

To view oneself with self-contempt is not only to view oneself as lacking integrity; it *is* to lack integrity. It is to lose the sense of oneself as a separate and distinct person who is intrinsically important in one's own right. It is to have a categorical aversion to what one perceives oneself to be. The only life open to such a person is a life of self-contempt, of insanity, or of self-deception; in neither case is there an agent of integrity.

There are at least two forms of self-contempt that result from a blow to one's self-respect as the attitude of minimal self-tolerance. The first involves a blow that results from one's coming to believe that one is the kind of person who lacks the relevant R-qualities, even though one does not feel responsible for one's lack of worth. The second is the blow that results from coming to have one of two beliefs regarding responsibility. On the one hand is the belief that through one's actions one is responsible for being the kind of person who lacks the relevant R-qualities. On the other is the belief that through one's actions one is responsible for a threat to one's becoming the kind of person who lacks these qualities. The first form of self-contempt is the result of a blow of the first sort. I refer to it as shame. The second form of self-contempt, where one feels responsible for one's state of worth, results in two forms of guilt, only the first of which is also a form of shame.[3]

Thus a person can meaningfully feel shame but not guilt for having or lacking a quality for which he or she does not feel responsible. Someone might feel shame on realizing both that he is a racist and that his racist attitudes are the result of his upbringing. If he truly values racial openness as an R-quality and believes that he lacks this quality but through no fault of his own, then he feels shame but not guilt. Similarly, if he believes that having a certain genetic background is a necessary R-quality but that he lacks this quality, he will feel shame but not guilt for not having it. This is because he does not believe he is responsible for what he believes to be his intolerable status.

Still it is impossible in the first sense of guilt to speak of feeling guilt

---

3. The analysis here is influenced greatly by that of Gabriele Taylor, though it differs in detail. See Gabriele Taylor, *Pride, Shame and Guilt: Emotions of Self-Assessment* (Oxford: Clarendon Press, 1985).

without shame. For shame, in this sense, is a form of self-contempt for the kind of person one perceives oneself to be. The first form of guilt carries with it this perception plus the belief that one is responsible for being an intolerable person. The second form of guilt does not include shame, because it does not include the belief that one lacks R-qualities. Those experiencing guilt in the second sense feel responsible for an action that is characteristic of an intolerable person who lacks R-qualities but believe the action is nonetheless not indicative of their true qualities. Consequently, the guilt is experienced only as a threat to the agent's becoming an intolerable person. It is experienced as a threat to the agent's R-qualities. For this reason, those who feel guilt in the second sense also feel remorse, which includes the disposition to repudiate their intolerable actions. But they do not feel shame, for they are not disposed to repudiate their basic sense of self. Those who feel guilt in the first sense might feel remorse as well, but not necessarily. For they might believe that there is no longer anything they can do for self-redemption. This is to believe that they cannot do anything to reverse the status of being persons who lack R-qualities and become persons who have them. Thus self-repudiation is the only course available to them.

All three emotions involve self-assessment; they all function as regulative norms within a psychology; and they all illuminate relationships between self-respect and integrity and the meaning of an agent's life from his or her own point of view. Not only do they indicate that a person who experiences these emotions lacks the sense of himself or herself as intrinsically important as a distinct and separate person, but they also indicate that a person who experiences these emotions either lacks the unity of self required for integrity or that the destruction of such unity is imminent. Finally, they reveal that the agent repudiates the meaningfulness of lives thought to be the objects of such contempt. In this way, these emotions of self-assessment reveal the deeper values in terms of which an agent is able to find meaning in life and maintain the elements of integrity. What we see implicit in these emotions are the criteria of finality and self-sufficiency at work on the emotional level. All these emotions repudiate in various degrees a way of life that does not include the agent as an end worthy of respect.

Shame and guilt of the first type indicate the presence of two senses of self. One is valued as having the relevant R-qualities; the other, as predominant but as lacking these qualities. In this way, self-contempt always indicates a serious degree of alienation from oneself. This experience comes both as a loss of a sense of one's intrinsic worth as a separate and distinct person and as involving a bifurcation and loss of unity of the self. Guilt in the second sense is not properly a form of self-contempt but the recognition that one is on the course to ruin and that something must be done about it. Undoubtedly the most intolerable form of self-contempt is the experience of guilt of the first form, plus the thought that there is nothing the agent can do for self-redemption.

Self-contempt and loss of self-respect are also related to integrity in other significant ways. They tend to destabilize the status of other goods and lead to a loss of the will to live. They involve a serious disunity of the self and often lead to a life of self-deception. Among humans, there is a causal relationship between their dispositional states regarding their self-worth and their dispositional responses to other goods. Even the goods of love are diminished in importance when we find ourselves intolerable, for then we perceive ourselves as unworthy of the love of others. In this way, the person who experiences self-contempt feels that his or her reasons for living are threatened. But, as we have seen, the person of integrity has reasons for living. The course of self-deception is a response to this threat, but it succeeds only with the bifurcation of the self and the loss of integrity, which is a direct function of the loss of meaning in one's life. For the respectful agent, the attempt to live a disrespectful life leads to loss of integrity and to agent breakdown. Thus for the respectful agent, the attempt to invest meaning in a disrespectful life is doomed to failure. Respect for self and others, then, cannot be accounted for on externalist concepts.

3.

Here it is important to say something about the relationship between the goods of respect and the other goods of the person of integrity. The good of self-respect is not only a categorical good, and fundamental in this sense; it is also fundamental in another sense. It is a good the absence of which tends to diminish the importance of other goods in an agent's reasons for living. In this sense, the other goods of a person of integrity are evaluatively dependent on the good of self-respect. But there are other ways in which the good of self-respect is evaluatively dependent on other goods, which means that self-respect is a foundational good as well as a dependent good. Here I will merely preview the evaluative dependence and foundational value of self-respect. I leave further discussion until the relevant foundational and dependent goods are discussed in later chapters.

Consider the dispositions of someone for whom simple respect and self-respect involve R-qualities that include the qualities of the person categorically committed to the goods of love. This person's sense of respect is evaluatively dependent on the goods of love and the virtues of a loving person. In this sense, the goods of love are foundational goods in terms of the goods of respect. Thus if the goods of love are universal categorical goods, then the qualities of a loving person—L-qualities, let us say—are among the R-qualities of any human agent of integrity. In any event, the person with this sense of respect will find persons totally lacking in L-qualities intolerable. This is true even if the claim that L-qualities are among the R-qualities of any human agent of integrity is false. The same can be said for other possible qualities related to other possible categorical goods.

As we have already observed, however, even the goods of love tend to lose their allure for the person who has self-contempt. For such a person, the belief that he or she lacks L-qualities, and thereby R-qualities, will causally tend to impair that person's dispositional sensitivity to the goods of love. To the extent that we perceive ourselves to be intolerable in terms of the lack of R-qualities, we find being loved intolerable. For it is difficult, if not impossible, to find oneself intolerable and to be the proper object of love. In this way, self-respect is a foundational value in relationship to the goods of love. Therefore, those (of a mature age) with a categorical interest in the goods of love can have these goods only to the degree to which they have self-respect.[4]

One final comment on evaluative dependence: From what I have said it follows that there is one R-quality that is a component in any conception of self-respect and the concept of integrity. It is the quality of being a respectful person. Similarly, we can conclude that there is one R-quality that is a component in any conception of simple respect for others and integrity. It is the quality of being a self-evaluative person, a person whose sense of self is regulated by respect as a regulative norm. To this extent the Aristotelian and the Kantian internalist can agree. This is one interpretation of Socrates' claim that the unexamined life is not worth living. But just how this dimension of self-evaluation is regulated by other concerns is a story yet to be told. Therefore, all I have shown at this point is that respect derives its place in practical reason as a good apart from which the respectful agent does not find life minimally worth living. This refutes traditional Kantianism, but it leaves internalist Kantianism intact.

4. I discuss what I call the pathological features of respect further in *Dignity and Vulnerability: Strength and Quality of Character* (Berkeley: University of California Press, 1997), 77–78.

7. The Categorical Value of the Goods of Respect

In this chapter, I focus more on what is categorical in the value of respect for the agent of integrity in the thick sense with an aim to providing criticisms of both traditional and internalist Kantianism. Throughout the discussion, I will keep a close eye on the implications of these observations for the integration test and for first-person deliberations. Section I centers on self-respect and how this good facilitates other intrinsic goods involving relationships with others. Section II focuses on the goods of being respected by others. The distinction between simple respect and special respect is crucial, for they provide different goods. Moreover, their relationship raises the issue of how they are related in their regulative functions. I will argue that the impartial norm of simple respect for others and the agent-centered form of special respect for others are symmetrical in their regulative functions. Thus the issue of the symmetrical relations among impartial and partial norms arises within respect itself, which raises criticisms of both traditional and internalist Kantianism. Section III centers on the goods of simple respect for others and special respect for others. Again, the symmetrical functions of these norms are illustrated as they make possible certain goods that are categorically valued by the agent of integrity in the thick sense. Sections IV and V discuss how the goods of self-respect enter the deliberations of an agent of integrity, and how simple respect for others is related to the meaningfulness of the agent's life from his or her own point of view. What we will see is that the role of respect in practical reason reflects the Aristotelian conception of reflective endorsement or rationality, all things considered. The claim, then, is that the Aristotelian model of practical reason and rational agency is best suited to accommodate the goods of respect.

1.

The value of self-respect in general is that it is a condition apart from which agents of integrity have a categorical aversion to themselves. To have this self-aversion is to lack a basic element of integrity, a sense of oneself as intrinsically important as a separate and numerically distinct person. Also, having self-respect is a condition apart from which such agents believe themselves to be objects of contempt for other respectable persons. To be without self-respect, then, is to be alienated both from oneself and from others in a very fundamental sense. To suffer self-aversion from a lack of self-respect for one's impartial R-qualities is also to be alienated from those one respects but to whom one is not specially related. To suffer from self-aversion from a lack of special self-respect for one's partial R-qualities is also to be alienated from those one respects and with whom one has a special relationship. One kind of self-contempt, then, alienates an agent from himself or herself and what we might call familiar strangers; the other from himself or herself and loved ones.

Thus one value to the agent of both simple self-respect and special self-respect is that it allows one to value oneself in a way that makes positive relationships possible from one's own point of view. The good of self-respect is a value that not only allows one to tolerate oneself in a nonsocial sense, as valuable apart from the perception of others, but also allows one to find oneself tolerable in the eyes of other respectable persons.

Consider, for example, those who labor under conceptions of self-respect that are excessively tied to physical appearance or physical prowess. The emphasis on these qualities among adolescents in our culture is often so out of proportion to other kinds of attributes that beauty-conferring qualities or prowess qualities are internalized as R-qualities. When the adolescent female, for instance, perceives herself as lacking these beauty-conferring qualities, asocial attitudes of various sorts result. The spectrum runs from excessive shyness to hopeless feelings of isolation. Very often these feelings are as much from the person's self-perception as from the behavior of others around her. It is her lack of self-tolerance that inhibits her openness to others.

Studies of anorexia nervosa confirm this, and, as such, constitute some evidence that when the integration test is applied to many human beings the goods of respect will be among their categorical values. Although anorexia nervosa is a syndrome rather than a disease with a known cause, researchers list several factors as probable causal elements in its occurrence.

Most prominent among these are both an ideal of thinness coupled with a fear of fatness and a vulnerable sense of self. In some patients, there is an unhealthy perfectionism that constantly promotes an ideal impossible to achieve. Such an ideal seems to reinforce an already vulnerable personality. Among the consequences of the syndrome is a diminished personal life, including the loss of interest in friends and sexual relations.[1]

Admittedly, in such cases the conception of self-respect is not a very mature one. But this does not change the fact that when self-respect is lacking, on whatever conception, openness to others is inhibited. To have self-contempt is to think oneself worthy of the contempt of respectable people. No wonder then that self-contempt breeds asocial attitudes, even the desire for isolation. That the isolation is so devastating shows that the value of meeting one's own standards for self-tolerance are of first importance to one's relationships with others.[2] This is one way, then, that the goods of respect are internal to the meaningfulness of life from the agent's own point of view. It is unclear how traditional, externalist Kantianism is to account for this.

2.

Closely related to the goods of self-respect are those of being respected by both familiar strangers and loved ones who are respected peers. I want here to draw attention to two important human goods that accrue to an agent from having the respect of others: the first is the good of having the confidence of others, and the second is the good of having the understanding of others.

Consider these goods where they are the attitudes of others to whom an agent is not specially related. I am thinking primarily of the attitudes of those I will call familiar strangers, persons with whom the agent is familiar but with whom he or she has no special, loving relationship. When respectable people perceive another as not respectful of others, they lack con-

---

1. See Arnold E. Anderson, *Practical Comprehensive Treatment of Anorexia Nervosa and Bulimia* (Baltimore: Johns Hopkins University Press, 1985). The syndrome occurs primarily in women but not entirely so. See Derek Scott, "Sex Differences Within Anorexia Nervosa," in *Anorexia Nervosa*, ed. Derek Scott (New York: New York University Press, 1988), 59–73.

2. Studies in shyness confirm this. See Lorne M. Hartman and Patricia A. Cleland, "Social Anxiety, Personality, and the Self," in *Shyness and Embarrassment: Perspectives from Social Psychology*, ed. W. Ray Crozier (Cambridge: Cambridge University Press, 1990), 315–55.

fidence that such a person is worthy of the trust involved in intrinsic social relationships. Thus to lack this confidence of others and to be aware that one lacks it is to see oneself as viewed with suspicion and mistrust by other respectable people, in this case, by familiar strangers. It is also to see oneself as a perceived threat by people one respects. Therefore, the good of confidence as a good of being held in simple respect by respectable peers is that it makes minimal social relationships with respected peers possible.

Such relationships are intrinsic goods rather than merely necessary to some independent good of the agent. The agent values the confidence as an element intrinsic to the relationships of which it is a part. So the confidence of others is good in part because it reflects the recognition by others of the kind of person the agent is. Thus the good of confidence is a good of respect in the sense that it supervenes from the viewpoint of others on their perception of the agent as a respectful person. The value the agent places on respect, then, could not be simply for the fact that respect has a certain payoff. The intrinsic value placed on respect by the agent is *explained* by the fact that the agent is a respectful agent. It is not *justified* by some independent standard.

It is very important to see that those who value such confidence categorically are psychologically constituted in such a way that their other concerns are restricted by simple respect for others as a regulative norm. Moreover, it is categorically important to them that others see and value this about them. And, again, this value is internal to the way of life that is minimally meaningful to the agent.

In addition to their confidence, however, it is also important that an agent has a certain kind of understanding from respectable strangers. This understanding pertains to their respect for the agent's concern for his or her own loved ones. First, they understand and respect the priorities of the agent, seeing that often the agent's concern for loved ones takes priority over the concern for them as respectable strangers. (This will become clearer in later chapters with the discussion of how love regulates respect.) Understanding this is crucial to their ability to maintain the confidence that when the agent sometimes favors loved ones this does not reveal disrespect for them. Meaningful social relationships are possible only where there is sufficient trust among persons. Here trust is founded on the confidence in the agent's respect. But if respect requires an equal place of loved ones and strangers in one's life, then love, being what it is, can only generate suspicion and the loss of confidence. That mature people understand that simple respect does not require *this* kind of equality is a tremendous good. It allows the agent who cares about loved ones and who has respect for others to be relieved of thinking that he or she is viewed with suspicion for having normal human relationships.

Those who categorically value such understanding from others reveal that simple respect for others is sometimes regulated by special respect for loved ones, which is a case of a partial norm regulating an impartial one. This fact is significant because it illustrates that the good of confidence involves different forms of respect: The special respect of familiar strangers for the agent regulates what these strangers see as required of the agent in terms of simple respect for themselves. I do not see how even internalist Kantianism can account for this, as long as that view requires that impartial respect is asymmetrical in its regulative function. For the special respect familiar strangers have for the agent is for the agent's partial commitments, commitments that reflect norms in which impartial respect is not asymmetrically dominant across deliberative contexts. This is no small point. Establishing that respect is regulative is not the same as establishing that impartial or simple respect is regulative. These observations about the goods of confidence as supervenient on the goods of respect show that the conception of respect at work in judgments about these goods is regulated by special respect for a person's loving commitments. And if it is shown that the place of the goods of respect in the lives of respectful persons does not accommodate the concept of asymmetrical impartial norms, then Kantian internalism is refuted on its own turf. However, a more complete discussion of this point must await the discussion of the goods of love.

Second, the understanding that familiar strangers have of the agent allows them to view the agent as potentially worthy of being involved in more intimate personal relationships. Thus this understanding is crucial to the confidence necessary for moving from agent-neutral, impartial relationships with others to agent-centered, partial relationships with them. A person, for example, might be viewed as scrupulously fair with strangers but incapable of maintaining the commitments of special relationships. Gandhi was at times very disrespectful to his wife—not simply as a person, but as his spouse.[3] This was not to his credit, and it undermines the degree of esteem he is due, as well as the confidence that he was a good candidate for intimate personal relationships. Indeed, it is an open question about many social reformers whether they were admirable in ways that recom-

3. See Robert Payne, *The Life and Death of Mahatma Gandhi* (New York: E. P. Dutton, 1969).

mended them as friends, parents, lovers, and neighbors. The point I am pushing here has to do with a good for the agent. Imagine how Gandhi would have felt if his wife had left him, not because she did not respect him for his commitment to others but because she could not respect him for his lack of respect for his loved ones. Also imagine the loss for Gandhi if no one lost respect for him for his impartial commitment to others but *everyone* lost respect for him as someone with whom to have a special relationship.

Once again, we have a categorical good, the good of the confidence of familiar strangers that is possible only where the norm of simple respect is regulated by the norm of special respect. This tells against traditional Kantianism because this good is internal to the categorical values of the agent, and it tells against both traditional and internalist Kantianism because it reveals a context in which the impartial norm of simple respect is regulated by the partial norm of special respect.

Consider now these goods of confidence and understanding where they involve special relationships. Those with whom the agent has a special relationship need the confidence that the agent's respect for them will have its due place in the agent's life. This is possible only if these loved ones have special respect for the agent in the agent-centered sense. To have this kind of respect, they must feel confident that the agent will sometimes give priority to respectable loved ones over other respectable people. Without this kind of confidence in the agent's priorities, it is difficult for these loved ones to see how they stand in a special relationship to the agent. Here think of Gandhi's wife or the wife of Tolstoy, who was also mistreated by her husband.[4] To lose this confidence of one's loved ones is to lose a good essential to personal living.

As with respectable strangers, the fully social agent needs not only the confidence of loved ones but also their understanding. The understanding is that in many significant contexts the agent must give priority to the interests of others who are respectable but who are not loved ones. To have this understanding, the agent's loved ones must have respect for the agent's respectfulness of others. Think, for example, what it would have been like for Martin Luther King, Jr., not to have had the understanding of Coretta, his wife, that his work required him *and* his family to make sacrifices. That she did not view these sacrifices as a sign of disrespect for her was a tremen-

---

4. See Henri Troyat, *Tolstoy* (New York: Dell Publishing, 1967); William Shirer, *Love and Hatred: The Troubled Marriage of Leo and Sonya Tolstoy* (New York: Simon and Schuster, 1994).

dous good for Dr. King.[5] To have this kind of understanding is essential to any agent who is respectful of others and who has deep intimate relationships. This is a case where the good of understanding of one's loved ones is predicated on a conception of special respect that is regulated by simple respect for others. Thus both special respect for others and simple respect for others are symmetrical in their regulative functions regarding each other. This is consistent with the Aristotelian conception of practical reason as I have defined it but inconsistent with any version of impartialism.

One way of seeing the importance of these goods is in the connection with an agent's sense of shame. To lack the goods of self-respect is, for any remotely normal social being, a source of shame. It is to view oneself as unworthy of minimal self-affirmation and of the minimal affirmation of others. To lack this affirmation from respectable strangers is to view oneself as worthy of their contempt. To lack this affirmation from respectable loved ones is to view oneself as a source of shame to them. To be a person of integrity, then, as a normal social being is to be dispositionally sensitive to one's own R-qualities and to the beliefs of others regarding them. To believe that one lacks these qualities and that others rightly believe that one lacks these qualities is to suffer a severe disruption in one's identifying thoughts. This exemplifies itself in shame, which is the recognition of the kind of person one is without the minimal ability to tolerate oneself. What could better illustrate the connection between the goods of respect and the meaningfulness of an agent's life from his or her own point of view? And what could better illustrate the deficiencies of any externalist account of the role of respect in practical reason?

3.

Understanding of the value of self-respect and of having the respect of others should make clearer some of what is involved in the value to a respectful agent of the goods of respect for others. Consider first the value to the agent of having simple respect for those who have simple respect for others. It allows the agent to be free of suspicion and mistrust of others, which is the good of confidence in others. Simple respect for others for their special respect for their loved ones provides the agent with a very important good. It is the good of understanding that when others often favor their own respectable loved ones over the agent this is not cause for alarm or sus-

5. See Stephen B. Oates, *Let the Trumpet Sound: The Life of Martin Luther King, Jr.* (New York: Mentor, 1985).

picion. Some degree of this is part of what it is to be a loving person and of what is admired in such persons. Of course, this special respect for others is also crucial to another good. It is the good of the agent having the confidence that there are those around who are worthy candidates for future personal relationships.

This brings us to the agent's special respect for his or her own loved ones. What is the value of this to the agent? Remember that this is an agent-centered kind of respect for loved ones, reflecting admiration for their R-qualities. Among these qualities are both simple respect for others and special respect for the agent as a loved one. Not only does the agent have the confidence that these respectable loved ones will treat the agent as a respectable loved one, the agent also has the understanding that when they must favor other respectable persons over the agent this is not an act of abandonment or betrayal. Rather, the agent admires this concern for respectable, familiar strangers, even when it comes at some cost to the agent. This is a case that both Aristotelians and internalist Kantians can agree involves a partial norm being regulated by an impartial one. Again, imagine Coretta Scott King's admiration for her husband in this regard as a benefit to her. Earlier, we saw how it was a benefit to him. So, once again, there are crucial human goods that reveal symmetrical relations between simple respect and special respect as regulative norms.

To lack the goods of simple respect for others is to live a life of contempt for those to whom one is not specially related. To lack special respect for others is to live a life of shame for those whom one loves. For any remotely normal social being, neither life is worth living without self-deception. The first is not worth living, in part, because the agent despairs of developing social relationships with others. One is unable to tolerate them in even the minimal sense that is necessary for forming such relationships. Imagine having access only to Nazi fanatics. The anticipation of friendship, neighborliness, or romance would be impossible. Indeed, to form such relationships with such contemptible people would be to give up one's own integrity. It would be to forfeit one's identifying thoughts. In this sense, such a life is the object of a categorical aversion to a social being who is a person of integrity. Similarly, a life filled only with shame for one's loved ones would be equally unworthy of living.

A fictional example that shows the importance of the good of respect for loved ones in a person's life is in the film *The Music Box*.[6] The protagonist

---

6. See Constantin Costa-Gavras, *The Music Box* (1989). For historical examples involving shame for loved ones, see Peter Sichrovsky, *Born Guilty* (New York: Ba-

is a Chicago lawyer whose father emigrated from Hungary to the United States after World War II. The U.S. government charges the father with committing war crimes as a guard in one of the concentration camps. Since the daughter—the lawyer—has known her father only to be a model, loving parent, she understandably finds the charges incredible. Against contrary advice, she decides to represent him as his defense attorney. The rest of the film traces her slow realization that he is indeed guilty of the most heinous of crimes. The realization of his guilt, however, comes only after she has succeeded in having the charges against him dropped. Faced with what to do with the knowledge of his guilt, she first confronts him and then turns in the evidence that results in his conviction. The confrontation and subsequent release of the evidence are the daughter's repudiation of her relationship with her father, whom she holds in contempt but clearly loves.

Note that in this example the daughter's beliefs regarding the impartial R-qualities of the father render it psychologically impossible for her to maintain the relationship without self-deception. Her contempt for her father makes it psychologically impossible for her to endorse a loving relationship with him. This is certainly no small loss. Imagine by extension that she had discovered similar facts regarding all her loved ones. But also imagine the loss from the father's perspective. Here I mean the loss of his daughter's love through the loss of her respect, where he believes (though this is not in the film) that her contempt is justified. Surely, without self-deception, this would be a psychologically unendurable punishment for any loving parent.

A social being, especially a loving one, cannot survive in isolation, for such a being has an intrinsic interest in relationships with others. With protracted isolation, the social being either loses its will to live or suffers a loss of integrity in one of the ways in which that is possible. When faced with ways of life that involve either significant isolation from others or a life of self-deception, a social being often suffers from the latter.[7] The desire for communal relationships with loved ones often prevents an agent from clearly perceiving the contemptible qualities of loved ones. The loneliness

---

sic Books, 1988); and Gerald Posner, *Hitler's Children* (New York: Random House, 1991).

7. Studies of loneliness reveal that the isolation from others felt by the lonely often results in bitter denial of the importance of others to the lonely persons. See Warren H. Jones, "Loneliness and Social Behavior," in *Loneliness: A Sourcebook of Current Theory, Research, and Therapy,* ed. Letitia Anne Peplau and Daniel Perlman (New York: John Wiley, 1982), 238–52.

of isolation also often generates false beliefs about the qualities of others to allow them to become candidates for communal relationships. Yet sometimes the evidence is all too clear that one's loved ones as well as all the other persons around are contemptible. To perceive this fact and that there is no hope for change is to lose hope for a meaningful life, if one is a remotely normal social being. From the first-person perspective, integration is not possible. For the perception and lack of hope is to anticipate a life of solitary confinement, the evidence of the negative effects of which for human beings in general is overwhelming. This we know from the third-person point of view.[8] To the extent to which such isolation is traced to lack of respect, these observations show that the integration test as applied to most human beings reveals that the goods of respect are categorical goods and essential to personality integration.

The goods of respect, then, are important in several ways. First, they are basic to the ability of both the agent and others to view the agent as intrinsically important as a separate and numerically distinct person. Second, they are crucial to the confidence and understanding essential to the agent entering social relationships, relationships valued intrinsically both by the agent and by others. Finally, for any deeply social being, they are basic to the agent's having reasons for living. It is not that the goods of respect give

8. Studies distinguish between social isolation due to physical isolation and that due to psychological isolation. Loneliness due to psychological isolation is much more difficult to cure. The lonely person is often isolated from others because of a lack of self-approval, especially in adolescents. But whether loneliness is the result of the inability to find oneself worthy of the approval of others or the inability to approve of those by whom one is surrounded, it can have differing effects on the person suffering from it. It is a major factor in college dropouts and in both alcohol abuse and suicides on college campuses. Researchers also distinguish between depressed and nondepressed loneliness. Suicide often correlates with the former. Also, the thought of solitary confinement as punishment makes little sense apart from the assumption that social relations are primary goods from the point of view of the criminal. Otherwise, confinement seems a reward for asocial behavior. The confinement is not only meant as a punishment in the form of withholding a good but also as a corrective by reminding criminals of how important cooperation with others is from their own points of view. Otherwise, the practice makes little sense.

Still one should not equate the negative effects of loneliness with the view that aloneness is always a bad thing. Aloneness also has its importance within the lives of healthy people, and some more than others. See Tim Brennan, "Loneliness at Adolescence," Carolyn E. Cutrona, "Transition to College: Loneliness and the Process of Social Adjustment," Karen S. Rook and Letitia Anne Peplau, "Perspectives on Helping the Lonely," and Peter Suedfield, "Aloneness as a Healing Experience," all in Peplau and Perlman, *Loneliness*.

the agent reasons for living; far more is necessary for that than merely the ability to tolerate oneself and others. But without the goods of respect, many other goods are not forthcoming without self-deception and loss of integrity. In this way, the norms of respect have a tremendous regulatory role over other norms within a life found minimally meaningful for the agent of the sort described in the thick conception of integrity. But this does not confirm internalist Kantianism, for some forms of respect are impartial and others are partial. And the regulative functions between these norms are symmetrical rather than asymmetrical as either form of Kantianism would have it. This gives us some reasons for thinking that the Aristotelian conception of practical reason can better accommodate our conception of respect than either form of Kantianism can.

4.

Two other issues reveal the categorical value of the goods of respect in the lives of human agents. One involves how the goods of self-respect enter into the deliberations of the agent of integrity, and the other involves how deliberations involving simple respect for others are related to the meaningfulness of the agent's life from his or her own point of view. Consider the first issue.

Any categorical changes in an agent's values and interests are either complete or incomplete. If they are incomplete, it is possible for such changes to be deliberative. But any incomplete deliberative change in an agent's conception of the R-qualities of self-respect has its origin in values already embedded in the agent's identifying thoughts. That is, the change has its source in some of the R-qualities already recognized by the agent. Among these are those that reflect the values on which the value of self-respect depends. Since it is not possible for deliberations about one's R-qualities to be noncategorical, all the associated values of self-respect are categorical. Thus there is no way for an agent with self-respect to deliberate to a way of life that requires a complete change in the agent's conception of self-respect.

Yet, whatever the possibilities of deliberative changes in one's conception of respect are, deliberations regarding the forfeit of self-respect are another issue still. The dispositions of an agent of integrity make it psychologically impossible for one to deliberate to the conclusion that one should forfeit self-respect. Such a prospect would fill one with self-contempt, preempting deliberation regarding the forfeit of self-respect. This is due to the dispositional sensitivity of self-contempt to beliefs regarding the agent's lack of the relevant R-qualities. Thus it is not that self-contempt is a compelling deliberative consideration that gives the agent a reason for not sacrificing the good of self-respect. Rather, the dispositional sensitivity of self-respect to beliefs about R-qualities precludes any such deliberation from the start.

Therefore, it is possible that one can deliberate to a conclusion regarding an incomplete change in one's own conception of respect. This is even possible regarding the conclusion that one ought to take actions that are designed to result in nondeliberative changes in someone else's conception of respect. But one cannot deliberate to a conclusion regarding a complete change in one's own conception of respect. Nor can one conclude that one should forfeit one's self-respect. To deny this is either to presuppose a mysterious source of practical deliberation or to deny the claims made about the goods of self-respect. Internalist Kantians will surely agree with this, but I will try to show that the fact that one cannot deliberate to the conclusion that one ought to sacrifice one's self-respect for some other good does not require a conception of self-respect as an asymmetrical regulative norm.

Still it might be thought that there are many examples of practical deliberation in which the forfeit of self-respect is a deliberative option, in which one's self-respect appears within one's deliberative field as a kind of bargaining chip, albeit a highly prized one. Before considering any such example, note that it must be one assuming the deliberations of a person who possesses self-respect and considers forfeiting it for some other good. The other good that I will consider involves romantic love. I consider love because those we love have a kind of power over us that other people and other things do not. Good people are far more tempted to compromise themselves for love than for money.

Imagine, then, the following person. Romeo loves Juliet, whom he initially perceives to be both beautiful and admirable. Yet despite his love for her, time reveals that she is a cheat, a liar, and a person of vanity. Romeo is torn, for his life seems meaningless without Juliet. But his association with her (she is quite demanding) requires him to participate in a life that undermines his commitment to honesty, truthfulness, and the well-being of others. All are qualities apart from which Romeo cannot find himself tolerable. Ultimately, the point of decision comes: Either he must end the relationship with Juliet and retain those qualities central to his self-respect or he must sacrifice the qualities central to his self-respect to retain the relationship. In either case, the issue about self-respect appears within his deliberative field as an issue about his R-qualities, not so much about his self-respect. He is worried about becoming dishonest, a liar, and insensitive.

How are we to understand Romeo's dilemma as presenting him with a matter of deliberation? For Romeo could recognize the alternatives without a resulting deliberation. On realizing his options, he might simply see straightaway that there is no question regarding his self-respect and that he must end the relationship. If this occurs too readily, we can only wonder whether it is really love he feels for Juliet. But if he is too ready to sacrifice his self-respect, similar questions arise regarding the reality of his integrity. There must be at least some tension between the two values in a case like this for us to make sense of the situation. Moreover, given the two values at stake it is puzzling how the tension could be other than one involving a categorical conflict.

Yet it does not follow from there being some conflict between the two values that the resolution must be one of deliberation. First, there is the possibility of a deliberative impasse.[9] Romeo might simply find that the values are incommensurable or of equal commensurable value. In neither case is there a way to make sense of a deliberative resolution, because there is no way to make sense of an evaluative foundation for the deliberation. This is because when such conflicts emerge the attempt at reflective endorsement fails. Why? Because the agent cannot imaginatively project a coherent way of life that resolves the problematic situation and in which his deepest values can coherently express themselves. Second, there is the possibility of resolution by self-deception. Here self-deception is the response of a human organism to a conflict between or among the agent's categorical interests. This resolution involves an implicit recognition that a deliberative resolution is impossible for the agent. Thus we are still without a way of understanding Romeo's dilemma as providing a deliberative context.

There are, I believe, two other possibilities of construing the situation as involving a deliberative context. The first involves what we might call "the forgetfulness scenario." Knowing the facts about self-deception, Romeo might reason that if he chooses to retain his relationship with Juliet, he

9. The concept of deliberative impasse as employed here is more evidence for Michael Stocker's thesis regarding the plurality of values, namely, that values cannot be measured on some singular scale. See Stocker's, *Plural and Conflicting Values* (Oxford: Clarendon Press, 1990). Also see Isaiah Berlin, *The Crooked Timber of Humanity* (Princeton: Princeton University Press, 1990).

must endure self-contempt for a time. Yet self-deception will soon come as a relief, he reasons, allowing him to forget what he has done to himself.

The second involves what we might call "the resigned contempt scenario." Here Romeo does not reason that his choice to retain the relationship with Juliet will soon bring the relief of self-deception. Rather, he simply resigns himself to a life of self-contempt for his relationship with his beloved, for whom he has contempt.

Either strategy is possible, however, only if the attachment to Juliet has already significantly altered the dispositional states of Romeo. Once one has at all seriously considered forfeiting features of oneself central to one's self-respect, one has already had thoughts inimical to having those features in any stable way. A self-respecting person values his or her R-qualities, not how thoughts of having those qualities make him or her feel. To construe the value of one's R-qualities in this way is to misconstrue their value as ends. Assuming that one was once truly self-respecting, then, such misconstrual can only be the result of an unstable character. But this move from stability to instability is a nondeliberative change that has the result of a loss of an R-quality necessary for self-respect, namely, the quality of being able to withstand threats to those qualities most basic to one's sense of self-worth. Remember that Romeo is a person who is dispositionally sensitive to beliefs about R-qualities. He appears within his own deliberative field as an end worthy of respect only insofar as he appears there with the relevant R-qualities. To recognize that he has considered the sacrifice of his R-qualities is for him to recognize that he has changed in a way that fills him with self-contempt. It is for him to recognize that his deliberations are not those that he can endorse, despite the fact that he is ruled by them. The forgetfulness scenario and the resigned contempt scenario are, therefore, far from being deliberations that consider self-respect as a deliberative concern. Rather, they exhibit Romeo's recognition that he has a diminished deliberative capacity because he is too weak to stand by his most cherished values. To forfeit self-respect through weakness of will is not to deliberate to forfeit one's R-qualities for some other, more cherished good. In this regard, it seems that the same analysis is available both to the internalist Kantian and to the Aristotelian.

Another construal of Romeo's dilemma might be more promising as providing a deliberative context in which the sacrifice of Romeo's R-qualities (and thereby his self-respect) is a deliberative consideration. On this construal, Juliet is all that she initially appeared to be. Juliet's father, however, is opposed to the relationship. He threatens, and let us assume that he has the power, to force one of them into cocaine or heroin addiction. Doing so will have radical effects on human character, turning the addicted person into a cheat, a liar, and a person insensitive to others. If Romeo persists in pursuing the relationship, the father will force Juliet into addiction. Yet if Romeo will end the relationship, it is Romeo who faces addiction.

Romeo's dilemma, then, seems to be this: Either he can retain his relationship with Juliet and she will lose her R-qualities (and thereby her self-respect) or he can end his relationship with Juliet and he will lose his R-qualities (and thereby his self-respect). Thus, on this construal of the dilemma, it seems, Romeo's love for Juliet provides him with a deliberative reason for sacrificing his own R-qualities.

If we rule out scenarios based on incommensurable conflicts, there is no doubt that this construal involves a deliberative context. Yet it is not at all clear that it provides a deliberative context involving a conflict between two types of values. The problem is this: How can we understand Romeo's decision to become addicted himself on a rationale excluding reference to his beliefs about the values on which R-qualities are dependent? His dispositional sensitivity to his own beliefs regarding Juliet's beliefs about her own R-qualities is inseparable from both his love for her and his own R-qualities. How can he love her, rob her of the good of self-respect, and retain his self-respect? It is misleading, then, to construe the deliberative context as involving love on the one side and self-respect on the other, where love provides reasons for forfeiting one's R-qualities and thereby one's self-respect.

Rather, it is best to view the conflict as occurring within Romeo's sense of self-respect where love and respect are inextricably linked. If the situation allows him to remember or otherwise retain his reason for his addiction, his self-respect will be ambivalent. He will lose self-respect in the light of his new qualities. But he will gain self-respect for acting out of respect and love for Juliet. On the other hand, if Romeo anticipates forgetting his reasons for becoming addicted, his decision is to terminate his identifying thoughts. But this is a decision founded on his current conception of self-tolerance. Now, if this is the sense of Romeo's reasoning, the deliberative context does not involve alternatives that include a way of life he could find minimally worthwhile, for neither alternative involves a deliberative field in which he can appear as an end worthy of respect from his own point of view. Neither way of life, then, is even in a minimal way either self-sufficient or final, for both are lacking a fundamental good. Thus it is not a deliberative context in which the forfeit of self-respect is a deliberative option. Given his choices, there simply is no way for him to retain his self-respect. This is true because Romeo's conception of self-respect exhibits the regulative effect of personal love. Therefore, this is not a case that illustrates that self-respect is an asymmetrical regulative norm.

Barring some other interpretation to the contrary, then, it is plausible to conclude that there are no such deliberative contexts. There are no contexts in which an agent deliberates to the conclusion to sacrifice his or her R qualities for some other good, where that good is a component in a minimally worthwhile life. Only one context makes sense of an agent's deliberating to the sacrifice of R-qualities. It is where there are no alternatives that allow the agent access to a minimally worthwhile life. From the first-person point of view, then, these observations show how for the agent of integrity in the thick sense the attempt to integrate the goods of life without self-respect comes to impasse and is doomed to failure. Yet because an agent's conception of self-respect exhibits the regulative effects of other norms and reflective endorsement fails from the point of view of life as a whole, this does not support internalist Kantianism but the Aristotelian conception of the integrative function of practical reason.

5.

I turn now to the issue of how simple respect for others enters into the deliberations of the agent of integrity and how this is related to the meaningfulness of the agent's life from his or her own point of view. I focus on how simple respect for others can give one reasons for dying.

From what I have said, it follows that one can have reasons founded on one's sense of respect for ruling out a way of life as permissible. If this applies to all the ways of life available, one will have reasons for giving up one's life. In such cases, one always has both agent-neutral and agent-centered reasons for taking actions that will result in one's death. One's sense of respect for others will not allow the thought that there is a permissible way of life left open. One's sense of self-respect will not allow the thought that there is a worthwhile way of life left open. Such contexts, when fully understood by the respectful agent, do not give rise to a concern for morality and impartiality on the one side and a meaningful life on the other, thoughts about which function as a contrary inclination to doing what impartiality requires. Those moral conceptual schemes that construe these contexts in this way simply misconstrue the role of respect in the deliberations of a respectful agent. Dietrich Bonhoeffer found the prospects of a life made possible by passivity to Nazi evil both morally unthinkable and not the least worthwhile.[10] In this, both internalist Kantians and Aristotelians can agree that traditional Kantianism is seriously flawed.

Kantians of both kinds are right, however, that respect is a regulative norm in relationship to all other norms. Thus it can be the source of one's reasons for dying. But when it is, it is so because it involves a categorical aversion traceable to respect as a basic sentiment; it is not because the demands of pure practical reason check our inclinations to pursue morally impermissible but meaningful ways of life. When one's respect for self and others requires one's death, one does not arrive at this conclusion through an impartial CI procedure; rather it is because no alternative way of life appears within one's deliberative field in which oneself and others appear as fundamental goods, goods that are necessary to make a life minimally self-sufficient and worthy of final choice. In short, the alternatives lack the kind of meaning they need in order to be the objects of choice and practical reason. Nor should we think that since respect can give us reasons for dying, it is asymmetrical in its regulative function. That there are contexts in which respect regulates other norms at the cost of any further meaning to life does not mean that there are not other contexts in which respect would be regulated by other norms with the same result. We will see how this can occur in what follows.

10. Bonhoeffer was a German theologian who was killed in the Nazi concentration camps. See Mary Bosanquet, *The Life and Death of Dietrich Bonhoeffer* (New York: Harper and Row, 1968).

Part 3

THE GOODS OF LOVE

Thin love ain't no love at all.

Toni Morrison, Beloved

I hold it true, whate'er befall;
I feel it when I sorrow most—
'Tis better to have loved and lost
Than never to have loved at all.

Alfred, Lord Tennyson, In Memoriam

The goal of part 3 is to accomplish three things. The first is to elaborate in considerable detail a conception of a rational agent who is both respectful and loving in a variety of ways. The issue is how a rational agent can integrate both the interests of respect and the interests of personal love in a way that preserves the basic elements of integrity. In order for the analysis to confirm the Aristotelian scheme, it will have to illustrate how the agent can be reflective without the aid of an impartial decision procedure and how the rightness of action is the nonaccidental result of its motive. Here the Aristotelian criteria of finality and self-sufficiency will prove crucial in the analysis of full rationality and reflective endorsement. The second thing to be accomplished in part 3 is to show that on the Aristotelian conception the impartial and partial norms of a respectful and loving agent are both symmetrical in their regulative functions and rational. This part of the argument is designed to show that Kantian internalism is false. Having given reasons in part 2 for thinking that traditional Kantianism cannot account for the role of respect in the moral life, the critical focus of part 3 is on the debate between Kantian and Aristotelian internalism. Finally, the third goal is to show through the integration test how the norms of respect and love, both partial and impartial, have their foundation in the goods that provide unity and meaning to most of our lives in a way that makes integrity possible. If I succeed on all these points, I will have developed a conceptual scheme in some detail; I will have presented a rational alternative to

Kantian internalism; and I will have given reasons for thinking that the Aristotelian scheme is rational for a significant portion of humanity.

The analysis has several dimensions or layers. The first involves analysis of various forms of personal love in terms of intentional dispositional states. As in part 2, the goods of love, like the goods of respect, will be analyzed in terms of the objects of such states. General features that distinguish personal love and impartial respect must be delineated, and then different forms of personal love must be distinguished from each other. I will especially be concerned with parental love for a child, the love involved in friendship, and what I call neighborly love, the love of a group or community. What we must imagine in this analysis is the deliberative field of an agent of a certain sort. To do so, we must get a detailed picture of how things appear within that field as good, as things to be pursued, nurtured, maintained, cherished, respected, loved, and so on. Only after getting a sense of these things can we proceed to the issue of how these goods are to be reflectively integrated. At this level, the analysis is further work in philosophical psychology, though at a more concrete stage than the general psychology set out in chapters 3 and 4. As will become clear, however, this analysis builds on the earlier general psychology involving categorical and noncategorical interests.

The second layer of analysis involves the concept of rationality. In the introduction, I said that I would defend the thesis that practical rationality is character-relative. I will try to show how this is true regarding the agent of integrity in the thick sense. The argumentative strategy employed to establish this involves the evaluation of what I call deliberative patterns for their rationality. A deliberative pattern is the pattern of deliberation leading to a practical conclusion. To take a simple example, consider the distinction between a "maximization pattern" and a "worst outcomes pattern." In some contexts, it is undeniably rational to deliberate in a way that reflects a maximization pattern. That is, it is sometimes rational, especially where resources are scarce, to try to get as much as one can of something, or put another way, to try to bring about the best available state of affairs where states of affairs are ranked from best to worst on some value criteria. Everything else being equal, if gasoline is in short supply and one needs lots of it, then one should attempt to get as much as one can. In other contexts, it is sometimes rational to try to avoid worst outcomes, to try to bring about the least worst of several possibilities. Everything else being equal, if faced with being hanged or being tortured, one should weigh the evils and choose the lesser.

Moreover, there are many other kinds of deliberative patterns that lead to practical conclusions. Among these are impartial and partial patterns. For example, both maximization and worst outcome patterns have impartial and partial forms. Act utilitarians take impartial maximization to be the most fundamental form of moral deliberation, whereas egoists take as fundamental a very partial conception of maximization. Although there are many other possibilities, I will argue that there is no deliberative pattern, partial or impartial, for an agent of integrity in the thick sense that will yield rational results across all deliberative contexts. The argument will be that the rationality of a deliberative pattern is determined by its ability to solve the integration problems faced by the agent in the context and that there is no deliberative pattern, partial or impartial, that will solve such integration problems across a wide range of deliberative contexts. Thus what makes a particular pattern rational is a function of the context and the character of the agent doing the deliberating. In this regard, although it is true on the version of Aristotelianism defended here that the criteria of finality and self-sufficiency will be satisfied by any rational pattern in any context, it is only in the most reflective contexts that these criteria will be explicitly applied in deliberation. Furthermore, there are contexts, I will argue, in which not even the criteria of finality and self-sufficiency can achieve integrative success.

It is in the context of this analysis that I will distinguish between different versions of Kantian internalism, between deontological versions and consequentialist versions. The task is to specify the deliberative patterns that lead to practical conclusions in various contexts that are claimed to be rational by Kantians. Here the goal is to see what the rival Kantian views are when they are spelled out in a way that is both contextually sensitive and contextually thorough. And we will see that deontological Kantians have not been at all sensitive and thorough in this regard. As for Kantian consequentialism: I will argue that the deliberative strategies available to such a conception of impartialism are not rational across deliberative contexts for the agent of integrity in the thick sense.

The contexts will be distinguished in terms of the kinds of interests at stake for those involved in conflict situations. Suppose we are evaluating whether a deliberative pattern, Alpha, is rational for a particular agent, A, in a particular context or situation, S. S will be analyzed in terms of the kinds of conflicts that are at stake and for whom. Suppose the interests at stake are those of A and B. But what kind of interests? If A is a respectful person, much will turn on what kind of interest is at stake and for whom.

Suppose the conflict is between a categorical interest of one person and a minor noncategorical interest of another. Everything else being equal, it is difficult to see how it could be respectful to give priority to the minor interest over the categorical interest. For a respectful person, then, the issue of whose interests to give priority to often turns on whose interest is categorical and whose is not. Were the conflict one involving a conflict only among minor interests, the deliberative pattern would be different for a rational, respectful agent. Whether Alpha is rational in S, then, turns very much on the nature of S and the character of A, or so I will argue. As it turns out, the analysis of the interests of respect and love when combined with the distinctions involving categorical and noncategorical interests generates a rich array of contexts in which deliberative patterns emerge. It is within this range of contexts that the second level of analysis regarding rationality must take place. And it is in this context that I will argue for the rationality of norms that are symmetrical in their regulative functions, that is, for the Aristotelian model of practical reason as it applies to an agent of integrity in the thick sense. Moreover, and this is of utmost importance, I will show how the agent can make a rational decision without the aid of an impartial decision procedure sought for by Enlightenment conceptions of morality. Recall that on the Aristotelian model there is no impartial decision procedure; yet there is rational reflection.

The third layer of analysis involves the integration test. Analysis at the second layer was in a sense hypothetical. The issue there was what would rationality come to for an agent of a certain sort, namely, of the sort described in the thick conception of integrity. It is possible that this analysis, the second layer of analysis, could be correct but that it applies to humanity in a marginal way at best. Whether it does or not turns on the results of the integration test when applied to a wide range of the human population. In chapter 15, I apply the integration test and argue that as a matter of empirical fact the analysis at the second layer applies to a rather large portion of humanity. If this is true, then the Aristotelian model of practical reason, and the conception of morality embedded in it, is applicable to most of us. In the process of this analysis, I will try to show how progressive a conception of morality Aristotelianism is when properly attuned to the facts.

I turn now to the first layer of analysis and the general features of personal love as an intentional dispositional state.

8.   General Features of Love

Although the contours of personal love differ with its various forms, there are some features that seem common to them all. As understood here, they all take persons or groups of persons as their intentional objects; they all express some core interests in their objects; they differ somewhat in their evaluations of their objects; and they all involve beliefs about the identities of their objects in a way that is crucial to activating the dispositions inherent in them. The aim of this chapter is to provide a general understanding of these features as a preliminary to the in-depth discussion that follows in subsequent chapters of personal love and its regulative functions. Section I discusses the various interests the loving person takes in those who are loved; sections II and III, some evaluative beliefs involved in personal love; and section IV, the role of the loved one's identity in activating love's dispositions. All these features are fundamental to understanding how a loved one appears within the deliberative field of the agent of integrity in the thick sense.

1.

If you are a loving person, you will have at least five important interests in your loved ones as the intentional objects of your love. You will be interested (i) in their mutual affections, (ii) in a shared relationship with them, (iii) in their welfare, and (iv) in being their benefactor. The fifth interest, which I will argue for in the next section, is (v) in their being good persons. All these interests factor into how your loved ones appear as ends within your deliberative field as a loving person.

Consider the first of these interests. How do we make sense of you as a loving person where your dispositions toward your loved ones are completely devoid of any interests in their mutual affections.[1] What would it be to be romantically in love with someone and have no interest in being the object of that person's sexual interests? What would it be to love someone as a friend and be altogether indifferent to your place in his or her affections and loyalties? And what would it be to love a child and not care at all about its feelings for you?

It is similarly difficult to make sense of not having an interest in a shared relationship with loved ones. The romantic lover has not only an interest in mutual sexual attraction, but also in sharing that interest in sexual activity. The interests mutually held between friends also find their satisfaction in the activities of a shared relationship, which is behind Aristotle's claim that friendship involves living together.[2] And though the mutuality requirement is different for the parent/child relationship, it is puzzling how you could love your children and be indifferently disposed to any shared relationship with them.

Still there might be arguments that mutuality and sharedness are not requirements of the concept of love. The first might involve showing that sometimes as a lover you might have reasons for deciding to keep your love a secret from a loved one. The reasons I have in mind are not because you lack the character to reveal the vulnerability that love involves but because you think it best for the loved one that he or she not know of your affections. A teacher who falls in love with a student might feel this, as might a biological parent who loves a child given up for adoption. The second argument might involve showing that as a lover you might sometimes love someone despite the fact that the love is not reciprocated. No doubt, romantic love provides many examples. The third argument might try to show that sometimes external circumstances prevent you from sharing a relationship with a loved one. Physical distance might cause this in any form of love, and with romantic love the condition of AIDS sufferers certainly comes to mind. The claim behind all three arguments is that despite the undeniable presence of such phenomena it is still obvious in some cases that you truly love the loved one.

We can admit these observations, however, without undermining the thesis. In all these cases, it remains true that as a loving person you retain an interest in the mutual affections of and a shared relationship with your loved one. It is just that in these special circumstances it is rational for you

---

1. For an interesting discussion, see Robert Brown, *Analyzing Love* (Cambridge: Cambridge University Press, 1987), 14–46.
2. See *NE* 1157b:19–21 and 1172a:1–5.

not to pursue these interests. This is clear in our conception of what a person's dispositions must be like to be those of a loving person. If from the very start you are indifferent to the fact that the feelings of another are not reciprocated or that no shared relationship with another is possible, then surely this shows, if anything does, that you do not love the other person. Absent, then, a belief that stress occurs, at least initially, in these special circumstances, it is simply contrary to our conception of the dispositional state of love to think of someone with such indifference as a loving person. As was true with shared affection, loved ones appear within the deliberative field of the loving agent as someone with whom to share a relationship.

Another important interest you will have in your loved ones is an intrinsic interest in their welfare. Even where nothing can be done, indifference to the plight of another is not a disposition we attribute to a loving person of whatever variety. Of course, this interest does not always take priority over other interests you might have, but it is nonetheless there.

Moreover, this concern for the welfare of loved ones is by its very nature a stronger concern than that for other persons who appear within the loving person's deliberative field. One can be interested in the welfare of another in ways that are independent of personal love. Respect is one such way, as we have seen, but so are pity, sympathy, and generosity. As a loving person you might even be moved in some contexts by respect or pity to give priority to the welfare of someone other than your loved one, especially for someone whose plight you perceive as severe in a way that your loved one's is not. Nevertheless, where everything else is equal, two conditions are sufficient for saying that you do not love another person, B. They are that you know that you do not love C and you care about the welfare of B and C to the same degree, regardless of context. This is a fundamental fact about how loved ones appear within the loving person's deliberative field, and it is true even where C appears within your field as someone worthy of respect. Remember that we are concerned with an agent who is not only loving but respectful of self and others as well.

Equally important is the fact that your interest in the welfare of loved ones sometimes expresses itself in your subordinating some of your own interests to those you love. Without some disposition to put the interests of loved ones above your own, you are simply unrecognizable as a loving person. What would it be to love another and yet hesitate to make even the slightest sacrifice for the sake of some central concern of that person? Thus, if you are a loving person, it is another fact about how loved ones appear within your deliberative field that they are taken to be goods that are more important than the good of satisfying some of your other interests.

Indeed, we hesitate to say that you love another unless we are willing to say that you are disposed in some contexts to subordinate some significant interests for the sake of that person. Among these significant interests are some that belong to you and some that belong to others. If you were disposed to subordinate only minor interests of yours and others for the sake of another's interests, we might be inclined to say that you liked the other person but never that you loved that person. This is especially true if the interests at stake for the other person are very important ones.

Of special significance to a loving person are the categorical interests of loved ones. First, they are among the loved ones' welfare interests, since they are what life is most about from their own point of view. Thus we can apply our previous point in the present context: If you know that you do not love C and you care about the categorical interests of B and C to the same degree, then, everything else being equal, you do not love B. Therefore, and this is the second point, the categorical interests of loved ones are more important to a loving person than the categorical interests of others, which is a fundamental fact about how loved ones appear within the loving person's deliberative field.

Finally, there is the loving person's interest in being the benefactor of his or her loved ones. Here I do not have in mind the truth that as a loving person you desire to give your affections and loyalties to your loved ones. Clearly you do want to bestow these goods on your loved ones in a way that is inconsistent with your being content with the fact that they already have the affections and loyalties of others. Rather, what I have in mind is another truth connected with the concept of the welfare of loved ones. There are some benefits that could be conferred on a person by a lover or a nonlover, and there are others that only a lover could confer.[3] Some of the former are welfare benefits. The clearest case involves a parent's love for a child. Anyone can provide the welfare benefit of adequate shelter for a child, but only a parent can provide a child the benefit of parental affection. Also, the parent's love includes not only the interest in the child's welfare needs being met but also the interest in meeting at least some of these needs. This does not mean that the parent would oppose these needs being met by someone else when it is not possible for the parent to do so. After all, the primary interest the parent has in this regard is that the child's needs are met. However, it does mean that when the parent is unable to meet *any* of the child's

---

3. Here, see Lawrence Blum, *Friendship, Altruism and Morality* (London: Routledge and Kegan Paul, 1980), 140–68.

welfare needs, the dispositions of parental love result in a sense of loss for the parent. The lack of any sense of loss where the child's needs are always met by someone other than the parent signifies a lack of love. Such indifference is simply inconsistent with the dispositions of a parent who loves her child, although a nonloving parent might have some other concern for the child's welfare.

Personal love includes an interest in being the benefactor of loved ones in this sense because personal love includes nurturing. This is true not only of parental love but of the other kinds of personal love as well. The romantic lover is not only concerned with the sexual interests and the welfare of her partner, she is also concerned with playing a nurturing role in his life. Absent such an interest, she is merely sexually attracted to him and has some impersonal concern for his welfare. Nor is there love for friends or neighborly love without nurturing, though it need not play the same role as in parental love.

To nurture is to be concerned with and to desire to contribute to the growth and development of another. In parental love, at least for the immature child, nurturing is not a part of the mutual affections of lover and loved one. But in friendship and other forms of peer love, it is. To love another as a friend is to be concerned with and to desire to contribute to the friend's growth and development. But here, unlike the case of parental love, the nurturing of love is mutual. It is the nurturing of peers. To see oneself as the friend of another, then, involves seeing oneself as both the beneficiary and the benefactor of the friend in terms of personal growth and development. It is, of course, many other things as well. The same can be said for other types of peer love. In this regard, it is one sign that patriotic talk is mere talk when there is no evidence of a nurturing disposition toward the welfare needs of fellow citizens. This is true, of course, unless the patriot is thought of as the staunch adherent of an ideology, who need not love his or her fellow citizens at all. In any event, if you are a loving person, loved ones appear within your deliberative field as others on whom you are to confer benefits of various sorts.

I conclude, then, that the intentional object of personal love is a person or persons and that, if you are a loving person, embedded in your loving dispositions toward your loved ones are the interests in their mutual affections, in a shared relationship with them, in their welfare, and in being their benefactor. Moreover, loved ones will appear within your deliberative field as persons whose welfare and categorical interests are significantly more important to you than the welfare and categorical interests of others, even those you respect but do not love. And as a loving person it will be especially important to you that some of the benefits that accrue to your loved ones come from you rather than from someone else.

2.

The evaluative element of personal love is problematic, as is the role of beliefs in love. It is even unclear that there is an evaluative component to some kinds of love. One important issue, then, is this: Are there any kinds of evaluative beliefs that you must have regarding another person in order to make sense of our saying that you love that person?

It is certainly doubtful that you must, qua loving person, believe that the loved one is in some sense good. Romantic and parental love, especially, seem vulnerable to having intentional objects accompanied with negative evaluative beliefs regarding their goodness. It seems mere linguistic legislation to say that a romantic lover does not *really* love the person he or she clearly believes is despicable. This seems even more obvious in a parent's love for a wayward child. The love of friends and the love of fellow citizens seem less tolerant in this regard. Yet even here, the love for the friend or fellow citizen is certainly not proportionate to the belief that the friend or fellow citizen is good.

A more plausible candidate for such a belief is the evaluation of the loved one as capable of being good, on values reflected in the dispositions of a loving person. Embedded in this conception of love is a denial that anyone can love that which he or she evaluates as hopelessly without value. An argument in favor of this is the fact that those who obviously love despicable persons often must resort to self-deception concerning their loved ones' goodness to maintain the love. Such self-deception does not always yield the belief that loved ones are good. Rather, it sometimes yields the unfounded belief, despite ample contrary evidence, that loved ones are capable of being good as the grounds for false hope of their reform.

Still having an intrinsic concern for your loved ones does not entail that you believe that they are good or even capable of being good. The conclusion that it does needs an argument, and I do not see that the observations concerning self-deception are conclusive. Some seem to love their children, friends, and lovers, while clearly believing that their loved ones are hopelessly without merit and unworthy of even simple respect.

Two factors might motivate the intuition, for some, that love requires a positive evaluation of the loved one as good or as capable of being good. The first involves the fact that as a loving person you are concerned with your loved one's welfare. It is difficult to see how you could care about the welfare of a loved one and not care whether he has the good of self-respect. Yet if your loved one truly has the good of self-respect on values that you endorse, you see your loved one as at least minimally good. Also, it seems plausible that the good of self-respect is good for a person only if the person is capable of recognizing, appreciating, or having that good. Thus it seems that your concern for your loved one's welfare includes your having the evaluative belief that he is at least capable of being good. Here the sense of goodness is the minimally tolerable sense of being capable of being worthy of respect. It is also difficult to see how you could care about your loved one's welfare and not care whether he has the good of self-esteem. And by parity of reasoning, the same argument would apply to the relationships between welfare, the good of self-esteem, and your loved one's being good. Thus your evaluative belief that self-respect and self-esteem are goods for your loved one allegedly shows that as a loving person you have other implicit beliefs about your loved one. They are that your loved one is capable of the relevant respect- and esteem-conferring qualities and therefore capable of having good-making qualities.

Despite the apparent strength of this argument, it is only partially successful. The degree of both its success and its failure is reflected in the fact that it succeeds regarding some but not all kinds of personal love. It succeeds, in part, regarding love among persons who must be in some sense peers. The love of friends and the love of fellow community members require the notion of love among peers as a basis for mutual affections and shared relationships. As a part of this, peer love requires not just the ability to tolerate loved ones but the ability to hold them in esteem as well. Yet even here, the success is only partial. All that is required is that somewhere in the history of the love for the friend, say, was the implicit belief that he was worthy or capable of being worthy of respect and esteem. For you can meaningfully love a friend for whom you have lost respect.[4] In these cases, the friend for whom one has lost respect appears within one's deliberative field as someone who was once good, which, of course, is one of life's saddest experiences.

That the argument does not work at all for some kinds of personal love reflects the degree of the argument's failure. It seems entirely clear that a

---

4. Actually, this might be misleading. If at an earlier time A loves B and respects and esteems B but at a later time A comes to believe that B is no longer respectable and no longer a peer, though it does not follow that A no longer loves B, it might be best to say that the love is no longer that involved in friendship.

parent could love a child, be concerned with the child's welfare, believe that the child would have a better life if it had and thus was capable of having the good of self-respect, and yet believe that the child was incapable of self-respect. A parent's love for a severely retarded child is a good example. Another is the love for an elderly person in the advanced stages of Alzheimer's disease.

One response is that the objects of love in these cases are not really persons and thus the examples do not involve "personal" love. But this seems mere linguistic fiat that dictates that all personal love must be peer love to some degree. What we have in these cases is not love that includes the belief that the loved one is good or capable of being good. Rather, it is love that includes the *desire* that the loved one have these qualities. So we can add to the interests that loving persons have in their loved ones a fifth interest: the interest that they are of good character. But this is different from having the *belief* that they are good. It is one thing for your loved ones to appear within your deliberative field as good and quite another for you to desire this.

Now consider the second source that might motivate the intuition that loving persons must believe that their loved ones are good or at least capable of being good. It is the failure to distinguish, on the one hand, the evaluation of the lover's love and the loved one's goodness and, on the other, the belief that a person's loving another is always a good thing. It is very difficult for some people to say that love is ever a bad thing. One reason for this is that most people who disparage love are clearly either bitter or lack the character traits to face the risks that love involves. Combine this with some belief or hope that being loved will bring out the good in someone apparently devoid of any goodness, and this might lead some to assert that the lover must believe, however subconsciously, that the loved one is at least capable of being good.

Often appeals to subconsciously held beliefs are the last grasps of a view in trouble. It is one thing to have an implicit belief and quite another for the belief to be subconscious. An implicit belief can be made explicit to the believer by showing that his or her other beliefs logically require the "implicit" belief. But this cannot be what a subconscious belief is. For the claim is still unproven that there is anything contradictory about the beliefs of the lover, qua personal lover, who claims that the loved one is hopelessly without merit.

Rather than insist on a tight conceptual link between love and a positive evaluation of the loved one, we should simply deny that love is always a human good. In would-be peer love, it is not a human good, either for the lover or the loved one, when the lover correctly believes that the loved one is hopelessly without good qualities. Loving in such a case is not a good for the lover due to the recognition that the mutuality and sharedness of love are impossible with a contemptible loved one. Being loved is not good for the loved one, since it would be a sign of some goodness in him if he recognized love as a good. Thus it is not a part of the dispositional state of all forms of personal love that the lover believes that the loved one is either good or capable of being good. Later, we will see that a positive evaluation of loved ones is crucial to peer love in its central form, and this will prove crucial to an understanding of the normative thoughts generated by the various forms of personal love.[5]

3.

So far in the analysis of the intentionality of love and evaluative beliefs, we have been considering this: Does the proposition "A loves B" entail some proposition of the sort "A believes _____ about B" within an adequate account of personal love? Specifically, we have been considering whether "A loves B" entails "A believes that B is either good or capable of being good." Now, I want to focus on a different possibility regarding the beliefs that A must have if we are to say that A loves B. It is this: Does the proposition "A loves B" entail the proposition "A loves B *because* she believes _____ about B"? I confine myself to cases of peer love. These require that at some point in the history of the lover's dispositions the lover must believe that the loved one is good regarding the qualities of respect and esteem. I also will assume cases where such love is a human good, where the non-self-deceived and adequately informed lover unmistakenly finds that love for the loved one is a good thing.

In these cases, analysis requires that "A loves B" entails "A believes that B has the good-making qualities of being worthy of respect and esteem." But it seems mistaken to say that "A loves B" entails "A loves B *because*

---

5. There might be a weaker connection between A's loving B and A's beliefs regarding B's qualities. It might be this: It makes sense to say that A currently loves B only if we believe that there was some earlier time at which A did not love B and did *not* have the belief that B was incapable of good-making qualities. This would preclude speaking of someone coming to love someone he or she believed from the beginning to be hopelessly without merit but would allow that A can love B without having the belief that B is either good or capable of being good. Whether this connection is included in our conception of love, I do not know. I thank Mark Katz for bringing this to my attention.

she believes that he has the good-making qualities of being worthy of respect and esteem." For it is clearly sensible to say that "A believes that B is worthy of respect and esteem and A does not love B."

Someone might maintain that it is not in terms of good-making qualities that A must be said to love B but some other qualities. These might be beloved-making qualities—B-qualities, let us call them—in terms of which A evaluates B as being "lovable." On this view, love is like respect in one regard. Beliefs about what qualities are the relevant B-qualities are evaluative beliefs, but beliefs about whether a person has the relevant B-qualities are factual beliefs. Whether these beliefs are true is discernible by those who do not share the evaluative beliefs.

The most plausible kind of peer love to which this analysis might apply is romantic love. It might indeed be true that A romantically loves B, only if A believes that B is lovable, where A has some conscious or subconscious evaluative beliefs about B-qualities. For the sake of argument, let us assume so. It is entirely unclear that this means that A loves B because A believes that B has these qualities. For it might be true that A finds that certain qualities are lovable in B, that C has the same qualities, that all other factors are equal, but that A does not love C. It is difficult to see, then, that there is some set of qualities that A believes B to possess that causes her to love him. In this regard, the dispositions of love and respect are quite different. For the belief that B has the relevant R-qualities will, under normal circumstances, cause A to respect him, if she is a respectful person.

The objection is not that the concept of B-qualities is mysterious, or vacuous, or lacks meaning. Such objections are mistaken, I believe. To have peer love for another, under normal circumstances, is to love another in some sense as an equal. This includes—however implicitly—the judgment that the loved one is a peer. Thus, in peer love, there are B-qualities in a limited sense. If you are a peer-loving person, there are some qualities you must, at some point in the history of your love for your loved one, believe him to possess. But there are no B-qualities in the stronger sense that your believing them to be present will cause you to love him. For you could have the evaluative belief that he is a peer and believe that he has all the relevant peer love interests in you, yet you could lack peer love for him.

Nor is love dispositionally sensitive to beliefs about the loved one's qualities in the same way that respect is. Where love need not include the peer evaluation, it is difficult to see that such love is necessarily sensitive to beliefs about the qualities of the loved one at all. The parent's love for the severely retarded child is a good example. Even in peer love, the love is not only disproportionate to the beliefs about some set of qualities of the loved one but also flexible regarding beliefs about the qualities of the intentional object in a way that simple respect is not. One can go on loving a friend long after coming to believe that he has undergone extensive changes in personal qualities. Sometimes this is long after coming to believe that he is no longer worthy of respect and esteem. This contrasts with the comparative rigidity of simple respect, which vanishes the moment one becomes convinced that the intentional object of respect no longer has the relevant R-qualities. These are fundamental differences in how the objects of love and respect appear within a loving and respectful agent's deliberative field.

4.

There is one belief, however, that plays an essential role in your loving another, namely, your belief that the other is numerically identical to your loved one. The idea is that your dispositional state uniquely has your loved one as its object and not someone you perceive to be qualitatively similar but numerically distinct from him. In this way, personal love as a dispositional state is sensitive to identity beliefs regarding its intentional object. Thus you love another only if you are sensitive to the belief that the person perceived as your loved one is indeed your loved one. Your love for a third party, on the other hand, involves a different disposition toward that person, although it might be the same *type* of disposition. Rather, it is another disposition that is sensitive to the belief that the numerically distinct third party is its intentional object. Not only, then, does love differ from simple respect in terms of the dispositional sensitivity to beliefs about the *qualities* of the intentional object; it also differs from simple respect in terms of the dispositional sensitivity to beliefs about the *identity* of the intentional object.

If you believe that another person has the relevant R-qualities and discover that you are mistaken about the person's identity, then, under normal circumstances, you will still respect that person. But suppose you love another and mistake another person for your loved one. If you discover your mistaken identity belief and that this person is not your loved one, you will not have the same disposition toward the person you mistook for your loved one. This is true even if this person's set of qualities is indiscernible from your loved one's. You might in fact be indifferent or even hostile toward the person on such a discovery. In this way, beliefs about the identity of the intentional object of love play a causal role in love that they do not play in simple respect, and this is very crucial to understanding how others appear within the deliberative field of a respectful and loving agent.

If I could magically produce multiple identical duplicates (including memory or quasi-memory experiences) of the person you love most, I would not have multiplied your benefits in life. Rather, I would have robbed you of one of life's most precious goods. I would have done this by rendering it impossible for you to *identify* your loved one within your deliberative field. Without an identity belief, there would be no way for your dispositions to find their expression, and thus a precious relationship would be lost.[6]

We also must consider another causal role beliefs might play in love that they do not play in simple respect. It concerns the issue of whether beliefs about the identity of the *lover* play a causal role in the lover's love. Previous analysis shows that simple respect involves a disposition indifferent to identity beliefs regarding the agent of an action where concern for action arises from respect. But where there is indifference in simple respect, there is sensitivity in personal love. Your interests in the mutual affections of and a shared relationship with your loved ones establish this. So, too, does the interest in being their benefactor.

The romantic lover, for example, has an interest not only in the loved one having romantic interests but also in the focus of those interests. They must focus on the lover rather than someone else. Parental love for a child includes not only the interest in the child's welfare needs being met but also the interest in the parent being the one who meets these needs as the parental benefactor of the child. All this is made clear in the fact that the loved one appears within the deliberative field as "my lover," "my child," "my friend," and "my neighbor." There is no analogue with respect. We do not think of someone we respect as "my respectable one," even where we can think of another as "my respectable friend."

The goods of personal love, then, are agent-centered goods and objects of agent-centered interests. Because they involve identity beliefs in the way they do, they generate partial reasons for action. Because they involve an intrinsic interest in the interests of others, they are social rather than individual interests. Because they involve a desire for intimacy not found in im-

---

6. See Derek Parfit, *Reasons and Persons* (Oxford: Clarendon Press, 1984), 293–97. There Parfit attempts to refute Bernard Williams's view that loving another as a person-token rather than as a person-type involves loving a particular body. But he denies that this means that loving another involves loving a person-type. For Parfit, the object of love is a series-person, and a series-person is a particular individual. Whether this means he would agree with the above claims about identity beliefs, I do not know. For Williams's view, see Bernard Williams, *Problems of the Self* (Cambridge: Cambridge University Press, 1973), 80–81.

partial relationships, they are communal interests. When accompanied in our lives with the commitment of an agent of integrity, they generate many of our partial norms. Since it is clear that we relate to others differently through the partial norms of love and the impartial norms of simple respect, it remains to be seen how they are related in their regulative functions. For this, we need an account of the normative thoughts of a person who is both personally loving in a variety of ways and respectful of others. In the next chapter, I will address these issues as they pertain to respect and parental love.

9. The Normative Thoughts of Parental Love, Part I

Self-Restricting Normative Beliefs

1.

In part 2, I addressed the issue of how those who are believed to be worthy of respect appear within the deliberative field of a respectful person, and in chapter 8, I showed how in general loved ones appear within the deliberative field of the agent who is both respectful and personally loving. Here, I begin to address the integration problems faced by the agent of integrity in the thick sense, starting with the issue of how respect for self and others is to be integrated with parental love for a child.

In chapter 1, I argued that any acceptable theory must satisfy certain methodological requirements, among them that the theory must be context-sensitive and contextually thorough and that the theory must be subject to the integration test. The relationship between these requirements is that the integration test cannot be applied without thorough sensitivity to context. Nowhere is this more essential than in the individual chapters on the normative thoughts associated with various forms of personal love, beginning here with parental love for a child and continuing in chapters 10 through 14. The sensitivity and the thoroughness of these chapters are necessary for the argument regarding the integration test in chapter 15. The reader, then, should expect the arguments to turn on the details of the analysis. There is no shortcut method available. Moreover, the analysis is cumulative: Later analysis builds on and is dependent on previous analysis. Indeed, much of the framework for the analysis in the chapters that follow depends on the framework developed in this and the next chapter. I say all this in part to explain why there are two chapters on parental love and to set the expectations of the reader; careful and patient work here is to pay off later.

The goal of this chapter is to give a structural account of the normative thoughts of a person who has self-respect and who is also a loving parent. The next chapter focuses on someone who is respectful of others and who is a loving parent. What we need to imagine is a person whose deliberative field is such that his or her children appear in consciousness as good, as something to be cherished, nurtured, supported, and the like. But also within that deliberative field appear thoughts of the agent and others as persons worthy of respect. In addition, we need to imagine various kinds of problematic situations (to recall Peirce's phrase) such an agent might face. I hope to show that when we employ the previous features of our analysis, we can understand a great deal about what is rational for such a person in these contexts.

The account, I believe, will solve three problems. The first I call Stocker's problem, a problem regarding relationships between obligation and motivation. The idea here is to give an account of how a sense of obligation arises within the psychology of a person who is both respectful in the relevant senses and who is parentally loving. In the end, I hope to show that the Aristotelian scheme can accommodate a strong sense of obligation, though not the one Kant sought or the one the "peculiar institution" conception of morality requires. The second problem I call the integration problem. It involves the issue of how to understand the normative thoughts of a person who is both personally loving and respectful of self and others in a way that integrates all the normative concerns of the agent. So construed the integration problem reflects a direct concern with the notion of full rationality, and I show how the Aristotelian criteria of finality and self-sufficiency function in this regard. The third and final problem is the priorities problem. It involves the issue of how to understand the priorities of a loving agent regarding loved ones, on the one hand, and those the agent respects but does not love, on the other. The solution to this problem provides the solution to the integration problem and demonstrates that the partial norms of personal love and the impartial norms of simple respect are symmetrical in their regulative functions. Moreover, the analysis shows how reflective endorsement can achieve full rationality without an impartial decision procedure. If I am successful, then I will have shown how the Aristotelian conception of practical reason is better equipped to provide an account of parental love and impartial respect than any Kantian account. More important, the analysis provides a filling out of the Aristotelian model as it applies to the thick conception of integrity.

One of the difficulties to be encountered is that the topic of parental love is not one that is discussed much among Kantians. This is certainly not because Kantians somehow love their children less than Aristotelians, any more than Aristotelians respect others less than Kantians. It is because love has little, if anything, to do with morality on their view, which is not to say that love is unimportant to them. Nevertheless, one would expect some extensive discussion of parental obligations, since a great deal of a parent's life is devoted to caring for the child. It is hardly the case, as Kant himself claimed about friendship, that parenthood develops only the minor virtues of life.[1] Anyone believing so has simply not been a parent. Yet there is very little at all said about parental obligations in the current proliferation of internalist readings of Kant. Search as you may the writings of Barbara Herman, David Cummiskey, Henry Allison, Christine Korsgaard, Marcia Baron, Onora O'Neill, Thomas Hill, and Alan Donagan and you will find very little on how the CI procedure generates parental obligations and what those obligations are.[2] To be fair to Korsgaard: Her view, as I understand it in *The Sources of Normativity*, is that personal relationships are independent sources of obligation, and hence parental obligations are not generated through the CI procedure.[3] But this seems a revision of Kant, though it is open to question whether it is a friendly amendment to his agenda. It is certainly from my point of view a sensible departure. Cummiskey's account has the advantage over the others that there is a general principle for determining the role of such obligations. They are determined by the consequences of parental roles in maximizing respect for Kantian dignity. As far as I know, all the other Kantian internalists are nonconsequentialists. How, then, does the CI procedure on their view settle the priorities of a respectful and loving parent in the various contexts in which conflicts might arise in a way that allows such an agent to integrate these kinds of concerns? Without an answer to this question, an answer that must be given in some

1. See Immanuel Kant, *Lectures on Ethics*, trans. Louis Infield (Indianapolis: Hackett, 1963), 209.

2. O'Neill has discussed parental obligations in "Begetting, Bearing, and Rearing," in *Having Children: Philosophical and Legal Reflections on Parenthood*, eds. Onora O'Neill and William Ruddick (New York: Oxford University Press, 1979), 25–38, but there is no discussion of Kant there. I will say more about O'Neill later.

3. This might seem to raise the possibility of the irrationality of morality in cases in which the obligations from independent sources override the obligations of morality from a practical point of view. Though this seems to be suggested by Korsgaard in *The Sources of Normativity*, it is not her view. Rather, she believes only the weaker view that morality does not *always* override these independent obligations, which is different from the view that these independent obligations *sometimes* override moral obligations. Korsgaard has confirmed that it is the weaker view she holds in personal correspondence. To maintain the stronger view would be too great a departure from Kant to call a revision.

detail, the claim that Kantian respect for persons is an asymmetrical regulative norm in relationship to parental love is not one that can be philosophically tested. Currently, we have no account of parental obligations from the internalist Kantians; thus we are forced to construct various possibilities. Consequently, I will simply do my best to consider what are plausible "Kantian" deliberative patterns, along with other kinds of impartial patterns, in arguing for the Aristotelian view. In doing so, I will studiously avoid the kind of caricature that sometimes arises on both sides of debates about Kant.

2.

Recall from chapter 2 the dispute between Michael Stocker and the Kantians, Marcia Baron and Barbara Herman. There I argued that the Kantians were right against Stocker that as his examples are formulated they do not adequately recognize the regulative function of impartial norms. But I also argued that there are contexts that are marked by three features. These are contexts in which (i) we feel obligated to our loved ones, and (ii) were it not for them we would feel obligated by respect for others to reverse our priorities, yet (iii) to act on this sense of obligation in such contexts is not to act disrespectfully. To claim that there are such contexts is to claim that in some contexts impartial respect is a not a dominant norm. It is also to claim that in some contexts love is a dominant norm relative to impartial respect. Such contexts raise special motivational problems regarding a sense of obligation.

According to Stocker, loving acts must be motivated directly by love, and when apparently loving acts are done from nonloving motives they cease to be loving acts.[4] This is true, but Stocker suggests that if an act is done from a sense of obligation, it cannot be done from love, and this, I believe, is false. For although it is true that if some acts are done from a sense of obligation they are not loving acts, it does not follow that all loving acts are devoid of a sense of obligation. I say this because I cannot see what it would mean to say that one person loves another—at least in the central cases—without implying that the lover has some sense of obligation toward the loved one. Nevertheless, Stocker is right about the second point, that loving acts cannot be externally motivated and remain loving acts. The prob-

4. See Michael Stocker, "The Schizophrenia of Modern Ethical Theories," in *The Virtues: Contemporary Essays on Moral Character*, ed. Robert B. Kruschwitz and Robert C. Roberts (Belmont, Calif.: Wadsworth, 1986), 36–45.

lem then is to show that there is a sense of obligation that is generated by love itself in cases where one has a sense of obligation to one's loved ones. The task of matching love as a motive to a sense of obligation in these cases I refer to as Stocker's problem. I turn now to its solution.

3.

To clarify the view of felt obligation I endorse here and its Kantian contrast, I distinguish between what I call a normative belief and a deontic belief. A normative belief is one that can be expressed in the form, A ought to do x. A deontic belief is a normative belief that, in normal circumstances, results in a felt sense of obligation when the agent sincerely believes it. This is despite whether the agent actually does what the agent believes he or she ought to do. The concept of felt obligation, then, is a phenomenological concept that requires explanation in terms of an agent's normative beliefs and other factors.

Influenced by Kant, many thinkers understand the notion of acting from a felt sense of obligation as acting contrary to inclination or, at least, a willingness to so act should contrary inclination arise to oppose one's moral beliefs. Themselves sufficient for motivation, moral beliefs require (for Kant) an affective contrast for the emergence of a felt sense of obligation. This affective contrast is natural inclination. Therefore, for Kant, while natural inclination plays no positive role in moral motivation, it is nonetheless crucial to explaining the phenomenological features of deontic beliefs and a felt sense of duty.

Kant imagined three different kinds of beings in relationship to normative beliefs and a felt sense of obligation: God, who is a purely rational being without natural inclinations, for whom normative beliefs are never deontic beliefs; human beings, who are impurely rational beings who have both natural inclinations and a felt sense of obligation, for whom normative beliefs are deontic beliefs; and nonhuman animals, who are purely nonrational beings who have only natural inclinations, who lack both deontic beliefs and a sense of obligation. The reason that only beings of the second sort can have a felt sense of obligation and whose normative beliefs are deontic beliefs is that a felt sense of obligation cannot arise except for a being who can experience a conflict of motives of different kinds. God has only moral motives. Thus God's moral beliefs do not come into conflict with inclination in a way that can produce a felt sense of obligation. Similarly, the nonrational being of pure inclination does not experience a conflict of different kinds of motives in a way that can produce the relevant phenomenon.

Insofar as the Kantian view of moral motivation turns on this account of a felt sense of obligation, it is simply mistaken. It is clearly mistaken in the case of a parent's love for a child, as well as in other cases of personal love. The mistake is not that a felt sense of obligation cannot arise within the consciousness of a being incapable of experiencing a conflict between different kinds of motives. This much is correct. The mistake is that such conflicts cannot arise within "natural inclinations," which is a mistake founded on the Kantian claim that all human inclinations are of the same kind. They are not. The discussion of the interests of the person of integrity shows this, as will the discussion of the various forms of personal love.

Central to understanding the argument that follows in this regard is a distinction between self-restricting and other-restricting normative beliefs and their structure. Suppose you believe that you ought to do something for another person. So stated, we cannot tell whether this is a self-restricting or an other-restricting belief. Put in the second person, the explicit logical form of a self-restricting belief is "You ought to do x for B rather than do y for yourself." Implied in this form is that there is some interest of yours that is being restricted for the sake of some interest of B. If you have such a belief, then you believe that in the context B has an interest that is normatively prior to some interest of your own. Call B's interest in such a context a restricting interest, since it is the interest that you see as rationally serving as the grounds for restricting the pursuit of another interest. It is self-restricting because it restricts one of your own interests. Call your interest that is being restricted a restricted interest. Any normative belief, then, at least of the sort we will be concerned with, has two dimensions: a restricting base, which is a set of interests for the sake of which restrictions apply, and a restricted scope, which is a set of interests that are restricted for the sake of other interests.

The logical form of an other-restricting normative belief (again, put in the second person) is "You ought to do x for B rather than do y for C." What makes this "other-restricting" is not that you are restricted from satisfying one of your own interests for the sake of B's interests but from satisfying the interests of a third party, C, for the sake of B's interests. The restricting base is the same in both cases, namely, some interest belonging to B, but the restricted scope differs. In self-restricting beliefs, the scope is some set of interests that belong to the agent, in this case, yourself. In other-restricting beliefs, the scope is some set of interests that belong to a third party, C. The thought is that our love for our loved ones gives some priority to their interests over other interests of our own, and this is reflected in our normative beliefs. On the other hand, our love for our loved ones gives some priority to their interests over the interests of other people, and this too is reflected in our normative beliefs.

In what follows, I will show how parental love itself can generate a sense of obligation that accompanies both self-restricting and other-restricting normative beliefs. This contrasts with the Kantian view that only impartial respect construed as a function of pure practical reason can generate a sense of obligation, either as a regulative or as a determinate norm. Recall that on the Kantian view a motive is a moral one only if it arises from impartial respect either in its regulative or in its determinate function. I will show, however, that it is the determinate norm of parental love itself that often generates the sense of obligation, even though such love is regulated by respect for others. Moreover, even when impartial respect is the determinate norm, it alone does not generate the sense of obligation. This is because in contexts in which such respect is determinate parental love functions and motivates as a regulative norm. I will begin with self-restricting normative beliefs and take up other-restricting beliefs in the next chapter.

4.

Consider the conditions under which we would be willing to say that a person has parental love, as opposed to some other kind of concern, for a child. Suppose that prompted by your fondness for children you were considering becoming a parent, yet you were unsure of whether you were willing to take on the commitments of nurturing and caring for the child. Given the complexities of modern life, there is certainly room for doubt about taking on such commitments. There is even room for doubt that one wants children more than one wants other things. But what if you had *no* inclination to take on such commitments or to evaluate yourself in terms of such commitments? Whatever sense of fondness you might have for children it would certainly not be one of incipient parental love. For it is intrinsic to parental love that it includes the notion of commitment to one's children. Of course, one might love one's children and fail in one's commitments, but indifference to evaluating oneself in the light of such failures is surely one of the most telling signs of a lack of parental love. Thus the person who has parental love is dispositionally sensitive to beliefs about his or her qualities as a committed parent.

This sensitivity of disposition naturally leads to a sense of obligation that has its source in parental love. The first step in seeing this is under-standing how, as a loving parent, you could acquire the self-restricting nor-mative belief that you ought to do something for the sake of your child. The second step is understanding how such a normative belief under some normal circumstances results in a felt sense of obligation. This is to see how such a normative belief could be a deontic belief. Taken together, the two steps result in an understanding of how parental love can generate deontic beliefs in loving parents toward their children.

Consider the first step.

To have parental love for a child is to have the five interests of personal love for the child as set out in chapter 8, on the general features of love. Your child will be deeply interested in your affection, in sharing a relation-ship with you, and in being your beneficiary in a variety of ways, and it will be deeply important to you that these interests of your child are satisfied. Your child will also be interested in his or her own welfare, and, again, that these interests are satisfied will be deeply important to you. Finally, you will have a deep interest in your child's character, as a good for the child fundamental to his or her own self-respect. Moreover, you will experience these parental interests in a way that your child's interests in these regards are felt to be significantly more important than some of your nonparental interests. Also, you will feel that these interests of your child are signifi-cantly more important than at least some other interests, even categorical ones, of persons you do not love. All this follows from the previous analy-sis of how a loved one appears within the loving person's deliberative field. Thus it is easy to see that by way of your love for a child, you could have normative beliefs of various sorts regarding her.[5]

For example, you might consider the various factors you think to be relevant to a particular decision. As a result, you might believe that you ought to show your affections to your child rather than devote time to your entertainment interests. Surely if you never believe that your child's inter-ests in your affections are of such importance, then your love for your child is doubtful. The point here is that from what we know about love as an in-tentional dispositional state and what we assume about your character (that you are a loving parent) we can know that you cannot have parental love for your child and in all contexts be without self-restricting normative be-liefs regarding her.

5. This would make sense of Korsgaard's claim previously alluded to that per-sonal relationships are independent sources of normativity.

As a loving parent, some of your self-restricting normative beliefs will include restrictions on behalf of your child's interest in your parental affections. Others will include restrictions on behalf of the other interests mentioned above: the child's interests in a shared relationship with you, in being your beneficiary, and the child's welfare and character interests. As a dimension of your normative beliefs as a loving parent, these interests constitute the base of restricting interests alluded to earlier. Thus you have parental love for your child only if you have some self-restricting normative beliefs regarding these interests of your child in some contexts.

The scope dimension of restricted interests will vary, depending on what is at stake for the child and the parent. But, in any event, you have parental love for your child only if, in some contexts, you have this self-restricting normative belief: that some of your important noncategorical interests ought to be restricted on behalf of some of the interests mentioned above regarding your child. Thus your parental love for your child involves a commitment to her, which, in turn, involves self-restricting normative beliefs of various scope and base dimensions.

Theoretically, the base and scope dimensions of self-restricting normative beliefs can be related to each other in a wide variety of ways. The restricing concern for the child's character, for example, might restrict in scope the parent's interest in associating with another person, especially if the other person's influence would be detrimental to the development of the child's character. Another possibility is that the restricting concern for the child's interest in being the beneficiary of the parent might restrict the parent's interest in recreation. At a deeper level, concern for the child's welfare might restrict the parent's vital interests, the interests in being alive. For it is clearly not a thought foreign to parental love that the importance of the child's life might come before the parent's own. This is true at least in some contexts. In these cases and many more, if you are a loving parent, you have *as a function of loving* your child the self-restricting normative belief that you ought to do something for the sake of your child rather than do something for the sake of yourself in terms of your nonparental interests. Absent these normative beliefs, we are unable to make sense of a person as a loving parent.

Thus we have a partial solution to Stocker's problem. We see that the dispositional state of parental love generates normative beliefs. To complete the solution, we must see how parental love generates deontic beliefs and a felt sense of obligation. I will turn to that issue later, but before I do I must address the integration problem and the priorities problem as they involve self-restricting normative beliefs.

5.

Here the integration problem is this: How does one, as an agent, integrate the base concerns in the love for a child with the various concerns for oneself? This problem arises only when we recognize that the agent has at least these two different kinds of concerns to incorporate into his or her life. Integration is necessary because of the multiplicity of goods that appear within the agent's deliberative field. The solution to this problem requires that the agent has some reasonably settled set of priorities that allows for integrating these concerns across deliberative contexts. What this set of priorities is to be for a loving parent is the priorities problem.

We have seen that if one settles conflicts between the interests of the child and one's other interests by always favoring these other interests one is simply not a loving parent. Thus an egoistic deliberative pattern as the fundamental mode of practical reasoning is irrational for a loving parent. In Aristotelian terms, the child would not have the proper place as an end in the egoistic life, which shows that the egoistic life fails to satisfy the criterion of finality for a loving parent. In Kantian terms, the child would not be an end-in-itself. But it is difficult to see how parental love would require the opposite set of priorities of always favoring the interests of the child over his or her own, regardless of the deliberative context. Love is not that demanding. Nor is that set of priorities consistent with self-respect, and what we are seeking is the priorities of a person who is both personally loving and self-respectful. In Aristotelian terms, the agent himself would not, on the priorities in question, sufficiently appear as an end in the way of life structured by those priorities; hence, a failure regarding the criterion of finality. From this we can conclude unsurprisingly that a purely altruistic deliberative pattern is irrational for a loving parent who has self-respect. Thus the solution to the priorities problem must construe the priorities to allow *both* for self-concern and for concern for the child. An examination of the contexts in which these concerns can emerge will show that the patterns of practical deliberation open to a self-respecting and parentally loving parent are best accounted for on the Aristotelian model. This is because the norms of self-respect and parental love are symmetrical in their regulative functions.

Consider in this regard the following contexts, bearing in mind the deliberative patterns that are rational in these contexts. If the Aristotelian analysis is correct, it should show what is rational in these contexts for the agent and should demonstrate how the agent could be rational without an impartial decision procedure. Now, consider the contexts.

Contexts in Which the Interests of the Child Are Categorical and the Interests of the Parent Are Noncategorical

The previous analysis has already shown that in contexts in which the interests of the child appear within the parent's deliberative field as categorical and the parent's as noncategorical the loving parent will give priority to the interests of the child. No doubt a Kantian analysis would agree. But it is important here to see how the Aristotelian agent would reflectively endorse these priorities. The denial of these priorities projected over a life would leave no place for the loved one as the kind of end she appears to be within the parent's deliberative field. If the child appears within the loving parent's deliberative field as a categorical good, which is surely the case with a loving parent, then the child cannot be seen as a good that allows noncategorical interests of the parent or anyone else to be of more importance than the child's categorical interests. Reflective endorsement of these priorities is achieved not by means of an impartial decision procedure but simply by getting a clear picture of everything of importance within the deliberative field and placed in the context of a life as a whole. Once this picture is clear, the agent's character draws him to the alternative that includes a place for the relevant goods. Also, it is equally important to see that the alternative set of priorities, once vividly pictured in a way of life by the agent, fails the criteria of finality and self-sufficiency in two ways. For the way of life envisioned on the alternative priorities does not include a place for the child as a beloved end, nor does the agent himself appear there as an end worthy of respect. No loving parent could possibly maintain self-respect at the clear and persistent neglect of the child's categorical interests in favor of his or her own noncategorical interests. Hence the way of life envisioned by the alternative set of priorities is viewed by a respectful and loving parent as neither final nor self-sufficient. Consequently, the norms of parental love and self-respect converge as determinate norms in contexts of this sort, and the rightness of action is the nonaccidental result of its motives.

We should note here the Aristotelian form of practical deliberation and reflective endorsement. First practical alternatives are projected in terms of how they structure a way of life, and then that way of life is evaluated in terms of finality and self-sufficiency in relationship to the goods that appear within the agent's deliberative field. When we enrich this process by structuring practical contexts in terms of the philosophical psychology that employs the categorical/noncategorical distinction regarding interests, we get a more informative conception of practical reason than is found in Aristotle's doctrine of the mean. In fact, what we get is an enriched notion of the mean. The search for the mean is simply the filtering of one's desires, sentiments, and values through the process of envisioning how alternative priorities structure different ways of life relative to what appear within one's deliberative field. Notice that when we do this in the current context, we have no problem rationally choosing between the alternatives without the aid of an impartial decision procedure. Hence the rationality and rightness of action is found in the mean, that is, in the alternative that structures a way of life that achieves integrative success vis-à-vis finality and self-sufficiency. What Aristotle lacked to make his doctrine of the mean workable was a more fine tuned philosophical psychology.

Contexts in Which the Interests of the Parent Are Categorical and the Interests of the Child Are Noncategorical

Before considering these contexts, it is important to be clear that, at least in central cases, the interests of a loving parent in the base concerns of the child are categorical for the parent when they are categorical for the child, once the parent reflectively sees what is involved. This means that the concerns that are central to the psychology of the child are central to the psychology of the loving parent, with two qualifications for the central cases: (i) the interests at stake are indeed categorical interests rather than ones merely thought to be so by the child, and (ii) the categorical interests of the child are consistent with the most fundamental categorical commitments of the parent. This would mean that the loving parent would have the normative belief that the categorical interests of the child are actually worthwhile and worthy of respect. With these qualifications, then, the claim stands, I believe. For example, not every instance of a child's concern for a parent's affection is categorical, but the interest in some threshold level of such affection is. Thus, when parental affection is a categorical concern for the child, it is a categorical concern for the loving parent. Therefore, any conflict of interest the loving parent experiences regarding the categorical interests of the child involves a conflict *within* the parent's categorical interests.

The kind of conflict important here is one in which the parent's self-respect is in conflict with the noncategorical base concerns of the child. Where these concerns do not reach the categorical threshold level, the self-respecting and loving parent will not give priority to the base concerns of the child. To do so would reveal dispositions antithetical to self-respect. A self-respecting but loving parent does not feel self-reproach for requiring the child to make some sacrifices for the sake of the parent, especially where the interests for the child are noncategorical and the interests of the parent are categorical. In this regard, the concept of parental love reveals within our conceptual scheme the regulating influence of self-respect. But note that in such a context, the thoughts that are sufficient for guidance are simply those that reveal the kinds of interests at stake. Once these thoughts are clear, given the character of the agent, there is no need for a decision procedure. Given the options, the problematic situation is resolved the moment the agent sees that on one option the agent appears as an end within a way of life that satisfies the criterion of finality and on the other a crucial good is missing and the criterion of self-sufficiency is not met. Assuming that these options include in the context all the relevant variables, the agent does the right thing for the right reason, namely, it is the rational thing to do, all things considered. Reflective endorsement is achieved without the need for an impartial decision procedure, which is what we expect on the Aristotelian view. What is needed, however, for an agent of the sort in question, is a clear understanding of what is at stake for both the parent and the child. It is this that presents the alternatives to the agent as elements in different ways of life.

That these contexts unquestionably reveal the regulative influence of self-respect on parental love can be seen in another way. To cater to the non-categorical interests of the child in such contexts at the expense of the parent's categorical interests would be tantamount to servility. And though there are servile conceptions of parenthood, it is important to see that both the Kantian and the Aristotelian models preclude such conceptions. The Kantian model precludes servility by requiring that self-respect is asymmetrical in its regulative function regarding parental love. The Aristotelian model precludes servility by requiring a symmetrical relationship between the norms of parental love and self-respect, which is explained by the fact that the interests at stake for the parent play a certain role in his psychology. On the other hand, the kind of catering considered here is one in which parental love is an asymmetrical regulative norm. I see no reason, then, why the best interpretation of the CI procedure would have any difficulties yielding rational results in these contexts in terms of setting the agent's priorities. But then the Aristotelian model has no difficulties either, as long as parental love functions as a regulative norm in these contexts, which the analysis of the previous contexts reveals is true. The Kantian model, however, fails in context-sensitivity here, not because it requires that self-respect is the determinate norm in these contexts, but because it cannot explain in these contexts the regulative function of parental love.

Contexts in Which Both the Interests of the Parent and the Interests of the Child are Categorical

These are philosophically very interesting contexts, and they have important implications for a conception of practical reason. Where the concerns of both the parent and the child do reach the categorical threshold level, the self-respecting and loving parent will reach a deliberative impasse, experience a nondeliberative change in his or her identifying thoughts, or experience a categorical aversion to life. Recall here the discussion of practical deliberation in chapter 4 in the context of the thin conception of integrity.

In the case of a deliberative impasse, the problem is that priorities have no way of being established. For a self-respecting and loving parent, there is a problem here. It is seeing how self-respect could be retained for a loving parent by deliberating to a sacrifice of the categorical goods of the beloved child. So it is difficult to think of a deliberative impasse here in the sense of the inability to sacrifice one of *two* competing categorical goods. Recall the discussion of Romeo's dilemma in chapter 7. Yet there could be an impasse in the sense that the situation presents no acceptable alternatives for the agent. In this regard, should such a conflict arise, what conception of self-respect could be saved for a loving parent? Put in Aristotelian terms, there is no way for the agent to see through to the future to a life that provides a place for either of the goods most fundamental to a self-respecting and loving parent, let alone those that make a way of life self-sufficient and final. Some such contexts will lead to the deliberative conclusion that one should end one's life, but this is not a case of deliberative impasse. Deliberative impasse is reached when not even that decision is possible; the agent is simply stultified about the direction of life. This is why not even reflection that employs the criteria of finality and self-sufficiency can always yield a rational result.

Imagine a woman who has a categorical aversion to bringing a child into the world because she cannot tolerate thoughts of herself as a procreator. The thoughts of being pregnant, giving birth, and either giving the child up for adoption or becoming a parent are practically inaccessible to her. Any reflection on such prospects threatens the deepest and most debilitating forms of depression. Yet, on the other hand, she has a categorical commitment that abortion is always wrong. Any reflection on the prospects of having ended the life of a fetus through abortion is just as devastating as the reflection on the previous thoughts about pregnancy. Imagine that she is raped and becomes pregnant. Assuming that these commitments are indeed categorical and that the situation does not force a change in her commitments, the woman is simply caught in a deliberative impasse. None of her alternatives gives her a way of maintaining her commitments, all of which reflect on her self-respect. Reflective endorsement of an alternative cannot be achieved due to the character of the agent and what she cares about, which is the point of the example. Of course, a self-respecting and loving parent need not have this woman's beliefs. Nevertheless, deliberative impasse is possible, even for the agent of integrity in the thick sense.

Now consider the second possibility of a nondeliberative change in the agent's identifying thoughts. Here I am imagining a case in which the demands of children are so extreme that they exterminate either love or self-respect. The conditions under which many women and some men have had to be parents have been such as to test either their loving capacities or their capacities for self-respect, or both. Think of how difficult it would be to maintain self-respect and be thought of merely as a servant of others. Also think of how such a struggle for a sense of dignity could test one's love. Moreover, these pressures could arise in contexts in which their origins were in conditions independent of the bad character of the children. To love is to be able to give of oneself, but it is not a necessary condition of love to be able to give of oneself endlessly. When the effort to give endlessly exhausts itself and there is no resource to give at all anymore, love has spent itself. When love has spent itself, the deliberative capacities of an agent have changed. Perhaps this is what happens in some contexts in which parents walk out on their families in order to preserve their sanity and self-respect. Notice that the account of rationality in these contexts is predicated on a change in the agent's character. Only by this change is the agent able to see through the problematic situation to a way of life that can meet the conditions of finality and self-sufficiency. Rationality and reflective endorsement become possible only with a nondeliberative change of character.

In some contexts, the loving and self-respecting parent will have a categorical aversion to life. This is because the agent will not undergo a nondeliberative change and will not perceive any alternative way of life that will allow for the preservation of both self-respect and the categorical goods of the child. In some of these cases, the agent's sense of self-respect— embedded as it is in parental love—will *require* the sacrifice of the agent's vital interests for the sake of the categorical interests of the child. This requirement will be from the agent's own point of view. Imagine, for example, a loving parent facing the choice of either being sent to the concentration camps or sending his or her child there.[6] Thus, from parental love for your child, you might have a categorical aversion that generates the normative belief, "I ought to give up my life for my child." Parental love, then, like self-respect, can give one reasons for dying. From the first-person point of view, you can foresee in these contexts a future way of life, but that life does not include you; yet it does include those things you value more than your own life. This is a perfectly coherent Aristotelian thought on the objectivist understanding of eudaimonia

These observations regarding contexts involving the categorical interests of both the child and the parent reveal that there are four subcontexts: one in which there is no conflict between the interests of parent and child and three in which there is tension that might involve the parent's self-respect. The first sort of context is not one that presents the parent with a problematic situation, because the categorical interests of the child and the parent coincide. Tragically, this is not always possible. It is when conflict does occur that the latter three contexts become possibilities. As we have seen, one possibility involves deliberative impasse, another nondeliberative change in the agent's conception of self-respect, and the third agent breakdown in the form of a categorical aversion to life. I cannot see how to explain the phenomena of the last three subcontexts without abandoning the concept of respect as an asymmetrical regulative norm.

In the case of deliberative impasse, the norm of self-respect in relationship to the norm of parental love is indeterminate. Neither love nor respect can regulate the other, and it is just this that prevents deliberative resolution. What this shows is that our sense of self-respect runs up against our sense of love in contexts in which it gives us no guidance. This seems clearly contrary to the Kantian commitment to the asymmetry of respect as a regulative norm in practical reason. It will not do here to claim that this is a caricature of Kant, unless the Kantian can successfully show how (i) the CI procedure yields a clear result in such contexts and (ii) following this result is something of which we are psychologically capable. I am unaware of any place in the literature where such contexts are discussed by Kantians, especially as these contexts are presented as cases in which the CI procedure is to be applied. The failure to take seriously the importance of categorical interests to practical reason has led Kantians to overlook important decision contexts. In this sense, they have been lacking in both context-sensitivity

6. This is, of course, a variation on Sophie's situation in William Styron's novel, *Sophie's Choice* (New York: Random House, 1976).

and contextual thoroughness. Moreover, the same problem arises for any imaginable impartial norm, including utilitarian sympathy.

Of course, Kantians can say that I have the facts of human psychology right here but that these facts only reveal that humans, at least those who are loving parents, are not fully rational. To make this response, however, is to revert to a methodology that begins with an a priori conception of rational agency. And I have already given reasons for rejecting that methodology: Our conception of rational agency should be tightly connected to the study of ourselves.[7] Moreover, on the enriched Aristotelian account, we have a very clear explanation of why impasse occurs. *It is only by not considering how the criteria of finality and self-sufficiency are employed in practical reason that we are tempted to call persons who are broken by these contexts irrational.*

In the case of nondeliberative change that allows resolution, what we find is a conception of love and a conception of self-respect that cannot maintain themselves. Neither adequately makes room for the other, and this too undermines the asymmetry of respect as a regulative norm. It is only where both love and respect conflict in a way that pushes the agent to revise both conceptions that we have nondeliberative change. That one's sense of self-respect is subject to pressures of this sort reveals that we do not think that self-respect is invulnerable to partial regulating influences. Had both the agent's sense of self-respect and his conception of parental love been sufficiently sensitive to the regulative influences of each other deliberation would not have stymied in the way that forces nondeliberative change.

Finally, there are contexts in which the only choice left open results in a categorical aversion to life. These too reveal the lack of asymmetry in our conception of self-respect. If one cannot will to go on living because of tragic choice involving one's children and this is consistent with a conception of self-respect, then surely self-respect on this conception is sensitive to the regulating influences of parental love in practical reason. That is, practical reason just is a complex integrative function of our consciousness, including our cognitive, conative, and affective capacities. It is not a function of respect as a purely cognitive faculty regulating the more pathological features of our psychology. It is the commitment to the latter that led Kant to

7. I made this point earlier against Korsgaard, but I do not think it applies to her in this context. This is because she thinks there can be deep, real conflicts between independent sources of normativity. But this, as she recognizes, is a departure from Kant.

deny the rationality of suicide in these contexts. But those who commit suicide in these contexts are not necessarily lacking in self-respect.[8] We are led to thinking so only by not seeing how the criteria of finality and self-sufficiency bear on some of these choices, which explains a certain kind of insensitivity on Kant's part. The so-called Kantian perfect duty not to commit suicide is predicated either on a strict procedural interpretation of Kantian universalizability tests or on the substantive interpretation of human dignity as being absolute, nonscalar, nonadditive, and immune to trade-offs. But what is insensitive about either interpretation is that each obscures our view of what is actually happening in many cases of suicide. On the other hand, if we employ the criteria of finality and self-sufficiency, we can see very clearly what is at stake.

Contexts in Which the Interests of the Child Are Important Noncategorical Interests and the Interests of the Parent Are Minor

It is tempting to say that the parent will give priority to the child's interests, but reflection reveals that such conflicts are hard to imagine. The reason is that if an interest is important to the child, it is important (on reflection) to the loving parent. Of course, it is possible that the parent has other important interests and that they are more important than the child's interests. Usually the gauge in these cases for a loving parent is the relative importance to the child of its interests versus the relative importance of the other interests of the parent. Also, there is the additional parental preference for a child's satisfaction. This is why, barring other considerations, there are so few close calls for a loving parent. The child's interests come first unless there is a significantly greater degree of relative importance of the parent's other interests. To deny this seems contrary to both self-respect and parental love. What would it be to be a self-respecting and loving parent and yet give priority to one's minor interests over the important, even though noncategorical, interests of one's child? That we think in this way seems best explained by the fact that our conception of self-respect for a loving parent is regulated by parental love and that our conception of parental love for a self-respecting parent is regulated by self-respect. If so, then these contexts too reveal the Aristotelian model of practical reason.

8. I discuss this issue extensively in *Dignity and Vulnerability: Strength and Quality of Character* (Berkeley: University of California Press, 1997), especially in chapter 7.

They reveal that from the viewpoint of life as a whole the beloved child can take its proper place in the loving parent's priorities only in a way that places more importance on the child's important noncategorical interests than on the parent's minor interests. Only so can the loving and self-respecting parent see his or her way of life as final and self-sufficient.

Contexts in Which the Child's Minor Noncategorical Interests Come Last in the Priorities of the Self-Respecting and Loving Parent, except for the Parent's Minor Interests

The parent's minor interests have a similar relative importance to the minor interests of the child as in conflicts between the parent's and child's important noncategorical interests.

These, then, are priorities built into the dispositions of a loving parent. They generate normative thoughts that, along with other thoughts, provide guidance for the loving and self-respecting parent in how to resolve practical matters of living the life of a parent. In this case, they are priorities that set the goals and limits of self-restriction as they apply to the parent's interests relative to those of the child. If you are a loving parent to your child as well as a self-respecting person, you will have these priorities reflected in your normative thoughts. The difficulty with the Kantian account is that it is not contextually sensitive to the regulative role parental love plays in practical reason in these contexts. Of course, parental love does not play this role for those who are either not self-respecting or not parentally loving. This is why the rationality of these norms is character-relative.

6.

It does not follow, of course, from your having a normative belief that it is for you a deontic belief. Showing how the self-restricting normative beliefs of parental love can generate a felt sense of obligation is the second step in the solution to Stocker's problem. Here we are to imagine those contexts in which parental love is the determinate norm that generates a self-restricting normative belief. In these contexts, the experienced conflict between nonparental interests and parental interests in the concerns for the child might be so slight that there is no felt sense of obligation. But, even for the most loving and dedicated parent, this will not always be so. That a parent sometimes feels a real conflict between parental responsibilities and even minor noncategorical interests is not a sign of a lack of parental love for the

child. Indeed, any child who expects a loving parent never to feel such conflict is overly demanding and should see the parent's sense of obligation as
a sign of love. The source of this sense of obligation is the parent's loving
concern for the interests of the child, and this concern operates to check the
contrary inclinations of the parent. On such occasions, the parent's self-
restricting normative belief is a deontic belief because it results in the phenomenon of a felt sense of obligation.

The loving parent's disposition to self-reproach is also illuminating in
this regard. Even in cases in which there is no significant contrary inclination, the normative beliefs are deontic beliefs in an important sense. The
parent *would* feel self-reproach were there a significant contrary inclination and the parent did not act on the self-restricting norms built into the
dispositions of a loving parent. Here it is not a decision procedure in the
sense associated with modern moral theory that yields the self-restricting
belief. Nor is the normative belief a belief in a *principle* that motivates the
action and serves to check contrary inclination. Thus there are not the kinds
of externalities Stocker rightly finds objectionable. Rather, both the belief
and the check on contrary inclination come directly from the source of parental love for the child, the direct concern for another. That is, the determinate norm in both the justificatory and motivational senses is parental
love. This is not to deny that respect is a regulative norm in this context, but
so are many other norms in the agent's life. The point is that the determinate norm generates both a normative belief and a sense of obligation.

Consider two examples. The first is quite like Stocker's example of Smith's
visit, except it is John visiting his daughter, Ann, in the hospital. When Ann
begins to praise John for his being such a loving father, he gives her the
Smith line about obligation: It really is "duty" rather than anything personal that brings him. This clearly will not do if we are to think of John as
a loving parent, and we can imagine the alienation Ann might feel toward
her father. Love is not like that. End of story.[9]

But consider another story about John and Ann. After several truly loving visits from her father, Ann comes home for her final period of conva-
lescence. Having received much attention from John, she becomes a bit demanding. The demands gradually increase to the point of trying her father's
well-known patience. He attempts to settle down for some leisurely reading after having been interrupted by Ann several times for some minor
thing just to get his attention. His impulse is to rebuke her harshly, more

9. Of course, by now it should be obvious that Kantian duty is not like that either, at least on the best interpretation of Kantian duty.

harshly than he would feel comfortable with afterward. But he catches himself. He believes that he ought not to speak harshly to her, despite his current inclination. Though he is clearly upset with her, he explains that she needs to show some concern for him. Ann, being the little psychologist she is, perceives the whole process. What she perceives is that her father loves her and that this allows him to treat her with love even when he is upset with her. She also perceives that his love for her does not permit her everything. That he has a contrary inclination does not alienate her from her father. Rather, that his love checks his contrary inclination reassures her of her place in her father's affections.

Without the notion of love as a check on contrary inclination, the phenomenon of parental self-reproach would not be as we know it. Of course, it is possible that out of a sense of duty someone could act as a loving parent would act toward a child, and this too could function as a check on contrary inclination. But this is clearly not the way we understand loving parents. So, embedded in the notion of parental self-reproach is the notion of parental self-restricting normative beliefs. These are sometimes accompanied by a felt sense of obligation on the part of the parent. When they are, they are deontic beliefs. Thus we have a solution to Stocker's problem, the integration problem, and the priorities problem as they pertain to the self-restricting normative and deontic beliefs of parental love. Admittedly, this is not the sense of obligation associated with what Bernard Williams has called "the peculiar institution." But I am not defending that conception of morality, for I do not believe it is defensible. Nevertheless, the sense of obligation associated with the conception of morality defended here does come from an all things considered point of view, a point of view of life as a whole in which some things are valued as ends and evaluated in terms of finality and self-sufficiency. It is just that "all things" are those things the agent cares about on reflection, namely, the kinds of things about which the agent of integrity in the thick sense cares.

7.

Thus far I have been speaking only of the parent's self-restricting thoughts. But these are not the only kinds of normative thoughts the loving parent will have. Such a parent will also have other-restricting normative beliefs, and as with self-restricting beliefs, we need a solution to Stocker's problem, the integration problem, and the priorities problem regarding them. I turn to these topics in the next chapter.

10. The Normative Thoughts of Parental Love, Part II
Other-restricting Normative Beliefs

1.

In the last chapter, I discussed the self-restricting normative thoughts of parental love. I showed in the process how the Aristotelian model can accommodate a strong sense of obligation—one that reflects a set of priorities that solves the integration problems of the agent of integrity who is both respectful and parentally loving. Moreover, the analysis was applied across a wide range of contexts and revealed that the regulative functions of parental love and self-respect are symmetrical in their regulative effects. The deficiency of the Kantian model was shown to be that it cannot accommodate the function of parental love as a regulative and determinate self-restricting norm.

In this chapter, I attempt to provide similar results regarding the other-restricting normative beliefs of the agent who is both parentally loving and respectful of others. Because other-restricting beliefs involve the interests of third parties, they are especially relevant to impartial norms. They raise the issue of how the respectful and parentally loving agent is to integrate impartial concern for third parties with the partial concern for a beloved child. This complicates matters because it requires an argument for the Aristotelian model that employs a two-pronged defense, one against Kantian consequentialism and another against Kantian deontology, both of which take internalist forms. Thus I begin with some discussion of how to understand that distinction, with the goal of laying some foundation for the arguments not only of this chapter but of later chapters as well. I argue that neither deontological nor consequentialist deliberative patterns, when given Kantian interpretations, are rational across the complete range of deliberative contexts faced by an agent of integrity who is both impartially respectful of others and parentally loving. I also consider another alternative represented by Samuel Scheffler's notion of an agent-centered prerogative.[1] But more on that later. In the process of the argument, I demonstrate the rationality of the Aristotelian model with its symmetrically regulating norms. I start, then, with some discussion of the difference between Kantian deontology and Kantian consequentialism.

2.

Taxonomies can be tiresome and irrelevant, but when it comes to evaluating rival conceptual schemes they are indispensable. As preparation for the argument for the Aristotelian model, I will try to keep the tedium to a minimum, consistent with what is necessary for the inquiry. Important here is the following general taxonomy of normative conceptual schemes:

I. Impartial consequentialism
  A. Direct
  B. Indirect

II. Nonconsequentialism
  A. Prerogative
  B. Deontology
    1. Action-type
    2. Personal relations

As we gain some understanding of this general taxonomy, I will attempt to show how it can take Kantian forms. Thus there will be Kantian consequentialism of both direct and indirect versions: Kantian nonconsequentialism of the prerogative and the deontological sort; and Kantian deontology of an action-type and a personal relations sort.

An impartial consequentialist conceptual scheme is one that has both a conception of value and a conception of obligation. (Hereafter, when I refer to consequentialism I will mean impartial consequentialism, unless otherwise noted.) The conception of obligation states that what one ought to do is to maximize good consequences, to act in a way that is most likely to result in the best available state of affairs. The conception of value is one that provides impartial criteria for ranking consequences or states of affairs from best to worst. Thus the theory of value makes possible the implementation of the theory of obligation: Ranking consequences or states of affairs from best to worst is necessary for maximizing good consequences. Utilitarianism is, of course, the clearest case of impartial consequentialism.

So understood, consequentialism comes in both direct and indirect ver-

---

1. See Samuel Scheffler, *The Rejection of Consequentialism* (Oxford: Oxford University Press, 1982); George W. Harris, "A Paradoxical Departure from Consequentialism," *Journal of Philosophy* 86, no. 2 (February 1989): 90–102.

sions. Direct versions construe good consequences as the causal consequence of individual acts; indirect versions construe good consequences as the causal consequence of any one thing or a combination of a variety of things. Most prominent among these are either the adoption of a set of rules for a general practice or the development of a set of character traits for living a life. In each case, the general practice and the set of character traits are determined to be "optimific" in terms of whether they result in the best state of affairs on impartial criteria.

With these distinctions, we can formulate two kinds of consequentialist deliberative patterns, patterns of deliberation that result in practical conclusions. A direct consequentialist deliberative pattern has the form, A ought to do x because x is likely to result in the best available state of affairs on some impartial value, V. With one caveat, an indirect consequentialist deliberative pattern has a rather complicated form, which can vary depending on the pattern of indirection. If formulated in terms of rules for a practice, it can be stated as: A ought to do x because x is required by a rule in a rule-governed practice that is most likely to result in the best available state of affairs on some impartial value, V. Stated in terms of a set of character traits, it can read: A ought to do x because x is necessary to develop and maintain a set of character traits that are essential to a way of life that contributes to the impartially optimific state of affairs according to V. The caveat is that there are indirect versions of consequentialism that would deny that they have this form. According to some, indirect consequentialism does not provide a decision procedure and hence does not recommend a deliberative pattern. Rather, it provides an account of moral "objectivity," an account for evaluating the truth of moral claims.[2] I believe there are several problems with this view, but they need not concern us here. What we are trying to do here is to evaluate different conceptions of morality that are based on practical reason, not on some independent notion of moral objectivity. On conceptions of morality that are based on practical reason, the objectivity or truth of a normative claim is cashed out in terms of whether it meets conditions of rationality. Thus if indirect consequentialism is to be a competitor for a conception of practical reason, then it must recommend indirection as a deliberative pattern.

Nonconsequentialism, then, is the view that it is not always, either directly or indirectly, obligatory to act in a way that is designed to bring about the best available state of affairs on impartial criteria. Here we will consider

2. If I am not mistaken, this is Richard Brandt's view. See his *A Theory of the Good and the Right* (New York: Oxford University Press, 1979), 183–99.

two versions. The first is prerogative nonconsequentialism, which is a weak denial of consequentialism. Introduced by Samuel Scheffler, it asserts that while it is sometimes permissible to act in ways that are *not* impartially optimific, it is never wrong to act in an impartially maximizing way.[3] This ensures that sometimes (though not always) an agent has the "prerogative" either to maximize on impartial criteria or to pursue more personal projects. Prerogative nonconsequentialism is motivated by the thought that sometimes consequentialism can be too demanding for an individual agent. Thus a prerogative deliberative pattern has the form, A may do x rather than y because y is too demanding. The second version of nonconsequentialism is deontology, which is a strong denial of consequentialism in that it asserts that it is sometimes wrong to act in ways that are designed to bring about impartially specified states of affairs. In asserting this, deontology employs what has become known as agent-centered or deontological restrictions, moral restrictions on the agent from acting on impartial, consequentialist criteria. Deontology, then, is motivated by the thought that consequentialism can demand the wrong thing. We cannot say much yet in general about what a deontological deliberative pattern is since different versions of deontology might arrive at agent-centered restrictions through different deliberative routes. As we will see, the Aristotelian model is a form of deontology that includes agent-centered restrictions significantly different from any Kantian model. What we can say at this point is that a deontological deliberative pattern of whatever variety has the form, A ought not to act on impartial maximizing criteria because doing so would be wrong. However, the rationale for thinking that impartial maximizing would be wrong is not revealed in this form. What we need is a form that reflects the rationale behind the restriction, and this we can formulate only on different versions of deontology. We can note, however, that the rationale for the Kantian version must be revealed through the CI procedure on either the procedural or substantive interpretation of that procedure. In the former case, it must be revealed through the universalizability tests of the first two formulations of the categorical imperative. In the latter case, the rationale must be accessible through practical judgment guided by respect for human dignity, where human dignity is absolute, nonscalar, nonadditive, and immune to trade-offs in terms of other values. Later, I will argue that it is difficult to see what that procedure is in some relevant contexts and

3. See Scheffler, *The Rejection of Consequentialism*.

in others that practical judgment is clearly inconsistent with affording human dignity such a value. This will be to argue that whatever latitude for judgment is left on the substantive Kantian view, the requirement that such judgment be guided by thoughts of human dignity so conceived is incompatible with the commitments of the agent of integrity in the thick sense.

Finally, deontology can employ different kinds of restrictions: action-type restrictions or personal relations restrictions. Action-type restrictions specify action-types that are not to be engaged in, even if they will bring about a better state of affairs on impartial criteria. For example, one might believe that promoting good consequences, such as social utility, is a good thing, even obligatory in some contexts, but that it is wrong to do so if doing so requires one to break a promise, tell a lie, or torture an innocent person. Here breaking-a-promise, telling-a-lie, torturing-an-innocent-person are all action-types. An action-type deliberative pattern has the form that A ought or ought not to do x because of its action-type, regardless of whether it is impartially optimific.

Personal relations restrictions, on the other hand, are restrictions against impartial maximization based on the agent's personal relations. For example, a personal relations restriction might require you to do something for the sake of a loved one, even where there are other acts available to you that would bring about a better state of affairs on impartial criteria. In this chapter, the major focus is on whether there are such restrictions regarding parental love and what account is to be given of them. I argue that the Aristotelian model provides the best account, for it provides a rationale that is elusive on Kantian versions of deontology. Logically, such a restriction takes the form of an other-restricting normative belief, A ought to do x for B rather than do y for C, where what can be done for C (and others) would result in a better state of affairs from an impartial point of view.

As I understand at least some versions of Kantian deontology, action-type restrictions are generated by an application of the CI procedure sometimes called the conceivability test. According to these versions, we can sometimes conclude that impartial maximizing would be wrong because the maxim that would allow it fails the conceivability test. According to this test, a maxim is not to be acted on unless one could conceive of that maxim as a law in a system of nature where that system could sustain itself. Put another way, if the system of nature could not be conceived as self-sustaining because it includes that maxim, then that maxim is not to be acted on. There has been much dispute about how to interpret this test, but I will employ Korsgaard's practical contradiction interpretation, even though she denies that the test generates duties against action-types.[4] I employ this interpretation because it seems to me the right one for the reasons she gives, though there is clearly room for debate on this point.[5] Whether it has the connection to action-types is a further question I will come to later. On this interpretation, there is a special kind of contradiction involved in the attempt to universalize certain maxims of action. The contradiction is not strictly that of contradictory beliefs, as in, say, formal logic or some purely theoretical enterprise. Rather, it is a practical contradiction in the following sense. We are supposed to imagine that we live in a universe in which the maxims we act on actually turn into laws of nature. Thus if we act on a maxim, all our future actions as well as all the actions of other persons are governed by these natural laws that we create through our own willings. Some such maxims would be self-defeating in the sense that they would will a certain purpose but that purpose could not be achieved because of the content of the maxim. Kant's example involves false promises. He imagines a person acting on the maxim of borrowing money knowing that he will never pay it back.[6] The maxim is supposed to be something to the effect that the agent intends to borrow money promising to pay it back but with the intent not to do so if doing so is at all inconvenient. In a world where our maxims become natural laws once acted on, this maxim would be self-defeating because it would result in the downfall of the promise-making/promise-keeping convention once everyone realized that one could not keep a promise were it at all inconvenient to do so. More specifically, in the present case, the purpose of borrowing money, which is the goal of the maxim, could not be achieved through that maxim in our imaginary world because everyone would know that it is a law of nature that the money could not be repaid and consequently no one would make the loan. Hence if it can be determined that false promises fail this test, then those (unlike Korsgaard) who want to put the emphasis on action-types would say that any maximization pattern that would allow false promises is a prohibited pattern because of the action-types they involve. The same might be said for

4. For a discussion of alternative interpretations of the test—the Logical Contradiction Interpretation and the Teleological Contradiction Interpretation—as well as the Practical Contradiction Interpretation, see Christine M. Korsgaard, *Creating the Kingdom of Ends* (Cambridge: Cambridge University Press, 1996), 77–105.

5. For an interesting discussion, see Nancy Sherman, *Making a Necessity of Virtue: Aristotle and Kant on Virtue* (Cambridge: Cambridge University Press, 1997), 305–11.

6. Immanuel Kant, *Groundwork of the Metaphysic of Morals*, trans. H. J. Paton (New York: Harper Torchbooks, 1964), 89, 90.

lying, cheating, violating contracts, and torturing innocent persons. I will say more about this later, but let us call a deliberative pattern of this sort a perfect duty deliberative pattern, since the conceivability test was said by Kant to generate perfect duties.

Most Kantians also want to assert that we have special obligations to our loved ones, but it is unclear how these obligations are generated. One possibility, of course, is that they are action-type restrictions. If so, the CI procedure in its deployment of the conceivability test must reveal what the content of these obligations are and that they are perfect duties. Another possibility is that personal relations restrictions are generated by another implementation of the CI procedure sometimes called the volitional test. In order to understand this test, we must assume that it is applied to maxims that pass the conceivability test. For Kant, duties or obligations are always generated when a maxim fails a test. Should a maxim fail the conceivability test, there is no need to employ the volitional test, for that maxim has already been shown to be one that cannot be universalized. However, it is possible that a maxim could pass the conceivability test yet still be one that is not universalizable. The volitional test is supposed to show this.

Very generally, the volitional test requires us to imagine that a maxim could be a law in a possible, self-sustaining system of nature but that somehow a rational agent could not will to live in that system of nature. Though there is a good deal of dispute about what this comes to, I will interpret the test in the following way. Kant is not having us imagine that a self-interested rational agent could not will to live in this system of nature. Rather, he is having us imagine that if the agent acts on a particular maxim, then that maxim will become a natural law that will govern the actions of all rational agents who live in that system of nature. Since rational agents are all motivated by impartial respect for persons, the construction of a system of nature through one's will must be such that it is consistent with the willings of every other rational being who must live in the same environment. Hence what I can will for myself without concern for others is not the issue, but what I can will for myself and any other rational being who is affected by my maxims as possible natural laws.

Kant believed that this version of the CI procedure generated a duty of mutual aid.[7] Here actions are not required because they are of a type that can be evaluated for the kind of inconsistency found in false promises. There are many ways to render aid. For this reason, there is a great deal

7. Ibid., 90, 91.

more latitude in just what is required in the way of specific acts by this test.[8] Thus maxims are prohibited by this test not because they attach to action-types but because they are inconsistent with the motivation of being concerned with the agency of impurely rational beings, beings who are both rational and have inclinations that can be thwarted in various ways. This is why Kant called obligations generated by the volitional test imperfect duties. I propose, then, that we understand a deliberative pattern that employs this form of the CI procedure an imperfect duties deliberative pattern. Later, I will argue that Kantians have not shown how such a pattern generates agent-centered restrictions involving personal relations, including those of parental love. Either they have failed to show on a purely procedural interpretation of the test how this is done, or they have failed to show on a substantive interpretation how such restrictions are rational when judgment is guided by the thought that human dignity is absolute, nonscalar, nonadditive, and immune to trade-offs in terms of other values.

Finally, I must say something about Kantian consequentialism. Historically, Kantian deontology has been contrasted with utilitarianism, and it has been thought that it is sufficient to be a deontologist that one believes that it is sometimes wrong to seek to maximize social utility, either directly or indirectly. It should be easy to see that identifying deontology with this belief is a mistake. One could believe that the wrongness of pursuing one impartial goal is made wrong by the priority of some other impartial goal. If this is the reasoning behind the rejection of utilitarianism, then it is not one that leads to deontology. For deontology asserts that it is sometimes wrong to seek to promote impartial goals, no matter what they are. Kantian consequentialism rejects utilitarianism, not because it is consequentialist, but because it employs the wrong criteria for ranking states of affairs from best to worst.

David Cummiskey has defended a view of this sort in his book, *Kantian Consequentialism*. As it turns out, on Cummiskey's view, a Kantian consequentialist deliberative pattern is two-tiered: it aims at promoting the conditions for the exercise of rational agency throughout the network of rational agents, and it aims at promoting the happiness of rational beings. Actually, Cummiskey says that this two-tiered view involves three things: "First, each agent should promote the conditions necessary for forming, revising, and effectively pursuing a conception of the good. Second, since all agents are equal, each agent should adjust his or her personal ends in light

---

8. I will discuss the latitude of imperfect duties in more detail in chapter 18 when I discuss Marcia Baron's work in more detail.

of the equal status of all other agents and their ends. Third, since others' ends are just as important as my own, each agent should recognize the equal value of the ends of others, and thus promote the happiness of others—provided that the ends of others are not inconsistent with the previous two conditions and are thus permissible." He says also that "in deciding difficult cases of conflict between individuals . . . we must adjudicate in light of the equal status of each person and his or her interest in realizing a self-chosen conception of the good."[9]

Though Cummiskey does not give us a crystal-clear picture of how these deliberations in difficult cases are to take place, the general spirit of the view is clear enough. In the general context of duties to others, obligations derive from a concern either to respect autonomy or to promote happiness, with the former ordinally prior to the latter. Adjusted to accommodate the distinctions regarding categorical and noncategorical interests, Cummiskey's view can be interpreted to distinguish between two Kantian deliberative patterns. The first I call a Kantian ordinal pattern. The idea is that when rational agents are parties to a conflict their interests are to be lexically ordered with categorical interests being the most important, important noncategorical interests the next important, and minor interests the least important. The ordinal pattern requires that, everything else being equal, the interests higher up the scale are to be given priority in deciding what to do because they are more central to the autonomy of a rational agent's life plan. The second pattern I call a Kantian maximization pattern. This pattern comes into play only when conflicts are between interests on the same level of the lexical ordering. It requires that when interests on the same level of the ordinal scale conflict, then one ought to act in a way that is most likely to satisfy the highest number of interests at that level without regard to persons. In what follows, I will argue that neither of these patterns is rational across the complete range of contexts a respectful and personal loving agent might face.

Before turning to the issue of the other-restricting beliefs of parental love, let me indicate Cummiskey's deepest worries about Kantian deontology. His major worry is about action-type deontological restrictions. The worry, expressed by many others, is that it is difficult to see what rationale such restrictions could have. Restrictions against torturing innocent persons is a good example. Any moral person is concerned to avoid and prevent the torture of innocent persons. But suppose that there are only two

9. David Cummiskey, *Kantian Consequentialism* (New York: Oxford University Press, 1996), 98, 98–99.

options: You can prevent either the torture of one innocent person or the torture of many other innocent persons, and everything else is equal. On what grounds could it be rational to choose to prevent the torture of only the one person? If it is the fact that an action is of a certain type that gives one reasons for thinking it to be wrong or irrational, then how could it not be worse or more irrational to allow for more instances of it, everything else being equal? I cannot see how to reject the implications of this question. For this reason, I am as skeptical of action-type deontologies as Cummiskey. More crucial, however, is the fact that if he is right about the irrationality of action-type deontology, then there is something incoherent about the employment of the CI procedure in testing for perfect duties if it tests for action-types. For there is no maxim involving action-types that would fail the conceivability test, if that test is to be understood as generating moral prohibitions against action-types. Why? Because it would always be rational on Cummiskey's view to perform an action-type to prevent further actions of that type. In this, I think he is right. Moreover, he is right that Kantian action-type deontologists do not address this issue.[10] But it does not follow that deontology has been refuted, because there remains the issue of a personal relations deontology. In what follows, then, I will give an account of the other-restricting normative beliefs of parental love that rejects action-type deontology of any sort for Cummiskey's reasons and leave it to those who would endorse such deontology to give us reasons for changing our minds. This leaves open the possibility that the conceivability test can be seen not to generate duties against action-types but should be understood in a way that avoids consequentialism, provides a basis for personal relations restrictions in the conceivability test, and has a clear rationale. One of my main tasks in the rest of this chapter, then, is to show that none of the following deliberative patterns—a Kantian ordinal pattern, a Kantian maximization pattern, and a Kantian imperfect duties pattern— is rational across the complete relevant range of deliberative contexts. I will also consider a utility maximization pattern, as well as a prerogative pattern. Though there are no Kantians who would defend all these patterns, the point is to consider a wide range of deliberative patterns that might be called "Kantian" and argue that they all fail in important ways. In this way, I avoid the task of determining what the "real" Kantian view is.

Finally, I can reject Cummiskey's claim that only an indirect justification is possible for our deontological intuitions, if I can show that there is a ra-

---

10. Ibid., 11–15, 92, 93; and see Korsgaard, *Creating the Kingdom of Ends,* 100–101.

tionale for them that does not fall prey to the problems of action-type de-ontology.[11] I argue that the Aristotelian model provides a direct rationale for personal relations restrictions.

3.

Recall that an other-restricting normative belief concerns the interests of third parties. "A ought to do x for the sake of B rather than do y for the sake of C" is the logical form of such a belief. If the restriction is such that do-ing y for C (and others) would result in a better state of affairs on impar-tial criteria than doing x for B, then it is a personal relations deontological restriction. In this section, I address the integration and priorities problems as they arise across a significant range of contexts. After doing so, I address Stocker's problem and how the sense of obligation arises in these contexts.

Here the integration problem is this: How does one integrate the vari-ous concerns in the love for a child with the various concerns for others, es-pecially those of respect? Again, this problem arises only when we recog-nize that the agent has a multiplicity of goods that appear within his or her deliberative field that must be integrated within a coherent way of life. The solution requires some reasonably settled set of priorities that allows for integrating these concerns across deliberative contexts.

To achieve integration, three alternative sets of priorities are ruled out. First, lexical priority to the interests of the child over the interests of oth-ers regardless of deliberative context leaves insufficient room for respect for others. If you cater to your child's whims while others suffer miser-ably in ways you could easily prevent, you are not a respectful person. My previous analysis of respect should have made this clear. Reflective en-dorsement of a way of life in which this set of priorities held would not be possible for an agent of integrity in the thick sense, because the criterion of finality would rule it out. For a respectful agent, other respectable people must appear as ends in the way of life that meets the finality criterion, and, on this set of priorities, they do not. Second, the same kind of priority to

11. Cummiskey says, "If one rejects deontological intuitionism, then an indi-rect consequentialist account of our deontological intuitions and commitments is the only reasonable justification that remains." See *Kantian Consequentialism*, 100. I cannot see that Cummiskey ever gives an argument for this conclusion. First, it might be that there are only two possible justifications for deontological intu-itions but neither of them succeeds. Second, what is the argument that there are only two reasonable alternatives? I intend to show here that an Aristotelian concep-tual scheme can provide a direct justification for personal relations restrictions.

the interests of others over those of the child regardless of context leaves insufficient room for parental love. What would it be to love your child and always put the interests of others above those of your child? Even Cummiskey admits this, although his justification for some of the most important cases is only indirectly a function of the concern to maximize the network of Kantian autonomy.[12] But on the Aristotelian view, this set of priorities is ruled out because of the criteria of finality and self-sufficiency: finality, because the child does not have the proper place as a beloved end within the way of life ordered by these priorities; and self-sufficiency, because that way of life is missing something good, namely, the child as a beloved end. A third alternative—the equal treatment of others and the child across deliberative contexts—is also to be rejected. No plausible conception of respect requires this, and no plausible conception of parental love permits it. The general analysis of personal love is sufficient to establish this point. The child appears within the respectful and parentally loving agent's deliberative field as important in ways that preclude such an ordering of his or her priorities. Thus the respectful and parentally loving agent is able to order his or her priorities without the aid of an impartial decision procedure in a way that rules out all three alternatives. Rather, the priorities are set by the vision of a way of life that makes a place within that way of life for the goods that appear within the agent's deliberative field. This is just what the Aristotelian conception of practical reason promised to provide.

Yet, if these priorities are to be rejected, what are the priorities of an agent who has parental love and respect for a child and is respectful of others? What do these priorities show about the symmetry of regulative function between parental love, impartial respect, and impartial sympathy for others? And how can a successful solution to the priorities problem show that the rightness of the agent's actions is the nonaccidental result of his or her motives? To answer these questions, we must consider a range of contexts and the deliberative patterns that are rational in them.

1. When the interests at stake for the child are categorical, they have first priority over any noncategorical interests of others who are respected but not loved by the agent. This is true no matter how many noncategorical interests are at stake for others and no matter how many other persons have such interests at stake. To make this point vivid, consider whether you would sacrifice the fundamental psychological well-being of your child to

---

12. Cummiskey, *Kantian Consequentialism*, 11–15, 146 ff.

prevent the temporary, minor irritation of everyone on earth. Or to make the point more strongly, what would you do to protect the fundamental psychological well-being of your child in the way of causing others the kind of temporary depression that might come with the frustration of an important noncategorical interest? If we take temporary but nondebilitating depression as the strongest indicator that an important noncategorical interest has been frustrated, I cannot see how the concern to prevent such depression in itself, without regard to its impact on the categorical interests of others, could ever give a loving parent reasons for sacrificing the things crucial to the child's finding life meaningful, no matter how many people were so depressed. Suppose, for example, that sexually abusing your child, with the kind of deep long-lasting trauma caused by such an experience, would prevent the rest of the human population from being depressed for, say, a month. Or imagine the kind of deep psychological effects on your child of *your* locking him or her in a closet for a month with only the most sparse diet. Would you do this if the only bad effects were confined to your child and the only good effects were the relief of the kind of nonclinical depression alluded to for the rest of the human population for a month? These considerations should establish that a loving parent does not deliberate about utility calculations in such contexts. The loving parent's deliberations do not reflect a utility maximization pattern. The reason for this is that the place the child has in the parent's deliberations is determined by parental love. For on a way of life ordered by the set of priorities leading to the utility calculus the child could not have a place in that way of life as a beloved end, and the finality criterion would not be satisfied. Nor would that way of life be self-sufficient in even a minimal sense, since it would omit a good that is categorical from the parent's point of view. Thus the priorities leading to the utility calculus are rejected because they would not order a life in which the agent's ends would have their perceived value. In rejecting these priorities, the agent does the right thing in a way that the rightness of his or her action is the nonaccidental result of its motive. That is, the agent orders his or her priorities and the actions entailed by them in a way that takes into account all the relevant values from the widest possible position of reflective endorsement. Although this might seem a case of parental love for your child regulating your impartial sympathy for others, I will give reasons shortly for thinking that sympathy and love would converge in these cases.

Certainly the priorities of simple respect and parental love would converge. For if you respect a third party and both respect and love your child, you will be disposed to give priority to your child's interests in any case in which the interest at stake for your child is categorical and the third party's is noncategorical. And it will not matter to you how many minor interests of others, including the third party's, are at stake. Nor would you as respectful agent deliberate about utility payoffs in such contexts, even if your child was not involved. As a respectful person, let alone a loving one, you would not deliberate about utility payoffs when faced with a conflict of this sort between the interests of two children neither of which were your own and to which you were not specially related. Why? Because the priorities that lead to the utility calculus clearly preclude the kind of value placed on those worthy of respect who are to be treated as ends. This is how respectable people appear within the deliberative field of a respectful person. Though this conclusion is not sufficient to establish that respect attaches to a conception of human dignity that is absolute, nonscalar, and immune to trade-offs, it is sufficient to establish that respect reflects a commitment to a value that is immune to trade-offs of this sort, as is parental love. Thus parental love and simple respect do not differ in their priorities in this regard, and there is no need for regulation between them, which is to say that the deliberative patterns of parental love and a Kantian ordinal pattern would converge in these contexts. Of course, the Kantian and the Aristotelian reach these priorities through different routes: allegedly the Kantian through the CI procedure and the Aristotelian through the criteria of finality and self-sufficiency as applied to how a set of priorities orders goods within a way of life. But how is it that one can deny that for the Aristotelian the rightness of action is the nonaccidental result of its motive, despite the fact that the Aristotelian's deliberations do not employ an impartial decision procedure?

A similar analysis applies, I believe, regarding impartial sympathy, regardless of what many direct utilitarians say about maximizing happiness. Suppose we could determine through interpersonal comparisons of utility that if you do x C will get 10 units of utility, your child, B, will get 1, and that there are twenty other people affected by your doing x. Suppose that they receive 10 units each. If you are impartially sympathetic, say some utilitarians, you will be disposed to do x if you believe that there is no alternative with a better overall sum of utility. But suppose that if you do y, then your child will receive 2 units of utility and C and the others will receive 5 units. According to either total sum or average utilitarianism, if you are impartially sympathetic, you will believe that you ought to do x rather than y. But I do not believe that you will necessarily have such a sense of priorities, even discounting your parental love for B, but certainly not where your love for your child is included.

Consider first the case in which B is just one among others and not your child, that your concern for her is impartial sympathy. What if you believe correctly that 1 unit of utility measures an attachment to life that makes it minimally worth living? Anything less and life becomes pointless. Anything more only adds to a meaningful but far from perfect life. Add to this that you correctly believe that 5 units measure the satisfaction of a life with great meaning and that 10 units measure a life of ecstasy. It is anything but clear that your sympathy would lead you to sacrifice the meaningfulness of B's life for the increase from great meaning to ecstasy in the lives of the others. But there are two things that are clear. First, not just any marginal increase (either in average or total sum) of utility would allow you as a sympathetic person to do x rather than y. The base concern for the categorical interests of one person over the noncategorical interests of others would not allow you to make such a sacrifice. Second, this is most certainly the case if you have either simple respect or personal love for B.

On the first point regarding sympathy alone: Just imagine cases in which the total or average fluctuates only marginally in the meaning assigned to the units of utility. What this shows is that the solution to the problem of interpersonal comparisons of utility does not solve the problem of ranking states of affairs from best to worst from an impartial point of view. Being able to assign cardinal measurements to utility received for each person affected does not tell us what to do with those numbers in evaluating overall states of affairs. Do we add them, add and divide, or do we need some interpretive device to give them significance for evaluating states of affairs? I believe that the distinctions involving categorical and noncategorical interests are needed even to understand the concept of impartial sympathy. In this sense, I have serious doubts that the utilitarian's conception of impartial sympathy is adequate to give us a notion of social utility.[13]

13. See Derek Parfit's discussion of the repugnant conclusion in *Reasons and Persons* (London: Clarendon Press, 1984), 381–90.
What is important is that the mathematical model for *social utility* track the concept we employ in judging the well-being of one population over another. Neither average nor total sum utilitarianism does this very well, once one interprets the numbers in a way that makes vivid what the numbers might mean. That there might be some mathematical model that captures our notion of the well-being of a population I do not deny (though I do not affirm it either), but the math tracks the concept rather than the other way around. And the concept is not revealed in the

On the second point in which either respect or love is involved: Good people who are either loving parents or respectful of others, or both, do not participate in some kinds of consequentialist thinking (which is not to deny that they participate in others). This shows, I believe, that there need be no conflict between Kantians and the dispositions of parental love when it comes to *this* kind of conflict. What I mean is that the priorities of the parentally loving but respectful person are extensionally equivalent on the Kantian ordinal pattern and the Aristotelian model for these contexts. The difference is that this set of priorities for the Aristotelian is a function of reflection on whether a set of priorities can make an adequate place within a way of life for the things that appear good within the agent's deliberative field; whereas on the Kantian view it is a function of the employment of the CI procedure on a certain interpretation. In order to understand the latter, a richer account of what it is to respect another as an end is needed than is sometimes found among Kantians. There must be a clearer understanding of how categorical interests are crucial to personhood and how personal love often allows one to be the person one is.

To this point, then, we have evaluated the rationality of deliberative patterns for contexts in which the categorical interests of the beloved child are in conflict with the noncategorical interests of third parties. We have seen that for a parentally loving and respectful parent, the categorical interests of the child have first priority over the noncategorical interests of others. This is what we would expect on an Aristotelian view, but it also converges with a Kantian ordinal pattern. But what about the rationality of the other three deliberative patterns, the Kantian maximization pattern, the imperfect duties pattern, and the prerogative pattern? We need not spend much time on these for three reasons. First, the Kantian maximization pattern applies only in contexts in which there are conflicts of interests on the same level within the lexical ordering of the categorical/noncategorical scale, and this is not a context of that sort. Second, since we have a plausible Kantian account for these contexts, there is no need to evaluate the imperfect duties pattern. And third, this is not a context in which the loving parent feels that a reverse set of priorities would be rational and permissible, which rules out the prerogative pattern.

2. When the interests at stake for the child and the interests at stake for others are important noncategorical interests, numbers of people involved

---

numbers produced by the solution to the problem of interpersonal comparisons of utility.

or interests at stake might matter. If it is only a conflict between your child's interests and C's interests, and everything else is equal, then the numbers will not factor. As a loving parent, you will give priority to your child's interests. This follows from the general analysis of personal love as an intentional dispositional state and how the beloved appears within the deliberative field of an agent who is *both* respectful of others and parentally loving. Such a set of priorities orders a way of life in which C appears as an end worthy of respect and your child as a beloved end. Both finality and self-sufficiency are satisfied on the Aristotelian view, and no one is treated as a mere means on the Kantian view.

But if there are large numbers of other respectable people who have equally important (though noncategorical) interests at stake, what are we then to say about the priorities of the loving parent who is also respectful and sympathetic toward others? Suppose, for example, that if you were to contribute to a Christmas fund for disadvantaged children you could be practically certain that the amount of your contribution would bring a certain amount of joy to a large number of children during the holidays. If you do not contribute, the same number of children will be somewhat depressed for a week or so. Your child, however, has her heart set on a particular, relatively expensive gift. If she does not get it, she will be somewhat depressed for a similar amount of time. In neither case—neither the disadvantaged children nor your daughter—will there be anything like agent breakdown as a result of disappointment; still, the disappointment is no minor matter, which is demonstrated by the depression. The reason the same sum of money will meet either the interests of the disadvantaged children or the interest of your own child is explained by the different expectations generated by social and economic background. Your child, say, wants a new, upgraded computer, and the other children want inexpensive dolls. What we are to imagine in the case of your daughter is that the difference between her old computer and the new one is understandably significant for her, no mere indulgence, but not crucial in ways that would make the interest in it seem more than the other children's interests in the dolls. We should also imagine the circumstance as being rare. For too many instances of deferring to others in this way might undermine the relationship between the parent and the child and hence would introduce the interest in the relationship into the equation, and that interest is categorical. What I have in mind is the fact that some acts represent patterns that express deep commitments and sentiments, and establishing and maintaining such patterns are crucial to the categorical interests involved in loving relationships. Here I am trying to imagine a case where doing something for others would not undermine such patterns but would nonetheless come at some cost to a loved one. The purchase of that cost, however, is not the prevention of catastrophe or tragedy for others; rather, it is something of real importance, but not categorically so.

What would we make of a parent who considered the numbers in such contexts and eventually yielded to the interests of others? I, myself, do not see that such a parent would be unloving for having such priorities, though I must report that some people I know who clearly care a great deal about other people and who love their children cannot see how a loving parent could be moved by such considerations. This gives me reservations about asserting that the numbers must eventually add up or the person is not respectful and sympathetic toward the other children. I suspect this says something about the underdeterminate nature of our conceptions of parental love, on the one hand, and simple respect and sympathy, on the other. Perhaps it says something about getting a clear picture of just what is at stake in such contexts.

At any rate, I want to say rather tentatively that I can see nothing contrary to parental love in making such calculations in some contexts and eventually acting on them. A set of priorities that would allow for such calculations in such circumstances would not to my mind preclude a place to the child as a beloved end within a loving way of life. For example, one can imagine explaining to one's child the reason for going with the larger numbers in some cases, her understanding such a reason, and her still being disappointed in (though not disapproving of) the results. Examples of this sort show the regulating influence of simple respect and sympathy on the priorities of parental love. (Moreover, the fact that thoughts about these contexts are tentative shows the same regulative tension.) But precision here seems to be both unattainable and undesirable. Both respect and parental love are underdeterminate norms. Just how much others' important non-categorical interests can be trumped (if at all) by the same kinds of interests of a beloved child from the point of view of a loving parent is not subject to precise formulation. It will certainly not be at the precise point of marginal differences, for, as we have seen, the beloved child does not get into the way of life ordered by those priorities in a way that matches how she appears within the parent's deliberative field. Moreover, others do find a place as ends within a way of life that does not take the borders of marginal difference as crucial. Where others do not find their place as ends worthy of respect and sympathy is where the numbers never seem to matter, regardless of how high they are and no matter how crucial the interests. These observations suggest the symmetrically regulating influence of parental love and simple respect on each other in the priorities of a person who is both a loving parent and a respectful person. All this seems to be explained by the fact of reflection on these priorities and how they order the goods that appear within the deliberative field of one who is both respectful of others and parentally loving. The underdeterminate nature of our concepts here seems easily explained by the Aristotelian model of practical reason. The internalist Kantians, especially advocates of the deontological versions of that view, must either affirm this result or deny it. In either case, they must show *how* the CI procedure, on either the purely procedural interpretation or the substantive interpretation, leads to what they take to be the correct result. If they affirm this result, they need to show how respect is operating as an asymmetrical regulative norm, which seems puzzling. To show this on the substantive interpretation of imperfect duties, they must show how the concept of human dignity as absolute, nonscalar, nonadditive, and immune to trade-offs properly restricts the latitude of the agent's reasoning. They cannot merely allude to the latitude of imperfect duties. If they deny this result, they need to show what is irrational about such a parent.

These observations should be sufficient to reject a utilitarian maximization pattern for these contexts. Slight marginal increases in utility at this level do not give a loving parent reasons for favoring others over a beloved child. How could they and the child's interests appear within the parent's deliberative field to be more important, even significantly more important, than the interests of others? Nor can I see any reason for thinking that a Kantian maximization pattern is any more rational than the utilitarian pattern. It is only when increases in utility or autonomy go well past the marginal borders that the loving parent's priorities might change. A prerogative pattern does not seem to account for these priorities, because the loving parent in these contexts seems to feel that either the numbers add up to the point of being compelling or they do not. Either way, the parent does not feel that it would be equally rational to reverse the priorities.

We are left, then, with a Kantian ordinal pattern and an imperfect duties pattern. The Kantian ordinal pattern does not apply because the conflicts are within the same level on the lexical scale. What about the imperfect duties pattern? The problem here is that we do not have an account from Kantians of how this pattern is supposed to work in contexts of this sort.

The person who has written most from a Kantian perspective about children has been Onora O'Neill, but she does not address the issue of how the

CI procedure generates parental obligations. She has discussed parental obligations in "Begetting, Bearing, and Rearing," in *Having Children*.[14] However, she does not discuss Kant in that work. She also discusses children in *Constructions of Reason*, chapter 10, "Children's Rights and Children's Lives."[15] There she is concerned to show that a rights-based account of obligations to children is incomplete and blurred because it fails to take into account imperfect duties. In closing she says, "There are good reasons to think that paternalism may be much of what is ethically required in dealing with children, even if it is inadequate in dealings with mature and maturing minors. Nothing is lost in debates about the allocation of obligations to children between families and public institutions if we do not suppose that fundamental rights are the basis of those obligations. However, a fuller account of fundamental obligations to children and of their appropriate institutionalization in families and in public institutions is a further story. The task of this essay has been to show why that story needs telling."[16] This is, as far as I know, a promissory note as yet unfulfilled by either O'Neill or any other Kantian.[17] Nor is there in her discussion an indication of how the CI procedure would apply in the various kinds of contexts we are considering here. Recall from chapter 2 that this must be done in a way that does not involve the filtering of respect through considerations of parental

14. See Onora O'Neill, "Begetting, Bearing, and Rearing," in *Having Children: Philosophical and Legal Reflections on Parenthood*, ed. Onora O'Neill and William Ruddick (New York: Oxford University Press, 1979), 25–38.

15. Onora O'Neill, *Constructions of Reason: Explorations of Kant Practical Philosophy* (Cambridge: Cambridge University Press, 1989), 187–205.

16. Ibid., 205–6.

17. In *Towards Justice and Virtue: A Constructive Account of Practical Reason* (Cambridge: Cambridge University Press, 1996), O'Neill says the following:

Good parents usually think they are bound in *many* ways to their children. They will take it that they owe their children (and others) certain obligations which they also owe all others, to whose observance their children (like others) have rights: for example, they will take it that they are obliged not to injure. These are the *universal perfect obligations*, which abusing parents, and other child abusers, violate. They will also take it that they owe their children care and support, which their particular children, but not all children, let alone all others, have a right to receive from them: these are the *special perfect obligations* that neglectful parents violate. They will also take it that they owe their children, as they owe others, a measure of courtesy and concern: these *universal imperfect obligations* are virtues that rigid or fanatical or cold people lack, and whose lack rigid, fanatical or cold parents inflict specifically on their children, even when they scrupulously observe all their children's rights. Finally, good parents will take it that they owe their children certain sorts of love, attention and support which they do not owe to all, which are quite specific to the relationship to the child, but to which their children have no right. Certain sorts of fun, warmth and encouragement might come under this heading: these are *special imperfect obligations* which parents see as part of what is required of good parents, and which may be neglected even by parents who both

love. Moreover, it must be done in a way that affords human dignity a value that is absolute, nonscalar, nonadditive, and immune to trade-offs. It is difficult, then, to see how Kantians can be confident of their theory without having worked out these details. Indeed, it is as puzzling as how a scientist could be confident of a test for a hypothesis without controls. I will come back to this issue when I consider the normative thoughts of friendship. But I doubt very seriously that the CI procedure could succeed here, because these are contexts in which parental love and impartial respect are symmetrical in their regulative effects. And whatever the interpretation of the CI procedure, it cannot allow for such symmetry of regulative function. If this is true, then these are contexts in which the Aristotelian model provides an account of the rightness of action being the nonaccidental result of its motive where the CI procedure does not.

3. One might think that a similar analysis is true regarding conflicts between the minor interests of the child and others. There might be contexts in which as a loving parent you are in a special role vis-à-vis your children and other children and because of that context the numbers might matter. In the ordinary life of a parent, however, unmindfulness of the minor interests of other children and attention to the minor interests of one's own is certainly no mark of a lack of either sympathy or respect for others. Theories that try to fine-tune normative conceptions of respect and sympathy to cover cases of this sort do so only arbitrarily and at the cost of showing how silly theories can become. If this is correct, then, in a small way, these contexts reveal the regulative effect of parental love on our conceptions of simple respect and sympathy.

4. Conflicts between the categorical interests of the child and the categorical interests of others who are respected but not loved raise special difficulties. Only in very extreme cases can numbers matter for the loving parent, but at some point the numbers will have to add up if the parent is respectful of others. Often consequentialists offer as argument against nonconsequentialist forms of reasoning that if things get bad enough it is

---

observe their children's universal and special rights scrupulously and accord their children the same help and concern they habitually show all others—but no more. (151–52)
What is said here is anything but sufficient to fill the aforementioned promissory note. This is nothing more than a taxonomy of parental obligations. We are told nothing about how this taxonomy works out in detail in different contexts; nor are we told anything about how to get from the CI procedure to an understanding of how obligations falling under the categories of this taxonomy take shape in particular contexts. It is one thing to provide a taxonomy and quite another to show how that taxonomy reflects a theory of practical reason that is both context-sensitive and contextually thorough.

absurd to stand by certain personal commitments. Of course it is, but to offer this as an argument is puzzling. There is a difference between impartialist maximizing rationality, impartialist minimizing rationality, and what might be called catastrophic reasoning. It does not follow that if I am willing to sacrifice my life to avoid a catastrophe for others that I am willing to sacrifice it either to maximize some impartial good or to minimize some social evil. The same applies regarding a loving parent's willingness to sacrifice the categorical interests of a beloved child. But, in such catastrophic cases, it is important to note that the loving parent is often likely to experience a deliberative impasse.

In contexts in which you are a loving parent and C is someone for whom you have only simple respect, if your child's categorical interests conflict with C's, and everything else is equal, you will give priority to your child's interests and have great sadness at C's loss. We can explain both the choice to favor your own child and the sadness on the Aristotelian model. The context is one in which there is no alternative that will save all the goods that are within your deliberative field; hence you must choose the most final of less than ideal choices. Because your child's categorical interests appear within your deliberative field as more important than those of the other person, the rational choice is the one that preserves your child's categorical interests. The sadness is explained by the wish for an alternative that would preserve the categorical interests of everyone involved.

A similar analysis is true, I believe, even if a significant number of losses of this sort accrue to other people, except that there will be greater sadness involved. This is the reaction we expect from loving parents who are respectful of others. It testifies to the regulative tension between parental love and respect for others, which would not be true if we thought of respect or parental love as asymmetrical in their regulative functions. Were parental love asymmetrical in its regulative function, we would have a difficult time explaining the sadness, and were impartial respect asymmetrical, we would have a difficult time explaining the choice in these contexts.

But if we think of agents in such contexts as respectful, at some point we expect them to have difficulties giving priority to their children. This might simply be due to the large numbers involved, or it might be the numbers plus a relative difference in the character of one's children versus the character and interests of others. If you have a bad child, you might love the child and still favor its categorical interests over the categorical interests of other respectable people. In fact, unless your child were totally evil, this seems certainly the case. But it would be inconsistent with the disposition of simple respect to be *as* disposed to allow for the categorical sacrifices of others for the sake of such a child. Further, to the extent that parental love would allow the agent to permit such sacrifices, the sadness would be greater. Both the contexts leading to sadness and those in which the threshold reverses the priorities make evident the regulative influence of respect on our conception of personal love. But the lack of bright-line criteria for drawing the line signals the regulative influence of parental love on our conception of impartial respect. The thought process that reveals that this is true is simply the projection of how a set of priorities would structure a way of life relative to the goods that appear within one's deliberative field. If seeing what life would be like for persons with the character of loving, respectful parents on each of the alternatives does not settle the issue, there simply is no rational way to settle it. If Kantians are to deny this, they must show precisely how their theory avoids it; they cannot simply assert that this objection is a caricature of Kant. Nor can they merely allude to the latitude of imperfect duties, because there are competing accounts of the latitude allowed within practical reason: one Kantian and one Aristotelian. The former must explain the latitude in a way that is guided by the value of human dignity as absolute, nonscalar, nonadditive, and immune to trade-offs, which seems clearly false in these contexts. The latter explains the latitude in terms of the criteria of finality and self-sufficiency and the need to balance a variety of goods that symmetrically regulate each other.

There are rather mundane as well as dramatic situations involving the contexts in question that illustrate the priorities of a loving and respectful parent in this regard. The mundane situations are those everyday situations in which we apportion a percentage of our budgets to assist others. Most of us do not have a conception of respect such that, even on reflection, we would view ourselves as disrespectful of others unless we would be willing to reduce the well-being of our children to the point of diminishing marginal utility (or some Kantian standard) in the service of the categorical well-being of others. That we admire people who make exceptional sacrifices in this regard is clear, but it is not lack of respect for others that keeps loving parents from requiring categorical sacrifices of their children in this regard. What we would be willing on reflection to do with our everyday lives confirms this in rather mundane and undramatic ways. Of course, there may be those who do think that this is disrespectful, but then it is unclear what their conception of a loving parent is. Unless we are to reject the view that loving parents are in that regard good people, it is simply philosophically unacceptable to assert that some behavior is disrespectful unless one can say how avoiding such behavior is consistent with being a loving parent. Kantians owe us a carefully worked out conception of what a loving parent is *before* they can tell us what respect for others requires of a loving parent. I cannot see that this has even been attempted.[18] Morever, they must show how that account is consistent with a view of respect for human dignity as a value that is absolute, nonscalar, and immune to trade-offs in terms of other values. They cannot simply allude to latitude allowed by the universalizability tests. But if anything could be clearer than that these contexts show that respectful agents do allow for trade-offs, it is difficult to imagine what it would be. That parental love involves giving priority to the categorical interests of one's child over others in this way, at the cost of the very meaning of life to others beyond marginal differences in numbers, shows that respect does not function as absolute, nonscalar, nonadditive, and immune to trade-offs. So whatever latitude is involved in these contexts, it is not governed by the concept of respect for human dignity claimed by Kantians.

The point can be seen more dramatically by thinking about people who are put in witness protection programs in order to protect their families. Imagine being in a position to provide information that might undermine a drug cartel and the human misery such cartels inflict on large numbers of people. There can be no doubt that viewed impartially your own life and the life of your children are not as important as the many lives you might save through cooperation. But suppose that testifying would expose your children to very real and horrible dangers of recrimination by the cartel. You might be quite willing to risk recriminations against yourself, but would you be willing to risk the categorical well-being of your children, regardless of how small the numbers beyond the threshold of impartial value

18. In this regard, I am expressing a frustration with Kantian ethicists similar to the frustration expressed by Annette Baier. One frustration she has expressed is that Kantians do not seem interested in telling us very much about parent/child relations. Of course, she doubts that the Kantian framework is at all equipped in a way that would allow them to do so, primarily because she believes that the role of trust in the moral life is crucial, especially to women's experience, and that when contracts, promises, and voluntary exchanges are taken as the primary models for moral understanding, we lose sight of the kinds of trust that are essential to much of personal life. Moreover, I believe she is right that to gain a conceptual scheme that is more sensitive to matters of trust, we need to appeal to a tradition that makes much more out of human sentiments than the Kantian tradition can. Moreover, I believe this is as true for loving fathers as for loving mothers. For these reasons, I think Baier has done far more to shed light on what it is to be a good parent than anything found among Kantian writers. See especially her book, *Moral Prejudices* (Cambridge, Mass.: Harvard University Press, 1995).

that you might save by testifying? In fact, I think such considerations reveal that your insistence on witness protection as a condition for testifying when even some rather large numbers are involved illustrates how much more important one's children are to a loving parent than those for whom the parent has only impartial respect. We would not think of you as at all disrespectful were you to insist on witness protection as a condition of your testifying. Those who want to insist that you would be disrespectful inherit the burden of giving us a clear picture of what a loving parent is.

On the other hand, there are dramatic cases that illustrate that at some point the consequences to others of favoring the categorical well-being of one's own children would be disrespectful and uncaring. Reflections on actual recent events in Bosnia are illuminating in this regard. In *A Bridge Betrayed*, Michael Sells provides a vivid account of the kind of context faced by many Serbs in which the Serbian army was carrying out a policy of genocide against Muslims. First, he reports:

> Serbs who refused to participate in the persecution of Muslims were killed. In a Serb-army occupied area of Sarajevo, Serb militants killed a Serb officer who objected to atrocities against civilians; they left his body on the street for over a week as an object lesson. During one of the "selections" carried out by Serb militants in Sarajevo, an old Serb named Ljubo objected to being separated out from his Muslims friends and neighbors; they beat him to death on the spot. In Zvornik, Serb militiamen slit the throat of a seventeen-year-old Serb girl who protested the shooting of Muslim civilians. In the Prijedor region, Serb militants put Serbs accused of helping non-Serb neighbors into the camps with those they tried to help. Similar incidents occurred throughout areas controlled by the Bosnian military.[19]

And later:

> When fighting broke out in Croatia in 1991, Serb irregular militiamen wore ski-masks or face paint. Survivors of atrocities reported trying to discern the accent of their masked torturers to determine where they came from. Sometimes a victim would recognize the voice of a neighbor. In many cases the man behind the mask was content to allow his identity to be known through his voice, and in some cases even taunted his victim with the fact that they knew each other.[20]

19. Michael A. Sells, *The Bridge Betrayed: Religion and Genocide in Bosnia* (Berkeley: University of California Press, 1996), 73.
20. Ibid., 77.

Yet even in the face of such terror, some Serbs came to the aid of Muslims at the cost of putting their families at risk. In this regard, Sells reports:

> Despite the effort of Serb religious nationalists to dehumanize both their own population and their target population, many Serbs have resisted and kept their humanity. Bosnian Muslim survivors commonly reported that a Serb or (in the case of Croat extremist violence) a Croat helped them escape. A soldier or border guard may have turned a blind eye as a Bosnian slipped away from an atrocity or fled to safe territory. A family might shelter a fugitive in their home, at great risk. A Muslim survivor of the killing camp at Susica mentioned that a Serb priest tried to help him. Bogdan Bogdanovic, the Serb former mayor of Belgrade, has spoken out courageously against the systematic annihilation of mosques and other cultural monuments. Many of the stories of resistance and courage cannot be told at this time, because the resisters or their families are still vulnerable to reprisals.[21]

What we have in this kind of context is a catastrophe of monumental proportions, and it is here that we can make sense of a loving parent being willing to put the categorical well-being of his or her children at risk for the sake of others. The regulative influence of respect on parental love is seen in a very graphic way. But these contexts are not contexts involving the marginal borders of impartial considerations; they are catastrophic.

Thus the loss that other respectable people might have to bear in order for the loving and respectful parent to favor his or her child's categorical interests might become so acute that there can be no question that the interests of others prevail. Sells's observations about Bosnia show this. But if a loving parent is forced into catastrophic contexts like those in Bosnia, he or she—as a loving parent and as a respectful agent—will experience a categorical conflict. Even if there is a deliberative resolution, it will come at a categorical cost to the agent, and such costs always involve some degree of loss of integrity, should tragedy result. One might be the loss of the will to live. Justifying thoughts are not always consoling thoughts, and that one has had to sacrifice one's child for the sake of others might be justifying, but it is not consoling for a loving parent. Reflection might reveal that there is a way of life that one can endorse from among the alternatives in the context, but that way of life will fail in a significant way to be self-sufficient. It will lack a good fundamental to the meaning the agent sees in the best life. The parent's deliberative field will be haunted by the ghost of the child for some time to come. Thus, even in extreme cases, it is the exceptional per-

21. Ibid., 78.

son who is a loving parent who can have the normative thought that he or she ought to sacrifice a beloved child. The inability to do so even in these extreme cases is more a sign of the limits of human agency than a lack of respect.

Here it is important to note a difference between the priorities inherent in simple respect and parental love. If Cummiskey is correct (and I think he is), simple respect, considered in itself, can be forced into consequentialist reasoning that is not open to parental love. If you, only as a respectful agent concerned with the autonomy of others, can do x or y, where y will result in marginally less intrusions of individual autonomy than x to a larger number of people, and everything else is equal, then you will believe that you ought to do y. When, for example, rights of equal weight conflict, the Kantian can no longer resort to ranking rights. The only rational pattern left is optimizing across persons, a Kantian maximization pattern. Until Kantian deontologists have shown us a clear rationale for avoiding this conclusion, we are justified in believing it. Our belief that saving many human lives at the expense of far fewer innocent human lives is stronger than our belief that human dignity is absolute, nonscalar, nonadditive, and immune to trade-offs. In fact, I do not believe there is *any* evidence that we believe the latter. The evidence of moral reflection supports only the view that the value we place on human dignity resists some kinds of trade-offs. But parental love, considered in itself, does not allow such optimizing for the sake of others. To do so would leave no place in a way of life for a fundamental good that appears within the loving parent's deliberative field. Nor, except for the catastrophic contexts, does parental love allow for impartial consequentialist thinking even when combined with the dispositions of respect. For this reason, the agent who is personally loving and respectful of self and others has other-restricting normative beliefs that reflect thoughts of agent-centered restrictions. Thus parental love is not consistent with a conception of simple respect where simple respect is conceived in isolation from other dispositions and norms an agent might have. This, I believe, is why the Kantians give us a distorted picture of what simple respect is for human agents. It is not for a value that is absolute, nonscalar, nonadditive, and immune to trade-offs in terms of other values. Cummiskey, then, is wrong to think that *these* personal relations restrictions have no direct rationale. They are the direct result of reflective endorsement: The loving and respectful agent sees the priorities embedded within these restrictions as ordering the goods of his or her deliberative field in a way of life that is the most final and self-sufficient among the alternatives. Moreover, were simple respect taken as an asymmetrical regulative norm that required the

Kantian maximization pattern it would not guarantee the rightness of action in these contexts, for it would set the agent's priorities in the wrong way. On the other hand, where simple respect and parental love are symmetrical in their regulative functions, as they are on the Aristotelian view, priorities are set in a way that the agent's actions are the nonaccidental result of his or her motives.

In any event, the loving parent's dispositions toward a child and respectful dispositions toward other respectable people are not egalitarian, in either a Kantian or a utilitarian sense. The latitude of the loving and respectful parent's deliberations is not restricted by the concern for human dignity as the kind of value Kantians assert it to be. Nevertheless, the priorities described here allow and require considerable weight to be given to the interests of other respectable people. They certainly require that the parent be willing to sacrifice important noncategorical interests of the child, even for noncategorical interests of others. Under extreme conditions, there is even some room for the horrifying thought that the categorical interests of the child are to be sacrificed. Room for such thoughts, however, is limited by the place of parental love in an agent's life. Still, this set of priorities hardly reflects an overly conservative commitment to the welfare of those an agent is related to in only agent-neutral or impartial ways. To this extent worries that any view that takes its departure from Aristotle will be overly conservative and lack progressive vision are unfounded. It is the symmetry of regulative effect as exemplified in these contexts that constitutes the Aristotelian yet progressive view. And note that these priorities are arrived at without the need for an impartial decision procedure and that the rightness of the agent's actions is the nonaccidental result of his or her motives. Thus the account of full rationality and reflective endorsement in these contexts confirms the Aristotelian conception of practical reason.

I turn now to a discussion of Stocker's problem and how parental love can generate a sense of obligation in terms of other-restricting normative beliefs.

4.

Without other-restricting normative beliefs, it is impossible for us to make sense of the place a child has in the sentiments and dispositions of the loving parent. The previous discussion has established that these beliefs reflect a symmetrical regulative function between parental love and impartial respect. It remains, then, for me to show how these normative beliefs can be deontic beliefs and carry a strong sense of obligation. To see this, we must understand how your respectful interest in another person can act as a contrary inclination to your parental interest in your child. This is where you have, relative to your child and the other person, an other-restricting normative belief. In what circumstances, then, are these normative beliefs deontic beliefs?

It is easy enough to imagine cases in which you would feel contrary inclination to favor your child over another person where you have an other-restricting normative belief regarding the other person. A good example is where you are the teacher of both and are grading their papers or deciding on academic awards. The point of mentioning this is to show that one other-regarding interest can act as a contrary inclination to another. In this case, parental love for your child acts as a contrary inclination to simple respect and esteem for the other person. But the kind of case we are seeking is different; it is either one of two kinds. The first is where an impartial interest (respect, esteem, sympathy) acts as a contrary inclination to an agent-centered one (parental love). The second is where a partial interest (parental love) acts as a contrary inclination to another partial interest, that is, to some other form of personal love.

The first kind of example might involve situations where the exhilaration of working in the cause of justice is pitted against the sometimes humdrum of parenting.[22] Here we must imagine that in such a situation you truly care about the other person's just treatment rather than about your own moral self-aggrandizement. It is the simple respect for the other person plus the numbing effects of routine parenting that have led you to the *neglect* of parental commitment. Strongly inclined to help the other person, you are reminded of your child's plight. You then come to believe that you ought to do x for the sake of your child rather than do y for the sake of the other person. On some occasions of such reminders, your normative belief will not become a deontic belief. For sometimes the reminder will evoke feelings of love that will eliminate any competition between the partial interest in your child and the impartial one in the other person. But these reminders do not always eliminate the felt competition between these interests.

You might, for example, feel the competition between the two interests, even after recognizing that the parental commitment to your child comes

22. The film *A World Apart* deals with a woman and her relationship to her daughter as conflicts arise as a result of her commitment against the injustices of the apartheid policies of South Africa. See Chris Menges, *A World Apart* (Atlantic Entertainment and British Screen, 1988).

before the concern for the other person. You might especially feel this way when caring for your child is particularly burdensome and attending to the concern for the other is not as personally taxing. This is often true of the commitments of personal relationships. The concerns that often lead good people to do things that are wrong are not like those that lead others (especially the elusive egoist) to do things that are wrong. It is a mistake born of a certain way of reading Kantian thought to overlook this. In itself, it is a praiseworthy concern that leads the biased parent to sometimes wrongly favor his or her own child when he or she should not. To remove the objectionable element in the bias, it is not love that needs to be subtracted but respect that needs to be added. Likewise, it is an intrinsically praiseworthy concern for another child or person that might sometimes lead a parent to wrongly favor the third party over the child. This is especially true in the humdrum-type contexts. Respect does not need to be subtracted, but love brought to the forefront.

When you are reminded of your child's plight and feel a conflict between your interests in your child and the other person, the conflict does not show that you do not love your child. Rather, it is your parental love for your child that acts as a check on the contrary inclination to help the other person instead. Suppose you are currently justifiably frustrated with your child. You might *need* to be reminded that this is indeed your child in order to avoid the kind of neglect that can come about through what are otherwise admirable motives.

Here it is your love for your child that allows you to check the contrary inclination to help the other person. The competing nature of this contrary inclination is properly analyzed as a combination of two factors. One is your simple respect for the other person; the other is your justifiable frustration with your child. But the frustration with your child is not itself a motive. Rather, it is a psychological influence that serves to detract attention from the rightful place of your child in your sentiments and commitments. This is contrasted with a case in which you might help the other person rather than your child for the express purpose of venting the frustration with your child. Parental love comes in to deal with the frustration in such a way that allows you not to eliminate it but to check it. This is why the interest in the other person remains a psychologically competing interest. It is also why your other-restricting normative belief regarding the interests of your child and the other person is a deontic belief for you, because it results in your having a felt sense of obligation in this and similar contexts.

Of course, if you always find the parental routine numbing and frustrating so that the concern for others leads to your neglecting your child, we must question your parental love. But the presence of some such frustration goes with being psychologically normal, as does the ability to manage these effects with being a normal, loving parent. Thus without the ability to check the contrary inclinations of a normal person with impartial concerns for others, your sentiments, commitments, and dispositions would be incomplete. They would be incomplete as those of a loving parent and would not properly reflect the place of your child in your life. Perhaps this is why patience is such an indispensable parental virtue.

Another way in which contrary inclination might arise regarding an other-restricting normative belief is where the scope restriction applies to the interests of another loved one. You might, for example, have personal love for both your child and your spouse and have the other-restricting normative belief that you ought to do something for the sake of your child rather than do something for the sake of your spouse. There will certainly be situations where the above belief will be accompanied with frustration with the child. And it is your parental love that will act as a check on the contrary inclination of your romantic love for your spouse. Your spouse, for example, might want to spend the evening at the cinema, whereas your child might need help preparing for an algebra exam, partly due to the fact that she has been negligent in her studies. That your daughter has been negligent is frustrating to both you and your spouse, but certainly in some such cases there could be no doubt that the child's interest comes first. Of course, as a loving spouse who is also a good parent, your spouse will understand this. In other cases, he or she rightfully and lovingly will not.

5.

I conclude, then, that if you have parental love for your child, you will, in many normal contexts, have both self-restricting and other-restricting normative beliefs regarding your child. Often these will be deontic beliefs, resulting in your having a felt sense of obligation. The significance of this is that there is a set of normative beliefs that comes with the disposition of personal love in its parental form. This precludes a person from having the dispositions of parental love and giving lexical priority to impartial concerns in all contexts in which they conflict with partial ones. In fact, the dispositional sensitivity of parental love is such that it requires, in some normal contexts, a reverse ordering of priorities. But contrary to the worry of some, parental love, despite its favoring of the child, leaves significant room for commitment and concern for others. Moreover, respect requires it, though not in the ways or for the reasons that the Kantian or the utilitarian would require. Thus the priorities reflected in the normative thoughts of an agent who is both a loving parent and a respectful person reveal the symmetry between the agent's impartial and partial regulative norms. And the agent's deliberations that reveal the structure of these norms take place without an impartial decision procedure. Rather, they are the result of rational reflection by an agent with a respectful and loving character on priorities that structure a way of life in terms of finality and self-sufficiency. This argues for the Aristotelian conception of practical reason as it applies to the agent of integrity in the thick sense as thus far understood.

This completes my sketch of a solution to Stocker's problem, the integration problem, and the priorities problem as they apply to parental love. The sketch not only indicates what the priorities of a loving parent who is respectful of self and others cannot be; it also provides an outline of what they must be. In this regard, it provides an account of how parental love and respect together, as forms of direct concern for others, generate the normative beliefs of a respectful and loving parent. Finally, it gives an account of the motivational match between concern and normative belief in a way that is consistent with a sense of obligation that avoids the problems associated with acting on principles foreign to that sense. In Herman's terms, right action is the nonaccidental result of its motive. In the next several chapters, we will see how this analysis applies to other forms of personal love. These are forms of what I call peer love: friendship and neighborly love.

11. Peer Love

Some people we consider our peers, and others we do not. Those whom we do, we consider our equals in some important sense. Thus if we do not think of others as peers, there is an important sense in which we do not think of them as our equals. For example, most people who believe in God do not believe themselves to be God's peers because they consider him to be superior to themselves. Nor do most people believe small children to be their peers, because they consider themselves to be superior to small children in some important sense. That is, they think of small children as their moral and intellectual inferiors.

It is possible, of course, that we might love our inferiors. Parents do this when they love their small children, but it is possible in other ways as well. Loving elderly parents who have lost their faculties and elements of their character to the effects of aging is an example. Still there are other ways. The wife who loves an abusive husband, the boy who loves his indifferent mother, the citizen who loves an unjust country, all are cases of people loving their inferiors. Although I will address some of these latter cases here, I will do so only in order to elucidate another form of love, one that does not involve love for an inferior but for a peer. Similarly, I will not address the issue of loving our superiors, as theists claim to do when they love God.

Of course, we do not always love our peers, but we nonetheless value them as we value ourselves as objects of respect and esteem. Yet some of our peers we do love, and this gives them a different place in our lives and our priorities than those we either do not value as peers or whom we value as peers but do not love. What, then, is the difference between loving another as a peer and loving another as an inferior? And what is the difference between loving another as a peer and simply valuing another as a peer? Finally, what are the different forms of loving another as a peer?

In this chapter, I address all these issues in a way that prepares for later discussion. Thus the function of this chapter is to gain some clarity about how another appears within the deliberative field of one who is respectful of others and who is peer loving in a variety of ways. Section I distinguishes peer love from other forms of love, particularly from parental love. Sections II and III are given to distinguishing different forms of peer love from each other: friendship and the concept of neighborly love, both of which are forms of loving others as peers. In later chapters I will discuss the integration and priorities problems as they pertain to these forms of love.

1.

The first task is to distinguish peer love from other forms of love. Since I have put aside the topic of loving one's superiors, the task is to distinguish peer love from loving one's inferiors. For convenience, I use parental love as the contrasting case, pointing out differences in terms of intentional features.

The major difference between peer love and parental love is in the evaluative beliefs regarding their intentional objects. Both forms of personal love take only persons and groups of persons as intentional objects; both include the five interests of personal love discussed earlier; and both include identity beliefs regarding their intentional objects. Just as numerical identity—rather than mere descriptive identity—is essential in a parent's love for a child, it is equally essential in a friend's love for a friend, in a romantic lover's love for the beloved, and in a neighbor's love for the community. All these features apply to an adequate understanding of how in general a loved one appears within the deliberative field of a loving person. But, as I have argued earlier, parental love does not require, even in the central case, that the loving parent evaluate the beloved child as either good or even capable of being good. With peer love, however, a positive evaluation of the loved one is essential.

What is essential to peer love are two kinds of evaluative beliefs, and both emanate from the fact that peer love is the love for another as an equal. First, any person of integrity has self-respect and hence the evaluative belief that he or she has the R-qualities essential to respect. Thus if you have self-respect and love another as an equal, then you have the evaluative belief that the other person is worthy of respect and has the relevant R-qualities. Second, any person of integrity has some level of self-esteem and hence the evaluative belief that he or she has the E-qualities (esteem-conferring qualities) essential to esteem. Esteem, remember, is the attitude one takes toward someone as having exceeded the qualities necessary for mere tolerance. Thus if you have self-esteem and love another as an equal, then you have the evaluative belief that the other person is worthy of esteem and has the relevant E-qualities. Moreover, the belief is that the other person has a set of qualities that confer a level of esteem similar to that of which you consider yourself worthy.

Thus it is the notion of E-qualities that provides the basis for the evaluative beliefs relevant to peer love. As we have seen, not all kinds of personal love include the evaluative belief that the loved one is good. Parental love does not require this, nor do deviant cases of friendship, romantic love, or neighborly love. But where these forms of love are forms of peer love the lover has the evaluative belief that both he or she and the loved one have the relevant R-qualities and a measure of E-qualities that confer a similar degree of esteem.

Two qualifications, however, are in order. The first concerns the notion of approximate equality. Suppose, for example, that you are able to love another only if you believe that she has the E-quality of being kind. You may perhaps be able to respect people who lack kindness, but you cannot hold them in esteem or love them. Assume further that it is in terms of this quality, among others, that you believe you and the other person are peers. To say that for you to have peer love for this person requires that you believe that you and she are strictly equal in terms of kindness would simply not be true to the facts. Rather, the sensitivity of peer love to beliefs concerning comparisons of the lover and the loved one in terms of E-qualities is dispositionally flexible. It is flexible in the sense that the disposition of peer love is tolerant of your believing that there is some range of difference between you and the other person in this regard. Thus peer love requires the belief that the loved one is approximately equal to the lover in terms of E-qualities. Nonetheless, if it is peer love that you have for another, you cannot be dispositionally indifferent to beliefs in all disparities of range between your E-qualities and those of the other person. For without some such sensitivity, we are without a way of understanding how it is that you love the other person as a peer.

The second qualification concerns the degree to which your having peer love for another requires your ability to specify those E-qualities in terms of which you see yourself and the other person as peers. The view that seems correct is that your beliefs about the other person's peer qualities must be *in principle* explicable for you. It is not required that any of your beliefs about her peer qualities are explicit. Nor is it required that they are implicit as hidden premises in some readily available set of beliefs you have about the comparative qualities of the two of you. Yet they cannot be sub-conscious in a way that if they were made conscious they would be incompatible with your loving her as a peer. What, then, does it mean to say that such beliefs must be explicable in principle for you? It is to say that, whether you realize it or not, there are some qualities that you value in persons as E-qualities. It is to say that if you came to believe that the other person did not have those qualities, then your dispositional state toward her would be different: Either your love for her would become a deviant of peer love or you would cease to love her at all. And it is to say that your love for her is compatible with your being explicitly aware of these beliefs. These beliefs, then, are explicable in principle, because they are beliefs that you could explicitly hold without threat to your love and esteem for her. With enough experience, you could discover what these beliefs are and explicitly recognize the qualities apart from which you could no longer hold her in esteem and love her as a peer. Thus you cannot love another as a peer, in the central case, without valuing the other person as approximately equal to you regarding some set of E-qualities. Yet none of these beliefs are necessarily explicit for you. In fact, they often will be neither explicit nor readily available to you.

Of course, the belief that another is a peer is not sufficient for peer love. You, for example, might believe that you and both B and C, say, are approximately equal in terms of E-qualities, but you might love only B. Indeed, you might love only B even where you believe that B and C have identical E-qualities. Again, numerical identity matters in peer love, as in all cases of personal love. Just as I would have harmed you if I had made it impossible for you to identify your beloved child, I would have harmed you if I had made it impossible for you to identify your beloved spouse, friend, or neighbor. Such harm is avoided only by the ability to recognize numerical identity rather than mere qualitative, exact similarity.

Another likeness between peer love and parental love bears on the priorities problem. Recall that it is a general feature of personal love that it is sufficient for saying that you do not love B if you know that you do not love C and you care about the welfare of B and C to the same degree. This is no less true about the appearance of a loved one within the loving person's deliberative field in peer love than in parental love. Thus you can esteem B and C to the same degree, but if you have peer love only for B, you will care more for B's welfare than for C's. You will also have interests in B—the interests in a shared relationship, in her mutual affections, in being her benefactor, and in her character—that you do not have in C. These interests along with the differences in the degree of concern will generate both self-restricting and other-restricting normative beliefs that take the form of agent-centered restrictions. In later chapters, I will consider these normative beliefs in the context of the integration and priorities problems regarding the separate forms of peer love.

Here, however, it is important to note additional complexities regarding the agent of integrity as now described. To this point we have been concerned with how an agent of integrity can integrate the interests and commitments of respect with those of parental love. This concern required a solution to Stocker's problem and the integration and priorities problems. We must now add to the agent's interests and commitments the interests of peer love and those of esteem, especially of self-esteem and simple esteem for others. The integration problem, therefore, is more complex. We must consider not only how such an agent can integrate parental love with self-respect and simple respect but also how such an agent can integrate these concerns with peer love and with self-esteem and simple esteem. Moreover, we must consider how one integrates the love for one's inferiors with the love for one's equals. Before I can address any of these complex issues, however, I must make some attempt to distinguish between the various forms of peer love.

2.

There is a kind of human relationship in which persons are bonded together in personal love that is the most intimate form of bonding as equals. This is friendship, in the central case. It includes among other things a one-to-one relationship with another person where each has mutual respect and esteem for the other as a peer. To love another as a friend, then, one must love another in a nonderivative sense. That is, loving another as a friend does not depend on some mediated relationship between the friends. If one's love for another requires that the other belongs to some beloved group, then the love is not that of friendship. Belonging to the Kingdom of God, the Kiwanis Club, the Democratic Party, the Women's Caucus, or the Skull and Bones cannot be prerequisites for the kind of love involved in friendship. This is because friendship is the kind of peer relationship that involves the most extensive sharing of mutual love and esteem between persons. We would not call two people friends in this strong sense if the relationship was threatened by loss of group membership where there was no loss of personal qualities. It is not a personal quality, let alone an E-quality, that one belongs to a group. That one belongs to a group that fosters the mutual love and esteem of friendship could only be accidental to that group. Hence group membership is not a requirement of friendship.

It is, however, a requirement of friendship in the central case that the loved one is approximately equal to the lover in E-qualities. Indeed, there is no other form of personal love where a person's qualities matter more to the relationship than in friendship—more than in parental love, more than in filial love, and more than in neighborly love. Thus to say that another is your friend in this sense is to make an evaluative judgment about yourself and another peculiar to friendship. It is to say that you are equals in the most extensive sense among the persons that you love.

There are, of course, deviant cases of friendship, and it is crucial to understand these differences. For, as it turns out, the priorities of friendship depend on whether the friendship is one of the central case or one of the deviants. Later, this will prove essential in the defense of the Aristotelian model, and Aristotle himself clearly recognized the problem. In the *Nicomachean Ethics*, he says: "A further problem is whether or not a friendship should be broken off when the friend does not remain what he was" (*NE* 1165b:1), and he later distinguishes between two kinds of change, which represent two deviant forms of friendship. Sometimes Kantian criticisms of friendship apply to the deviant forms but not the central case, and Kantians assume that Aristotelian claims about friendship apply, no matter what form friendship takes. As we will see, loved ones appear within the loving person's deliberative field differently in the central case and in the deviant cases, and this fact has implications for the loving person's normative thoughts. It has implications for the regulative functions of personal love within practical reason.

None of the deviant forms of friendship include a requirement of group membership, but some involve loving an inferior. I am interested here primarily in only two kinds of cases. One sort of case is one in which a friend has permanently lost qualities central to being a peer through trauma, disease, or the effects of aging. Certainly the dispositions of love do not disappear with the realization that such effects are permanent. We would be more than a little suspicious that friendship had existed at all should someone claiming to be a friend lose interest at such a point. It sounds a bit odd to deny that the loved one is your friend, although clearly no longer your peer. But this case is not one of the two that I want to emphasize. I mention it only in order to make clear the two kinds of cases I have in mind.

We can make the distinction in terms of a passage from Aristotle. In the *Nicomachean Ethics*, he says:

If we accept a person as a friend assuming that he is good, but he becomes, and we think he has become, wicked, do we still owe him affection? Surely, that is impossible, since only the good—not just anything—is the object of affection. What is evil neither is nor should be an object of affection, for a man must not be a lover of evil, nor must he become like what is base. As we have said, like is the friend of like. Should the friendship, then, be broken off at once? Probably not in every case, but only when a friend's wickedness has become incurable. But if there is a chance of reforming him, we must come to the aid of character more than to the aid of his property, inasmuch as character is the better thing and a more integral part of friendship. But no one would regard a person who breaks off such a friendship as acting strangely, because the man who was his friend was not the kind of man [he turned out to be]: his friend has changed, and since he is unable to save him, he severs his connections with him. (*NE* 1165b:12–23)

We need not agree with everything in this passage to learn from it. What I am most interested in is the distinction between two kinds of change, one possibly temporary and the other permanent. The first sort of case is one in which a friend has lost, with the possibility of redemption, qualities central to being a peer through changes in his or her way of life. The deterioration in character has come not as the result of trauma, disease, or the effects of aging but through life-affecting choices. The less extreme instances involve the loss of E-qualities; the more extreme, the loss of R-qualities. In the former, a friend might have slipped into neglect of community care, into lethargy regarding personal relationships, or into accepting mediocrity in the pursuit of excellence. Changes of this sort result in a loss of esteem, displayed in a sense of humility or modesty regarding the person as a loved one. Thus the loved one appears within the deliberative field as having a different status than the friend who has not changed in these ways. In the latter (where R-qualities are lost), a friend might have let a personal habit inhibit concern for others, a bad feeling grow into malicious intent, or a minor prejudice evolve into gross unfairness. Changes of this sort result in a loss of respect, displayed in a sense of shame and contempt for the friend as a person. Both kinds of changes are inimical to a relationship remaining one of friendship, and, without hope of redemption, there is no long-term hope for the friendship. So the first sort of case, the first deviant form of friendship, is one in which the change is due to the agent's choices and results either in a loss of E-qualities or a loss of R-qualities but the resulting change in character is "curable." As in the central case, friendship of this sort has normative thoughts peculiar to it. Later, I will address this issue, when discussing friendship's behavioral manifestations.

The second sort of case that might be considered a deviant form of friendship involving the love of an inferior is like that set out in the previous paragraph, except the loss of peer qualities is beyond redemption. Here a friend has undergone changes either in E-qualities or in R-qualities that have become permanent due to a change in a way of life. The loss of esteem carries with it the loss of expectations—expectations of sharing the most prized aspects of oneself with a loved one. The loss of respect and the resulting shame and contempt preclude sharing a life that threatens one's own self-respect. Though over time it is difficult and often improbable, it is possible to love such persons, contrary to what Aristotle says. But even where love remains, if we are to call this friendship—which is highly suspect—it is the most deviant form of friendship of the three mentioned. Later, I will discuss the possibility of there being normative thoughts peculiar to this kind of relationship. For now it should be clear that the loved one in these cases appears within the loving person's deliberative field in a radically different way than in the central case. However, I must delay the discussion of the behavioral manifestations and the normative thoughts of friendship until I have discussed neighborly love and its deviants.

3.

Neighborly love, as I intend it, is the love of another person as a member of a community. Here the term "neighborly love" is strictly a technical one used to designate relevant phenomena. Falling under its rubric, I intend the dispositions involved in relationships that might exist in local neighborhoods, plus those that might exist on both larger and smaller community levels. On the smaller end of the spectrum are the relationships that might exist among club members. Excluded are the friendships and other love relationships that exist between one individual and another, independent of some larger group attachment. On the larger end of the spectrum are relationships that might exist among persons as fellow citizens of a country or as members of a common culture. Excluded here are the relationships that exist among persons qua persons, independent of any smaller group attachment.

Mere group attachment, however, is not sufficient for neighborly love in the sense I intend. Such attachment must be accompanied by the five interests of personal love. Thus no purely extrinsic attachment to a group can count as a case of neighborly love. Moreover, the group attachment must be such that the relationship among the members of the group is taken by the neighborly lover to be a relationship among peers. Thus neighborly love is a form of peer love. In this way, it differs from parental love. It differs from the love of friends in that it involves the notion of group membership and the degree of equality need not be as approximate. It differs from romantic love in that it does not necessarily involve sexual interests.

As I intend it, neighborly love does not require friendship. Friendship I take to be a deeper form of personal love than neighborly love, though someone might be loved both as a friend and as a community member. To be loved as a friend is to be the object of an intrinsic interest, independent of some larger social whole or unit. To be loved as a community member, on the other hand, is to be the object of an intrinsic interest as a *part* of a larger social unit. Thus if you have neighborly love for another person, then you must, in the central case, believe that she has the peer qualities of being a functional part of the community, or has been or will be such.

This does not mean that all functional roles that require certain qualities of the persons who fill them are of equal importance to the whole as a social unit. One person, for example, might be a community leader, whereas another might contribute in some other way to the social unit being what it is. Thus your peer love for another as a member of the community need not include the belief that one member's contribution to the community equals that of any other member. But if you have neighborly love for another in the sense in which I intend, you must believe that you and she are approximately equal in one sense. It is that you are both persons with the qualities of a community-minded person and contribute, in one role or another, to the social unit being what it is.

Another mistake is thinking that since the intentional object of neighborly love is a person-in-a-functional-community-role, then the neighbor is loved as a means. But it is one thing to be valued as a means to some social good and still another to be loved as a part of the community. In the latter case, the community would not be what it is without its parts. Even where a means is necessary to a certain end, the end is still what it is apart from the necessary means of coming to be what it is. The partiality of neighborly love shows that the neighbor, though loved as a part of a social unit, is loved as an end rather than valued merely as a means. This is essential to how the beloved neighbor appears within the deliberative field.

To love a community is not simply to be attached to it as falling under a certain description and thus to value any of the necessary means to it. Rather, it is to value as an end that very particular community and the particular individuals who are the member parts of that community. This distinguishes your mere instrumental or extrinsic value of the community from your love of the community. It also distinguishes your love of the community from your simple respect and esteem for it. Thus if you love your community, you are dispositionally sensitive to beliefs about its identity in a way that you are not to communities you believe to be descriptively similar but numerically distinct. Also, since no particular community is what it is apart from its particular parts, you will be sensitive to beliefs about the identity of the individuals who are the member parts of the community you love. Valuing something only as a means does not have this partial feature.

The problem, however, of how identity beliefs function within the dispositions of neighborly love raises special difficulties. According to what I have said, if you love your community, then you will be dispositionally sensitive not only to the qualities of the members of your community but also to identity beliefs of two sorts. First, you will be sensitive to beliefs about the identity of your community. It will be important to you that you properly identify *your* community rather than one that is exactly similar to it in its description. But, second, it will be important that you identify the individual members of your group or community. In small groups, this seems correct. If one loves one's bridge club, one will be sensitive to the identity of each of its members. Outsiders sitting in might be appreciated, but not loved. They are not part of the beloved group. Player substitutions are possible, but not as beloved members of the community. What, then, is the problem?

The problem is that on my analysis some kinds of neighborly love require that we love those we do not even know. This is true even in groups of moderate size. Think, for example, of really loving one's alma mater, one's professional group (the Aristotelian Society or the Southwestern Philosophical Society), one's church, or even one's local neighborhood. Larger groups are also relevant. Here think of being Irish or Scottish and loving Ireland or Scotland, of being a New Englander or a Southerner and loving New England or the South, or of being a Texan or a New Yorker and loving Texas or New York. In all these cases, I mean to refer to someone who really loves these groups, not to someone who is merely fond of them. The person I am referring to is dedicated to these groups and has a commitment to them. Also, it is not simply place that is important, but the communities that live in these places. But in none of these cases can one claim to know all the members of these communities.

One possibility, of course, is that despite the sentiments attached to proper names in these kinds of cases, the names do not in fact attach to communities in any significant sense. What we have in these cases, it might be argued, are simulacra of neighborly love rather than neighborly love itself.

In many cases, I think this is quite right. But I do not believe that it would be true to human experience to say that all such cases are mere imitations. If they are not, then we are left with saying that it is possible to love some people we do not even know.

Let me give an example, and, though it is both anecdotal and personal, it should illustrate the point. Some years ago when the *Challenger* shuttle exploded killing all those on board, I found myself, as did many other Americans, in a profound state of shock. I simply could not accept it. It seemed impossible that these wonderful people could be dead. My reaction, however, could not be explained simply as caring about some wonderful people who were tragically killed. For I was also moved at the loss of the people at Chernobyl, but not in the same way. The difference was not that I thought the crew of the *Challenger* were more wonderful people than those who made the heroic efforts at the Soviet nuclear plant. The *Challenger* crew were Americans, and, to my surprise, *that* mattered a great deal to me. I grieved at their death. I did not—because I could not—grieve at the death of those at Chernobyl. This does not mean that I felt no sorrow for their loss. I did. But I did not love them, however else I might have cared for them. That I grieved at the loss of fellow Americans reveals to me a kind of connectedness that is communal in nature. I see no reason for not calling this a form of love, when it is not mere sentimentality but includes the other features of personal love. Nonetheless, I did not know any of the crew of the *Challenger*. That they were identified as Americans, however, triggered in me the dispositions of neighborly love.

Grief is a very revealing emotion regarding communal relationships. It is an agent-centered emotion in that it is an emotional response to tragic events affecting those to whom one is specially related, which means that identity beliefs are central to triggering the disposition of grief. Other forms of sorrow do not require this. For example, to refer to a group as a group of persons rather than as a group of chimpanzees is not to identify them numerically. It is to identify them descriptively. When the events of Chernobyl were reported to me, descriptive identity was sufficient to trigger my sorrow. All that mattered was that this tragedy happened to some decent people. Their national and numerical identity did not matter at all. But when I heard about the *Challenger* tragedy, the belief that those who died were Americans did matter to my response. I cared more, and the sorrow was more personal, and it is crucial to understand that to call the victims Americans is not just to describe them but to identify them numerically, that is, as members of a numerically identifiable community.

Of course, the more intimate the personal connection, the more intense the sorrow and grief on a tragic loss. The grief at losses involving one-to-one personal relationships—as in friendship and romantic relationships or in parental love for a child—is more intense than in any form of neighborly love. Similarly, the closer bonding of small communities lends itself to greater possibilities of grievous losses than do the less intimate relationships of larger communities. Nevertheless, when one experiences grief, there are at least two central features of the experience. The first is that someone of intrinsic importance in his or her own right has met with tragedy. This happened both with the *Challenger* and at Chernobyl. The second is that the person or persons lost have been lost *to the grieving agent*. The latter can happen only if there is some agent-centered relationship between the agent and the person or persons lost. In my case, the agent-centered relationship with the *Challenger* crew was that we were all Americans and functional members of the same beloved community.

Thus the role of identity beliefs in neighborly love is different from that in friendship, romance, or parental love. In these forms of personal love, identity beliefs must be specific enough to identify numerically a specific individual independent of group attachments. This is because these forms of personal love involve a one-to-one communal relationship. Neighborly love, however, does not require this. All that is required is an identity belief sufficient to identify an individual as a member of the community, which no purely descriptive belief can do. In larger groups this allows that one can have neighborly love for those one does not know. Later I will argue that this has implications for the normative thoughts of neighborly love that are different from both simple respect and esteem as well as the other forms of personal love.

Before I turn to the deviant cases of neighborly love, I must make one more qualification on neighborly love in the central case. When persons are bonded together through neighborly love, a central feature of their bonding is that they share some positive values. If they are bonded, however tightly, through mere opposition to a perceived threat or something of that sort, they are not bonded together through neighborly love. For this reason I do not recognize as communities in the relevant sense groups of people who are bonded together simply through a common hatred generated by irrational prejudice toward others. My reasons for this are not based on a concern for the victims of such prejudice (although I certainly have that concern). Rather, it is because a life of prejudice is not a good life for those who live it. There is not a racist or a sexist alive who would not have a better life by losing the prejudice. Anything that is intrinsically good in their lives owes none of its value to the prejudice. Certainly nothing that could be called love in their lives owes itself to malicious prejudice. That racists and sexists cannot see this shows only how great is the tragedy that has befallen them. Though this sounds somewhat sermonic, I do not mean it thus. I mean these claims as straightforward claims about the psychological well-being of those suffering from malicious prejudice toward others.

Indeed, there is a kind of paradox about irrational and malicious prejudice being at the core of someone's way of life. Take the Nazis, for example. The fact is (as someone has said, I believe) if the Jews had not existed, the Nazis would have had to invent them. Not having any positive basis for communal relationships, the Nazis were thrown back on their hatred and resentment of others. And, of course, like all such people they had to make a virtue of it. But what if the final solution had worked? What if all the Jews had been eliminated, voluntarily moving to another planet in a far-off solar system? This would not have preserved the Nazi way of life. There would have been no one to focus their bonding (assuming, very generously, that there was anything like that among them). Seeking to preserve their bonding they would have had to find others so evil that they would have felt compelled to eliminate them. Only in this way could they preserve not only their way of life but also their character. Thus the paradox of such prejudice is that it requires as a categorical good something it considers a categorical evil. This kind of paradox creates a categorical tension within the lives of those suffering from such bigotry, which is a fact of the psychology of malicious prejudice. It is not an invention of the sermonizing of moral theory.

In the central case, then, neighborly love is a bonding of persons as members of a beloved community who share some positive goals and values. It involves a relationship among peers who hold each other in esteem, though the esteem need not be either as high or as approximate as in friendship. And the identity beliefs central to neighborly love need be only sufficient enough to identify a person as a functional member of the beloved community.

The deviant cases of neighborly love I will consider are analogous to the two deviants to friendship in the central case involving love for one's inferiors. The first is where members of the community have lost valued peer qualities through changes in their way of life, though redemption is still possible. Here I have in mind that it is not just a few members of the community but enough so that the community has lost these qualities, though with the possibility of redemption. Included in this case are some members who have hopelessly lost their peer qualities. I will focus primarily on cases where the lost qualities are R-qualities and where the response is shame and contempt. The second deviant case—which is a suspect case of neighborly love—is where the community, through the deterioration of the character of its members, has hopelessly lost its status as a community of estimable peers. Otherwise, the second case is like the first. In both cases, I have in mind especially those where communities have become insensitive in one way or another either to their members or to outsiders. One kind of special case of this sort is the unjust community.

It is, of course, possible for some members of a community to lose their peer qualities without the community as a whole losing its status as a community of peers. Thus there are deviant cases of neighborly love in which a member fits the description indicated in the second and third deviations above but the community as a whole does not. That is, one can be an unjust member of the community in the second or third deviant senses without the community being unjust.

For now this completes the general characterization of peer love and the distinctions among its most important forms. In the three chapters that follow, I will consider how friendship and neighborly love generate their own normative thoughts and how these thoughts confirm the Aristotelian conception of practical reason. It is crucial to that account, however, that it be kept in mind that loved ones appear within the loving person's deliberative field as beloved ends and that respectable and estimable strangers appear there as ends worthy of respect and esteem. Any priorities that order a way of life that does not give persons the status as the kinds of ends they are taken to be by the agent will not be true to the goods appearing within the agent's deliberative field. Such priorities will fail the criteria of finality and self-sufficiency, for they will not construct a way of life that includes all that is good in a way of life that is worthy of final choice for the agent of integrity in the thick sense.

12. The Normative Thoughts of Friendship

Since the commitments of peer love add to the complexities of the integration problem for the agent of integrity, they must now be integrated with those of self-respect and self-esteem, with those of simple respect and esteem for others, and with those of parental love. Eventually, friendship and neighborly love must be integrated with each other. To accomplish this there must be a solution to the priorities problem. Thus the goal of this chapter is to provide a partial solution to the integration problem by giving a partial account of the priorities of an agent of integrity who has respect and esteem for self and others and who has the commitments of peer love as in friendship.

The solution is partial in the sense that I address here only the issue of priorities as they bear on the agent's other-restricting normative beliefs. The self-restricting beliefs of friendship are important in their own right, but I believe the continuity of the inquiry and the development of the conceptual scheme I wish to defend is best served at this point by providing an analysis of the other-restricting normative beliefs of friendship parallel to the other-restricting normative beliefs of parental love. Here, then, I consider the agent's priorities regarding what he or she ought to do in cases in which there are conflicts between the interests of a friend and the interests of others who are peers but not loved ones. The analysis focuses on what agent-centered restrictions might emerge in the normative thoughts of an agent who has simple respect and esteem for others and who loves his or her friends. The analysis includes both the central cases and their deviants.

The deviants are very important. If one looks at the work of the ancients on friendship, one will find a persistent concern for the influence of friendship on other matters and for what the limit of such influence should be.

This is true whether one is considering Plato, Aristotle, Cicero, or Seneca.[1] Contrary to being a moral hobbyhorse, as Kant once called it,[2] the concept of friendship was always discussed in the context of other goods among the ancients. It is no less important that we should so understand friendship in relationship to the goods of respect and other goods. How we understand this relationship turns on how far from the central case an instance of friendship is. Deviants involving friends with bad character do not yield the same normative dimensions as the central case. For friends with bad character enter the loving agent's deliberative field in a different way than those with good character. And, as we will see, the regulative functions of impartial respect are different for the deviant cases than for the central case, with the determinate function of friendship in the central case being much more extensive than in the deviant cases.

In this regard, some preliminary comments on current Kantian literature are in order. The treatment of friendship is more extensive among Kantian internalists than is their treatment of parental obligations. That said, however, the treatment of friendship is nonetheless very incomplete. Marcia Baron probably has written more about friendship than any of the other Kantians and has shown quite admirably that we do not accept a conception of friendship that is not regulated by impartial respect.[3] But even in her work we do not get any developed treatment of how the CI procedure settles the priorities of friendship and impartial respect across a range of deliberative contexts. She merely alludes to the latitude allowed by imperfect duties. Baron also shows quite well that some treatments of Kant on friendship are caricatures.[4] However, it is not enough to show that some conceptions of friendship are objectionable because they do not exhibit the regulative effects of impartial norms. Nor is it enough to show this and that some criticisms of Kant are based on caricatures. What the Kantian must show is that there is a clear rational procedure for setting the priorities of an agent who is a loving friend and who is respectful of others where that procedure employs impartial respect as an asymmetrical regulative norm. I cannot see

1. See Plato's *Lysis*, books 9 and 10 of Aristotle's *Nicomachean Ethics*, Cicero's *De Amicitia*, and Seneca's *Epistle 60* and *Epistle 63*.
2. See Immanuel Kant, *Lectures on Ethics*, trans. Louis Infield (Indianapolis: Hackett, 1963), 209.
3. See Marcia Baron, *Kantian Ethics Almost Without Apology* (Ithaca: Cornell University Press, 1995), esp. chap. 4, 117–45.
4. See Marcia Baron, "Was Effi Briest a Victim of Kantian Morality?" in *Friendship: A Philosophical Reader*, ed. Neera Kapur Badhwar (Ithaca: Cornell University Press, 1993), 192–210.

that the Kantian literature even addresses this issue. To do so requires extensive analysis of different kinds of contexts and how the CI procedure works for those contexts. To be sure, it is open to the Kantian to abandon the purely procedural interpretation of the CI procedure and appeal to the substantive interpretation with its emphasis on the Formula of Humanity in accounting for latitude. But it is still a requirement of inquiry that the account of that latitude be shown to be restricted by a conception of respect for human dignity that is absolute, nonscalar, nonadditive, and immune to trade-offs in terms of other values. Currently we do not have such an analysis from the Kantian perspective, despite the recent work by Baron, Nancy Sherman, and Allen Wood.[5] Consequently, in what follows I will provide what appears to me plausible Kantian possibilities in arguing for the Aristotelian conception. Central to the discussion will be the issue of agent-centered restrictions.

1.

The issue of agent-centered restrictions involved in friendship is an issue of other-restricting norms that prohibit the agent from acting on impartial norms in order to bring about the best available state of affairs from an impartial point of view. That is, they restrict what the agent can do for others in the name of simple respect and esteem and impartial sympathy. To the extent to which these norms are rational, I will argue, they exemplify the regulative function of our concept of friendship on our concept of impartiality. They do not reflect the rational result of treating human dignity as a value that is absolute, nonscalar, nonadditive, and immune to trade-offs. I will attempt to give an account of the scope and limits of such restrictions and how they emerge within an Aristotelian framework.

The important thing here is to understand the contexts in which these restrictions can have a place in the norms of a person who has simple respect and esteem for others among his or her categorical commitments. We can distinguish these contexts both by the kinds of interests at stake and by the kinds of deliberative patterns that emerge in these contexts, as we did in chapter 10. Broadly, the possibilities of contexts for conflicts between the

5. See Baron's *Kantian Ethics Almost Without Apology;* Nancy Sherman's *Making a Necessity of Virtue: Aristotle and Kant on Virtue* (Cambridge: Cambridge University Press, 1997); and Allen Wood's "The Final Form of Kant's Practical Philosophy," in *Kant's "Metaphysics of Morals,"* ed. Nelson Potter and Mark Timmons, Spindel Conference 1997, *Southern Journal of Philosophy* 36, supplement (1998): 1–20.

interests of a friend and the interests of others held in simple respect or esteem are the following: (i) where categorical interests of the friend conflict with noncategorical interests of others, (ii) where noncategorical interests of the friend conflict with categorical interests of others, (iii) where categorical interests of the friend conflict with categorical interests of others, and (iv) where noncategorical interests of the friend conflict with noncategorical interests of others.

Within these contexts, we can evaluate certain kinds of impartial deliberative patterns for their rationality. Here it is important to understand that what follows is not the sketch of a decision procedure so much as a description of a moral psychology. It assumes that the agent in these situations has a reasonably clear picture of what is at stake in these contexts. It then describes the deliberative pattern rational for agents with a certain character in these contexts. I say this to avoid the misunderstanding that I am attributing some mechanical decision procedure to an agent of this sort. The reason the agent deliberates in a certain way in the context is simply the fact that such a deliberation solves the integration problems the agent faces. This is consistent with the view of practical reason as an integrative function of consciousness that seeks an equilibrium of the goods valued in various ways by the agent. My thesis is that the rationality of these patterns is dependent on the character of the agent and the contexts in which the patterns emerge. I will consider several impartial patterns—some Kantian and some non-Kantian—and show how the impartial norms reflected in these patterns and the norms of friendship are symmetrical in their regulative functions. This could not be true on a Kantian view of any variety. But my purpose here is not simply either to create problems for Kantians or to restate the conclusions of chapter 2. Rather, the aim of my discussion of these patterns is to provide a developed account of the structure of the norms of simple respect and friendship and to show how they emerge in practical reason understood on the Aristotelian model as defined in the introduction.

Among the impartial norms to be considered here are some that were considered in the discussion of parental love: a utility maximization pattern, a Kantian ordinal pattern, a Kantian maximization pattern, and an imperfect duties pattern. The point is not that all Kantians endorse these patterns but that an array of "Kantian" perspectives be evaluated for the sake of thoroughness. In addition to these "Kantian" patterns, I consider two other impartial patterns: one I call a catastrophe avoidance pattern; the other, a great benefits pattern.

A catastrophe avoidance pattern emerges only in contexts involving bad outcomes and requires avoiding bad outcomes only when they are extreme. It can attach to utilitarian or to Kantian considerations. But mere marginal losses of utility or of persons' autonomy are not to count as catastrophic outcomes. Such losses must be "significant" for this pattern to be at work. I will say more about the distinction between "marginal" and "significant" later.[6]

A great benefits pattern emerges only in contexts in which relative social well-being is already good in some sense but can move to being much better by the agent's acting one way rather than another. Thus if things are in a good state of affairs from an impartial point of view and the agent can improve things significantly by doing x but does not damage things by doing y, then the agent ought to do x on this pattern. However, if doing x will only marginally improve things from an impartial point of view, then doing x is not required. A great benefits pattern, then, is not a simple maximizing pattern of either a Kantian or a utilitarian sort.

The scope and limits of agent-centered restrictions generated by friendship are measured by the degree to which impartial deliberative patterns are rational in these contexts. To the extent that the friend's interests require avoiding impartial deliberative patterns, considerations of the friend's interests generate agent-centered restrictions. To the extent that impartial deliberative patterns are rational in these contexts, the friend's interests do not generate agent-centered restrictions. A combined analysis of these contexts will give us an account of the scope and limits of the agent-centered restrictions generated by friendship as a partial norm. It will also confirm the Aristotelian model of both simple respect and friendship as symmetrically regulating norms.[7] I begin with friendship in the central case.

6. Korsgaard seems to worry over related matters in "The Right to Lie: Kant on Dealing with Evil," in *Creating the Kingdom of Ends* (Cambridge: Cambridge University Press, 1996), 133–58.

7. Consequentialists will object that I have not included *indirect* impartial patterns. Cummiskey defers to Parfit in this regard but does not develop just what the indirect duties of special personal relations are. We are to assume, I suppose, that they will be just the right ones. As I note in chapter 2, Herman rejects indirect patterns in these matters, and I think she is correct. Moreover, I have nothing new to say to those who think that indirection accounts for our obligations along these lines. And I do not see what would count as convincing to those who are still unconvinced that if there are special duties to loved ones they are direct rather than indirect. Similarly, I do not know how to convince someone who insists that we have only indirect duties to animals that many of our duties to animals are direct. From my own point of view, that I have an obligation *to animals* not to torture

2.

Consider contexts of the first sort in which the friend's categorical interests conflict with the noncategorical interests of others. In these contexts, a loving friend never engages in the "moral mathematics" of utility maximization. Here *numbers do not count*, and it would be irrational for a loving friend to employ a utility maximization pattern in these contexts. No matter how many noncategorical interests of others are at stake, a loving friend's deliberations are at an end about numbers once it is perceived that the friend's categorical interests are at stake *in these contexts*. Here just imagine the person you believe to be your best friend even considering the possibility that if enough people would somewhat enjoy an evening at Disney World it might just be worth your life from his or her point of view. If you cannot imagine this, then you cannot imagine your friend doing the same thing where it is not your vital interests at stake but the categorical interests in terms of which your very life is meaningful to you. From this we can see that for these contexts a maximization pattern would order your priorities in a way that would not allow your friend a place as an end in a way of life that would capture the good he appears to be within your deliberative field. And it is this fact that makes the maximization pattern irrational in these contexts.

As far as what one ought to do is concerned, this resistance to maximizing is consistent with a Kantian understanding of respect for persons and a Kantian ordinal pattern. For Kantians, utility alone cannot add up to reasons for violating the personhood of others. No matter how many units of utility are generated by satisfying the noncategorical interests of others, these numbers cannot be a reason for violating the categorical interests of a person worthy of respect on a Kantian view. This would be to treat the person as a mere means and would violate the ordinal priority of categorical interests over noncategorical interests. It is important to note, however, that we can get the result that human dignity blocks consequentialist reasoning of the utilitarian sort without going on to say that the value of human dignity is absolute, nonscalar, and immune to trade-offs in terms of other values. All we need say is that human dignity is immune to trade-offs of *this* sort. But on a utilitarian view, at some point the numbers (however

---

them for pleasure is clearer than the theory-laden claim that only rational nature has moral value. It is equally clear to me that my obligations to my children are *to them* rather than an indirect consequent of my concern for maximizing the respect for rational nature.

small in individual cases) involved in adding up the minor satisfactions of others outweigh whatever utility is assigned to the satisfaction of a single person's categorical interests.[8] What I am asserting here is that people who have simple respect and esteem for others and who love their friends *do not* and *cannot* think like utilitarians. The Kantian asserts that a person who has just simple respect for others (let alone friendship) cannot think like a utilitarian in this regard. To this extent, I agree with the Kantian.

There is, however, a difference between the Kantian view (on the ordinal pattern interpretation) and the Aristotelian view. The rationality of the Kantian view is traced through the employment of the impartial CI procedure and has nothing special to do with friendship. On the Aristotelian view, the irrationality of a maximization pattern for these contexts is that neither the agent's respect nor the agent's love for the friend will tolerate a utility maximization pattern because such a pattern will not order the agent's priorities in a way that makes a place for the goods that appear within the agent's deliberative field. This is seen at once when those priorities are placed within the context of how they would order a way of life and the goods valued by the agent. What the agent sees is that something good has either been distorted or is not within that way of life at all. And, given what that good is, the way of life is not worthy of choice. Clearly, these thoughts reflect the fact that the criteria of finality and self-sufficiency are at work in the perception of a way of life from the agent's point of view. Consequently, the agent's doing the right thing in these contexts is the nonaccidental result of his or her motives.

The Kantian can reply here that the normative thoughts of friendship do indeed have the structure I assert and that the criteria of self-sufficiency and finality are also reflected in these thoughts, but this does not undermine the claim that the simple respect that leads to the ordinal pattern is a regulative norm in these contexts. For if friendship were not involved, the simple respect that leads to the ordinal pattern would require the same priorities of friendship that make utility maximization irrational and wrong.

This response is partially successful, because it is true that simple respect would require the ordinal pattern rather than the utility maximization pattern in these contexts were friendship not involved. The beauty of the Aristotelian view is that it covers both norms. The reason that the ordinal pattern would be rational in these contexts were friendship not involved is that

---

8. This is at least true on total sum utilitarian view. Again see Derek Parfit's discussion of the repugnant conclusion in *Reasons and Persons* (London: Clarendon Press, 1984), 381–90.

it is the only pattern that orders priorities in a way that structures a way of life in which the goods of that way of life are self-sufficient and final from the agent's own point of view. Thus there is a simplicity to the Aristotelian model that is lacking on the Kantian model: The kind of explanation for the rationality of friendship as a norm is the same as for the rationality of respect as a norm.

I believe that a similar analysis applies to the first deviant case of friendship, where the friend has lost R-qualities but has the possibility of redemption. Of course, a great deal depends on how bad the change in character of the friend is, how likely redemption is, and how the change in character is related to the interests of those involved. For present purposes, I will assume contexts in which the change is a significant one involving a serious flaw, the likelihood of redemption is reasonably probable, and the change forces a conflict involving the friend's categorical interests. To fix intuitions, imagine that a friend's ambitions have grown to the point that they have eclipsed his sense of fairness in dealing with the important but noncategorical interests of others. His relationship with you is such that it is the only really personal relationship he has. He loves you, and without you not even his ambitions will carry enough meaning to motivate his life. Yet the mere threat of withdrawal will not move him to fairness regarding the important noncategorical interests of others. If his ambitions are curtailed through his collapse as a result of your actual withdrawal from the relationship, other respectable people will receive what they fairly deserve regarding some of their important noncategorical interests. What would the priorities of a loving friend and respectful person be in such a context?

Even disregarding friendship, most of us believe that any reasonable probability of redemption from even some fairly significant character flaws is worth some significant noncategorical sacrifices on the part of respectable people. This is simply to say that retrieving lost character is worth more than minimal costs. Here there are two issues, and both involve the concept of hope. First, is it consistent with having simple respect for others to abandon hope for a person who has lost R-qualities where redemption seems reasonably probable? Second, does this hope generate normative thoughts about giving priority to the categorical interests of a person who stands a reasonable chance at redemption over the noncategorical interests of others? The answer to the first question, I believe, is no. At least it is where the failings are not overwhelmingly short of tolerable and where the probabilities of redemption are reasonable. As to the second question, the answer, I believe, is yes, given the same assumptions about the failings and the probabilities of redemption.

But if this is true of simple respect and esteem, there can be no doubt about friendship: Under these conditions the answer to the first question is no and to the second yes. If the agent is not disposed to hope in these contexts, the agent simply is not a loving agent. Of course, simple respect and esteem for others will require that this hope has a foundation in fact if it is to be normative for the agent. But if the hope does have a foundation in fact, the hope will be normative. It will set the agent's priorities regarding the friend's categorical interests far above any number of noncategorical interests of others. This is enough to foreclose, from the loving and respectful agent's point of view, the consideration of a utility maximization procedure in these contexts.

The second deviant of the central case of friendship is different, however. This is where, due to a change in the friend's way of life, the friend has lost R-qualities without the possibility (or at least the significant probability) of redemption. Although it is possible to love "friends" of this sort and to have simple respect and esteem for others, it does not seem that such love is as normative as in the previous cases of friendship. Can one have simple respect and esteem for others and consider it an *obligation* to sacrifice their important noncategorical interests for the sake of the categorical interests of an incorrigibly contemptible loved one?

Perhaps this depends on how awful the loved one is.[9] It does not seem that our public conceptions of what it is to respect, esteem, and love people in these contexts are clear enough to be determinate and to provide guidance except in the extreme cases. These are cases in which the loved one has become thoroughly rotten and the noncategorical interests are important ones of estimable persons. But one thing is certain: There is no room for the normative thoughts of hope in these contexts.

If what I have said here is correct, we can conclude some things about the scope of agent-centered restrictions from observations about the first kind of context. First, friendship generates agent-centered restrictions against utility maximization patterns in the central case of friendship and its first deviant. The second deviant is unclear. Second, there are no agent-centered restrictions against giving priority to simple respect and esteem for others in these contexts. That is, there are no agent-centered restrictions against

9. In *NE* 1165b:31–36, Aristotle says, "Should, then, a former friend be treated just as if he had never been a friend at all? No; we should remember our past familiarity with him, and just as we feel more obliged to do favors for friends than for strangers, we must show some consideration to him for old friendship's sake, provided that it was not excessive wickedness on his part that broke the friendship."

a Kantian ordinal pattern in these contexts. This is because Kantian respect, like friendship, would give priority to the categorical interests independent of the numbers. Kantian maximization patterns do not emerge in these contexts, because there are no conflicts of similar kinds of interests. Thus there are no agent-centered restrictions against either a Kantian maximization pattern or a Kantian ordinal pattern in these contexts, though for different reasons. Nevertheless, consideration of the role of personal love in these contexts explains something about the motivational structure of the agent's deliberations on the Aristotelian view that the Kantian analysis does not, namely, that the structure of the agent's reflective endorsement of a set of priorities for these contexts involves the criteria of finality and self-sufficiency for both simple respect and friendship in exactly the same way.

3.

Now consider contexts of the second kind in which the noncategorical interests of the friend conflict with the categorical interests of others for whom the agent has simple respect and esteem. We need only consider friendship in the central case because friendship in the central case does not generate agent-centered restrictions in these contexts. If this is true, then the weaker deviants of friendship with their diminished normative structures certainly do not.

The priorities of the agent of integrity who is respectful of others and who is a loving friend are reversed in these contexts as to what they were in the previous contexts. Nothing about friendship in the central case requires giving priority to the friend's noncategorical interests, and simple respect for others will not allow it. If this is true, then a Kantian ordinal pattern is rational relative to these contexts. Also, if this is true, the Kantian ordinal pattern restricts the rationality of both utility maximization patterns and the agent-centered concerns of friendship.

As to the latter point, consider the case of Diane. Diane has a great love for opera and wants to share this with her friend, Karen. This is very important but not categorically important to Diane, and being very important to her it is very important to Karen. Besides, Karen thinks exposing herself to opera is an important thing on its own. When Diane discovers that one of her favorite operas is scheduled for the upcoming weekend, she invites Karen to attend. Unfortunately, Karen cannot attend due to a previous commitment that involves developing a reading skills program for functionally illiterate adults who are trying to become productive members of society. (If Karen does not keep her commitment, the program will fold, not to be taken up by others.) Diane becomes angry and alienated from Karen because of the declined invitation.

Now, it seems that we can conclude two things about Diane, one about respect and the other about friendship. Clearly she does not have the disposition of respect for others that either the Kantian or any mature person would want us to have. But, equally clear, she knows very little about friendship, because she does not recognize the nature of her friend's commitments.

Worries that friendship does not allow significant room for simple respect and esteem for others are simply misplaced. Diane's negligence and indifference to others is not due to her love for Karen and the opera but to a lack of concern for others. After all, we can assume that Karen has an equal concern for sharing the opera with Diane as Diane has with sharing it with her. But Karen has the concern for others, which affects her normative thoughts in these contexts. By forgoing the opera she is not being a bad friend, but if she neglected these admirable people she would be showing a lack of respect. Indeed, it is Diane who is lacking not only in respect for others but in friendship as well. Karen's conception of friendship is regulated by simple respect and esteem for others; Diane's is not. To the extent to which Diane is a friend, she illustrates a deviant case, because if she were a friend in the central case she would understand Karen's priorities. Unfortunately, friends like Diane are familiar to us all.

Consider also how this might be thought to apply to the addiction to smoking. Suppose your friend's addiction to smoking conflicts with the vital and categorical interests of others for whom you have simple respect and esteem. I am thinking here primarily of the dangers of secondhand smoke. In this context, it will be important to consider a special feature of a responsible agent's sense of obligation to be a reliable critic. If you are a respectful and sympathetic agent, you will have a sense of obligation to be a reliable critic on behalf of those worthy of respect and sympathy. To be unwilling to criticize others for acting disrespectfully and unsympathetically toward others when the circumstances indicate that effective criticism is in order is simply to be lacking in respect and sympathy. In this sense, respect and sympathy are intolerant dispositions. Moreover, as a respectful person you will, on reflection, think of it as a good thing that others can be relied on in this regard, even if you at times come up for criticism. One of the goods of simple respect, then, is that there are others who are reliable critics of your behavior, and one of the roles of being a respectful person is being a reliable critic of others. How do these thoughts bear on the present context?

One of the categorical interests of friendship is the interest in the friend's character. Remember that friendship is a peer relationship and that one feature of equality in this regard is that your friend is your moral equal. Thus the loving friend in the central case will be especially concerned to be a reliable moral critic for his or her friends. As a loving friend and as a respectful and sympathetic agent, then, you will have two sources of your concern to be a reliable critic: One attaches to your concern as expressed in your respect and sympathy for others; the other, to your concern for your friend's character. Now, in cases like the one involving smoking and the dangers of your friend's secondhand smoke harming others, it is important to keep in mind both roles regarding criticism.

One might think that the kind of smoking issue described is a straightforward case of a deliberative context of the second sort in which noncategorical interests of the friend conflict with categorical interests of others. But this would be a mistake. True, there are noncategorical interests at stake for the friend and vital and therefore categorical interests at stake for others. The fact that the addiction to smoking is in a way compelling to your friend does not make that interest a categorical one. It is not that your friend thinks that smoking is more important than the health and well-being of others. Rather, the addiction simply blinds your friend to the values at stake. Apparently, this is often one of the features of addiction. But the context is complicated by your interest in a continued relationship with the friend and in the friend's character. Given the influence and possibly alienating consequences of criticism, you have a contrary inclination to being critical and to giving priority to the interests of others. Nevertheless, if the context is one in which it is plausible that criticism might prove effective (even at the cost of some alienation) the agent of integrity in these contexts will give priority to the categorical interests of others. But note that this involves categorical risk—risk required for the sake of others. The reason I say that you will give priority to the categorical interests of others is because there is no sense to be made of saying that your doing so in these contexts is a sign of being a bad friend. Thus if anyone is being a bad friend, it is the addicted person who puts the relationship at risk for the sake of an addiction. Of course, if your friend is one in the central case, he or she will take criticism that is thoughtfully given for what it is, and to the extent that you understand your friend to be a friend in this sense you will have less anxiety about the criticism causing an end to the relationship. The problem is that such addictions are simply difficult to maintain and retain the kind of character to be a friend in the central case, which is one of the major reasons for avoiding addictions.

Of course, this analysis can apply to many, many contexts involving addiction and other forms of irrationality, not the least of which are those including racism and sexism. Still the categorical interests of those affected by these attitudes are so important to the respectful and esteeming agent of integrity that not even the categorical risk involved in putting one's friendships in jeopardy is enough to justify (from the agent's point of view) the tolerance of such behavior. To be sure, we often fail to live up to our own norms here, and we understand why this is sometimes so. But admitting our failures only reinforces the claims here about what the priorities of simple respect and esteem are relative to friendship in these contexts. Without thoughts of self-reproach for such failures, an agent is simply unrecognizable as being respectful of others. Friendship in the central case, however, does not have this result, because friends in the central case are open to the reliable criticism of their friends, as well as that of others who are held in respect and esteem.

Yet let me add that when we do act in accordance with our commitments in these contexts we act not only for the sake of others; we also act for the sake of our friends and in accordance with our own good (if not for the sake of it). This is because as loving friends we act in the role of reliable critics for them, and we expect from them that they act as reliable critics for us. In this way, our partial and impartial norms coordinate in these contexts. Without such coordination we cannot make sense of our concern in these contexts both for our friends and for others. Therefore, although friendship can generate conflicts here, it is also part of the solution: Good friends do not stand by idly while friends are failing in serious ways. They stand their ground as reliable critics, acting not only for the sake of the categorical good of others but also for the sake of the categorical good of the friend's character. Thus these contexts are not of the second sort. Rather, they are contexts that involve multiple categorical conflicts. This is why they are so difficult to manage.

I conclude, then, that contexts of the second sort are not ones in which agent-centered restrictions are even permissible from the perspective of a respectful and loving agent of integrity. This is due to the fact that simple respect and esteem is reflected in the rationality of a Kantian ordinal pattern in these contexts. Since this is true of the central case of friendship, there is no need to consider the deviant forms. Finally, it is also important to point out that there is no need for a disagreement between a Kantian account and my account of the priorities of an agent of integrity in these contexts. Once again, the Kantian ordinal pattern is consistent with the priorities of friendship. However, the structure of the agent's deliberations can be described more accurately on the Aristotelian view. The right set of priorities in these contexts structures a way of life in which both other respectable people and one's friends are ends in their respectively relevant senses. The choice of that way of life with its priorities reflects the criteria of finality and self-sufficiency: The way of life includes both one's friends and others as ends and is chosen for itself. So, once again, the rightness of the Aristotelian agent's actions is the nonaccidental result of their motives, as Herman and Kant require, but without the need for an impartial decision procedure.

4.

Contexts of the third sort, however, are ones in which the categorical interests of friends come into conflict with the categorical interests of others for whom the agent has simple respect and esteem. Here, I believe, an adequate solution to the priorities problem clearly conflicts with three of the impartial deliberative patterns mentioned above: a utility maximization pattern, a Kantian ordinal pattern, and a Kantian maximization pattern. Since it is unclear what an imperfect duties pattern would be in these contexts, it is difficult to assess its relevance. Whatever that pattern is, however, it must be consistent with the value of human dignity as absolute, nonscalar, nonadditive, and immune to trade-offs in terms of other values. I will argue that our thinking about these contexts reveals that we do not endorse that conception of the value of human dignity, and hence we have reasons for rejecting a Kantian analysis of latitude, even where we recognize a role for latitude. The role for latitude can best be made sense of on the Aristotelian model that does not treat human dignity as having the kind of value Kantians claim it has. Rather, it treats human dignity as it appears within one's deliberative field as a very important intrinsic value but one the overall value of which is affected by the need to make a place for other intrinsic values. Great benefits patterns are not contextually relevant because these contexts involve bad outcomes. Some of these contexts, however, involve not only bad outcomes but outcomes that are catastrophic. In some such cases, I will argue, impartial deliberative patterns are rational for the personally loving friend who also has simple respect and esteem for others. Thus, in some of these contexts, agent-centered restrictions are not generated by friendship but antithetical to the commitments of respect and esteem. The sum of these observations defines the symmetrical regulative relations between the norms of friendship and the agent's impartial norms.

In some sense, all contexts of the third sort are catastrophic, because someone worthy of respect loses categorically. But there is another sense in which some are catastrophic in ways that others are not. This sense involves the sheer numbers of similarly worthy people involved in the conflict situation. In some situations, the friend's categorical interests conflict with those of someone else equally worthy of respect and esteem. Given the influence of love and the greater interest in the friend, the agent's norms will prioritize the friend's interests over those of the other person. If this is true, then a Kantian ordinal pattern is irrational in these contexts, for it allows but does not require giving priority to either the friend's interests or the interests of the other person. In other contexts, there will be marginally more equally worthy persons with categorical interests at stake than the friend. Still, given the priorities of deep personal love, the friend's categorical interests will hold first in the agent's normative thoughts. If this is true, then neither a Kantian nor a utilitarian maximization pattern is rational in these contexts. In still other contexts, there will be extremely large numbers of equally worthy persons with categorical interests at stake. It is these that I am calling catastrophic contexts, and it is in these that friendship does not generate agent-centered restrictions.

Friendship prevents treating the categorical interests of a friend on an equal par with similar interests of another equally worthy person, everything else being equal.[10] This is true even for a person who undeniably has simple respect and esteem for others. Of course, having to do something with the foreseen consequence of destroying the categorical structure of another person will fill the respectful and esteeming person with sadness.[11] Indeed, without this sadness, we would be hesitant about the person's respect and esteem for others. But if the agent did not give priority to the friend's interests, we would be clear about the absence of friendship. Still,

10. It might seem that there are clear counterexamples to this. For instance, it seems that in *official* contexts agents often treat the interests of friends and others equally. Reflection reveals, however, that we do not usually allow an agent to fill an official role in contexts in which the categorical interests of his or her loved ones are likely to come into conflict with the interests of others in a way that requires the agent to adjudicate the conflict.

11. Isaiah Berlin was probably right that for any way of life to succeed in its own terms for any substantial number of people other ways of life will be ruled out for other people. This is an unpleasant fact, but it should be kept in mind when criticizing ways of life. One should not assume that as long as it can be pointed out that a way of life has a price for other people that this in itself counts as a criticism. For this can probably be pointed out for most any meaningful way of life whatever. Otherworldly criticisms of this sort have their home in utopian instincts, instincts

where there is both sadness at the loss of others and the disposition to give priority to the friend's interests, we have no hesitation at all in these contexts regarding the agent's simple respect and esteem for others. No one would say that a person choosing to save a beloved friend from a fire instead of an equally worthy stranger was being disrespectful to the stranger.

Nor can I see that anyone would be inclined to say that a person choosing in this kind of context to save a beloved friend rather than some marginally greater number of equally worthy strangers was being disrespectful to the strangers. Yet there would be serious doubts about friendship if the love for the friend operated only as a tie-breaker criterion. The priorities of friendship and other forms of love give significantly greater weight to the categorical interests of the loved one than to others worthy of respect and esteem. Of course, the dispositions of the loving friend in these contexts are coupled with simple respect and esteem for others. This means that having to act in a way that results in these categorical losses for others means even more sadness for the agent than in the previous case. Without this sadness, we are at a loss to ascribe the dispositions of respect and esteem for others to the agent, even in the face of deep personal friendship. Such sadness is one regulatory effect of simple respect on friendship, but it is also evidence of friendship as a determinate and dominant partial norm. I do not see how the Kantian can account for this, even on an imperfect duties pattern with its emphasis on latitude and appeal to the Formula of Humanity.

Clearly, loving friends do not have the latitude to employ either a tie-breaker criterion or a maximizing pattern by appealing to the value of human dignity in these contexts. To do so would violate the criterion of self-sufficiency in regard to how friends appear within the loving agent's deliberative field, even where others appear there as worthy of respect. What explains the latitude is not the value of human dignity as absolute, nonscalar, nonadditive, and immune to trade-offs. If human dignity were absolute, how could we explain a person allowing friendship to provide the latitude for deliberation on marginal and significant differences in the way that makes sense of catastrophe avoidance patterns at some point but not others? If human dignity is immune to trade-offs in terms of other values, then how do we explain the fact that the loving friend in such contexts does make such trade-offs without denying his or her respect for the value of

---

that have probably introduced as much misery into the world as anything else. See Berlin's *The Crooked Timber of Humanity* (Princeton: Princeton University Press, 1990).

human dignity? "Just so" stories that allude to latitude regarding the actions of friendship will not do; rigorous analysis is called for, analysis that shows how the latitude employed is restricted by the value of human dignity as absolute, nonscalar, nonadditive, and immune to trade-offs. Too often, the Kantian literature makes valid points about the regulatory effect of impartial respect on partial norms but then leaves it to intuition to fill in the details of the rest of the theory. But it is just those intuitions that I am challenging here. If I am wrong, there should be some clear specification of the CI procedure in its imperfect duties deployment that accounts for these thoughts. What is it, and how is it compatible with the Kantian account of the value of human dignity?

Imperfect duties are said to allow for latitude in what the agent does in ways that perfect duties do not. Baron's work makes a great deal of this.[12] In addition to latitude about just what one does, there is also latitude in many contexts about how much we are to do, even whether we are required to do anything at all. No doubt there are contexts in which these kinds of latitude would make sense of our judgments. However, it does not follow from this that the CI procedure explains the rationality of the agent's actions in these contexts. There are many distinctions in Kant's ethics, especially in *The Metaphysics of Morals*, but there is less argument than one would desire that shows that it is the CI procedure when applied to human beings that generates these distinctions. Rather, it often seems that these distinctions are generated by our intuitive judgments and the CI procedure is assumed to make a place for them. What is needed is the kind of careful casuistry that links the distinctions to the CI procedure in the way that Korsgaard does regarding perfect duties. I cannot see that Baron ever does this regarding friendship and the kind of context in question. Instead, she focuses on contexts in which respect regulates friendship. At any rate, the context in question leaves little latitude for choice about how much to do or whether to do anything at all. Yet the latitude makes perfect sense on the Aristotelian view: It is required to make sense of the place of both friends and other respectable people within a life that is self-sufficient and final. Any other set of priorities would distort the way that friends and others appear within the loving and respectful agent's deliberative field. When friends appear within one's deliberative field as more important than oth-

12. I will address Baron's views on imperfect duties in much more detail in chapter 18. For her views in this regard, see *Kantian Ethics Almost Without Apology*, esp. 88–110.

ers with equal dignity, it can hardly be the case that the notion of respect that generates that field is one that conceives of human dignity as absolute, nonscalar, nonadditive, and immune to trade-offs.

There comes a point, however, at which the categorical losses for others become considerably more than marginal and therefore catastrophic in the strong sense. There are, I believe, two kinds of cases here.

First, in some of these contexts simple respect and esteem for others and deep personal friendship come incommensurably into conflict. At some point—and I cannot see that there is any algorithm for this—the losses on both sides are stultifying to the agent. Yet there cannot be any thought of flipping a coin: No arbitrary tie-breaker criterion is conceivable to the agent. Try to imagine in this regard the features of a context in which flipping a coin would be appropriate to resolve a conflict between the categorical interests of a friend and those of others. Either the numbers are decisive, or stultifying, or they just do not add up. When they are stultifying, the agent cannot resolve the conflict, priorities cannot be established, and there is a deliberative impasse. When this occurs, the agent breaks down in ways that are indicative of a loss of integrity—a loss of the will to live, hysteria, self-deception, denial, debilitating depression, and so on.

Breakdowns of this sort teach us three very important lessons about stultifying catastrophic contexts. First, they give us a barometer for measuring the adequacy of a theory of human rationality. Any theory that does not recognize stultifying decision contexts by requiring the equivalent of flipping a coin to resolve the conflict is an inadequate theory of human rationality. It fails to recognize the psychological features of agent rationality as it applies to human organisms. Breakdowns in these contexts are a function of the presence rather than the absence of human rationality. Second, these contexts do not generate either agent-centered restrictions or impartial catastrophe avoidance patterns. Rather, they result in agent breakdown and reflect the limits of regulative norms, whatever their type. Finally, they show that there is no value, either of human dignity or of friendship, that is absolute, nonscalar, nonadditive, and immune to trade-offs. If there were such a value appearing within the agent's deliberative field, there would be no such stultifying contexts.

Yet there is a straightforward explanation for this on the Aristotelian model, as it is interpreted here. In such contexts, there is no set of priorities that will allow the agent to project a vision of a way of life in which all the categorically important parts are within it in a way that makes that way of life even minimally worthy of choice from the agent's point of view. The criteria of self-sufficiency and finality applied to categorical goods yield the desired explanation. I do not see how the Kantian has an explanation for such phenomena other than attributing them to our nonmoral, pathological nature. If what I have said is correct, however, the phenomena are due to what is best about us.[13] It is the failure to see how the criteria of finality and self-sufficiency function in practical reason that leads some to think of breakdowns in these contexts as irrational human failure.

The second kind of response to catastrophic contexts involves commensurability. The agent is simply overwhelmed by the numbers of those who will suffer categorically if the friend's categorical interests are secured. Think, for example, of facing the choice of either saving one's friend or preventing the Holocaust. In this case, the agent is able and feels compelled to deliberate to the normative thought of sacrificing the friend's categorical interests. Indeed, it is a case of the agent deliberating to the normative thought that his or her categorical interests are to be sacrificed, and we have already seen how this is possible. Just as friendship can give one reasons for dying for the sake of another, simple respect and esteem can give one reasons for allowing the death of one's dearest friend for the sake of others. Yet engaging in such deliberations and acting on them come with categorical consequences to the agent. Whether they are survivable is dependent in part on what other commitments there are in an agent's complex ground project. But it should not be surprising that, more often than not, being forced by the contingencies of life into making catastrophic decisions of this sort simply destroys an agent.[14] In these contexts, the agent can reflectively endorse a set of priorities that will structure a life for the moment but will not project into the future as a way of life in which the agent has a clear role. It is more important that the way of life projected on the agent's priorities include a place for these respected people as ends than that either the agent or the friend has a clear place there. The most choice-worthy life available is not self-sufficient, and the goods that are missing are the agent and the friend. And it is important to note that these contexts reveal the plausibility of objective over subjective eudaimonism: What one projects into the

13. I argue this more extensively in *Dignity and Vulnerability: Strength and Quality of Character* (Berkeley: University of California Press, 1997).
14. In these contexts, the breakdown comes as a result of the deliberations and actions that are possible for the agent. In the previous case, breakdown is a function of deliberative impasse and incommensurability. That is, in some cases, a decision must be made, but, due to incommensurability, it cannot be made. In other cases, a decision can be made, but it cannot be lived with.

future is not one's virtuous activities or one's happiness but others and their well-being.

The conclusion is that in the central case of friendship and in contexts involving categorical conflicts between the interests of friends and equally estimable strangers, simple respect and esteem sometimes generate catastrophe avoidance patterns that are inconsistent with agent-centered restrictions. When the numbers are marginal rather than catastrophic, however, agent-centered restrictions are generated by friendship, which establishes that the relationship between simple respect and friendship is that of symmetrically regulating norms within practical reason. This, of course, confirms the Aristotelian view, and explains the latitude in these contexts in a way that appeals to human dignity as a value that is absolute, nonscalar, nonadditive, and immune to trade-offs in terms of other values cannot. As for the deviant forms of friendship, it seems that the instances of incommensurability become less as the deviation from the central case increases. In the second deviation (where redemption is unlikely), it is unclear that stultifying contexts apply here for persons with categorical commitments of simple respect and esteem for others. It is, after all, one thing to know what one's commitments are and another to have a competing contrary inclination to keeping them. This can happen with people we love but for whom we have no hope of respect.

5.

Finally, I must say something about contexts of the fourth kind in which the noncategorical interests of the friend conflict with the noncategorical interests of others the agent respects and esteems. The distinction between important and minor noncategorical interests is relevant, as are distinctions regarding different contexts. I have in mind those contexts in which the friend's noncategorical interests are important and others in which they are minor.

We must be aware, however, that the distinction between important and minor noncategorical interests is clear only at the extremes, which makes an account of an agent's normative thoughts difficult in terms of precision. Where the distinction is difficult to perceive, the agent's normative thoughts will be less clear, from the agent's own point of view. This, I believe, is a strength of my account rather than a weakness. Our normative thoughts simply are not always clear, nor can they always achieve clarity with reflection, except arbitrarily. It is a fault of some moral theories that they fail to recognize this complexity and why it exists. Yet I think that in these contexts there is more room under conditions of unclarity for arbitrary tie-breaker criteria than in the contexts involving categorical conflicts. Still some of these contexts are ones in which friendship generates agent-centered restrictions against both utility maximization patterns and in others against certain kinds of Kantian reasoning.

Consider first those contexts in which the friend's noncategorical interests are important.

In one kind of context, the friend's important interests conflict with the minor interests of others who are held in simple respect and esteem by the agent. Here friendship restricts utility calculations, as would a Kantian ordinal pattern. Neither a Kantian nor a good friend would think that calculations regarding the minor interests of any number of other people would permit the frustration of a clearly important interest of someone, whether it is one's friend or not. Reconsider here actions that would prevent Diane and Karen from attending the aforementioned opera. What if these actions had the sole benefit of preventing an infinite number of people from experiencing the normal unpleasantness of a very temporary itch? The stranger who would prevent the itch, it seems, would lack respect (and probably sympathy as well) for Diane and Karen. If Karen canceled plans for the opera on these grounds, Diane would be more than justified in her anger at Karen's priorities, even doubtful about the status of the friendship. At the very least, Karen would be a bad friend to have such a sense of priorities, for these priorities would not project a way of life that is both self-sufficient and final because her friend would not have her proper place there as a beloved end. Yet the alternative that does give her friend the proper place in a way of life is not one that makes inadequate room for respect for others.

Now consider the reverse situation: the important noncategorical interests of others conflict with the minor interests of the friend. Unless the priorities are reversed here, it is difficult to make sense of the place of simple respect and esteem in the life of an agent. A person who values relieving the normal unpleasantness of a friend's temporary itch over the clearly important (even if noncategorical) interests of others is simply puzzling as a respectful agent. How could a respectful person reflectively endorse as self-sufficient and final a way of life that allowed such treatment of others, and how could a loving friend see that friendship required such priorities? Indeed, such a person could be described as insensitive to or negligent of the interests of others, rather than respectful of them. Yet a set of priorities that reflects sensitivity and mindfulness in these contexts is not at all evidence of a lack of friendship. Thus preoccupation with Karen's minor interests might dominate Diane's sense of caring to the exclusion of concern for the important interests of others. But if it does, it is testimony neither to a respectful character nor to mature friendship. Therefore, friendship in such contexts does not conflict with simple respect and esteem for others but is regulated by them.

But what about contexts in which the conflicts are between equally important noncategorical interests of a friend and others held in respect and esteem? Does an analysis of the dispositions of simple respect and esteem and the personal love of friendship yield a clear solution to the priorities problem here?

One might think that these contexts should be analyzed in a way parallel to the contexts in which the categorical interests of friends and the categorical interests of other respectable people come into conflict. But this would be a mistake. First, these contexts are never catastrophic, simply because there is not enough at stake given the kinds of interests involved, which means that they never give rise to catastrophe avoidance patterns, and second, because there is not enough at stake, they are never stultifying contexts in the way that contexts involving categorical interests can be. If this is true, then the agent of integrity is always able to deliberate to a solution and resolve the conflict. The relevant questions, then, are, do these deliberations yield agent-centered restrictions and, if so, in what contexts?

First, consider a case in which a friend and one other equally respectable and esteemed person have equally important noncategorical interests in conflict. Surely, there can be no doubt here that favoring one's friend is not a sign of disrespect to the nonfriend. Yet, everything else being equal, failing to favor the friend would be contrary to friendship. Otherwise, we are unable to account for the status of the friend within the loving agent's deliberative field, given what we have said about the general features of love.

Imagine, for example, that Karen decides to share the opera with Paul instead of Diane and justifies this to Diane with the response that Paul wanted to go to the opera just as much as Diane. Everything else being equal, this would be a sign either (i) that Karen considers Paul at least an equally good friend as she does Diane or (ii) that Karen does not love Diane as a friend. If Diane could rule out the first alternative, it would seem that if she were not hurt and offended by Karen's priorities, we could only conclude that she does not care for Karen as a friend. Moreover, if Paul understands friendship and does not see himself as a friend to either Karen or Diane, he also will be puzzled by Karen's priorities rather than see them as a sign of respect. Thus even Paul will see Karen as appropriately having the other-restricting belief that Diane's interest ought to come first in these contexts.

This other-restricting belief is an agent-centered restriction, despite the fact that the states of affairs resulting from either alternative are equal from an impartial point of view alone. The fact remains that Karen's personal commitments restrict her impersonal commitments. She is not free from her point of view to employ an arbitrary tie-breaker criterion. To do so would violate her commitment to Diane, her friend. Her other-restricting norm, then, is an agent-centered restriction against giving priority to the interests of others on the basis of equal respect and esteem. Where this is contrary to at least some ways of reading Kant is that a Kantian ordinal pattern permits, but does not require, the woman to favor the friend as a tie breaker criterion.[15] But I fail to see how thinking of Karen's priorities as settled by appeal to friendship as a tie-breaker criterion, as a kind of moral permit to favor Diane, is a reflection of Karen's love. Love, as we have seen, is not like that. What matters to one's loved one is not just as important but more important than what matters to some other person, even if the other is an equally worthy person. This is a fact about how one's friend appears within the deliberative field, which does not deny at all that others appear there as ends as well. Thus, in these contexts, a Kantian ordinal pattern is not rational for an agent who is a loving friend and who is respectful of others, nor is a prerogative pattern. This leaves open the possibility of some other Kantian pattern, but it is unclear what it is. The concept of imperfect duties is so amorphous, despite the extensive Kantian taxonomy, that it is difficult to see how one gets from the CI procedure on either the purely procedural or the substantive interpretation to a clear enough concept of imperfect duties to set priorities in these contexts. Moreover, this problem is compounded by the fact that the employment of the CI procedure must avoid filtering respect through considerations of friendship, as indicated in chapter 2. The burden is on the Kantian to provide a clear account here, and I do not see that such an account has even been attempted. Given the fact that there is a clear account on the Aristotelian view vis-à-vis the criteria

15. See Marcia Baron, "The Alleged Repugnance of Acting from Duty," *Journal of Philosophy* 81 (April 1984): 197–220; Barbara Herman, "On the Value of Acting from the Motive of Duty," *Philosophical Review* 66, no. 2 (July 1981): 233–50; and Charles Fried, *An Anatomy of Values* (Cambridge, Mass.: Harvard University Press, 1970), 27.

of self-sufficiency and finality and the categorical/noncategorical interest distinction, we are justified in accepting the Aristotelian view.

But what of the contexts in which there are marginally more equally worthy persons with equally important noncategorical interests at stake as the friend and those in which there are substantially more equally worthy persons involved? Is either of these contexts one in which friendship generates agent-centered restrictions? The answer, I believe, is that in the first kind of context it does, but in the second it does not. Yet I do not believe that there is any bright-line and still nonarbitrary criterion for determining when numbers are marginal and when they are substantial.

If we return to the opera with Karen and Diane, I think we can see this. When the interest is an important one, friendship in the central case does not allow Karen to say to Diane, "I can't go to the opera with you because I must go with Paul and Don who want to go just as much as you, even if they are not my friends. You see, they are fine people from the homeless shelter who need a sponsor to get in. I know that you are also in need of a break from your heavy schedule and have been very much looking forward to this, but after all, there are *two* of them and *that* makes the difference." Clearly, these are not the thoughts of friendship. If this is correct, then friendship renders a Kantian maximization pattern irrational in these contexts. Can a Kantian imperfect duties pattern yield the desired result? Perhaps, but two points are crucial here. First, the account must be given in a way that does not simply allude to the latitude that comes with imperfect duties. It must show how to get from the CI procedure to the notion of an imperfect duty that covers the case in question without filtering and while employing a conception of the value of human dignity in a way that is absolute, nonscalar, nonadditive, and immune to trade-offs. That is, the account must be context-sensitive rather than a hand-wave in the direction of imperfect duties. Second, since we already have an account in the Aristotelian view that shows how the agent's actions in these contexts are the nonaccidental result of their motives, what is the need for the CI procedure, even assuming that some interpretation of the imperfect duties pattern can produce the desired result? What prevents the numbers from counting in the way imagined is simply a function of the fact that such a set of priorities would not structure a way of life in which the beloved friend has a place as the good she appears to be within the loving agent's deliberative field. Moreover, the alternative set of priorities does structure a way of life in which both the friend and the others have their perceived value. Practical reasoning in terms of the Aristotelian criteria of finality and self-sufficiency provides the rational choice.

On the other hand, imagine that you are faced with a choice involving the allocation of scarce time: Either you can devote a certain amount of time to a project that brings an important but not categorical benefit to a friend or you can devote the same amount of time to a project that will benefit in a similar way a large number of people with whom you do not have a loving relationship but for whom you have both sympathy and respect. Suppose, for example, that your regular job has been demanding a great deal of your time but now things have changed to the point that you have more time to devote to other things. One alternative is that you can spend more time on the weekend with a friend whose life would be importantly though not categorically enriched by sharing more time with you. It is not that your friend is depressed but that life would be significantly enriched by a more regular sharing of life with you. A second alternative is that you can spend your weekends working with an organization that teaches a large number of elderly people skills that will add to their lives to the same degree that your friend's life will be improved by sharing his weekends with you.

I am sure that many of those immersed in moral theory will think that the answer is obvious: You would, if you are respectful and esteeming of others, take the second alternative. Others, perhaps, will think that your friendship will require the first alternative. But is either of these clear? What if you take the first alternative and feel little joy in it because of what you could have done for all these other fine people? You do not feel guilty, or shameful, but simply bad that these fine people could benefit from your help. What would such feelings show: that you do not fully love your friend? Or what if you take the second alternative with similar feelings about what you could have done with your friend? Does this show that you do not fully respect and esteem these other worthy people?

It seems that you are simply faced with a somewhat unpleasant choice, despite the fact that on either alternative no one is going to be worse off than before and someone is going to benefit. I cannot see that either your love for your friend or your respect and esteem for others would *necessarily* settle your priorities. You might find that you simply cannot see that there is anything that you ought to do. Nonetheless, thoughts about permissibility might not be liberating. Flipping a coin would also seem odd as a deliberative alternative, at least as a means of relieving the stress. It is possible, however, that your respect and esteem would require that you take the second alternative. I do not think there is anything about the concept of friendship that is inconsistent with such a set of priorities. It is just that I do not see that the concept of respect and esteem is sufficiently clear across persons for us to predict this set of priorities. What is clear to me, however, is that there is nothing about the concept of friendship in the central case that requires you to deliberate to the first alternative. The good friend who has simple respect and esteem for others will understand another friend having a set of priorities that either allows or requires the second alternative. Without understanding of this sort, it is difficult to see how friendship could exist as a peer relationship between persons who value both their friends and other worthy people in these contexts.

If what I have said about this case is true, then deliberative contexts of this sort do not generate agent-centered restrictions. For if friendship can be integrated with simple respect and esteem in either of these two ways— as allowing or requiring the second alternative—then friendship does not generate agent-centered restrictions in these contexts. But note that the absence of agent-centered restrictions here is not accounted for on either a utilitarian or a Kantian basis. Nor is it accounted for on the basis of catastrophe avoidance considerations, for there will be no catastrophe either way. Rather, what is at work here are considerations of flourishing, not at the borders of marginal increases in utility, but at the rapidly expanding horizons of the well-being of many people. Thus what is at work here is a great benefits pattern.

Sometimes we are struck with the differences in alternatives because one alternative would produce a great deal of good by improving many already good lives in significant ways. Yet there are other alternatives we could choose that would not result in as much good but would not result in catastrophe. This is the kind of context we are considering. When the sacrifice of overall flourishing would be neither noncatastrophic nor merely marginal but significant, this sometimes affects what we think it is rational to do. In such a context, neither mere maximization nor catastrophe avoidance patterns are at work. It is the sheer greatness of the benefit, not just that it is better, that moves us. Why does it move us? Because it allows us to project a way of life that accommodates all that we see as good within our deliberative field where that way of life is worthy of choice for itself. This is the Aristotelian view.

What would make such a pattern rational over a mere maximization pattern that would require always selecting for *any* marginal increase in utility no matter what the context? One answer is this: It would be rational to employ a great benefits pattern in a context in which the costs in terms of flourishing for other good people weighs too heavily on an agent in terms of the important interests of his or her loved ones. I am sure that many moral theorists will cringe at this because of its messiness. But I cannot see what the philosophical argument is that there is a nonarbitrary way of achieving neatness here. Human rationality simply is not as neat as some people want to think, even under the most ideal cognitive conditions. My claim here is that the rationality of great benefits patterns is context dependent, as is the rationality of Kantian, utilitarian maximization, and catastrophe avoidance patterns. In contexts in which great benefit patterns are rational, one of the limits of agent-centered restrictions is reached. This I have argued applies in the current kind of context.

6.

A summary here reveals that friendship both limits and is limited by our concern for self and others. Where agent-centered restrictions are generated within the dispositions of a person who has simple respect and esteem for others but who is also a loving friend, friendship limits the concern for others in setting the priorities of the agent. Where impartial deliberative patterns generate a sense of obligation to others or even simply allow the agent to give priority to others, friendship's restrictions are limited by the concern for others. I have tried to argue that, in different contexts, depending on the kinds of interests at stake and the kinds of relationships that exist between persons, there is a significant place for agent-centered restrictions, on the one hand, and impartial patterns, on the other. In other contexts, friendship and impartial patterns converge. Within these boundaries lie the priorities of a well-integrated agent who is personally loving and respectful and esteeming of others. But it should be clear that this agent is neither a Kantian nor a utilitarian, because there is no one kind of concern—even the concern for human dignity—that is lexically privileged across deliberative contexts that can solve for the integration problems. Nor is there any one kind of concern that either directly or indirectly sets the priorities of an agent of integrity without regard to context. Moreover, it should be clear that the priorities expressed here are decidedly not those of an overly conservative conception of morality, nor is the Aristotelian conception of practical reason they reflect.

13. The Normative Thoughts of Neighborly Love, Part I
Autonomy and Subservience

The thick conception of integrity as we now have it includes a solution to Stocker's problem and the integration and priorities problems regarding an agent who has simple respect, esteem, and sympathy for others and who is both a loving parent and a friend. These problems become more complex now because we must add to the thick conception the component of neighborly love, the concern an agent has for a beloved group or community.

The complexities here are both enormous and daunting. So intimidating is the range of these difficulties that I will simply put certain of them aside, not because they are unimportant, but because I want to make progress on two other fronts. Among those put aside are Stocker's problem and the integration and priorities problems as they apply to integrating the commitments of neighborly love with parental love, friendship, and even different cases of neighborly love.

The first of the fronts on which I want to make progress involves the integration and priorities problems and the concept of individual autonomy, a concept of much importance to the liberal tradition. One of the major worries liberals have about views that place a great deal of emphasis on community is that they will involve values and practices that will violate the integrity of the individual.[1] Individuals, they worry, lose their status as intrinsically important as separate and numerically distinct persons due to the strong emphasis on community. However, it should be clear that on the view defended here no conception of community or neighborly love is ac-

---

1. See John Rawls, "A Kantian Conception of Equality," in *Readings in Social and Political Philosophy*, ed. Robert M. Stewart (New York: Oxford University Press, 1986), 190.

ceptable that violates any of the conditions for integrity in the thin sense. Therefore, a conception of neighborly love must solve the priorities problem in a way that is consistent with the commitments of the agent that are foundational for self-respect, for without self-respect an agent cannot have a sense of worth as a separate and numerically distinct person. Moreover, on the thick conception we are considering, the conception of neighborly love must be consistent with the agent's commitments that are foundational for self-esteem. Thus I hope to show here and in the next chapter that the Aristotelian framework, wherein neighborly love and self-respect are symmetrical in their regulative functions, is better equipped to account for the concept of autonomy than is the Kantian account.

The second front involves the concept of a just community, another concept usually thought best analyzed in Kantian terms. Here there are two issues. The first involves internal justice and the agent's relationships to others within the community. The second involves external justice and the agent's relationships to those outside the community. Although I will say some things about internal justice, the primary focus will be on the integration and priorities problems as they apply to the issue of external justice. As framed here, this is the issue of the scope and limits of agent-centered restrictions as generated by neighborly love. I hope to show that the Aristotelian account can provide a rationale for these restrictions in a way that also requires a very progressive agenda for external justice. I will address these issues in chapter 14, but first I must consider the self-restricting norms of neighborly love.

1.

The account here is not meant to be complete but to provide something of a picture of what an agent's autonomy comes to on the integrity-sensitive conceptual scheme I am considering. Central to this task is a distinction between autonomy of interest and autonomy of conscience. Autonomy of interest concerns the sense in which an agent's interests are free of extraneous influences. Among the standard worries here are those concerning the influences of coercion by others, psychological encumbrances of various sorts, false beliefs, and mistakes in reasoning.[2] Autonomy of conscience, on

2. See John Harsanyi's discussion of preference autonomy in "Morality and the Theory of Rational Behavior," in *Utilitarianism and Beyond*, ed. Amartya Sen and Bernard Williams (Cambridge: Cambridge University Press, 1982), esp. 54 ff.

the other hand, concerns the sense in which an agent's normative beliefs are free of extraneous influences. Though the standard worries apply here as well, it is less clear what counts as a psychological encumbrance. Whether and to what extent neighborly love is such an encumbrance in that it blinds an agent to other considerations is among the relevant issues.

As applied to the issue of autonomy of interest, which is the topic of this chapter, the issue regarding autonomy and neighborly love can be put in terms of the concept of subservience or servility. Can an Aristotelian conceptual scheme place a significant emphasis on community and neighborly love without requiring subservience or servility on the part of the agent in regard to his or her own interests? Can it do this in the sense that it does not require an agent to subordinate his or her interests in a servile way to the interests of the community? If it can, then at least one Kantian objection to the Aristotelian scheme will have been refuted. It is the purpose of this chapter to provide such a defense. Of course, this leaves open the possibility that the Aristotelian scheme cannot successfully be defended in terms of its account of autonomy of conscience. But I will address that problem in the next chapter.

I argued earlier that when an agent feels restricted in pursuing his or her own interests because of respect, esteem, or personal love for another, this is not viewed by the agent as a loss of a good for the agent. To the contrary, in the case of personal love, to prioritize a loved one's categorical interests over one's own noncategorical interests is a conceptual feature of a good for oneself, namely, the good of personal love. Things are a bit different with simple respect and other impartial sentiments, but still there is no sense that the self-restricting beliefs generated by these sentiments are violations of one's own good or of one's autonomy. One's autonomy, then, is found in the expression of the priorities of one's deepest commitments. Here we are considering the deepest commitments of an agent who has self-respect and who has neighborly love for others.

It is interesting in this regard that Kantians see no violation of an individual's autonomy in the dictates of respect for persons. The norms generated by the categorical imperative are the expression of individual autonomy from the Kantian point of view; they are not violations of it. Being rational agents, we find our autonomy in acting in accordance with the dictates of reason, which require respect for persons. This is true, on the traditional Kantian view, even if we are acting contrary to our own good, contrary to those things that provide unity and meaning to our lives. On the internalist Kantian view, rational agents only find those ways of life meaningful that are regulated by the requirements of the CI procedure. The restrictions of the procedure, then, are expressions of autonomy rather than violations of it.

Kantians, therefore, cannot object to a conceptual scheme on the grounds of autonomy if their only point is that the view in question imposes some self-restricting normative beliefs. Moreover, on their own view, it is a defense of a normative conceptual scheme that it can be shown that the agent's own deepest commitments require the norms of the scheme. Autonomy, as I conceive it, is not the capacity to act in accordance with reason in some purely cognitive sense. Rather, it is the capacity to act in accordance with and from a sense of the priorities of one's own deepest commitments, where one is not clearly influenced by objectionable irrational forces. Thus neighborly love is not an objectionable irrational force but a substantive basis for ordering the priorities of the agent of integrity in the thick sense. Of course, neighborly love must be integrated with the other components of the thick conception of integrity. But this only sets the integration and priorities problems, it does not treat these influences as mere input to a cognitive output capacity. It does not treat these concerns as the subjective matter on which a purely rational decision procedure (the CI procedure) imposes its a priori form. How these problems work out with a sense of community based on neighborly love is the subject of this chapter and the next.

2.

I will consider here only conflicts between the agent's interests and the interests of the community as a whole. Thus, in considering the self-restricting beliefs of the agent of integrity in the thick sense, I am considering the issue of autonomy of interest. It is only in chapter 14 when I consider the other-restricting beliefs of such an agent that the issues of autonomy of conscience and the just community take central stage.

Beginning with the central case (as opposed to the deviant cases of neighborly love described earlier), we should distinguish between nonspecialized and specialized communities. Not all communities have explicit goals, but if a group is a community, it has a unifying basis. A group of people might simply enjoy each other's company and be bonded together in that enjoyment, yet their goals as a group might be something else entirely, for example, turning out widgets. In this case, the unifying basis is not the goal of turning out widgets but enjoying each other's company. A nonspecialized community is one in which the unifying basis is a shared general way of life. A general way of life is one that has a broad basis in a variety of human concerns—raising a family, having and making friends, protecting and enhancing an environment, making a living, getting an education, pursuing one's work, and so on. A specialized community is one in which the unifying basis is a component in a general way of life. The local angler's society is a community that has as its unifying basis a shared interest in angling. The local college might have as its unifying basis the shared goal of promoting a liberal arts education within the local college community.

Of course, some communities are embedded within other communities. One nonspecialized community might be embedded within a larger non-specialized community, and a specialized community such as an academic department might be embedded within the larger specialized community of a college or university. But not all communities are so embedded. Suppose we could say with some significance that a state or a region or even a country is a community. Still it spreads the concept far too thin to assert that we are all embedded within the community of humanity. To say this is poetry, not philosophy. For it is false that we all share a general way of life and that we are all bonded together through love as members of a universal nonspecialized community. Therefore, some people are members of *other* communities and are either familiar or unfamiliar strangers to us.

Another important feature of communities is that there are membership criteria. The first of these involves the E-qualities of the members. To be a member in good standing, one must share the qualities central to the way of life shared by the community. This is true in both specialized and non-specialized communities. Being a good philosopher in some public sense is necessary for membership in a group of philosophers where that group is a community. Also, being a good neighbor in some public sense is necessary for membership in a local neighborhood where that neighborhood is indeed a community. Of course, the public criteria need only be internal to the local community and to the conception of the way of life, whether specialized or nonspecialized, shared by that community. Nevertheless, the criteria are public and social rather than private and individual.

The second criterion for membership is that one both loves and is loved by the community. We are considering the norms of neighborly love, and though there may be other sources of bonding within a community, they are not the present subject. Thus, in the central case, the agent concerning us is one who cares for and believes that he or she is cared for in a special way by the community.

With this in mind, we can pose the issue of autonomy in terms of membership criteria. Are the membership criteria of neighborly love threatening to the autonomy of the agent's interests? Specifically, do the requirements of membership impose a way of setting the agent's priorities contrary to the deepest commitments of a person who has self-respect and self-esteem? Put this way, the issue is whether the priorities of neighborly love require subservience or servility by requiring an objectionable subordination of the agent's interests to the interests of the community. Clearly, if we cannot avoid a concept of neighborly love that requires an agent to be obsequious, we cannot endorse both neighborly love and autonomy. And we do, in this sense, endorse autonomy. Thus to insist on a conception of neighborly love that will pass this test is to insist on a conception regulated by the norms of self-respect. At issue between the Aristotelian and Kantian accounts is whether such respect is asymmetrical in its regulative functions. It will take the arguments of both the current and the following chapter to establish that these functions are symmetrical.

3.

You are subservient to your community, let us say, if you lexically order the interests of your community over your own interests across all deliberative contexts. This, of course, is extreme subservience. Another form might be one in which you give priority to your own interests over the interests of the community only where the interests of the community are minor and your own are categorical. Surely this too is subservience, but less extreme than the first form. A final possible form of subservience might be one in which you give priority to your own interests over the interests of the community only where the interests of the community are noncategorical and your own are categorical; otherwise, you give priority to the interests of the community. The difference in this last form and the previous form of subservience is that on this last form you would be willing to ask the community to give up some things that are important but noncategorical from its point of view for your sake. On the previous form, you would not.

In order for any of these possible forms of subservience to occur, there must be an agent with complex ground projects and multiple bases for self-assessment. You could not in these cases subordinate your interests to the community unless you had some categorical interests distinct from those of the community. If, however, your identifying thoughts were exhausted by the priorities of the community, there could not be the kinds of conflicts that make subservience possible. The categorical interests of the community would be your categorical interests, as would the community's categorical aversions and noncategorical interests. What is required for subservience is a distinction between what is good for oneself and what is good for one's community and a willingness to subordinate the former to the latter. It is possible, however, that there are agents without this sense of distinction due to their identifying thoughts being solely based on community membership criteria. Call agents with such identifying thoughts C-agents.

Some, I am sure, would want to say that C-agents constitute the most extreme form of subservience there is. At least, one might say, the first form of subservience above assumes agents with a sense of themselves as distinct from the community. C-agents cannot even think of themselves apart from the community, let alone as important apart from the community. How, then, can we think of them as self-respecting or as in any sense autonomous?

Stated this baldly, this view of C-agents is hasty. Think of the Japanese kamikaze pilots of World War II. On one interpretation, they were C-agents merely acting out the priorities of their culture. They were not subordinating their interests to the cause of Japan. But to say that they thereby lacked a sense of self-worth as separate and numerically distinct individuals would be decidedly contrary to the facts. I say this because they had a basis for self-assessment in their commitments as good Japanese. Had they suffered weakness of will or otherwise been unable to stand by their commitments, they would have suffered utter shame and self-contempt. Their willingness to act in these ways was a primary basis for their individual self-worth. So it cannot be argued *simpliciter* that C-agents lack integrity on the grounds that they fail to have a sense of self-worth as separate and numerically distinct individuals. (Indeed, one would be hard-pressed to find a culture in which its members are more prone to individual self-assessment than the Japanese.) Therefore, there is nothing about C-agents per se that requires that we think of them as lacking autonomy because they lack a sense of self-worth as individuals.

Nevertheless, the agent of integrity in the thick sense is not a C-agent. One reason for this is that the agent of integrity in the thick sense has categorical commitments to those outside the community. But this is a very different kind of point, one that is relevant to the issue of external justice. For now, however, it is important to show that C-agents should not be disallowed as agents of integrity in the thin sense on the grounds that they are dominated by subservience and a lack of self-worth. For they are not. Still they are disallowed as agents of integrity in the thick sense because the latter have categorical interests other than the interests generated by neighborly love. I turn then to those senses of subservience that do not involve

C-agents and to the concept of autonomy appropriate to the agent of integrity in the thick sense.

4.

I am interested primarily in the two less extreme forms of subservience in which you are willing to ask the community to put your interests ahead of the community's in at least some deliberative contexts. For this to occur, the interests at stake for you must be other than the categorical interests shared by the community. Consider first the case where your interests are categorical and the community's are minor. Suppose the community is a non-specialized community that provides a general way of life in which you have a special interest but that accommodating this interest would come at the cost of a minor interest of the community. Imagine, for example, that you are a farmer by trade and tradition, that farming is central to your way of life, and that you own land the community wants but does not in any deep sense need.

The problem with this case is that it is difficult to see how there could be a normative conflict here in the central case. To be sure, the interests could conflict, but how there could be a normative conflict between you and the community is the issue. In the central case, not only do you have the five interests of personal love in the community; the community also has these interests in you. How, then, could there be a conflict between the minor interests of the community and your categorical interests where the community demands that you give priority to its interests? To do so would show that the community does not love you. Clearly, if you have self-respect and see the community as making demands of this sort, your doubts about membership will not focus on your qualities but on those of the community. You will see the community, rather than yourself, as unloving. Therefore, you will not have the self-restricting thought that the community's minor interests come before your categorical interests. Indeed, you will not have the self-restricting thought that any of the noncategorical interests of the community come before your own categorical interests. Nor in the central case will the community think that you should have such thoughts. Communities bonded together in personal love do not have such priorities. Moreover, the priorities of a loving community are inconsistent with the priorities of subservience. This is because subservience is incompatible with peer relationships, and peer relationships require the intrinsic importance of neighbors as separate and numerically distinct individuals. Put in Aristotelian terms, the point is that the priorities that would allow for subservience do not order a way of life in which you would have a place as a peer with those you both love and hold in esteem. It is the fact that you appear within your deliberative field as worthy of esteem that rules out this way of life as being alluring when imaginatively projected as your future. On the Kantian view, the CI procedure, I suspect, would rule out subservience as a perfect duty to yourself. But note that the Aristotelian view provides the right result without an impartial decision procedure and does so in a way that guarantees that the rightness of your action is the nonaccidental result of your motive.

Not all cases, however, are central cases. Some are deviant. For instance, what if you love the community but the community is demanding categorical sacrifices of you for the sake of minor interests of the community? Suppose this is due to a change in the general way of life of the community. Consider an example.

Jason is a member of a specialized community, a university, say, where the community has slipped from being a group of mutually concerned teachers and scholars to something else. What they have become is a highly competitive group of professionals who are more concerned with advancing the prestige of their individual careers than with nurturing an intellectual community. Thinking of the work that goes with such nurturing as trivial and unimportant for those on "the cutting edge," they increasingly transfer their share of it to people like Jason who desire not only to have an intellectual community but also to make their own contributions to scholarship. Here the minor interest at stake for Jason's colleagues is the interest in avoiding a small share of routine activities central to nurturing the intellectual health of the university. The categorical interest at stake is Jason's interest in having enough time himself to be a good scholar as well as an excellent teacher and colleague.

If we imagine that Jason is categorically committed to excellence as a teacher and a scholar and that the community is incorrigibly committed to a corrupt set of priorities, it is difficult to see how he could maintain a sense of community with the university. What would it mean to assert that there is any community of which Jason is a member when not even his categorical interests are considered important enough to reorder the community's priorities? Perhaps he could still love this group in some nostalgic sense, but he could see it neither as a community of which he is a part nor as a group to which he must subordinate his interests, categorical or otherwise. Self-respect does not allow such a set of priorities, and neighborly love does not require it. For it is never in terms of neighborly love itself that a community would make such demands, and neighborly love itself would always reverse the priorities. In Aristotelian terms, neighborly love is consistent only with a set of priorities that orders a way of life in which its members are all worthy of esteem; otherwise, that way of life is not worthy of choice, for it is lacking a fundamental good. In Jason's case, this would be the good of self-respect.

Jason's sense of neighborly love, then, will itself include the regulative norm that the community must treat him with respect and esteem. Indeed, he will have an aversion to membership in any community that does not treat him in this way. Any community that would subordinate his categorical interests to the community's noncategorical interests is one in which Jason is not treated with respect and esteem. Moreover, he will have the view that he should be treated not only with respect but also with esteem, as an equal in the community. Not being treated with respect and esteem will not so much be a sign to him that his rights have been violated as that he is not loved as a part of the community.

But what about the corrigibly deviant case where the community is willing or requires of Jason that he subordinate his categorical interests to the important noncategorical interests of the community? Suppose, for example, that the community is an embedded but still nonspecialized community that provides a general way of life in which Jason has a statistically deviant interest. Suppose, for instance, that he is homosexual and wants to be recognized as having a marital relationship with another man. The community feels uneasy about this, but it is far from having a categorical aversion to it. Still, in the presence of the larger community, it is embarrassed and pressures Jason just to keep things quiet. Here the community does not experience shame in regard to Jason, but it is nevertheless embarrassed. Why does he have to be so public about his relationships?

Now assume that Jason has plausible grounds for believing that his community is corrigible in this regard, that it can come to see that it has a poor set of priorities. That is, he believes the members of the community are truly loving people who are nonetheless a bit repressed sexually. Temporarily influenced by embarrassment, their priorities are distorted by a psychological encumbrance. What Jason believes is not necessarily that they will change their sexual preferences. Rather, he believes that once they see things clearly as loving neighbors, they will be proud of their commitment to him despite this kind of difference, and, most important, they will change their attitude toward those who disapprove of him because of his values. In a case like this, what will be Jason's self-restricting normative beliefs if he is an agent of integrity?

One self-restricting thought he will not have is that he should sacrifice his identifying thoughts as a homosexual to prevent embarrassment to the community. Only a servile person could think that. The servile person is one who does not appear within his own deliberative field as worthy of respect and esteem, and it is this fact that allows him to project a way of life on a set of priorities that does not give him equal standing with his peers. Given the description of Jason's situation, he will have the normative thought that the community has in its heart of hearts the self-restricting belief that they should subordinate their concerns about embarrassment to his categorical interest in his personal relationships. A subservient person could not understand the community as having such norms. The members of a subservient person's community appear within his deliberative field as superior to him and their interests as more important than his. But this is not true of Jason, for he is an agent of integrity in the thick sense, and it is this fact that will not allow him to choose a set of priorities that orders a way of life in which he has an inferior place to his peers. The Aristotelian criteria of finality and self-sufficiency are clearly at work in his normative thoughts, thoughts that preclude his being servile.

Yet it does not follow from this that Jason will not have any self-restricting norms in this kind of context. He might very well have such norms, for he might, without being servile, have a contrary inclination. A loving person does not want to embarrass a loved one. This is not a categorical commitment of a loving neighbor, but it is an important interest, an interest that can compete psychologically with a categorical interest. On such occasions, Jason will have the normative belief that he ought to give priority to his own interest over the community's noncategorical aversion to embarrassment. Also, as a loving neighbor committed to the categorical interest of his peers in being loving neighbors, he will have the commitment to being a reliable critic. He will, therefore, have the self-restricting normative belief that he should not give in to his contrary inclination for the sake of his neighbors. Indeed, he will not think that acting on the basis of such a contrary inclination is good for them, let alone for him, but contrary to their own integrity. These self-restricting norms are hardly those of servility or subservience. They are in fact the very opposite and are generated by neighborly love itself, not by some independent concern. Thus one of the motives that moves Jason to reject servile priorities is his love for his neighbors. When he considers the way of life ordered by servile priorities, his neighbors do not appear within that way of life as peers but as inferiors. Therefore, in these contexts, neighborly love and the Aristotelian criteria of finality and self-sufficiency are not only consistent with individual autonomy, they require it. For autonomy of this sort is essential to the peer relationships of community.

Still there is another feature of this kind of case we must consider. The above comments establish that as an agent of integrity who is a loving neighbor Jason will not have the normative thought that he ought to subordinate his categorical interests to the noncategorical interests of the community. Rather, he will have the thought that for its sake he ought not to treat its interests in this way. Yet, on the set of priorities we are considering, he will have the normative thought that he ought to subordinate his categorical interests to the categorical interests of the community should they conflict. Is this subservience? Are these thoughts consistent with the normative thoughts of an agent of integrity, and are they consistent with the normative thoughts of neighborly love? I will consider these issues only within the parameters of the central case of neighborly love. What I will argue is that in some but not all contexts an agent of integrity who is also a loving neighbor will have this set of priorities; therefore, if Jason has this set of priorities across all deliberative contexts, he is subservient and lacks autonomy. Thus if the argument works for the central case, there is no need to consider the deviant cases. For if Jason's subordinating his interests to the interests of the community would be subservient in the central case, it would be even more subservient in the deviant cases.

It is tempting to say that such cases cannot occur. After all, if there is mutual love between Jason and the community, the community will have a categorical interest in Jason's categorical interests, even if the objects of those interests themselves are not very important to them independent of their importance to Jason. Conversely, Jason will have a categorical interest in the categorical interests of the community. How, then, could there be a conflict?

Despite the temptation to think that such conflicts cannot occur, there is an answer to this question. The answer is that just as an individual can experience a categorical conflict, so can a community. In order to survive, a community can find itself having to require things that destroy some of its members. In some such cases, the community is being tyrannical; in others, it is simply performing acts of love in tragic circumstances. But since we are considering the central case, we are considering what a loving community would do under such circumstances. Similarly, issues of survival might place an individual in the position of requiring things that will destroy the community. In some such cases, the individual is being selfish; in others, he or she is simply acting as lovingly as one can under tragic conditions. But in either case, such occurrences are both rare and delicate in their logic.

First, consider a case in which a loving community might require categorical sacrifice from some of its members. One case involves a nonspecialized community. At stake from its point of view is the general way of life that is the unifying basis of the community. But what might be at stake for Jason as a member of the community? To make sense of the situation, we must say that Jason has two categorical interests at stake: his general way of life *with* this community and something else. Of course, it is possible that there are three things at stake, because this general way of life might be possible for Jason only with *this* community. For the community, then, there are at least two things of categorical value at stake: its way of life and its way of life *with* Jason. What we must suppose is that there is no way for either Jason or the community to have all of what they want categorically.

What is very crucial about this case is that it illustrates how quickly we are approaching the borders of autonomy. It does this by illustrating the limited room for deliberative resolution of such conflicts. Jason might discover from the situation that he loves his community more than he does this other thing. Facing the situation might actually change his sentiments rather than simply reveal to him what they are, and the same might be true for the community.

Consider, for example, a variation on the case in which Jason is homosexual. Imagine that he is a devoted Christian and is very much a part of the church. Also imagine that the church is very loving and supportive of Jason as a person and a Christian. However, the emergence of his homosexuality and his desire for a marital relationship with his lover results in a crisis.

The church believes that homosexuality is wrong but loves Jason. It is not worried about embarrassment or what other communities might think. To construe it in this way would be to misunderstand both its relationship to Jason and its religious commitments. Its members are religious people, not facsimiles. They are worried about Jason's standing with God. The crisis from their point of view is one involving the well-being of a loved one. They do not condemn Jason, but they cannot from their point of view allow the practice he desires, and this is as much for his sake from their point of view as for theirs.

Though Jason disagrees with them about homosexuality and God's attitude toward it, he shares their other commitments. He loves both the way of life the church provides and his fellow church members, otherwise he would not be so desirous of their approval of the homosexual marriage. What he wants is simply open acceptance of himself and his lover into the general way of life of the church. He is not concerned to humiliate the church for what he perceives as its backward ways or to transform it into something totally new and more modern. To construe him in this way would be to misunderstand both his relationship to the church and his religious commitments. Jason loves these people, and he is committed, by and large, to their way of life.

At first, both Jason and the community think that the other is simply mistaken about what is central. The community thinks that Jason can come to see that the church is right about homosexuality and that they are only standing by him as loved ones should when they do not accede to his views. Jason, on the other hand, thinks that they will soon come to see that God is indifferent to what a person's sexual preferences are, as long as love is involved.

Both are mistaken, however. Time reveals that there is a fundamental disagreement between persons that love each other. Of course, this need not happen. It might be that the situation changes the community. They might find in the context that loving Jason and his lover is simply more important than sexual preferences. That is, the situation might lead them to a change in their theological outlook. This might be because they discover a deeper meaning in the concept of God's love, or it might be because they are changed by the situation and thus come to have a different view of God. In the first case, the crisis is resolved deliberatively by a discovery of what their real priorities are. What they thought was categorical was not. In the second case, the crisis is resolved nondeliberatively. What was once categorical is no longer. In neither case is there any longer a categorical conflict. And, of course, such resolutions might occur as a result of such changes for Jason rather than for the community. Either way, it is only the resolution of categorical conflict that allows either Jason or the members of his community to deliberate to a set of priorities that orders a way of life in which both Jason and his neighbors are peers. Until the criteria of finality and self-sufficiency are satisfied, practical reason is stultified.

But by hypothesis I am supposing a case in which the conflict cannot be resolved in these ways. The church has *both* the commitment to Jason and the commitment to those things central to its perception of the community's general way of life. It cannot come to see either the love for Jason or its views on homosexuality in noncategorical terms. On the one hand, it can only accept Jason and his lover on pain of a loss of its way of life. On the other hand, it can only retain its way of life by excluding Jason from the community.

These are catastrophic circumstances from the point of view of a loving community, and I will argue later when talking about internal justice that only in catastrophic circumstances can a loving community think of subordinating the categorical interests of its members to those of the community. But the issue here is not the community's norms. Rather, it is what Jason's self-restricting norms will be. Will he deliberate to the conclusion of a categorical sacrifice, and what will it be? Will it be the sacrifice of his interest in the community or his relationship to his lover? And if he deliberates to the latter, is he being subservient?

Assuming no movement on the part of the church, the options for Jason are limited. He might experience a nondeliberative change in his priorities that places his homosexual interests lower than his interest in the church. Or he might simply discover that his homosexual interest was never categorical in the first place. If we assume that he is not self-deceived or something of that sort and that he truly has a categorical interest in the church, I cannot see that he is being subservient or failing to be autonomous in these cases. Rather, he is acting in accordance with his deepest commitments, given the situation.

There are other possibilities.

Suppose he experiences no change, deliberative or otherwise, in his categorical commitments but subordinates his homosexual interest to the interest in the church. Whether this is subservience depends, I think, on several factors. We cannot say that it is necessarily a case of subservience, because if we do, the situation would require that there is little way for him *not* to be subservient. On this logic, if he subordinates the homosexual interest to the interest in the church, he is subservient to the church. But, by parity of reasoning, if he subordinates the interest in the church to the homosexual interest, he is subservient to his lover. The only way he could avoid subservience, on this view, would be to quit both his lover and his church. But this is silly.

What we must believe, I think, in order to see him as acting autonomously and without subservience is that he deliberates to a categorical sacrifice on the basis of an even more important categorical commitment. As we have seen, it is possible that an agent can do this but only with a categorical cost. It might be that the situation simply destroys Jason. If it does, it does not seem that one can say that he is necessarily a subservient person. He has simply reached a deliberative impasse and the limits of autonomy. The costs are to be found among the severer forms of agent breakdown. But if he is able to make the choice and the competing commitments are indeed categorical, he will not be able to live without experiencing some form of agent breakdown. Whether he survives or not depends on many other factors, not the least of which is luck. Whether he is subservient or not, it seems, depends on three things. First are his beliefs about himself. Does he feel that he has been unable to stand by his deepest commitments? Has he betrayed his lover? Second is the truth of his beliefs about himself. Are his beliefs about his relationship to his deepest commitments unaffected by self-deception? Does he have perspicuity of self-perception? Third are his beliefs about the community, and the issues here are more complicated.

It is tempting to say that if Jason has not acted subserviently he must believe that the community is in the right about its priorities. For it would seem that if he does not come to believe this he can no longer have esteem for the community, thus altering the situation to a deviant rather than a central case of neighborly love. This, however, would be a mistake. To be sure, such a conflict might result in a change in Jason's respect and esteem for the community, but it need not. It is surely not a requirement of even simple respect that one has *no* categorical disagreements with another held in respect. Let alone is it a requirement of esteem or personal love in any of its varieties. What is required of esteem, however, is that when such conflicts occur there must be other categorical commitments held in common and a belief that the contrary commitments of the one esteemed are sincerely held.

Thus in order to make sense of Jason's subordinating decision in a way that avoids subservience, we must make certain assumptions. First, he must believe that he has not acted contrary to his deepest commitments. Second, his beliefs in this regard must be true, rather than the products of self-deception or something of that sort. Third, his esteem for the community must be predicated not on their views on homosexuality but on other commitments that he believes they sincerely hold. But if these assumptions obtain and he does subordinate his interest in this way, it follows that he values the other commitments of the community and its way of life more than his homosexual relationship.

However, it does not follow that his interest in the homosexual relationship was not categorical. By hypothesis, we are supposing it was, and thus we can expect some form of agent breakdown as a result of the decision. If he was acting autonomously, his decision involved a categorical sacrifice. Debilitating depression, grief, and despair in varying degrees are all possible forms of response. Not possible without other factors are a loss of self-respect, self-esteem, shame, or guilt. For, on this interpretation, Jason has acted autonomously and has done nothing to make himself believe that he has violated his deepest commitments. On the other hand, if he has violated his deepest commitments, then he has not acted autonomously but subserviently. Still, though, we can expect some form of agent breakdown. Assuming that he is not self-deceived we can expect guilt, shame, and a loss of self-respect, along with the possibilities of extreme despair, grief, or depression. Without these differences in agent breakdown, there is no way to distinguish autonomous decisions in such contexts from those that are servile. But, more important, with these differences, we are able to distinguish between autonomous and subservient subordinating decisions in such contexts. Therefore, some but not all categorically subordinating decisions reflect subservience on the part of the agent making them. Furthermore, it is difficult to see how this analysis could be correct where either self-respect or neighborly love is construed as an asymmetrical regulative norm. Were we to understand Jason as operating with a conception of self-respect not regulated by neighborly love, it is difficult to see how we could ever see him as anything but subservient, given his categorical sexual interest. And, of course, were we not employing a conception of neighborly love regulated by self-respect, we would never see him as subservient. For these reasons, the Aristotelian model of practical reason is superior to the Kantian model in its explanatory role regarding moral psychology.

5.

When, then, is Jason, as an agent of integrity, autonomous vis-à-vis neighborly love and his own interests? From what we have said, we can conclude that he does not have a set of priorities that allows for the subordination of his categorical interests to the noncategorical interests of the community. When the categorical interests of the community conflict with his other categorical interests, he will not subordinate these other interests to those of the community if they are more important categorically to him than those of the community. If they are less important categorically to him, he will. If they are equally important to him, he will not be able to decide autonomously because he will not be able to decide at all. Facing such a decision, assuming no change, will in effect destroy him. But this is the border of autonomy, not the outskirts of subservience. Moreover, those borders are marked as clearly as they can be without arbitrariness by the Aristotelian model of practical reason and the criteria of finality and self-sufficiency.

Now if this is correct, we can say some illuminating things about other autonomous priorities of neighborly love. As a loving neighbor, Jason will have the self-restricting belief that the categorical interests of the community come before his noncategorical interests without seeing this as a violation of his autonomy. Thus those who have a conception of rights on which this set of priorities is offensive to their autonomy are not people who have neighborly love as a categorical interest. That is, they have a conception of their rights that is not regulated by neighborly love. Jason will also have the self-restricting normative belief that the important noncategorical interests of the community come before his minor interests. Again, this will be an expression of his autonomy, not a servile denial of it. Therefore, there is nothing in this set of priorities that is inconsistent with autonomy of interest as long as one values neighborly love. Of course, there is something servile about it if neighborly love is not among one's values. But the categorical value of neighborly love is among the values of the agent of integrity in the thick sense. This is why the criteria of finality and self-sufficiency allow such an agent to order a way of life in which servility has no place but one's neighbors are central to life's meaning and crucial to one's priorities.

There remains one kind of case. This is the case in which Jason might sacrifice his life for the community. If he is categorically committed to the community through personal love, his love in some contexts will give him reasons for dying. This will be where his commitment to the community, its way of life, and its values comes into conflict with his vital interests and there are no more important categorical commitments among those of his ground project. But surely, one would have to be the worst kind of individualist to think that this is subservience in the central case or even in some deviant cases. I am thinking of the deviant case where Jason might reasonably believe that the cost of his life might bring his community back from corruption to its former integrity. Of course, if he is an agent of integrity, he will not consider sacrificing his life for an incorrigibly corrupt community. Thus it is only the most extreme deviant of neighborly love that precludes such dedication. Where such dedication is appropriate, the loving agent is unable to project a way of life that accommodates a way of life both for the agent and for his peers that is minimally worthy of choice. Again, this is the Aristotelian notion of reflective endorsement.

I cannot see, then, that conceptions of neighborly love and self-respect that are symmetrical in their regulative functions entail anything that is contrary to an acceptable understanding of individual autonomy of interest and the thick conception of integrity as elaborated on the Aristotelian model. I, therefore, turn to the issues of the just community and autonomy of conscience, beginning with the issue of external justice.

14. The Normative Thoughts of Neighborly Love, Part II

*Autonomy of Conscience
and the Unjust Community*

1.

Another worry liberals have about conceptual schemes that emphasize community is that they are in danger of being indifferent to the interests of those who are not members of the community; thus communities composed of agents governed by such schemes run an undue risk of being unjust.[1] So stated, this version of the unjust community objection is from the perspective of external justice.

The worry about the exclusion expressed in this objection is certainly legitimate. Indeed, it is difficult to imagine anything more legitimate. But it is not legitimate to reject all communal concepts because of some deficient schemes. The schemes that are deficient, I believe, are those that fail to see that it is peer love of a certain sort that is the source of healthy and admirable community bonds. Bonds that emerge from other sources might very well be subject to the present objection from justice, but I will show that a conception of neighborly love that both regulates and is regulated by simple respect and esteem for others is not vulnerable to this complaint. Indeed, it is the symmetrical regulative effects of impartial and partial norms that makes the Aristotelianism defended here accommodating to both community and cosmopolitan values.[2]

I will argue that neighborly love as understood on a plausible Aristotelian interpretation is inconsistent with indifference toward others who are

1. See Paul Gomberg, "Patriotism Is Like Racism," *Ethics* (October 1990): 144-50.
2. I discuss Aristotelian prospects for an adequate version of cosmopolitanism in "Aristotelian Ethics, Contemporary," in *Encyclopedia of Ethics*, vol. 1, 2d ed., ed. Charlotte Becker and Lawrence Becker (New York: Garland, 1999).

respected or esteemed outside the community. This I will do in the process of finding a solution to the integration and priorities problems for the agent who has not only neighborly love for his or her community but also simple respect and esteem for outsiders. This last sentence is important, for it expresses on my view what a conception of external justice is about. A conception of external justice simply is a proposed solution to the integration and priorities problems regarding simple respect and neighborly love. Normative schemes and their various components find their place in human agency as responses to problems of integration, where the agent is struggling to set his or her priorities. The external justice component of a normative scheme, as I conceive it, is that part of the scheme that addresses the integration of simple respect and esteem with neighborly love. Thus external justice simply is whatever is required as a solution to this problem.

Therefore, I will argue that the unjust community objection in its present form is mistaken by showing that there is a solution to the integration and priorities problems as applied to neighborly love and simple respect and esteem. But that solution is decidedly not a liberal one, where liberalism is interpreted as requiring neutrality regarding the good.[3] Despite the lack of neutrality, however, I will argue that the proposed solution gives great weight to the concerns of those outside the community and their liberty.

I will start with the central case. The issue is how you and your community will treat another community for whom the members of your community have simple respect and esteem. Both communities are internally and externally just and are perceived as such by each other. I stipulate this because we are considering contexts that fit the central case of neighborly love. Finally, the central case requires that the two communities are not embedded within the same network of communities. You do not love the other community; you have only simple respect and esteem for it and its members.

I will consider the various deliberative contexts appropriate to the central case and the rationality of the various deliberative patterns as they apply to these contexts. In the end, I will show what I think is a liberal deliberative pattern of the sort that requires neutrality and that this pattern is not rational across all deliberative contexts. I will argue that neighborly love generates agent-centered restrictions against liberal patterns in some limited contexts. To this extent, the conception of external justice I defend

3. For what is in my opinion the most sophisticated treatment of neutrality in the literature, see George Sher, *Beyond Neutrality: Perfectionism and Politics* (Cambridge: Cambridge University Press, 1997), 1–144.

here is not a liberal one of the sort that requires neutrality regarding the good. I will argue, however, that these agent-centered restrictions are consistent with respect and esteem for those outside the community and leave significant place for a categorical concern for their liberty and welfare. I will assume without argument that any community has some threshold interest in liberty that is categorical, that without some degree of liberty no community could survive, let alone flourish.

2.

The first kind of deliberative context is one in which the categorical interests of the other community conflict with the minor noncategorical interests of your community. Here the welfare interests of your community are not at stake: Minor interests are not welfare interests. Nor is it plausible to say that the interest in liberty has reached the categorical threshold for your community: If any liberty is noncategorical it is the liberty to pursue minor interests. On the other hand, the categorical interests at stake for the other community could involve both welfare and liberty interests. With this in mind, consider the rationality of various deliberative patterns when it is welfare interests that are stake for the other community.

The problem of integration in this context is quite simple, for priorities are easily set. There is nothing about neighborly love that requires you to give priority to the interests of the other community, and respect and esteem for the citizens of the other community are inconsistent with the indifference that would be expressed in such a set of priorities. Therefore, in this context, as both a loving neighbor to your fellow citizens and a just person motivated by simple respect and esteem for others, you will give priority to the welfare interests of the citizens of the other community. Respect and esteem for others is the determinate norm, and neighborly love the regulative norm.

Imagine, for example, that the other community and its citizens face famine due to an unexpected natural catastrophe beyond their control. Further assume that by a small increase in individual taxes, your community could raise the foreign aid to effectively relieve the famine and that there would be no significant economic costs to the citizens of your community and its economy. On what conception of neighborly love would your support for the tax increase be perceived as betrayal or a lack of concern for your fellow citizens? The only possible conception is one that makes no place for simple respect and esteem for others. But this is a conception that is inconsistent with the thick conception of integrity. Therefore, neighborly love as it is embedded within the thick conception of integrity is inconsistent with indifference toward the welfare of other deserving people in these contexts. Reflective endorsement of a set of priorities that makes no place for persons and communities that are worthy of esteem is impossible, because such priorities do not structure a way of life in which the ends that appear within the agent's deliberative field have their proper place and value. Given the agent's character, practical reason requires the rejection of such priorities.

Now consider the rationality of various deliberative patterns in these contexts. Some patterns are irrational simply because their criteria of application limit them to other contexts. Three patterns that do not apply are a Kantian maximization pattern, a catastrophe avoidance pattern, and a great benefits pattern. The Kantian maximization pattern does not apply because there is not a conflict of equal interests lexically ordered on a categorical scale: The interests at stake for you are noncategorical, and those at stake for the other community are categorical. A catastrophe avoidance pattern does not apply, but this is not because no catastrophe is in the wings; rather, it is because catastrophe can be avoided without a categorical cost. A great benefits pattern does not apply because the context is not one in which improvement in an already good state of affairs is the concern.

This leaves a utility maximization pattern and a Kantian ordinal pattern. Here it is important to see that a utility maximization pattern is not irrational in the way that the others are, namely, the description of the contexts alone makes them so. Rather, what makes a utility maximization pattern irrational is that it is inconsistent with simple respect and esteem for others. Assume a calculation of utility that allows that some number of minor satisfactions can eventually outweigh a categorical cost to the interests of a person worthy of respect and esteem. If you are an agent of integrity in the thick sense, you will not deliberate in this maximizing way in these contexts. Your respect and esteem for the citizens of the other community will not allow it. No matter how many minor interests are at stake for your fellow citizens, they will never add up in importance to the categorical interests of the citizens of the other community. Therefore, a Kantian ordinal pattern will be consistent with what is rational for you in these contexts. For in these contexts the kinds of interests at stake are essential to determining the priorities of a respectful and esteeming agent, and they are consistent with the dispositions of neighborly love. But it is important to realize that the rationality of the Kantian ordinal pattern can easily be accounted for in

Aristotelian terms. A way of life for your community that costs the citizens of another esteemed community would be inconsistent with how they appear as good within your deliberative field. There is a direct connection between the goods in terms of which you find life meaningful and the Aristotelian criteria of finality and self-sufficiency. Moreover, your actions are the nonaccidental result of their motives in these contexts because of the method of reflective endorsement fundamental to your character.

I conclude, therefore, that in contexts like this—where categorical interests of those outside the community conflict with minor interests of the community—neighborly love does not generate the other-restricting beliefs of agent-centered restrictions. That is, you will not have a set of priorities in these contexts that will generate the normative thought that you ought to favor your neighbors over outsiders for whom you have simple respect and esteem. Impartial norms dominate here, not partial ones.

A similar analysis applies when the categorical interests at stake for the citizens of the other community are liberty interests rather than welfare interests. Suppose that by adopting a certain economic policy your community could broaden its markets in the other community in a way that would be a minor benefit to its economy. But also suppose that another result of the policy would be the emergence of a regime in the other community that would repress basic liberties essential to participatory government. The effect would be that the citizens of the other community, people worthy of respect and esteem, would be governed, say, without due process of law. In order to isolate the relevant phenomena, assume that the regime, although repressive of liberties, was conscientious of the welfare of the other community's citizens.

The economic interests of your community are minor, but the liberty interests of the citizens of the other community are most plausibly categorical. I focus on due process because I cannot think of a stronger candidate for an interest in liberty that is categorical than the interest in due process, the interest in freedom from governmental interference without due process of law. Here communitarians and liberals should agree, although there might be disagreements on the details of what due process requires. Community bonds are not strong where individuals are anxious about the arbitrariness of judicial decisions.[4] Another way of putting this is that a community bonded in neighborly love does not exist where to be accused

---

4. Mill is aware of this in chapter 5 of *Utilitarianism*. See John Stuart Mill, *Utilitarianism* (Indianapolis: Bobbs-Merrill, 1957), 52–79.

is to be thought guilty until proven otherwise. Such assumptions are incompatible with caring about others as one's peers.

If the importance of the liberty guaranteed by due process is as I suggest, then your deliberations about the liberty interests of the citizens of the other community will reflect exactly the same rationality as in the case of welfare interests. I cannot see the slightest grounds for difference. Opposition to the economic policy will be required by your respect and esteem for the citizens of the other community. Though this will be inconsistent with a utility calculation that considers the possibility that the numbers of citizens frustrated in your community might make the difference, neighborly love as it is embedded within the thick conception of integrity will not even consider this possibility. Thus the deliberative patterns of neighborly love and the Kantian ordinal pattern converge here.

We can conclude, then, that in contexts in which the interests at stake for your community and its citizens are minor and the interests for the citizens of the other community are categorical, you will give priority to the latter's categorical interests. This is true whether the categorical interests at stake for the other community are those of welfare or liberty. Therefore, with these priorities, you can integrate the love for your neighbors with your respect and esteem for others.

3.

A similar solution to the integration problem is in order for the central case in which the context is one in which your community's interests are important noncategorical interests and those of the other community are categorical, for the same priorities apply. The difference is that the costs here for you and your fellow citizens begin to reflect how much value you place on the people of the other community, despite the fact that there is no special relationship between the two communities. Without these priorities, we could hardly say that the interest in simple respect and esteem for others is categorical for you and your fellow citizens. If the only interests you and your community would subordinate to the interests of the people of the other community were minor ones, we could hardly say that your community had a categorical commitment to others for whom you have simple respect and esteem. Your community, therefore, will not see the call to important sacrifice for the sake of such people as an abandonment of a commitment to each other but as an expression of one of the things that binds you together as the kind of people you are. Thus neighborly love and simple respect and esteem for others mutually support each other to promote a just community in these contexts. If there is a context in which neighborly love runs the risk of generating the priorities of an unjust community, then it must be some other context.

There are only a limited number of possibilities: those in which the interests for your community are categorical and those for the other community are minor, those in which the interests for your community are categorical and those for the other community are important but noncategorical, and those in which the interests are categorical for both communities. It should be obvious that in the first two cases the priorities will be the mirror opposite of what they were in the previous cases. Assuming that the other community is a just community, its citizens would mirror the priorities of your community in the previous cases, with the positions reversed. Also if you are willing to ask your fellow citizens to forgo important interests for the sake of the categorical interests of the worthy citizens of the other community, you are at least as willing to have the citizens of the other community forgo important interests for the sake of the categorical interests of your beloved neighbors. Not to have this set of priorities in these contexts would not only show that you do not love your neighbors but also that you do not have respect and esteem for them. Thus this set of priorities hardly reflects those of an unjust citizen of an unjust community, for it is the same set of priorities required by the Kantian ordinal pattern. The favoring of loved ones in these contexts, then, does not reflect a commitment that generates agent-centered restrictions, because the favoring is in principle extensionally equivalent with an impartial deliberative pattern. It is not, however, consistent with a utilitarian pattern, since neighborly love would never rank the noncategorical interests of others over the categorical interests of loved ones, no matter the numbers involved. In terms of a utility maximization pattern, the normative thoughts of neighborly love in these contexts are agent-centered restrictions but not ones contrary to a sense of justice.

4.

Remaining are contexts in which the conflicting interests are categorical for both communities. Within these, there are three types in terms of the kinds of deliberative patterns that might apply. The first is a context in which your doing x would come at a categorical cost to your community and prevent such a cost to the other community, but the populations of the communities are the same. The second is a context in which your doing x would come at a categorical cost to your community and prevent such a cost to the other community, but the population of the other community is marginally higher than yours. The third is a context in which your doing x would come at a categorical cost to your community and prevent such a cost to the other community, but the population of the other community is significantly higher than yours. Doing y, however, would reverse the costs to the two communities. For argument's sake, assume that all other factors are equal. What types of deliberative patterns will be rational for you, if you have both simple respect and esteem for others and neighborly love for your fellow citizens? Will your norms involve agent-centered restrictions? Finally, will your normative thoughts reflect a (neutralist) liberal deliberative pattern?

I take a liberal deliberative pattern of the sort that requires neutrality regarding the good to be one that construes deliberative contexts to be of three basic sorts: (i) one that calls for a randomizing procedure when relevant considerations are equal from an impartial point of view, (ii) one that calls for an ordinal ranking of liberties and the interests they serve on a categorical/noncategorical scale and adjudicates accordingly, or (iii) one that maximizes liberties and interests across persons who have similar interests at stake on the ordinal ranking. The first we might call a Kantian randomizing pattern; the second, a Kantian ordinal pattern, which is designed to accommodate the notion of autonomy and the place of categorical interests within the life of an autonomous agent; and the third, a Kantian maximization pattern. Together, these three patterns constitute the basic structure of a liberal conception of external justice that is fully neutral regarding the good, and it is this conception that I will evaluate here.[5] The idea in (ii) is that liberties are ranked in terms of the kinds of interests they serve; basic liberties serve the most basic interests. The idea in (iii) is that when liberties of the same order conflict it is rational to maximize the scope of those liberties for the greatest number. Finally, the idea in (i) is that when everything is equal under (iii), that is, when liberties of the same order conflict and there are equal numbers of persons affected, morality requires randomizing.

5. Consider, in this regard, the place of justifying differences in outcomes on Rawls's theory of justice and how this applies to the difference principle. See *A Theory of Justice* (Cambridge, Mass.: Harvard University Press, 1971), 152 ff. See also David Cummiskey's *Kantian Consequentialism* (New York: Oxford University Press, 1996). The point here is to extend these types of liberal conceptions of internal justice to an analysis of external justice.

Of course, liberalism itself is currently in the midst of reformulation in the light of a host of issues, among which are issues of multiculturalism, issues of the moral status of the nation-state within liberal theory, and issues of gender and the effects of speech.[6] The outcome of this reformulation might be much different than what has come to be known as neutral-state liberalism. My aim, then, is not to evaluate the project of liberalism itself but to evaluate a kind of core thought that is associated with liberalism that requires neutrality regarding the good. This allows for the possibility that the outcome of the current debate about liberalism will result in a revised view that avoids the criticisms I offer here.

Now, consider the contexts.

In the first context (in which your doing x would come at a categorical cost to your community and prevent such a cost to the other community, but the population of the other community is marginally higher than yours), the liberal could say that moral luck is sufficiently randomizing to allow you to favor your beloved neighbors. Others might say that liberal principles require something even more randomizing than moral luck. But since I do not see how to settle such an internal dispute, I will assume the first alternative simply because it seems more plausible than the second.

At first sight, this assumption might seem to accord with the priorities of neighborly love, since love would certainly give priority to loved ones in such a context. The problem, however, is that the randomizing pattern— on any interpretation—does not yield the normative thoughts of neighborly love or those that we would expect in such a context. What love says in such contexts is not that you *may* favor your loved ones but that you *ought* or *must* favor your loved ones. The randomizing pattern fails to capture the urgency of the normative thoughts here. To see this only imagine the kind of frustration that your fellow citizens would experience should you decide in favor of the other community. It clearly would be a misdescription to call the frustration mere disappointment at the results of the

6. For a sample of a variety of approaches, see Will Kymlicka, *Liberalism, Community and Culture* (Oxford: Clarendon Press, 1989) and *Multicultural Citizenship: A Liberal Theory of Minority Rights* (Oxford: Oxford University Press, 1995); William Galston, *Liberal Purposes: Goods, Virtues, and Diversity in the Liberal State* (New York: Cambridge University Press, 1991); Joseph Raz, *The Morality of Freedom* (Oxford: Clarendon Press, 1986); and, of course, John Rawls, *A Theory of Justice* (Cambridge, Mass.: Harvard University Press, 1971) and *Political Liberalism* (New York: Columbia University Press, 1993). For an argument that liberalism is compatible with nationalism in a way that does not require the kind of neutrality alluded to here, see Yael Tamir, *Liberal Nationalism* (Princeton: Princeton University Press, 1993).

moral lottery. Rather, it would be the frustration at being betrayed by someone perceived as a beloved neighbor. Shock could hardly be an inappropriate response of your neighbors if you met the situation with the comment, "After all they have just as much to lose as we do." The commitments of love bind one not just psychologically but normatively as well. In these contexts, then, neighborly love generates agent-centered restrictions against the impartial Kantian and liberal randomizing pattern. This, of course, argues for the Aristotelian conception of the symmetrical functions of simple respect and neighborly love. Aristotelian reflection on the way of life ordered by priorities that favor or randomly select the other community's interests yields the result that that way of life is unworthy of choice. Why? Because the way of life structured by those priorities does not include your beloved neighbors as ends in the way that they appear within your deliberative field. Yet the rejection of these priorities still leaves a place within a way of life where your neighbors are ends worthy of respect and esteem. Thus the criteria of finality and self-sufficiency generate agent-centered restrictions and provide them with a rationale that is at least not obvious on the Kantian or liberal view.

In the second context (in which your doing x would come at a categorical cost to your community and prevent such a cost to the other community, but the population of the other community is marginally higher than yours), liberal deliberations would reflect a Kantian maximization pattern. This is because the dispute could not be settled by simple appeal to an ordinal ranking on a categorical/noncategorical scale, yet there would be quantitative differences. No doubt, there are contexts in which it would be rational for you to adopt such a maximization pattern. This is basically where your community and its citizens are called on to adjudicate a dispute between two other communities for which you and your fellow citizens have equal simple respect and esteem but no communal bonds. If there are marginally more citizens of one of the communities than the other in such a context, this will make the difference, assuming everything else is equal. Why? Because there is no distinction between others as ends within your deliberative field in such contexts. For this reason, the numbers will select for the way of life that preserves the most people valued equally on the same criteria. But this will not be true in the present case: Your love and commitment to your fellow citizens will not allow it. You will in these contexts have the normative thought that you ought to do y for the sake of your beloved neighbors rather than do x for the citizens of the other community. This norm expresses an agent-centered restriction against a Kantian maximization pattern in these contexts and thereby against a liberal deliberative pattern, which, again, argues for the Aristotelian scheme of symmetrically regulating norms. The rationale provided for such a restriction involves the criteria of finality and self-sufficiency employed in reflectively ordering one's priorities within a way of life. And, as we have seen time and again, this does not involve an impartial decision procedure.

Without a deliberative pattern that reflects agent-centered restrictions of this sort, we are without a way of making sense of your love for and categorical commitment to your fellow citizens. In this sense, the blood of neighborly love is much thicker than the neutral-state liberal can allow. But this should not disturb those with these communal commitments, for I cannot see how there is much sense to be made of saying that your doing y in this context would be disrespectful to the citizens of the other community. Given that the citizens of the other community understand what it is to love their neighbors, they will see that your decision is not a sign of indifference to them but of your love for your community. Indeed, if we assume that they too are agents of integrity in the thick sense, this is one of the things they will admire in you, even in the face of the cost to themselves. Of course, they will expect such a decision to cost you and your fellow citizens psychologically. For without such costs, there would be an absence of the behavioral manifestations of simple respect and esteem. Still they will admire you for your loving commitments in these contexts and not see such commitments as incompatible with respect and esteem for them. If this is true, then the conceptions of simple respect and esteem at work in their attitudes reflect the influence of neighborly love as a regulative function, which, again, argues for the Aristotelian scheme.

The third contexts—in which your doing x would come at a categorical cost to your community and prevent such a cost to the other community, but the population of the other community is significantly higher than yours—are more complex. The complexities arise from the fact that not only are the borders of what counts as marginal and significant increases vague, but there is considerable territory between these extremes. Some increases in numbers will clearly be significant enough to reverse an agent's priorities; others will not. But still others will neither reverse nor sustain but stultify the agent's attempt to set priorities and achieve integration. When this happens, there is deliberative impasse and agent breakdown.

Where the increases are only marginal from your own point of view, you will maintain the priorities in favor of your beloved neighbors. This we have already seen: A Kantian maximization pattern is not rational for you if you have neighborly love for your fellow citizens and simple respect and esteem for others in such a context. But the minimum of what we can expect is that if you are a respectful person, the numbers at some point will become either stultifying or such that they reverse your priorities. In the latter case, a catastrophe avoidance pattern is rational relative to the context. Faced with saving one's community at the expense of preventable genocide of the sort practiced during World War II, a respectful agent is either going to risk all or become stultified to the point of agent breakdown. The citizens of the French village Le Chambon-sur-Lignon who saved so many Jewish children from the Nazis were good examples of the kind of agents who were willing to risk all.[7] Thus at some point a respectful agent will not find life worth living—no matter what it includes—if it comes at such a cost. And not finding life worth living when it comes at such cost, there is only either willingness to risk all or agent breakdown. Without a sense of such significance, we are without a way of recognizing the presence of respect, on the one hand, and neighborly love, on the other, in such contexts. Therefore, when the agent goes beyond the threshold of the marginal, the normative thoughts of neighborly love do not generate agent-centered restrictions in these contexts. Indeed, in some of these contexts, catastrophe avoidance patterns limit from the agent's own point of view how much he or she can allow others to pay for his or her loved ones. From the agent's point of view, the tragic consequences of preserving one's life with one's neighbors' will render that way of life unworthy of choice because it does not accommodate the value of others who are worthy of respect and esteem. These sentiments clearly reflect the criteria of finality and self-sufficiency as they are displayed in the practical reason of a loving and respectful person.

We should note two things here. The first is that the concept of marginal increases will certainly allow for more than a little difference on an impartial scale. We recognize this by the scale of sorrow we expect from those who are trapped in situations in which their love for their loved ones comes at a cost to so many others. To advance a formula for clarifying the borders of marginality here would be both arbitrary and foolish. Our normative concepts are not that precise, and they cannot be made that precise nonarbitrarily. The second thing we should notice is that the catastrophe avoidance pattern is not a liberal pattern that requires neutrality regarding the good. The neutral-state liberal will find the Kantian maximization pattern to be rational in these contexts, even in the area between marginal increases

7. See Philip Hallie, *Lest Innocent Blood Be Shed* (New York: Harper and Row, 1979).

and those significant enough to reverse the priorities for the agent who has both love for his fellow citizens and respect for outsiders. But the latitude allowed between the borders of marginality and catastrophe is not accounted for on the basis of human dignity as a value that is absolute, nonscalar, nonadditive, and immune to trade-offs but in terms of the criteria of finality and self-sufficiency as they reflect one's attempt to accommodate both a concern for loved ones and other worthy people.

This is a twofold indictment of neutral-state liberalism in these contexts. First, such liberalism fails to note that agent breakdown in the stultifying contexts is a function of rationality rather than a result of its absence. Second, it fails to note that avoiding catastrophic outcomes is different from maximizing across persons on an ordinal scale. Both failures are the result of a normative scheme that does not conceive of priorities problems as integration problems. Once again, we have a moral conception that is constructed on an impoverished conception of human agency.

5.

A summary here should allow for a return to the focus on the issue of whether a community based on neighborly love as it is embedded within the thick conception of integrity is unjust. What should be clear is that your priorities in this context leave significant room for simple respect and esteem for others. Indeed, much is required. The categorical interests of the other community are to take precedence over the noncategorical interests of yours. This extends to things that are very important to your community, even if they are not categorical, and this is no small degree of concern. Also, in some catastrophic contexts, your normative thoughts will call for a categorical sacrifice on your part and that of your fellow citizens. In some catastrophic contexts, your simple respect and esteem will give you reasons for dying for others, even where you have a way of life that includes many good things. That these things would come at such a cost would not allow you to think of these things as respectfully gained and enjoyed. For these reasons, that way of life would be neither self-sufficient nor worthy of choice for itself. Finally, though I have not addressed it yet, some contexts will call for a great benefits pattern for the sake of others held in simple respect and esteem. These are contexts in which you and your community could benefit the citizens of the other community a great deal without significant cost to yourselves. To refuse to confer benefits in such circumstances is to find meaning in a way of life that does include others as important. But the agent of integrity in the thick sense cares deeply about others, and for this reason, a life ordered by a great benefits pattern relative to the contexts of that life in which it is relevant is rational because of the agent's character.

All these contexts reflect the regulative influence of impartial respect and esteem on the conception of neighborly love as instantiated in the agent of integrity in the thick sense. What simple respect and esteem will not require of you and your fellow citizens, on the Aristotelian view, is to view your relationships as of equal importance to those of equally worthy outsiders in a way that requires either a randomizing or a maximizing pattern in these contexts. The agent-centered restrictions generated in these contexts reflect the regulative influence of neighborly love on the conception of impartial respect and esteem as instantiated in the agent of integrity in the thick sense. If this is being unjust, then loving one's neighbors in the central case is unjust, which is absurd.

6.

But what if your community is unjust? What if your community has a corrupt set of priorities? It pursues its noncategorical interests at the expense of the categorical interests of other, more worthy communities. It pursues its categorical interests with indifference to how many others might have to pay the price for its way of life. It stingily ignores the benefits it could easily bestow on other worthy communities at little or no cost to itself. And what if you love such a community? What if, that is, you have a deviant form of neighborly love? I can say only enough here to indicate some important things about the notion of autonomy of conscience in relationship to the problem of external justice.

I focus on the problem of autonomy of conscience because it involves a positive connection between the commitments of neighborly love and the commitment to external justice. As a form of peer love, neighborly love in the central case requires you to believe that your neighbors are your peers as agents of integrity. But we are assuming here that the community as a whole has deteriorated to an inferior status. The members of your community are no longer peers because they have become disrespectful to persons with the relevant R-qualities and E-qualities. If you are an agent of integrity, you see this and do not recoil from it through self-deception. By hypothesis, you love your community but lack a belief that makes that love a central case of neighborly love. Nonetheless, your love for the community includes an interest in its character and the character of its members. The concern for their R-qualities and E-qualities is a categorical commitment to you as part of your love for them. You will, therefore, have as one of your categorical commitments the commitment to being a reliable critic *for their sake*. As an agent of neighborly love, you will have a commitment to nurturing their characters as those of just and fair people. You will find it intolerable to surrender your conscience in this regard to their failures. In this way, autonomy of conscience as it relates to external justice is a function of your neighborly love for your fellow citizens. It is not simply a function of simple respect and esteem for others, though it is certainly also a function of this.

This commitment to criticism of your loved ones is not one that you have to communities you do not love. Of course, if you have simple respect and esteem for others, you will have a categorical commitment to resist the evils of injustice, wherever you find them. But this is a different commitment, far less personal than the first. Thus as long as you believe that your community is unjust and there are reasonable prospects of reform, your norms will require resisting the injustices of your community, not only for the sake of the people of the other community but also for the sake of your neighbors.

But what if your community is incorrigibly unjust to the people of the other community? The first thing to say is that this will fill you with contempt for your neighbors, which might very well destroy your love for them. In this case, the categorical commitments of neighborly love are off. Thus it could hardly be a fault of the conscience of neighborly love in this case that it lacks sufficient autonomy to stand on guard against injustice. After all, it is the lack of simple respect and esteem for others that has killed the love. But suppose that you continue to love your community, despite the resigned contempt you now have for it. I cannot see why this would be impossible, even for an agent of integrity. If a good parent can love an incorrigibly contemptible child, a good citizen can love an equally bad community. But, as we have seen, an agent of integrity will not see this love as a good thing; thus there will be no norms generated by this love for the sake of the community. No commitment to being a reliable critic on the community's behalf. No giving priority to the categorical interests of the community over the interests of others. Only categorical resistance to their unjust practices. As an agent of integrity in the thick sense you will therefore see such love as a bad thing and resist its influence. In no case will it be seen as a legitimate normative source. It will not appear within your deliberative field as good, and hence will give you no positive reason for action. Nor will it have an allure that will lead you into a way of life that is unjust.

When liberals object to personal love as a source of moral thinking, they must be careful not to bring to center stage deviant cases, especially the last. As philosophy, this is very poor procedure. One should start with central cases of concepts and put the deviants in contextual perspective. Neighborly love in the central case and in the deviant case involving an unjust but corrigible community is anything but lacking in autonomy of conscience. It is a positive force for justice. It never leads to injustice. It always mitigates against it. Thus failures regarding external justice are never traceable to the presence of neighborly love in the central case but to its absence. In the extreme deviant case of an incorrigibly unjust community, it can indeed be a threat to justice as a psychological influence, even for an agent of integrity. But it is not, for such an agent, a source of unjust normative thoughts. So I agree with liberals that neighborly love can sometimes be a horrible thing. But I say this from a much different perspective than the neutral-state liberal. The neutral-state liberal thinks that there is something essential about neighborly love per se that allows for injustice and compares this to impartial respect and esteem that does not allow it. I, however, think that there is something about neighborly love in the central case that is essentially intolerant of injustice and compare that to another form of love that is woefully inferior. But also inferior is a character that lacks the ability to bond with others in neighborly love but has only simple respect and esteem for others. Seeing how this is true and that these modes of concern are symmetrical in the regulative functions argues for the Aristotelian conceptual scheme against the Kantian.

7.

The issues of internal justice are far too complex to address here in any detail. I will say only enough to suggest how I see those issues as adequately conceptualized on a view that begins with considerations of human agency.

John Rawls, perhaps the most influential liberal philosopher of the twentieth century, has said that a constraint on a theory of justice is that it must be consistent with what he calls the integrity of the person. He was referring to a theory of internal justice as it applies to distributive goods and the basic institutions of society. But, of course, his point holds for any aspect of justice. I would only add that we must find a rationale for a particular conception of internal justice within the commitments of the agent of integrity in the thick sense. If we cannot, then we either reduce or drop our admiration for the agent who has these commitments or we reject the theory.

I agree with Rawls that considerations of the integrity of the person give us reasons for rejecting utility maximization patterns as rational across deliberative contexts. His reason is that utility maximization patterns fail to recognize the separateness of persons. This, as far as I can see, is correct. But my reasons include this and more. A utility maximization pattern violates the integrity of the person not just by conflating the distinctions between persons. It also violates the integrity of the person by imposing a set of priorities that is inconsistent with the commitments of an agent of integrity in the thick sense. But this point can be made against both utility maximization patterns and many Kantian patterns, whether they are randomizing, ordinal, or maximizing, within the deliberative contexts of internal justice. The reason this is true is that there are no deliberative patterns of a single kind—impartial or partial—that can solve the complexities of the integration problem.

Only when the issues of internal justice are formulated as integration problems arising within an agent's life do we get a slant on them that is consistent with being concerned about the integrity of the person. This is my most fundamental point. We cannot first formulate a theory of justice based on some independent value, say, equality of persons, and then as an afterthought ask if the theory is consistent with the integrity issue.

This gives us a clue as to how to proceed with a theory of internal justice. What are the commitments that must be integrated, and how will the agent of integrity set his or her priorities to achieve integration? For the agent of integrity in the thick sense, the commitments include categorical commitments of simple respect and esteem for others and various categorical commitments of personal love. They also include categorical commitments to many intrinsically meaningful activities and to excellence, to doing what one does well. This being the case, the integration and priorities problems are complex indeed. But the more complex the ground projects of persons of character, the thicker the conception of integrity that must be accommodated by a theory of internal justice. No thin conception will do, for it will oversimplify the nature of the integration problem. Therefore, a conception of internal justice will be a proposed solution to an integration problem of considerable complexity. What, then, is that problem?

First of all it is a problem for a social agent of a certain sort. That is, we begin to understand the concept of internal justice if we find its natural home. I believe that home is best understood as the contexts for integration problems involving agents of neighborly love in the central case. This is the case of an agent who is a part of a community of peers whose members have neighborly love for each other but are also embedded in a network of other personal and impersonal relationships of a categorical sort, namely, those of the thick conception of integrity. In contrast is a view of internal justice that sees the home context as one in which persons are alienated from each other, or indifferent to each other, or externally related to each other. That there is a problem of justice in such contexts I do not deny, but the concept of internal justice has its natural home in the context of community and the integration problems faced by its members who are bonded together in personal relationships. Most important, the appeal to the parties when they are in conflict is to those bonds of neighborly love in which they are united. Therefore, to begin with contexts of alienation, indifference, or external relationships is to start down the wrong path to understanding internal justice.

Here let me make reference to both egoism and Rawls's theory to make a point. If the egoist is someone who has no social or communal commitments or sentiments but cares only for himself or herself in some vague and narrow sense, then the egoist might face an integration problem having to do with the instrumental value of social cooperation, but this will not be a problem of justice for the egoist. Moreover, if cooperation is not rational for the egoist in some asocial sense, then there is no conception of justice, thick or thin, that will make it rational for the egoist to cooperate. The Greeks, understanding the natural home for the concept of internal justice, knew the solution for dealing with egoists and other asocial beings: If they are incorrigible, banish them from consideration. Do not construe them as moral subjects to which the demands of internal justice apply. Other kinds of concerns might apply—pity, contempt, rage, and so on—but not the concerns of love, respect, and esteem. To the extent, then, to which modern conceptions of internal justice try to take into account the equal intrinsic worth of all persons as the foundation value of justice, they will be preoccupied with what to do with the egoist, just as a certain epistemological tradition is preoccupied with the radical skeptic. This, I believe, leads nowhere, except perhaps to the cultural irrelevance of philosophy.

Now to Rawls and liberal conceptions of internal justice. I am not going to say that Rawls is irrelevant. Far from it. His is one of the most challenging theories of the modern era. But it is, I believe, badly misconceived. What is worse, it makes us think of ourselves and our relationships in ways that, I believe, distort our humanity, though there is no doubt about its humanistic intent.

One of the conditions of the original position in Rawls's theory is that the parties to the contract are mutually disinterested. This does not mean that they are egoists, as some might think, for they have a sense of justice.

In this sense, I believe, Rawls means that they have simple respect for each other. What they do not have is love for each other. They are not bound in a communal way. Thus, on Rawls's conception of internal justice, the integration problem is one involving commitments of simple respect and esteem for others and whatever other commitments and interests an agent might have. That this can be a problem, I do not deny. Indeed, it might be true that relationships *within* modern societies are more like foreign affairs than communal ties. It might also be true that Rawls's theory makes some sense for such contexts, though I have my reservations. What I do want to deny, however, is that this way of looking at justice is the natural home for the concept, and I want to assert that seeing this is terribly important to how we see ourselves and our moral concepts.

In contrast with Rawls's conception of the conditions of internal justice is one that begins with persons who are not mutually disinterested but whose life plans are intrinsically related through neighborly love. The integration problem in the context of internal justice, then, is not about how to integrate simple respect for others with whatever other commitments one might have. Rather, it is about how to integrate various forms of personal love with each other. Not only must different instances of neighborly love be integrated with each other within embedded communities, but neighborly love must be integrated with familial love, romantic love, and friendship. Respect and esteem play a central role because these commitments are essential to the commitments of peer love. Friendship, parental love, neighborly love, and the respect, esteem, and sympathy attached to these modes of caring, all make categorical claims on the agent. Therefore, a conception of internal justice simply is a proposed solution to *this* integration problem.

Why does seeing justice in this way make a difference, and how does it affect the way we see ourselves? Most fundamentally, it puts proper limits on the notion of impartial justification. We no longer seek to justify being human; we accept and endorse loving relationships simply because they give life its meaning for us. No longing for a priori proofs for ultimate commitments and categorical imperatives, no need for God's authority to live our lives in the light of love, no intuited moral properties, and no indirect appeals to utility. Simply the thoughts generated by the categorical commitments of a meaningful life, which include symmetrically regulated conceptions of love and respect.

The neutral-state liberal alternative distorts our humanity by making us think that we have to justify from an impartial point of view central aspects of our humanity and that we have to find justifying reasons for our most personal commitments. It does this by distorting the place in our lives of thoughts about moral equality. In a community of peers, people think of each other as moral equals. But some liberals, primarily under the influence of historically influential understandings of Kant, take thoughts about moral equality differently. For this reason, Rawls construes internal justice to impose a commitment to treating others equally unless not doing so is to the advantage of the least advantaged. The implication is that to deny this commitment to justifying unequal treatment is to deny the moral equality of others. But this is certainly not required by logic. "A believes that B and C are equally good persons, that treating them differently is not to B's advantage, the least advantaged of the two, but gives priority to C's interests" is by no means a contradiction in itself. It perhaps would be a contradiction in a certain context, namely, one in which basic welfare needs were at risk and A was related to B and C only through simple respect and esteem, or only through neighborly love within one community. But the context for internal justice involves integrating other kinds of categorical commitments, including forms of personal love other than neighborly love. One is not denying the equal worth of one's beloved neighbor just by giving priority to the interests of one's child or one's friend, even if everything else is equal. What the equal worth of one's neighbor requires is dependent on the context, not on some transcontextual moral value that creates a presumption of equal treatment. Indeed, it is bizarre to think that a loving parent stands under a prima facie duty to treat other equally worthy people equally but is justified in departing from that duty by overriding reasons. I say this because it is bizarre to think that a loving parent has to justify loving his or her child, although she might justify the conception of parental love she has in terms of the goods with which it is compatible within a way of life. But this is not impartial justification, any more than it is partial justification. Rather it is the most reflective viewpoint from which any agent can offer reasons for his or her commitments; it is the viewpoint of a way of life where the deliberative field reveals all the relevant goods that must be integrated within that life.

When you love your child more than your community, even when you deeply love your community and your fellow citizens, the categorical interests of your child will have a greater place in your normative thoughts than will those of the community. The same thing can be said about friendship. But does this mean that you do not value the equal worth of these others, who are loved in a different way? Hardly. The problem is how to integrate this good with other goods. The neutral-state liberal requires that this good is the one in terms of which all conflicts are resolved. But putting the problem this way fails to recognize the problem faced by real live human agents.

Integration of various categorical values is what is called for, not domination by one value. By misconstruing the natural home for internal justice, liberals generate an artificial moral axiom regarding the equal worth of persons. By so doing, they make us somewhat paranoid about whether we can endorse our better selves.

Some liberals fear, however, that once love gets in the door it will run the house to the detriment of a just society. But I cannot see that that fear is justified if we pay attention to the solution to the integration and priorities problems as specified in the central cases or in the deviant cases, especially the deviant cases of corrigible corruption. Loving neighbors will give priority to the categorical interests of their neighbors over the noncategorical interests of their friends and their children. They will also give priority to the important noncategorical interests of their neighbors over the minor interests of their friends and their children. In some catastrophic cases, they will even sacrifice the lives of these other loved ones for their fellow citizens. And in some contexts, they will simply be destroyed by the deliberative impasses created by such conflicts. Also, they will act with generosity rather than stinginess when they can greatly benefit their community at no categorical cost to their other loved ones. When their fellow citizens are internally unjust, they will function as reliable critics both on behalf of those who are being treated unjustly and on behalf of those who have strayed from their loving commitments. Finally, should the community become incorrigibly unjust, they will become categorically opposed to it. These are not the priorities of an unjust character but the essence of a character with a strong sense of internal justice. And, as we have repeatedly seen, these priorities can all be given a rational foundation without an impartial decision procedure from the point of view of the agent.

8.

Let me end this chapter with a story. Imagine, if you can, having been born in the mid-1940s, being a white male reared in the Deep South of the United States, with the typical (though not stereotypical) racial sentiments of that region and era. At nineteen, you are drafted and sent to Vietnam full of patriotic fervor and ready to defend your country, the country you love. Over time, however, two things happen to you: The first involves your fellow soldiers; the second, the Vietnamese.

One of the most difficult adjustments to the military for you involves your racial attitudes. All during training there is tension—sometimes latent, sometimes overt—between you and your fellow whites and the blacks of your outfit. When you arrive for active duty in Vietnam and for some time after, the tension grows, often breaking out in both verbal and physical altercations. You simply don't like them, and they don't like you. But the situation forces a certain degree of interdependence and cooperation. After a time, the demands of battle reveal the courage and dedication of all involved, both black and white. Grudgingly, at first, you come to have respect and esteem for each other where there was once contempt. As time moves on, the esteem that was once grudging is forthright and eager. "These men are every bit our equals" is the thought on both sides of the racial divide. Still there is a separation between you, a separate but equal social mentality.

At some point, however, the separateness begins to subside due to a bonding that goes beyond the exigencies of survival and mutual esteem. You have come to like each other and to care for each other in a deeper way. The disputes you have now take on a different tone. They are now no longer the confrontations of basic alienation. Some of you even form deep friendships that cut across racial divisions. In short, you have become a community. For sure, the war brought you together and sustained some of the conditions that keep you together. But now you share something more: Motown and Bob Dylan, anguish over the war and the domestic problems stateside, and hopes for the future. You have come not only to need each other and to have respect and esteem for each other; you have fallen in love with each other within the context of community.

A similar evolution takes place in your attitudes regarding the Vietnamese and the justness of the war. What you once saw as a defense of your country gradually appears to you as a travesty of justice. The killing, the dying, the suffering—all cry out for justification. Soldiers are put in positions where they must take the lives of children to survive. Others simply become murderers. The enemy are now "gooks," not people for whom sympathy, respect, and esteem apply. Where they were once "gooks" because they were a threat to the country, they are now so simply because they are the enemy, the people you have to think of as nonhuman in order to kill. To what end is all this? Former convictions gradually dissolve into empty platitudes, and what were once casualties in defense of home become categorical costs without clear categorical purpose. It is this that makes the war unjust.

After your stint in service, you return home with domestic problems festering and the war escalating and with a heightened sense of justice. But you still love your country. In fact, you love it even more, at least, more maturely. You are now more intimately bonded with its members, for you have now come to see the blacks of your society as neighbors. It is not just that you have come to see them as your equals in some impartial sense, though you surely do see them in this way. But you see them as loved ones, as beloved peers, as your neighbors. When you walk into a department store and recall the separate water fountains, your thought is not so much that such a practice violates the rights of black Americans. Rather it is, "How could *we* do this to *ourselves?* These people are our neighbors, our peers, our loved ones. What kind of people are we who betray our own?!" These are the terms in which your normative thoughts find expression. It is in these terms that your newly found conception of justice expresses it rage, and it is in these terms that internal justice speaks a domestic language.

Concurrent with the domestic crisis is your opposition to the war. Among your thoughts and objections are many expressions. Most basic are "This is intolerable; no decent person treats respectable people this way." These are impartial thoughts that are fundamental to your sense of external justice. But they are not complete in capturing the urgency of the situation. "*We* cannot do this. We are not *that kind* of people, and I cannot stand by while this is happening and allow us to violate our most cherished values." These additional thoughts are needed to fully express the urgency here, and these are normative thoughts of neighborly love, hardly the thoughts of an overly conservative conception of morality.

15. Loneliness, Intimacy, and the Integration Test

In the introduction, I distinguished between three conceptions of the integrative function of practical reason: traditional Kantianism, internalist Kantianism, and the Aristotelian conception. There I maintained that there are two very important features of the Aristotelian conception, the first of which is that there are no norms within practical reason that are asymmetrical in their regulative functions. It has been my purpose in the various chapters on personal love to show how this feature is true of the agent of integrity in the thick sense. The impartial norms of simple respect, sympathy, and esteem do regulate the partial norms of personal love. About this, the Kantians are right. However, I have also shown how for the agent of integrity in the thick sense the various partial norms of personal love regulate the impartial norms of respect, sympathy, and esteem. The arguments that demonstrate in which contexts agent-centered restrictions against impartial norms are rational show that this is true and how it is true. Moreover, they provide a rationale for these restrictions. Thus I take it that I have established a significant part of the argument for the Aristotelian model and that I have demonstrated a great deal of its structure.

If nonconsequentialist Kantians want to contest these arguments, they must address the same range of contexts I have discussed and show precisely how the CI procedure sets the agent's priorities and what those priorities are. They must show how the priorities of Kantian consequentialism are irrational and that the nonconsequentialist interpretation of the CI procedure would yield the same priorities as the Aristotelian conception, or they must show precisely how these priorities are irrational for human beings. Moreover, they must demonstrate that this can be done while employing impartial respect as a norm that is asymmetrical in its regulative functions. All this is to say that the Kantian project must be both context-sensitive and contextually thorough in testing its theory.

The other main feature of the Aristotelian model is that these norms with their symmetrical functions have their foundation in what gives meaning and unity to a particular kind of agent's life, namely, the life of the agent of integrity in the thick sense. Part of the argument for this feature of the Aristotelian model has already been provided by showing how the structure of these norms arises from an agent's categorical values. But I also said that the norms of the thick conception of integrity apply to a large portion of humanity. This chapter is intended to support this claim by suggesting how the integration test, when applied to a rather significant portion of humanity, lends support to the claim that for this population the goods of love are indeed categorical goods. If this is correct, then we should expect certain empirical results regarding the absence or loss of love in its various forms in the lives of many human beings. Those results will indicate that where love is missing, for whatever reason, the integrity of a psychology is compromised in a way that leads to agent breakdown. For the claim that personal love is categorical for an agent is the claim that the elements of integrity in the thin sense cannot be maintained over time where love is lost or missing. Thus the integration test gives us some empirical constraint on what can count as a defensible conception of practical reason.

1.

One way of seeing the importance of love in a person's life, even where that person has strong impartial norms, is by asking what happens to such a person on the loss of loved ones. And one way of seeing how important loving is to a person who has no loved ones is by asking how this absence affects such a person in terms of the basic elements of integrity. The answers to these questions reveal why, for most of us, love has a strong regulating influence on the place of respect in our practical reasoning.

The answer to the first question depends on what other elements are in a person's life at the time of the loss, as these elements bear on the anticipated prospects for the future. Most of us, after all, have experienced tragic losses of loved ones in ways that were staggering. Yet they might not have been disruptive of our identifying thoughts in a way that we lost contact with who we were or with having reasons for living. But even here, I would say that sometimes such losses are ultimately unbearable even for the strongest persons.[1] When they are survivable, it is because there is some other categorical motivating interest present that plays the role of a *consoling interest.*

I have argued in *Dignity and Vulnerability* that the impartial interests of respect and esteem cannot play the role of consoling interests in such contexts, nor can self-respect. Not even some other agent-centered interests can play such a role. If this is true, then, for most of us, the interests of personal love are central to our finding any meaning in life at all. But rather than pursue here this line of thought in answer to the first question, I want to focus on the second question and how it bears on the integration test.

2.

The issue of the widespread desire for the goods of personal love is not whether someone who has loved ones can survive their loss with the elements of integrity intact. It is rather the issue of whether a person can have the elements of integrity in the thin sense without ever loving or having been loved by another. It turns on the possibility of identifying thoughts for a person of integrity who has never had and has no interest in having the goods of personal love.

Certainly not everyone has an interest of any sort in being a parent. It does not follow from this, however, that parental love is not a widespread human good, even if it takes widely divergent cultural forms. For, still, persons might have a categorical interest in being a part of a loving parent/child relationship.

The argument that being a part of a love relationship involving these features is an extremely widespread human good focuses on the possibility of a basic element of integrity. It focuses on the child's forming a sense of self-worth—an essential element of integrity—and a sense of self-respect without being loved in a parental way.

Those never experiencing in their childhood or adolescence the belief that they are the objects of parental love have an extremely difficult time

1. See Ronald J. Knapp, *Beyond Endurance: When a Child Dies* (New York: Schocken Books, 1986); Colin Murray Parkes, *Bereavement: Studies of Grief in Adult Life* (New York: International Studies Press, 1972); and Wolfgang Stroebe and Margaret S. Stroebe, *Bereavement and Health: The Psychological and Physical Consequences of Partner Loss* (Cambridge: Cambridge University Press, 1987).

forming any lasting and coherent sense of self-worth.[2] Thinking of oneself as irreplaceable in the affections of another is formatively elementary and foundational to a sense of self-worth. It is clearly elementary to a child's ability to abstract from the peculiarities of its own worthwhile qualities. Moreover, it is difficult to see how a child could begin to develop a sense of self-worth from sources other than parental love. At least, it is difficult to see how this could result from sources other than those that have the essential features of such love.

The love need not be from a biological or a legal parent. It can be from a grandparent or a mature sibling. Nor must it come within a traditional family setting. But it must be love—or at least perceived by the child to be love—rather than mere generosity, kindness, or pity.[3] For what conveys the sense of the child's worth is its experience as irreplaceable in the affections and concerns of the parent. Contrary to highly individualistic views of psychological development, it is mysterious how the process by which a child attains its sense of self-worth could begin with the attitude of self-respect. Nor is it at all clear how a child could begin the development of its sense of the worth of others with simple respect and esteem for others. More plausibly, such development begins with the child's moving from needing the parent to loving the parent. The parent becomes irreplaceable in the affections of the child, and the child comes to feel itself as irreplaceable in the affections and concerns of the parent.[4] If this is true, then communal interests of the sort involved in love are categorically basic to being

2. See Richard L. Bednar, M. Gawain Wells, and Scott R. Peterson, *Self-Esteem: Paradoxes and Innovations in Clinical Theory and Practice* (Washington, D.C.: American Psychological Association, 1989). See especially chapter 9, "Family Relations and the Development of Self-Esteem," 257–92. This book addresses both the contributions and the limits of parental love in the development of self-esteem.

3. What is needed is the thought on the part of the child that he or she is central to the parents' lives. Generosity, kindness, and pity do not reflect this. As Bednar, Wells, and Peterson say in *Self-Esteem*, "To young children, nothing looms so large in their psychological world as their perception of being important in their parents' lives. The ubiquity of children's need to be loved, to feel that they occupy a central place in their parents' eyes, and to know that they belong in the family is evident in many aspects of child rearing, from sibling rivalry to the negative dependence of an adolescent. The child's experience of being accepted inside the family is vital throughout development, but it is critical in the formative years before adolescence" (276).

4. Here my thoughts are influenced greatly by the writings of George Herbert Mead. Mead is primarily concerned with the emergence of the self per se. My comments here are meant to take his observations and apply them to the notion of the emergence of a sense of self-worth. See George Herbert Mead, *Mind, Self, and Society*, ed. Charles W. Morris (Chicago: University of Chicago Press, 1962).

a person of integrity in the thin sense. They are basic in ways more elementary than individual interests, or the interests of self-respect and self-esteem, or any impartial interest.

3.

It is also difficult to see how life could be bearable for a person of any mature age whose life was completely devoid of any kind of peer love for any significant period of time. This is true no matter what else was in that person's life. My reasons for saying this involve the phenomenon of *loneliness*. Persons do not love other persons to avoid loneliness. They become lonely because it is natural for them to love and to desire to be loved by others. This is one feature of what it means from an Aristotelian perspective to be a social animal. Yet sometimes finding the prospects of love either remote or hopeless, they become isolated from others in a way that is often devastating to the will to live.[5] This is perhaps one reason that solitary confinement is often such an effective punishment. It is also a reason that there is no concept of hell that would be complete without the absence of peer love.[6]

One noteworthy fact about loneliness in this context is that a person need not have experienced love to experience loneliness. Of course, one can have loved and lost and experience loneliness as a result. But even those who have never been fortunate at love are subject to the ravaging effects of isolation from internal relations with others.[7]

This last point is crucial, because it is not just any kind of relationship with others that will eliminate loneliness. It is easy enough to see that those who are capable of loneliness cannot find solace in mere individual goods. For a life confined to such goods, however important and essential they might be, is so devastatingly lonely for the kinds of social beings most hu-

5. Correlations between depression, social isolation, and suicide confirm this. See F. V. Wenz, "Seasonal Suicide Attempts and Forms of Loneliness," *Psychological Reports* 40 (1977): 807–10.

6. It is worth considering in this regard the deepest stages of Hell in Dante's *Inferno* of *The Divine Comedy*. Among its population are those who betrayed their loved ones, with Judas Iscariot and Brutus and Cassius being the worst offenders. The story of Count Ugolino in Cantos 32 and 33 and his particular form of torment are also noteworthy. See Dante Alighieri, *The Inferno*, trans. John Ciardi (New York: New American Library, 1954, 1982).

7. In addition to the collection of essays in *Loneliness: A Sourcebook of Current Theory, Research and Therapy*, ed. Letitia Anne Peplau and Daniel Perlman (New York: John Wiley, 1982), see Robert S. Weiss, *Loneliness: The Experience of Emotional and Social Isolation* (Cambridge, Mass.: MIT Press, 1973).

mans are. The struggle for sanity by individuals of great creativity who have had to isolate themselves from others to do their work is testimony to this fact.[8] It is also easy enough to see that a life confined to nonsocial relationships with others is equally without solace. Solitude does not end with the mere arrival of useful people. In fact, the intensity of loneliness often increases with the presence of people one cannot relate to as a social being.[9]

What is not so easy to see is that devastating loneliness persists even in the presence of some forms of social relationships. Indeed, it persists even in the presence of some forms of personal love. Social relationships based on simple respect and esteem are not sufficient for the *intimacy* that dispels loneliness. Some of the loneliest people are those who have very strong commitments to social service, because the demands of those in need of such service often leave no time for personal intimacy. Also, the kind of concern expressed in such matters, though important, even urgent, is not intimate. Those who avoid the devastating effects of loneliness in the face of such impartial commitments are those who find a place for intimacy within such a lifestyle. They do this, I suspect, by managing to sustain—against the odds—a personal relationship with some other persons. But by doing so, they take on commitments that are not fully compatible with purely impartial commitments. Thus it is intimate relationships that dispel loneliness, and these are relationships based on personal love, rather than on impartial concerns for others.[10]

Not all varieties of personal love, however, are sufficient to dispel devastating loneliness in any lasting way. Parental love, for example, is not, in itself, sufficient. The reason it is not is due to the lack of intimacy. Here I do not mean that a parent cannot have the kind of intimacy with its child that

8. One researcher claims that the artistic are especially prone to severe loneliness. See F. Fromm-Reichmann, "Loneliness," *Psychiatry* 22 (1959): 1–15.

9. Most studies I have seen focus on social isolation due to an absence of others, a life among strangers, or alienation from others resulting from low self-regard. But another way to be isolated is to have a low regard for the people by which one is surrounded. This, of course, could be due to unreasonable standards, but it could also be due to reasonable standards and the bad luck of being around bad people. I have no knowledge of a scientific study of loneliness in such a context. Perhaps a context that would be important in this regard is one in which a person is socially isolated from others because he or she cannot find them interesting. Small-town life should provide plenty of study subjects, as might the lives of extremely gifted people.

10. See Dan P. McAdams, *Intimacy: The Need to Be Close* (New York: Doubleday, 1989), esp. 101–30. The author reports on the lives of medical students regarding the need for intimacy.

can dispel loneliness. But I do mean that it is not in virtue of parental love for the child that such intimacy can be sustained over time.

Imagine a mother who loves her infant daughter but whose life promises nothing further in the way of personal love. Unless the child were to develop past infancy, there could be very little that is shared between the parent and child. Yet without sharing there is an absence of intimacy, and without intimacy there is loneliness, where the product of absolute lack of intimacy is devastating loneliness. The more the child develops in relationship to the parent through love, the more the love involved takes on the elements of peer love. And it is the increased elements of peer love that promotes intimacy and dispels the loneliness.[11]

Neighborly love need not include friendship. If you love another as a neighbor—as a part of a community—you need not be attached to the person independent of your love of the community. But if you love another as a friend, then you care for another in ways that are independent of belonging to some larger social unit of which both you and your loved one are members. Thus neighborly love is not as intimate as the love of friendship, because the latter reflects a commitment that extends beyond the boundaries of community membership. Even so, despite the presence of all other forms of personal love, the lack of neighborly love is often difficult to bear. This is because other varieties of personal love are extremely taxing just because of the greater degree of intimacy and commitment involved, which is, of course, also the reason they are so effective in dispelling loneliness. But the comparable lightness of neighborly love provides expression to another kind of intimacy naturally desired among persons, the lack of which, I suspect, is one of the alienating conditions of modern society.

Modern persons increasingly face a choice of living a completely individualistic life or one in which the forms of intimacy are the most taxing. To be sure, in themselves, these are the most rewarding forms of personal commitment, but there are limitations. Imagine a society in which everyone would respect each other's rights but literally no one would be related to anyone else through neighborly love. If we add that each person had a few friends, a romantic lover, and loving children, we have clearly provided

11. One might be tempted to say that when the love between parent and child reaches this level, it is no longer parental love. But this would be a mistake, I think, and it is not one that I want to make. Yet if this form of personal love is parental love, then it would seem that my claim that parental love is not sufficient to dispel loneliness is false. What I should say, therefore, is that parental love that does not reach the level of peer love is insufficient to dispel loneliness in the ways suggested.

intimacy lacking in the previous case. Yet what would it be like once one left the confines of what would have to be a limited set of relationships due to the commitments involved? One would be among what could amount to little more than strangers. In any society at all complex, where much of one's time was spent apart from the sanctuary of personal relationships, life would be devastatingly lonely.

In less complex societies, the absence of neighborly love is unlikely. But its absence in small communities is even more conducive to devastating loneliness. Those who live in small communities devoid of neighborly relations should know what is meant here.

In this regard, neighborly love may not be universal as a categorical good. Possibly an agent of integrity with other forms of personal love in his or her life could survive, but not flourish, without neighborly love. But there is another sense in which neighborly love is a widespread categorical good. Just as a child cannot come to a sense of its own worth by beginning with self-respect, it is hard to imagine the emergence of friendship without neighborly love as a prelude. Exceptions are extremely rare.

4.

We must now consider the possibility of human beings who are immune to loneliness, not because they have the kind of intimacy in their lives that dispels it, but because they are incapable of it and do not have any interests in personal relationships at all. That there are such human beings seems not only possible but actual. Yet they are recognizable to the rest of us only as monsters or aliens. Most seem to be sociopaths, psychopaths, ruthless egoists, or ideological robots. For there is decisively not an actual class of human beings who are truly capable of simple respect, esteem, and sympathy and who are immune to loneliness. This is not because loneliness is attached to these attitudes in direct ways—I have argued that it is not—but because these attitudes and ways of caring evolve out of personal love, not the other way around.

Some will object that I have gained scope for the goods of personal love surreptitiously. I have done it by proscribing any connection between the concepts of human integrity and persons of certain sorts—sociopaths, psychopaths, egoists, and mechanical ideologues. It is easy enough to meet this objection regarding at least some, if not all, of these deviant forms of human personality. For example, a person of integrity is one who lives a life of commitment, and only a person with commitments can *compromise* his or her integrity. Perhaps this observation is insufficient to rule out the mechanical ideologue as a person of integrity, but it certainly rules out the sociopath, the psychopath, and the egoist.[12] For it is not in virtue of commitment that such persons' lives are structured. Perhaps one may generously understand the ideologue to be committed to a cause. Nevertheless, such a commitment hardly makes any sense apart from some sacrifice of the goods of personal love. Yet it is the neglect of the goods of personal love and its commitments that has hardened the ideologue and made mechanical his or her relationships with others. Thus the paradox of the ideologue is that he has become uncaring but supposedly still committed to others and has thus lost integrity as a humane, caring person.

Still there might be persons classifiable in ways that avoid this response but who lack any interests in personal love. Perhaps there are perfectly well adjusted hermits, who are in no sense monsters but are simply statistically abnormal. If this is true, then the statistical abnormality of their number confirms my general point that for most of us personal love is a categorical good the loss of which is inconsolable in terms of anything else.

5.

I conclude, then, that any person among a large portion of humanity has among his or her categorical interests, interests in goods of personal love, especially those of peer love. This will be reflected in the agent's identifying thoughts and in the regulative functions of the agent's partial norms. Without such goods, or at least the hope for them, such an agent will suffer in one or more ways. The most basic is a seriously distorted sense of self that significantly impairs the agent's ability to function as an ongoing agent of integrity. Others are a loss of the will to live, a life of self-deception, or a life of insanity. Anyone surviving any length of time without such goods without suffering these maladies either would be unrecognizable to us at all or would be recognizable to us only as a monstrosity or as an alien. These observations strongly suggest that for most of us the normative conceptual scheme that will pass the integration test is one that makes a place for the normative thoughts of personal love. We have seen that this is the Aristotelian—not the Kantian—scheme.

Since the goods of personal love come with attendant commitments,

12. This point is made well by Lynne McFall. See her article, "Integrity," *Ethics* 98 (October 1987): 5–20.

they involve the relevant self-restricting and other-restricting normative thoughts, including those involving agent-centered restrictions. Nevertheless, the person with loving dispositions can also have impartial commitments. The latter, however, are properly understood as including a set of priorities incompatible with impartial norms that are asymmetrical in their regulative functions. Specifically, the relationship between impartial respect and personal love is not one of authority to subject. Conceptual schemes that insist on this conception of authority fail to see how both impartial respect and personal love find their place within a psychology that reflects life's meaning to the individual agent. Here, I believe, Kantian internalism fails, where the Aristotelian view succeeds. Though life might be unbearable where it is lived at the expense of avoidable catastrophe to other respectable people, it is love that gives most meaning to life for most of us. And it is this that explains why love has the regulative function it does for us. Finally, that a human agent has a set of priorities that reflects those of a loving organism is no more a matter that needs impartial justification than are the priorities of a bird that lead it to flight.

Part 4

THE GOODS OF ACTIVITY
The Place of the Aesthetic in Practical Reason

Necessary meditations on the actual, including the mean bread-and-cheese question, dissipated the phantasmal for a while, and compelled Jude to smother high thinkings under immediate needs. He had to get up, and seek for work, manual work; the only kind deemed by many of its professors to be work at all.

Passing out into the streets on this errand he found that the colleges had treacherously changed their sympathetic countenances: some were pompous; some had put on the look of family vaults above ground; something barbaric loomed in the masonries of all. The spirits of the great men had disappeared.

Thomas Hardy, Jude the Obscure

Next to selfishness, the principal cause which makes life unsatisfactory is want of mental cultivation.

John Stuart Mill, Utilitarianism

In part 3, we saw that the goods of love provide a basis for many of the social norms we have. That we are creatures who care deeply about others in ways indicative of love is established in the facts of our psychology regarding our capacity for loneliness. It is this natural foundation that makes it crucial to any normative theory that it accommodate in a nondistorting way the normative thoughts of love. Those theories, like those of the ancient Stoics, that would have us extirpate our capacities for love are doomed to irrelevance because they cannot accommodate the goods most central to the meaning of life for most people, especially those we admire.[1] We have, then, in the case of a good number of our normative beliefs a fairly straightforward naturalistic explanation of why they would emerge in the lives of human beings. That there are other normative thoughts that are not accounted for in terms of any direct function of our capacity for intimacy is clear in those normative thoughts that derive from our notions of respect. Still, it is in terms of our proclivity for self-assessment that we find an explanation for why these impartial norms emerge. Without some foothold in our psychological capacities, explanations of the emergence of our normative conceptual schemes are mysterious, inadequate, or forced like a foot into a shoe too small. It has been one of the goals of part 2 and part 3 to show how this is true regarding the normative thoughts of respect and love when pressed into a Kantian framework. It has also been a goal of these parts of the book to show that the Aristotelian framework when properly revised provides relief in the way that only a proper fit can. Because practical reason emerges within the context of living a life, the task of practical reason must be defined in terms of the meaning of life from the perspective of the agent in whose life practical problems arise. It is for this reason that the criteria of finality and self-sufficiency fit the kind of problems relevant to practical reason. And it is because we are creatures who have the capacity for loneliness and the proclivity for self-assessment that the meaningfulness of life generates the normative thoughts of love and respect. Because we are creatures of this sort, we and others appear within our deliberative field in the way that we do.

There are, however, other normative thoughts that do not emerge from these concerns, especially for the agent of integrity in the thick sense. The thoughts I have in mind have to do with what I call the goods of activity. For these goods, we need at least a working taxonomy, a phenomenology of how they appear within an agent's deliberative field, an explanation of how they come to factor into practical reason, and an account of the normative thoughts they generate.

A rough designation of the activities I have in mind can be gained by thinking about how certain activities are central to integrity and practical reason. As human goods, the activities I have in mind are central in four ways. First, they are central in terms of their intrinsic worth to the agent, independent of how they reflect on the agent's conception of himself or her-

---

1. For a modern attempt at formulating a Stoic view that does not employ the extirpation strategy, see Lawrence C. Becker, *A New Stoicism* (Princeton: Princeton University Press, 1998).

self. Second, they are central to how the agent views his or her self-esteem. Third, they are central to the agent's view of how others regard him or her as a person worthy of esteem. And fourth, they are central to many ways in which the agent views others with esteem. The discussion that follows begins with an analysis of what I call the independent goods of activity. These are goods that attach to activities that have a value independent of the esteem they confer on the agent engaging in them. The discussion then proceeds to an analysis of the value of esteem as it is dependent on the agent's engaging in activities that are independently good. The latter topic involves the agent's commitment to excellence.

I am concerned to counter two Kantian themes relating to the goods of activity. The first is the Kantian account of how value comes to be a part of the world. In this regard, I address a view defended by Christine Korsgaard that value is the product of autonomous choice, understood along Kantian lines. The second involves the Kantian attempt to account for the commitment to excellence as a duty to develop our talents. In this regard, I focus on Marcia Baron's development of the Kantian notion of imperfect duties and her denial of the category of the supererogatory. In both cases, I contrast the Kantian conceptual scheme with a naturalistic account of our normative thoughts regarding the goods of activity and excellence that is plausibly Aristotelian. According to the latter account, the independent goods of activity have their value in the fact that they are natural to us in a way that neither inactivity nor other activities are. It is because the independent goods of activity have this value prior to choice that makes them the rational objects of choice, and this is contrary to Korsgaard's view that only rational choice confers value. Against Baron, I argue that though there is room for thoughts about an obligation to develop our talents, this does not account very well for our deepest thoughts about excellence. I argue that just as it is our capacities for love and loneliness that, in part, shape the kind of integration problems we face regarding our social nature, it is our capacity for boredom, along with the capacities that underwrite that capacity, and the engagement in certain kinds of activities for their own sake that give rise to the normative thoughts related to the goods of activity. It is in understanding how the goods of activity emerge within an agent's deliberative field and how they are integrated through the criteria of finality and self-sufficiency that makes the Aristotelian account of practical reason most fitting in regard to them.

Before proceeding, however, a note is in order on the extensive set of distinctions necessary for the analysis. I have struggled to contain technical vocabulary and distinctions to a minimum. Nevertheless, the set of distinctions that remains is fairly extensive and the vocabulary at points becomes technical. I have been unable to avoid this entirely, and the reason is to be found in the need for thoroughness. The variety of goods that fall under the heading of part 4 is extensive and complex. Failure to understand the complexity of these goods results in a failure to understand practical reason in human beings. Hence it is crucial to have a taxonomy that is true to the phenomena of practical experience. Detail, then, becomes absolutely essential to successful inquiry, even if keeping up with the details is sometimes taxing. I will try to provide mechanisms to reduce such taxation, but I cannot eliminate the need for work on the part of the reader. The subject matter just is complicated. Although I cannot pretend to be a Darwin or an Aristotle, I am guided by their commitment to a notion of theoretical adequacy that refuses to compromise the intricate details of the data.

I begin with the taxonomical task and some general distinctions regarding the possible activities of any particular agent. The first general distinction to note is this: one's engaging in an activity because one has the deontic belief that one ought to engage in that activity and one's engaging in an activity for its own sake without any such belief. Deontologists might object that doing x because one believes one ought to do x *is* to be doing x for its own sake. This may be true, but surely some cases of doing something for its own sake, like playing the piano, would *not* be cases of doing it because one believes one ought to. Thus we can distinguish between deontic and nondeontic activities. The latter are done for their own sake and have intrinsic rather than mere instrumental value to the agent, but they are not activities thought to be obligatory by the agent; if left undone by the agent, self-reproach would not be forthcoming on reflection.

Here I distinguish these activities primarily to put half of them aside for the moment. I want to put aside deontic activities and merely instrumental activities because they are not directly germane to the goods of activity as independent goods. Rather, the activities that I have in mind, as human goods, are those that are nondeontic activities of intrinsic value to a human agent.

For purposes of the discussion, I divide the independent goods of activity into three main groups: solitary individual activities, solitary benevolent activities, and shared activities. The first two I discuss in chapter 16; the third, in chapter 17. In each case, I begin with a general characterization of such activities and proceed to an account of subdivisions within each group, analyzing their role in the thick conception of integrity. But before turning to these tasks, I must make two further sets of distinctions.

The first set involves a division of activities into productive, contribution, and accomplishment activities. Productive activities are intended to result in a product. Building a house, cooking a meal, and writing a book are examples. Contribution activities, on the other hand, aim at enhancing the good of someone or some thing and need not involve a distinct product. Feeding the baby, advancing science, and protecting the environment are good examples. Of course, any productive activity might also be intended to contribute to the good of someone or some thing. In such case it is a productive/contribution activity. An example might be writing a book to advance clinical understanding of mental health. Finally, accomplishment activities result in some achievement, which is not necessarily a distinct product. Nor, as an achievement, is it necessarily a better state of well-being for someone or some thing. Good examples are playing a game, fighting a war, and earning a degree. Winning the game, winning the war, receiving the degree are the achievements—achievements specifiable apart from the well-being of those involved in these accomplishments. Nevertheless, many accomplishment activities are either productive or contributory, or include all three elements.

Another set of distinctions, which is neither exclusive nor exhaustive, is between work activities, play activities, and creative activities. In a vast number of cases, the distinction between work and play is very difficult to make out. What I will attempt to do is to make out distinctions that apply at least in the extremes. My purpose is not to come up with some essentialist definition of the difference between work and play but to pick out phenomena worthy of our attention given the current inquiry.

A work activity as I have in mind is an activity that involves labor to some degree. This contrasts with play activities that are done leisurely for their amusement or recreational features. Creative activities are those that involve the human urge to create, explore, and discover and may or may not involve labor. For an activity to involve labor is for it to involve some significant degree of taxing effort, though not necessarily of the physically taxing kind. For an activity to be done leisurely is for it to be untaxing in this sense. The distinction I am trying to capture is that between an agent's being in different dispositional states during the activity. On the one hand is a state of relative relaxation during the activity; on the other is a state that involves some noticeable taxing or draining effort. Another way of putting the distinction is that labor involves some degree of painstakingness, whereas play is lighthearted and free of painstakingness, or relatively so. The vagueness of the distinction is inherent in the phenomena. Just where the effort in an activity ceases to be leisurely or playful and when it becomes labor is not always easy to discern. But it is often clearly discernible, and this has something to do with how taxing the effort involved in the activity is. That it is taxing, however, is no reason for thinking that it is not fulfilling.

Perhaps a way of understanding the distinction between work and play is in one interpretation of Adam and Eve's fall from the Garden of Eden. According to the story in Genesis (2:5–3:24), Adam's punishment included the penalty that what once came to him with ease would now come to him only by the sweat of his brow. We might interpret this to mean that before the fall, Adam and Eve's activities were entirely of the playful sort. No taxing effort was involved at all. Whereas after the fall, what was once gained with mere playful effort would now require dreaded labor.

This interpretation assumes that all effort is either of the playful sort or dreaded labor. But it is simply false that all taxing effort is dreaded labor and that all labor is dreaded. Besides, it is implausible to think of Adam and Eve as human and of the Garden as heavenly if Adam and Eve could do nothing other than play all the time. Surely there was some work that required meaningful labor. For it is certainly an odd thought to humans that meaningful labor is a punishment while unending play is paradise. Still, many equate "labor" with "laborious" effort, and thus with some notion of dreaded effort. But, clearly, this is a mistake. Some effort is intrinsically meaningful; some is dreaded; and some of each involves labor. There is no reason, then, to think that talk of meaningful labor is at all odd. Playful effort, on the other hand, is not a type of labor in either sense. This is not because it is not meaningful but because it is not taxing in the relevant sense.

Thus what we have now is an understanding of human activities that divide into production activities, contribution activities, and accomplishment activities. These involve either labor or leisure and are either creative or routine. Production, contribution, and accomplishment activities are sometimes goods of work, sometimes goods of play, sometimes goods of creativity, and sometimes goods that exhibit some combination of these factors.

Yet it might be thought that goods involving production, contribution, and accomplishment are not of philosophical relevance here. Such activities, after all, are those an agent values for their ends—for their products, their contributions, and their achievements—rather than for their intrinsic value. This objection, however, is misplaced.

To be sure, failure in productive activity is a source of frustration to the person engaging in it. But this does not show that the activity is of mere instrumental value to the agent engaging in that activity when it is successfully productive. Two facts illustrate this. The first is that an agent values the products of some activities because of the kind of effort that goes into making them and because the products express and illustrate such effort. This is especially true of creative productive activities, such as artistic activity, for example. It is also true of productive play activities such as a child making sand castles on the beach.

The second fact that illustrates the intrinsic value of productive activities is that even where the products of such activities have instrumental value, they are often more easily and readily accessible through means other than the associated activities. The houses and meals that result from building and cooking clearly have instrumental value to the agents engaging in these productive activities. Yet there are often much easier ways of getting a house than by building it oneself or of getting a meal than by cooking it oneself. Here the presence of instrumental concerns does not vitiate the intrinsic value of productive activity.

The observations regarding the intrinsic value of productive activities apply in part or in whole to contribution activities and to accomplishment activities as well. Contribution activities always have an instrumental aspect to them. Still the improved or maintained states of their beneficiaries are sometimes very difficult to distinguish from the capacity to engage in the activities themselves. Jogging, for example, might be valued in part because it contributes to the maintenance or improvement of one's health. But the intrinsic enjoyment of one's health might sometimes be nothing more than the enjoyment of the activities that exemplify that state of health. A jogger's appreciation of his or her health may be nothing more than the appreciation of jogging itself. Yet, even where contribution activities have an intended benefit distinct from the ability to engage in the activities themselves, the presence of instrumental concerns does not preclude intrinsic value. Nowhere is this more evident than in the nondeontic activities associated with personal love. Parenting activities actually derive their intrinsic value from the fact that they are contributory to the well-being of the child. The interest in being the benefactor of the child as a source of nurturing clearly illustrates this. It is not simply that the child's welfare needs are met but that some of these needs are met through the activities of the parent, though they might have been more easily, but not better, met by others. A parent who does not intrinsically value some of these activities independent of any sense of obligation simply does not have parental love for the child. The same is true of a parent whose dispositions are sensitive only to the results of such activities without any desire to participate in the activities that procure these results.

The achievements of accomplishment activities are not always as distinct from the activities associated with them as one might think. The good of winning at chess, for example, cannot be specified without a description of the activity of playing chess itself. Such achievement cannot be intrinsically appreciated without an intrinsic appreciation for the activity that culminates in the victory. This is also true of earning a degree. Valuing a degree is one thing; valuing an earned degree is another. In fact, when accomplishment activities are valued intrinsically as nondeontic activities, they are of just this sort. Otherwise, it is only the results of such activities that are valued. Nevertheless, the value of the pursuit of knowledge, for example, does not diminish with the sometimes successful elimination of ignorance. Nor does it diminish when improvements in knowledge serve as stepping-stones to further achievements. Those who appreciate chess know that winning at it improves one's skills and enhances the appreciation of the activity, as long as there is some possibility of losing.

It should be clear then that the intrinsic value of productive activities, contribution activities, and accomplishment activities is not vitiated either by the fact that these activities have goals and ends or by their involving labor. Here I mean merely to assert that these are work activities only when they involve effort that is inconsistent with their being done with complete leisure. They involve some significant degree of taxing effort. Thus a work activity, as an intrinsic good, is inconsistent with an agent's aversion to all nonleisurely, taxing effort in such activity. Should someone be aversive in this way to these activities, either their value to the agent is merely extrinsic or they are not valued as goods of work. Work activities involve some significant degree of taxing effort, and this labor is part of their intrinsic value. Later I will argue that a world without opportunity for such labor would be an intolerable environment for human beings.

I turn now to the discussion of the independent goods of activity, beginning with individual solitary activities. In the course of this discussion, my first critical concern will be to evaluate Korsgaard's conception of value and how it applies to these goods. I will later discuss the topic of excellence and Baron's treatment of the duty to develop our talents.

16.   Solitary Activities

An activity is solitary if it is either done alone or if done with others, the sharing of the activity (as opposed to its results) has only instrumental significance to them. An activity is an individual one if the agent's interest in it is satisfiable apart from any intrinsic interest in the satisfaction of anyone else's interests. Thus not all solitary activities are individual activities, though some very important ones are. Some solitary activities, for example, do not have independent beneficiaries. In normal circumstances, playing chess with a computer is a good of this sort, because the benefit of the activity accrues only to the agent and the playing of the game is itself the benefit. Such activities we can call solitary individual activities. Other solitary activities do have independent beneficiaries and can appropriately be called solitary benevolent activities. Gift giving is often a good example, though there are others, as we will see. Personally benevolent solitary activities have intended beneficiaries who are personally related in an agent-centered way to the agent engaging in the activity. A mother nursing her infant is (under appropriate circumstances) an excellent example, as is a father building a playhouse for his children. Impartially benevolent solitary activities have intended beneficiaries who are not personally related to the agent. Providing Christmas gifts for disadvantaged children might take this form. In all these cases, I have in mind nondeontic activities, activities that if left undone would not result in the agent's self-reproach on reflection. We can summarize, then, as follows:

I. Solitary individual activities without independent beneficiaries

II. Solitary benevolent activities with independent beneficiaries

   A. Personally benevolent activities with loved ones (family, friends, neighbors) as independent beneficiaries

    B. Impartially benevolent activities with familiar and unfamiliar
       strangers as independent beneficiaries

The purpose of this chapter is to provide an analysis of these activities
with an eye to a better understanding of how they find their place within
the structure of the psychology of those we admire most. In section 1, I will
begin with some comments on our capacities for boredom and how this fact
about us is telling in regard to how these activities appear to us as good
within our deliberative field. They appear to us, I argue, as worthy of choice
in the Aristotelian sense that they, among other things, make life worthy
of choice from our point of view. Without some threshold level of these
goods, our own agency would not even matter to us. Hence an adequate
phenomenology of these values reveals that an ontology of value, like Korsgaard's, that starts with the value of rational agency distorts the value of
these goods as they appear within our deliberative field.[1] Section II discusses solitary individual activities; sections III and IV, personally benevolent solitary activities; and section V, impartially benevolent solitary activities. Only in a later chapter will I discuss Baron's views and the commitment
to excellence in some of these activities.

1.

In a delightful essay on boredom, Robert Nisbet has said that humans are
apparently unique in the capacity for boredom:

> We share with all forms of life periodic apathy, but apathy and bore-
> dom are different. Apathy is a depressed immobility that can come
> upon the organism, whether amoeba or man, when the environment
> can no longer be adequately assimilated by the nervous system, when
> the normal signals are either too faint or too conflicting. It is a kind of
> withdrawal from consciousness. Once sunk in apathy, the organism is
> inert and remains so until external stimulus jars it loose or else death
> ensues.
>
>   Boredom is much farther up the scale of afflictions than is apathy,
> and it is probable that only a nervous system as highly developed as
> man's is even capable of boredom. And within the human species, a
> level of mentality at least "normal" appears to be a requirement. The
> moron may know apathy but not boredom. Work of the mindlessly

---

   1. See Christine M. Korsgaard, *The Sources of Normativity* (Cambridge: Cambridge University Press, 1996), esp. chap. 4, 131–66.

repetitive kind, which is perfectly acceptable to the moron, all else being equal, quickly induces boredom in the normally intelligent worker.[2]

Both apathy and boredom are states of an organism in which the organism cannot take an interest in activity. In the case of apathy, the indifference to activity is because the stimuli within the organism's environment are either too faint or too demanding for the organism to assimilate. Ironically, too much stimuli can shut the organism down. Boredom, however, is not like this. Boredom is not due to faint stimuli or to the bombardment of stimuli but to the lack of anything in the organism's environment that is stimulating even when assimilated. It involves a lack of anything interesting to do.[3]

There is another difference between apathy and boredom that Nisbet does not mention, though it is implied in other things he says. Apathy is not a state of discontentment, but boredom is. Cats, for example, often seem apathetic but seldom bored. There is a limited range of activities that interest a cat. If these are not available, the cat simply goes to sleep. For the normal human this is not true. When a normal human has had a certain amount of sleep and there are no activities available of interest, eventually the normal human experiences a profound state of discontentment. This discontentment, of course, is the state of boredom, which involves an intense desire for meaningful activity where there is a lack of anything interesting to do.

Some have speculated that our capacity for boredom is in some sense an evolutionary function of the fact that, as a species, we had to develop a highly sophisticated nervous system in order to survive in our natural environment. The capacity for a state of highly pitched attentiveness together with highly developed cognitive powers, so the speculation goes, not only were adaptive to the environment but also rendered us vulnerable to boredom. In fact, boredom itself might be an adaptive mechanism, one that forces human organisms to develop their cognitive and perceptual ca-

2. Robert Nisbet, *Prejudices: A Philosophical Dictionary* (Cambridge, Mass.: Harvard University Press, 1982), 23.

3. See *Overload and Boredom: Essays on the Quality of Life in the Information Society,* ed. Orrin E. Klapp (New York: Greenwood Press, 1986). For a discussion with a focus more directed to physical health, see Augustin M. de la Peña, *The Psychobiology of Cancer: Automation and Boredom in Health and Disease* (New York: Praeger, 1983). See also, Martin E. P. Seligman, *Helplessness: On Depression, Development, and Death* (San Fransisco: W. H. Freeman, 1975).

pacities in a way that ensures creative adaptability. Without the restlessness that comes with inactivity, our cognitive and cultural development would have been much different. But be this speculation as it may, we are, in fact, extremely vulnerable to boredom. Left to boredom long and intense enough, we do not simply go to sleep; we go insane.

This fundamental fact about our psychology should play a central role in any conception of the human good and practical reason in at least two ways. The first has to do with the way in which the goods of activity are phenomenologically present within an agent's deliberative field. They must be present as intrinsic goods rather than mere instrumental goods, and they must fall under relevant value categories. Just as our capacities for self-assessment lead to ourselves appearing as ends within our deliberative field, and just as our loving capacities lead to our loved ones appearing there as beloved ends, our capacity for boredom and the capacities that underwrite it lead to some activities appearing within our deliberative field as ends, as activities to pursue for their own sake. Moreover, the goods of activity appear within an agent's deliberative field under relevant value categories. As goods that answer to our capacities for self-assessment, we appear within our deliberative field not only as ends but as ends worthy of respect. As goods that answer to our loving capacities, our loved ones appear within our deliberative field not only as ends but as beloved ends. These are, respectively, the relevant kinds of value categories for these goods. The goods of activity, however, appear within our deliberative field under other value categories. Among them are "interesting," "satisfying," "fascinating," "delightful," "amusing," and "captivating." That is, the nondeontic goods of activity appear within our deliberative field as activities that are good in that they are interesting, satisfying, fascinating, delightful, amusing, or captivating.

For now, the most important thing to notice about the value categories relevant to nondeontic activities is that they are all, in a broad sense, aesthetic categories. To be sure, these categories need not involve the kind of aesthetic appreciation involved in high art; nevertheless, to find something fascinating or delightful, for example, is often (though not always) far closer to involving the category of beauty or some other aesthetic category than the categories of respectable, loving, or morally good. Thus this fact about the value categories relevant to the goods of activity raises the important and largely neglected issue of the role of the aesthetic within practical reason. I will have much more to say about this as we go along.

The second way in which the fundamental facts about boredom and our psychology should play a central role in any conception of the human good and practical reason is that some threshold level of these goods is of categorical value to any remotely normal human agent. It is the fact that boredom is a threat to our very survival that makes the goods of activity categorical goods, and it is this fact that explains the phenomenology of the appearance of the goods of activity within our deliberative field as, in a broad sense, aesthetic goods. But if this is true, then our agency is a value to us, that is, it appears within our deliberative field as good to us, only if we do not find life utterly boring. And, in order for this to be true, we must have some activities that are available to us because they are in one way or another aesthetically appealing. If we do not find some activities available to us that are interesting, satisfying, fascinating, delightful, captivating, or the like, we will eventually either fall prey to apathy toward our existence or be driven insane by the effects of boredom. This, I believe, should lead us to reject the notion that value comes into the world only as the result of rational agency, as Korsgaard and Kant seem to have it. Rather, it seems that rational agency is valuable only if other things are valuable. And this is a comment on how things appear within our deliberative field: Our agency does not appear to us as good within our deliberative field when all the activities that appear there are cloaked in utter tedium and devoid of aesthetic appeal.[4] In Aristotelian terms, the life of agency without the goods of activity is unworthy of choice when the activities of that life are utterly tedious and boring.

I do not see how either Kant or Korsgaard can account for this fact about our valuing our lives and ourselves. Kant has it that respect for our rational agency prohibits our taking our own lives, regardless of how dreary life might be. Kantian internalists must give an account of this, and doing so is difficult. On the internalist view, just the thought that we are rational agents is enough to give us reasons for living, even if everything else about our lives is meaningless. Of course, this is just false. If everything else is meaningless, then our lives and our agency are meaningless from our own points of view. Nor will it do to say, as Korsgaard does, that the value of life is the foundation of all value. One can value one's life only when one can value a way of living. Were the value of life fundamental in Korsgaard's sense, then any way of life would be minimally worth living. She also says, "The price of denying that humanity is of value is complete normative

4. I will say more about this in the final chapter where I discuss the role of pain in practical reason.

scepticism."[5] No. The *consequence* of complete normative skepticism is the denial of the value of humanity, and were it the case that the only ways of life open to humans were utterly tedious and boring we *would* be complete normative skeptics. We would judge that human life and agency are not of much value because there would be no way of life open to humans that would make human life worthy of choice.

An understanding of boredom, then, is helpful in understanding the phenomenology of how the goods of activity appear within an agent's deliberative field. But it is also helpful in understanding the natural ontology of these values as the explanation for the phenomenology. The goods of activity, like the goods of respect and love, have their foundation in the psychological capacities of the agent.

In this regard, it is important to distinguish a capacity from the capacities that underwrite it, as it is equally important to understand the similarities between the accounts of the goods of love and respect and the goods of activity and their roles in practical reason. Loneliness is one psychological state for which most humans have the capacity. Those who have this capacity, however, have it as a result of other capacities they have, among which are the capacities for love and intimacy. But there are others; for instance, the capacities for memory and desire. Indeed, loneliness involves the desire for love and intimacy, often with some particular person. The remembering of a loved one who is absent with a desire for the loved one's company triggers the loneliness. Thus a being devoid of the capacities for love and intimacy and the desire for them would be immune to loneliness: If you are not a person who values others as ends of a certain sort, you are simply not capable of loneliness.

It is the fact that the capacity for loneliness is a function of the capacities of love and intimacy that loved ones cannot be taken as mere means to the amelioration of loneliness. Rather, loneliness is a function of the fact that a person's affective capacities include love, the valuing of specific others as ends of a certain sort. Hence the naturalized ontology of value explains the phenomenology of both how the goods of love appear within an agent's deliberative field and ultimately why the agent has the normative thoughts of love, why the agent justifies things in the way that he or she does. In other terms: An understanding of loneliness and the capacities that underwrite it explain the place of the goods of love within practical reason.

Something similar regarding the capacity for boredom and the capaci-

5. Korsgaard, *The Sources of Normativity*, 163.

ties that underwrite it explains the role of the goods of activity within practical reason. Among the capacities that underwrite the capacity for boredom are the capacities to find things interesting, satisfying, amusing, fascinating, or captivating. These latter capacities explain why activities appear within an agent's deliberative field as good under the relevant value categories and as ends of a certain sort. What is crucial to note is that these capacities are aesthetic capacities. Observations about the effects of boredom, then, show that aesthetic capacities are fundamental to the structure of our psychology, which explains why the goods associated with the capacities that underwrite the capacity for boredom are, at some threshold, categorical goods. This means that not only are some aesthetic goods categorical, but that any acceptable theory of practical reason must afford them this status. Otherwise, the theory is contrary to the natural ontology of value. But I will argue not only that the aesthetic goods of activity at some threshold level are categorical goods but also that the norms associated with these goods are symmetrical in their regulative functions regarding the goods of respect and love. If this is true, then, if we think of moral norms as those associated with respect, sympathy, and love for others, then aesthetic norms and moral norms are symmetrical in their regulative effects.[6] Hence an understanding of the capacity for boredom and the capacities that underwrite it explain why the goods of activity play the role they do within practical reason. As such, the account here provides a naturalistic ontology of value.

In what follows, I want to see how these thoughts gain credibility as we take a closer look at the goods of solitary activity.

2.

The first kind of activities to consider are solitary individual activities. These are activities that do not have independent beneficiaries and are either done alone or if done with others, the sharing of the activity has only instrumental value to the other participants.

6. Of course, one might not want to identify morality with only these concerns but with rationality all things considered, where full rationality and hence morality make a place for the aesthetic. Kant's view of full rationality has it that impartial respect regulates but is not regulated by the aesthetic. I do not believe his arguments succeed for the kinds of reasons given here in part 4. For other views on morality as involving rationality, all things considered, see Lawrence C. Becker, *Reciprocity* (London: Routledge and Kegan Paul, 1986), and my "Frankena and the Unity of Practical Reason," *Monist* (July 1981): 406–17.

Consider work activities. Again, Nisbet is interesting. He says:

> Work, more or less attuned to the worker's aptitudes, is undoubtedly
> the best defense against boredom. As Denis Gabor emphasized, work
> is the only visible activity to which man may be safely left.

And later:

> There have been workless strata before in the history of society. Think
> only of the half-million in imperial Rome on the dole . . . out of a total
> of two million people. The results were unsalutary, to say the least, and
> Toynbee gave this "internal proletariat," with its bored restlessness, its
> unproductivity, and its rising resentment of the government that fed it,
> credit for being, along with the "external proletariat" or invading bar-
> barians, one of the two key causes of the eventual collapse of the West-
> ern Roman Empire. In the modern day, chronic joblessness, especially
> among youth but in other strata as well, not overlooking the retired el-
> derly, produces its baneful results, ranging from the mindless violence
> of youth on the streets to the millions of elderly who, jobless and also
> functionless, lapse into boredom which all too often becomes apathy
> and depression.[7]

Though these observations are hardly the product of hard, systematic
social science, they do suggest as fact that where humans are not involved
in meaningful work destructive restlessness is the result. The point is not
simply that if people have to busy themselves with work they will have no
time for mischief. Rather, it is that there are no other kinds of activities that
engage humans deeply enough over time in a way that prevents the kind of
restlessness that results in such destructiveness.

Though there is much to be said for these general comments on work,
we need here to be more fine grained in our specification of work activities. Are there significant domains of work activity—activity that involves
labor—that are both solitary individual activities and of central importance
in many persons' lives as independent goods, as good independent of the esteem they confer? If so, are they productive activities, contribution activities, or accomplishment activities, or all of these? Must at least some be
creative, or can they all be routine? These are some of the questions that
must be addressed here. But remember that the emphasis in this context is
on the issue of survival, not the issue of flourishing. It is one thing to say
that someone's life is less flourishing than it could be if it lacks all opportu-

---

7. Nisbet, *Prejudices*, 23–24.

nity for meaningful work. It is quite another to say that such a life would not be worth living for many, regardless of what else life includes.

It is plausible that over time creative activities of both work and play are essential to avoid the debilitating effects of boredom for any normal human. For a person of average intelligence, the lightheartedness of play loses its appeal eventually and probably very quickly.[8] This is likely true of children as well. It is only from the perspective of an adult that most of the activities that appear meaningful to a child are play activities. Most probably involve the same kind of effort that goes into adult labor. Indeed, boredom sets in for an average child when its activities cease to challenge, to demand effort, to tax to some significant degree. Play actually seems to have its place in human psychology as a temporary leave from other types of activities. This explains why leisure soon becomes excruciatingly boring for the average person. That some of the activities of both play and work would not need to be solitary and individual in the relevant senses is implausible. Cognitive development alone would suggest that a significant portion of learning activities for both children and adults is solitary in this sense. That it is gives our lives much of its meaning when we are not engaged more socially. Learning activities of either work or play are often solitary in the relevant sense.

Also, a life full of every good thing except meaningful creative labor would no doubt soon become terribly burdensome for most. Play alone cannot relieve the weight of merely instrumental effort, of deontic activities, and of what can become humdrum routine. If not offset by the excitement of discovery and creativity that demands labor, it is simply insufficient as a panacea regarding boredom. Not even the knowledge that one is loved and that one loves others is sufficient over a protracted period. Love must become active, more than playful, and have some degree of discovery in it to be sustaining for very long. For it is a fact about personal love that if it does not remain dynamic it dies, and sometimes probably from boredom.

Regarding the aesthetic categories relevant to work activities: It is plausible to think that categories such as "fascinating" and "captivating" are the most relevant. To involve labor, the activities must be challenging, and, to

---

8. For a general study of play, see M. J. Ellis, *Why People Play* (Englewood Cliffs, N.J.: Prentice Hall, 1973). Also, see *Play: In Animals and Humans,* ed. Peter K. Smith (Oxford: Basil Blackwell, 1984). The reader should keep in mind that the concept of play in these studies is a broader concept than the one being evaluated here. The emphasis here is on play as a leisure activity, which is certainly not coextensive with the meaning of the word "play" in ordinary discourse.

avoid the dreaded kind, the labor must be to some degree fascinating and captivating. Without some threshold level of work activity that is both captivating and challenging, any reasonably intelligent person is vulnerable to the devastating effects of boredom; mere play will not suffice. Indeed, it is plausible that the more intelligent the creature, the larger the role aesthetic goods, especially aesthetic activities that are captivating and challenging, play in its psychology.

However, to argue that play is not sufficient to displace boredom is not to argue that it does not have an essential place in human experience. Just as play can become tiresome, so can work, even meaningful work. Periods of intense creative activity are very rewarding, but they are also draining. So are routine, uncreative work activities. This is because they involve labor, and protracted labor of any sort is exhausting. It leaves a person not only in need of rest—periods of inactivity—but in need of lightness of activity, in need of play. Imagine what life would be like if there were only the options of labor or inactivity. Not only would such a life exact a heavy toll on each person's individual interests; it would wreak havoc with personal relationships. For the only active associations with others a person would have would always have some taxing dimension to them. Over time, this would be more than an inconvenience; it would be unbearable. Yet this is only one thing that makes a life of mere work and rest so debilitating to those who find themselves forced into it. The children of the poor probably get more rest than they do play, and it is perhaps as much the lack of play as anything else that takes the sparkle from their eyes.

Recognition of the importance of creative activities, however, should not lead us to underestimate the value of routine activities. The inability to sustain creative engagement itself makes it imperative that if the human organism is to survive it must find much of routine activity inherently rewarding. That humans do find much of this activity rewarding goes a long way in explaining why humans have survived the vicissitudes of evolution. It explains why they have retained enough interest in themselves and their environment to find the struggle worthwhile. Thus the fact that an activity is routine should not in itself lead us to think that it is of mere instrumental significance in an agent's life. Rather, it is a life confined to the routine, without periods of creative work and leisure, that is debilitating.[9]

9. Whatever fails to survive of Karl Marx's economic thought, surely many of his observations on this topic are genuine contributions to social psychology. See especially his *Economic and Philosophic Manuscripts of 1844*. Selections are in-

Otherwise, the routine itself contains much activity that is intrinsically indispensable. Though meaningful routine might not be fascinating, some level of it is very satisfying, a less intense level of aesthetic experience. Were routine activities not at all satisfying, we would be hard-pressed to cope with life.

It is plausible then that the integration of routine work activities with creative work and play is not only necessary for a life of flourishing. Some degree of this seems necessary for the very survival of human integrity. The lack of it threatens the human ability to maintain an interest in life over time.

But why think that any of these activities must be solitary individual activities? The argument that some of them must be centers on two features of these kinds of activities. One involves creative activities; the other, routine contribution activities regarding one's own welfare.

There is a sphere of creative activity that is independent of the contribution feature of work activity. It exemplifies itself in the pursuit of art for art's sake and sport where the emphasis is not on winning but on how one plays the game. In both, the emphasis is not on contribution but on authenticity. In fact, the authenticity of creative activity with the concern for purity of pursuit is a mark of an agent's valuing creativity for its own sake. This is true whether it is in art, sport, the pursuit of knowledge, or wherever. Thus to engage in an activity to display for others one's cleverness at novelty may indeed be very creative, but it is not thereby valued for its creative dimension. Rather, the thought that there is a connection between the purity of one's activity and its being *one's own* is central to its being valued for its creative aspect. Therefore, the satisfaction of exercising one's own skill or insight is irreducibly individual in this aspect of the value of creativity, even when other more social dimensions are present.

On the other end of the spectrum are individual interests connected with the activities of routine everyday experience. These are basic welfare interests related to food, shelter, and health maintenance. The desire to contribute to one's own welfare and development is a normal desire for most of us. The valuing of such activity is not always reducible to the thought that it results in an acceptable state of welfare or personal development. For one might be disappointed that one's welfare has not resulted from an activity that is one's own. In fact, it is a feature of any plausible view of hu-

---

cluded in *The Marx-Engels Reader,* ed. Robert C. Tucker (New York: W. W. Norton, 1972).

man welfare that an agent makes some contribution, however small or indirect, to his or her own welfare. Another feature is that the agent values some activities of this sort for their own sake. What clearer sign could there be that a person is deeply self-alienated than that he or she finds *none* of the routine activities of self-care intrinsically rewarding?[10]

There are, of course, many cases in which some such contributions are not possible for any particular agent. Still it is hard to conceive of human welfare where it is not a loss for the agent that the agent could make no contribution of this sort. If this is true, then at least some (I suspect many) activities of contribution to one's own welfare are those an agent values intrinsically as individual goods. Some such activities would be pursued where possible by most people, even where they were completely and easily eliminable without loss of their other contributory ends. Being a mere patient, then, regarding one's welfare needs is a fantasy only for the overworked. Just as dreams of freedom from welfare needs and activities is one kind of nightmare, a world scarce in work activity is another. I also suspect that most people would pursue some work activities involving their own welfare needs, even at a significant cost to themselves.

Yet it might be objected that some people, due to extreme physical handicaps, cannot engage in contribution activities regarding their own welfare. Though their disabilities are a loss to them in just this regard, still they are among the most admirable and well adjusted people. They are certainly not people who have lost the basic elements of human integrity.

There are several things that must be said in response to this, none of which denies that there are indeed such people. The first is this: To argue that individual contribution activities are categorical goods is not to argue that they are universally so, however close they come to being so. It is to argue that they can and do function in a manner that often involves a person's identifying thoughts in important ways. The second thing to note is that we recognize as truly exceptional those who are well adjusted and admirable despite these handicaps. We stand in wonder of how they could survive, given their losses. Also, our attitude toward their integrity is admiration rather than pity, and our identifying thoughts reveal doubts that we could survive such misfortune.[11]

10. For an interesting study relevant to this issue, see Seligman, *Helplessness*.
11. Whether the hearing world and the signing world with its distinctive language are both impoverished when inaccessible to each other is an interesting and important issue. But it is not an issue of being physically handicapped in the sense that I intend here. See Oliver Sacks, *Seeing Voices: A Journey into the World of the Deaf* (New York: Harper Perennial, 1990).

Finally, we must understand the options of those who do survive with such handicaps regarding the ability to engage in these welfare contribution activities. If such a person is a talented person who has opportunity to develop that talent, his or her chances for survival increase tremendously. Why? Because an extremely physically handicapped person with significant intelligence but without opportunity for development must suffer through hours and hours of inactivity. But even where there is talent and opportunity for creative activity, the adjustment to the passivity in the routine regarding the agent's welfare needs will be most difficult. Those of us not physically handicapped can hardly appreciate the difficulties of adjusting to a routine filled with someone else's activities rather than our own. Our routines are active and interestingly so, even when they are uncreative, and this is a great blessing.

I conclude then that there are many intrinsically valued solitary activities of the individual sort. Many are in all probability of categorical importance to most of us as independent goods of activity. Writing a book is most valuable to its author (at least to an author of a certain sort) in that it is both challenging and fascinating. That it might make a contribution is, of course, a reason to think it worthy of publication, but writing a book and publishing a book are different activities. Any real writer, or artist, or musician, or scientist will tell you that what drives his or her work activity most is that it is fascinating and challenging. That some will take this claim with either dull surprise or disbelief only reflects their lack of understanding of what life is sometimes like for others. And though it is difficult for any of us to say what it is like to be a bat, some of us know what it is like to be a writer, an artist, a musician, or a scientist. It is to be taken with one's work, to be fascinated by it, to be captivated by it, to be lost in it. To be stripped of it is to be left in a world without color. The same, of course, can be said of many other workers and for many other kinds of work from carpentry to dentistry and from teaching to designing.

3.

In contrast with individual solitary activities is another group of activities that are done alone in the relevant sense and are of intrinsic value to the agent. But, unlike solitary individual activities, they have beneficiaries other than the agent. The agent is still an intrinsic beneficiary of the activity in the sense that these activities have intrinsic as well as (perhaps) instrumental value to the agent. But there are others who are independent beneficiaries of these activities in the sense that they either do not participate in the activities themselves or if they do, the activities themselves have only instrumental value to them. For this reason, these activities are solitary but are other- as well as self-regarding. The idea is that some activities are intrinsically valuable to an agent because they are intrinsically related to the satisfaction of someone else's interests. It is because these activities are both solitary and other-regarding that I call them solitary benevolent activities, remembering that they are nondeontic activities. Thus the issue for the remainder of this chapter is this: What role does the intrinsic interest in solitary benevolent activities play in the integrity of the agent of integrity in the thick sense?

Recall from earlier discussion that there are two types of these solitary activities, personally benevolent solitary activities and impartially benevolent solitary activities. Personally benevolent activities have independent beneficiaries personally related to the agent through some form of personal love or close personal attachment. Impartially benevolent activities have independent beneficiaries not specially related to the agent. I will say more about the latter activities later, but first I must address the former.

Personally benevolent solitary activities are done for the sake of one's loved ones, that is, for one's friends, family, neighbors, or community in some larger sense. As beneficiaries, loved ones are independent by virtue of not sharing the activity with the agent as an intrinsic good. Thus they are independently related to the activity as a good but personally related to the agent. Consequently, there are at least as many types of personally benevolent activities as there are personal relationships. Since my aim here has its limits in the structural significance of these goods to human integrity, I will restrict discussion to contribution activities of the personally benevolent sort. I will not attempt anything like a complete account.

Remember that contribution activities aim at enhancing the good of someone or some thing. Personally benevolent solitary activities of this sort, then, are those that aim at enhancing the good of someone with whom the agent has a loving relationship—a family member, a friend, or a member of the community. Of special importance are the agent's interest in the welfare of loved ones and the interest in being their benefactor.

Consider the nurturing activities of a parent toward a beloved child. Earlier we saw that any loving parent feels obligated to engage in some activities regarding the welfare interests of the child by virtue of parental love. Without such a feeling, we are at a loss to make sense of the parent's love. We are at a similar loss if we find the parent averse to all nondeontic activities regarding the child's welfare interests. Imagine a parent who looks with dread on any and all welfare-related activities regarding its child. Within the agent's deliberative field, all such activities are viewed as cloaked in tedium. All are done either out of some sense of obligation or simply as instrumentally important to the child's well-being. It is not that the parent does not want the child to prosper. Indeed, this parent wants benefits to accrue to the child in excess of what he or she feels an obligation to provide. But there remains an aversion to the activities that are the means that provide these benefits, an aversion that is outweighed by the concern for the child's welfare. Is this parental love?

Whatever else the concern such a person might have for the child, it is difficult to make sense of it as parental love. Personal love—of whatever type—takes delight in caring for loved ones. Some threshold level of these activities appears within the loving parent's deliberative field as delightful, which marks these activities as the kind of nondeontic activities in question. To force them into deontic or moral categories is to distort the kinds of goods they are. Thus, for example, never taking delight in providing the welfare benefit of emotional security for one's child through nurturing activities is simply incompatible with parental love.

To appreciate the kind of value these activities have, we need to pay careful attention to their phenomenology. What we need is a better understanding of when a delightful experience is aesthetic in the broad sense? Contrast three different cases of finding something delightful: (i) finding it delightful that a state of affairs obtains, for example, that your children are happy; (ii) taking delight in the results of your actions, for example, that your actions bring joy to your children; and (iii) taking delight in activities themselves, for example, taking delight in playing with and nurturing your children. In the first case, one could take delight in a state of affairs that is entirely unrelated to one's actions. Think, for example, of being away from home and learning that your children are doing well. The feeling that comes from such good news does not seem to me particularly aesthetic, even in a broad sense. Nor would the feeling that comes from knowing that your children are pleased that you had prepared their favorite meal for them while they were away all day at school, which would be an instance of (ii). You might find preparing the meal onerous except for the fact that it has the payoff of bringing joy to your children. But consider the person who would take delight not only in the fact of the payoff but also in preparing the meal itself. One of two things might be true. First, such a parent might take delight in cooking independent of the other delight in the payoff. Suppose this is true. There remains the question of whether the two delights are simply two instantiations of one kind of experience or whether they are two different kinds of experience. I believe there are good reasons for thinking that it is the latter and that this is important for practical reason.

One very important reason for thinking that the delights in this case are of different kinds is that approximate synonymous expressions for one experience cannot be substituted for the other. For example, instead of describing the experience of finding the cooking itself valuable, we might say that it is interesting, fascinating, or captivating. But to substitute these descriptions for the delight taken in the state of affairs of your children being pleased at having their favorite meal seems odd, to say the least. Imagine thinking that it is interesting that your child is pleased or finding such a fact fascinating or being captivated by it. None of these seems to capture the relevant sense of delight, yet they seem to apply rather straightforwardly to finding the cooking itself delightful.

The second possibility is that it is not cooking alone that you find delightful but cooking for your children, where the cooking is not valued merely instrumentally. In this kind of case, it seems that the activity of cooking also falls under another description. For instance, you might intrinsically value cooking as an instance of another kind of activity that you intrinsically value. If you see your cooking as a nurturing activity and if you intrinsically value nurturing activities, then you might intrinsically value your cooking for your children in a way that you might not value cooking per se. This would be to place intrinsic rather than mere instrumental value on your activity; hence you would not value your activity merely for its results. Now suppose that you take delight in cooking for your children and you take delight in the fact that your children are pleased with their favorite meal. Are these two different delights, and are they of different kinds? Are they phenomenologically distinct? I believe that they are, though their distinctness is easily overlooked.

One might find it interesting, fascinating, and captivating to cook for one's children in a way that one does not find it interesting, fascinating, or captivating to cook per se. To do so is to find the nurturing of one's children interesting, fascinating, and captivating. If you are a parent of this sort, then you take aesthetic delight in some of your nurturing activities in that you find them interesting, satisfying, fascinating, or captivating, but you also take nonaesthetic delight in the results of these activities. If this is true, then for some people the capacity for boredom is underwritten not only by the capacities to find some activities interesting, fascinating, captivating, and the like but also by social capacities, among which are loving capacities. The loving parent is not only one who can take loving delight in the results of her nurturing activities but also one who can take aesthetic delight in and be fascinated and captivated by nurturing activities. Any adequate conception of practical reason that applies to loving parents must therefore recognize the role of aesthetic reasons in their normative thoughts. Later, I will argue that these observations have previously unnoticed implications for a normative conceptual scheme, namely, that not only do various goods that give rise to deontic beliefs symmetrically regulate each other, but also the deontic and the nondeontic, the moral and the nonmoral, are symmetrical in their regulative functions.

There are, of course, moments when the delight subsides in the case of deontic activities, and the sense of obligation internal to personal love must take over. But the dispositions of a person who anticipates with dread *any* thought of welfare-related activities regarding loved ones are not those of love. Nor are those of the person who does not find intrinsic value in some such activities that are independent of what the lover feels is owed to loved ones. Thus the loving parent takes delight in some activities that contribute to the child's good independent of any sense of obligation he or she has toward the child. As a source of personal delight, the loving parent sees these activities not only as beneficial to the child but also as a part of the parent's own good. Without this conception of parental good as including contribution activities of this sort, we are unable to understand a person as a loving parent. If this is true, then our intrinsic interest in many loving activities underwrites our capacity not only for loneliness but for boredom as well. Without loving activities, we are vulnerable to the loneliness that fills the space where nonaesthetic delight should be, and without some loving activities being interesting, fascinating, and captivating, we are without the aesthetic delight that wards off boredom. That there should be a confluence of these interests and capacities should not be surprising on reflection. It is nature's way of getting us to enjoy what is good not only for us but also for the species.

One might admit this, however, and question whether any of these activities must include labor. Is it not enough simply to want to play with one's child and leave the labor to others, if one can? The problem with this suggestion is that it involves an impoverished conception of nurturing. If we confine the concept of nurturing to play activities, it is difficult to distinguish loving a child in a parental way from some lesser form of attachment. Suppose I enjoy playing with my neighbor's children, and I care for their welfare in that I am committed to their welfare needs being met. Being less affluent than myself, my neighbors need assistance that I am willing to provide in meeting the welfare needs of their children. The parents do the nurturing, enjoying a good bit of it; I pay the bills, without a trace of resentment; and I play with the children, aversive to any of the activities that constitute the nurturing. Perhaps I love the children, but there would be a clear distinction between the love I have for them and the love their parents have for them. Moreover, this judgment seems confirmed by the increasing difficulties we have with a conception of fatherhood confined exclusively to the role of secondary care: Too many secondary care responsibilities dull the capacity for primary care and thereby dull the capacity for parental love.

Furthermore, the degree of caring about the child's welfare and the delight in activities that secure it will not only exceed the feelings of obligation to the child. They will also exceed the feelings of obligation to others for whom the parent has impartial respect and esteem. Later, we will see how this works out regarding the priorities problem and the goods of activity. For now it is sufficient to point out that some commitments involving personal benevolence take priority over some impartial commitments. Here this is true of the intentional dispositional states of someone whose integrity involves parental love and the ground project of parenthood but who also has simple respect and esteem for others. But, in this case, the activities are nondeontic, solitary activities. Thus the integration problem is to be understood as the deontic having to make a place for the nondeontic. This is not an insignificant fact about a normative conceptual scheme, one I will discuss in more detail later when I discuss Baron's views.

For the moment, however, consider, a loving parent making a life-affecting choice that makes possible some significant degree of these contribution activities regarding a beloved child. Would this show a lack of respect for others, even if it diminished to some degree the capacity or opportunity to assist others with their rights? If so, the integration of parental affection and impartial respect can only take the form of subservience of the personal to the impersonal and the nondeontic to the deontic. But this is simply not our understanding of these concepts.

If we assume that you are a loving parent to your daughter, say, and a respectful person, it is *not* a sign that you do not respect others if in some contexts you give priority to personally benevolent activities regarding your daughter over some of the interests of respectable people. This is true even where these activities are not required by what you feel you ought to do for your daughter. We would have serious questions about the depth of your love for your daughter if you did not have such priorities, if you did not do some things for her simply because you find them delightful. Indeed, such priorities are a part of a loving parent's humanity and integrity. If this is true, then in some contexts you would have, as a function of having parental love for your child, the normative belief that you ought to do y for the sake of some respectable person or persons were it not for the delightfulness of doing x for your child, even where you do not view doing x for your child as an obligation. This is a new kind of normative belief, one as yet unanalyzed in terms of the priorities problem. If such beliefs are rational for us, then our conceptual scheme will reflect the fact that for us the deontic and the nondeontic, the aesthetic and the moral, are symmetrical in their regulative functions. Later, I will isolate the kinds of deliberative contexts in which such norms are rational and those in which they are irrational. For now it is enough to suggest that this kind of norm is a component in a loving parent's dispositions and that this is compatible with simple respect for others. Also, since all personal love includes the interests in the welfare of loved ones and in being their benefactor and in taking delight in loving activities, the analysis extends to all forms of loving relationships.

Of course, if your dispositional set includes both personal love for your child and respect for others, there are contexts in which you will believe that others' interests take priority over your nondeontic interest in the delightful activities of benefiting your child. You will believe in some contexts that it would be wrong for you to do x for the sake of your child, despite its delightfulness, because you will believe that you have an obligation to do y for other respectable people. This, of course, shows the regulative influence of impartial respect on the place of the goods of activity in our lives. Later, in addressing the priorities problem, I will isolate the deliberative contexts in which these thoughts emerge and show how the Aristotelian view accommodates them.

4.

Thus far the concern has been with the loved one as an extrinsic though independent beneficiary of the lover's activities. The loved one is an extrinsic beneficiary when the benefit is simply the result of the activity. Think of a baby benefiting from having its diaper changed. There are, however, other activities in which the loved one is intended as an intrinsic yet independent beneficiary. In these cases, the loved one is an intrinsic beneficiary because the activity itself is of intrinsic value to her. In both cases, however, she is an independent beneficiary in the sense that she is not an agent in the activities themselves.

Activities having an intrinsic independent beneficiary I call activities of recognition. I am not sure whether to say that such activities are a type of contribution activity or a separate category. The most important point is that the good of the activity is not entirely independent of the activity itself, yet the loved one is not an agent in the activity. I have in mind the lover's activities that express the importance of the loved one to the lover.

Some ways of expressing the importance of the loved one to the lover involve expressions of affection, but these are usually shared activities. Thus solitary activities of recognition involve either unilateral expressions of affection or some other expression of importance of the loved one to the lover. Sometimes these expressions involve "honoring" the loved one. Thus there are two types of unilateral activities of recognition: unilateral activities of affection and unilateral honoring activities.

We can summarize the distinctions regarding personally benevolent solitary activities as follows:

I.   Unilateral activities with extrinsic beneficiaries
II.   Unilateral activities of affection with intrinsic beneficiaries
III. Unilateral honoring activities with intrinsic beneficiaries

An example of a unilateral activity of affection might be one involving friendship, say, giving a gift to a friend. Your friend is not a participant in the activity but an intrinsic beneficiary of it. The giving expresses the affection, for the object that is the gift would not have the same meaning apart from the giving. Of course, some gifts have extrinsic benefits, but many of them either do not or they have dual benefits. Perhaps your gift to your friend involves the activity of preparing her favorite meal. In fact, it seems that the giving of gifts in some form—though not necessarily of material goods—is most certainly an essential element in human flourishing. The reason I say this is that it allows humans to express their *graciousness* to those they love. A gift well given is one that not only expresses love and thoughtfulness for what is given but also expresses grace in how it is given. Part of the way, then, in which gift giving appears within the loving agent's deliberative field as good is in terms of it graciousness, clearly an aesthetic category. Could a life totally without opportunities for graciousness to loved ones and delightfulness in it possibly be the best life for a communal being to live? The answer seems obvious to anyone not in the throes of a highly individualistic conception of the human good. Yet what might not be so obvious is that some level of the goods of unilateral activities of affection is necessary for the survival of human integrity.

One misleading argument for the categorical value of such activities is that if social beings are *never* the intrinsic beneficiaries of such activities, they will lose their sense of self-worth. The problem with such an argument is not its premises but its conclusion. The fact that such benefits are essential to the survival of a sense of self-worth does not show that the activities are the sorts of goods in question. What we are evaluating here is not whether your solitary activity of engaging in x is an intrinsic, extrinsic, or dual benefit to your friend. Rather, it is whether your engaging in doing x as an element in your way of life is a categorical good *for you* as a nondeontic activity. If the loss to you of never engaging in x for a friend is explained entirely in terms of her interests, then the activity is not the relevant sort. Nor are activities the absence of which from your life would result in your having a sense of guilt but no sense of personal loss. The reason in each case is that the activities must be intrinsic goods *for you* and they must be nondeontic activities.

Relative, then, to the class of agents of integrity in the thick sense, we can conclude that all such persons intrinsically value such activities of recognition. All such agents would unmistakenly find these activities an intrinsic part of the life most worth living. The issue here, though, concerns not that of human flourishing but that of human survival in the relevant sense. The question then is this: Could all such loving beings survive the complete loss of such activities in their lives with their integrity intact? Or could at least some of them survive by taking a categorically consoling interest in some other human good?

It does not seem plausible that there is any impartial interest that in itself could console for a complete loss of such goods in a person's life. Think what it would be like to sacrifice permanently any gracious communication of your affection to your children, your parents, your spouse or romantic lover, your friends, or your neighbors on the grounds of simple respect, sympathy, or esteem for others. It is difficult to see how such a sacrifice could be anything other than the sacrifice of one's life and one's reasons for living. As such, it would be the sacrifice of oneself as an ongoing agent, and this might occur only were there no way to be both a loving person and a person with self-respect. Our previous discussion of the role of the goods of love as nondeliberative goods is relevant here. The goods of love, where they exist, simply impose a deliberative limit on the concept of personal sacrifice in the name of impartial concerns. The goods of personally benevolent activities of the sort involving graciousness are another example of this. But what I am arguing here is that some threshold level of these goods is necessary in the lives of most for survival of the basic elements of integrity in the thin sense. I am not arguing that all conflicts between such goods and impartial concerns must give priority to these activities. Beyond a threshold level, these goods are nondeliberative goods in relationship to impartial concerns. It is in this sense that these activities are categorical goods for at least most of us.

More plausible as a consoling factor for the complete loss of unilateral activities of affection are shared activities of affection. Perhaps some persons could survive and even flourish without engaging in these unilateral activities, as long as there was some abundance of shared activities in their lives.

Although we should not underestimate the value of unilateral expressions of affection, let us suppose that they can be significantly consoled for by shared expressions of affection. But what if the only consoling interest sufficient to console for the loss of these solitary goods is the interest in personally shared goods? The same structural points regarding the place of agent-centered goods of activity in relationship to impartial concerns remain intact. My major concern here is to show that agent-centered goods of activity limit the demands of impartiality in the integrity of a normal human agent. Therefore, a concession to the relative categorical value of solitary activities to shared activities of the sort in question would not undermine the core of my analysis.

Yet there is reason to think that the unilateral aspect of these activities is more crucial than the previous paragraph suggests. The intrinsic benefits of such activities serve to convey not only that the loved one is important to the lover but also, because these activities are unilateral, that the loved one is important as a separate and numerically distinct person. Moreover, the interest in expressing this is to be found internal to the phenomenon of personal love itself. Thus such activities not only confer benefits on the loved one but are the objects of an intrinsic interest of the lover. To love another includes the interest in expressing not only how important the other is to oneself but also, quite simply, how important she is period.

A similar analysis applies to activities of recognition that "honor" loved ones. This is true, despite the fact that it is often difficult to draw a hard line between expressions of affection and honoring expressions in personal relationships. To honor a person is to hold that person in esteem, to value that person in some significant degree beyond the point of mere respect. It takes little to express toleration, but it takes greater attention to detail to honor a loved one. In the former case, one needs only to avoid actions that show contempt. But in the latter, there must be overt behavioral manifestation of the lover's recognition of the loved one's esteem-conferring qualities. In cases of peer love, honoring activities are no less important in the lover's love for the loved one than are the activities of affection. Thus unilateral honoring activities are no less important in the integrity of a loving person than are unilateral activities of affection.

Still an argument can be made that as unilateral activities there is a somewhat larger role for personal honoring activities than for activities of affection. The argument concerns the desire to confer the benefit of the lover's expression of the loved one's importance as a separate and numerically distinct person. E-qualities, like R-qualities, are in themselves the objects of impartial attitudes, as we have seen. But, for reasons already given, personal affection is not transferable across persons of similar qualities in the way that esteem is. Thus unilateral honoring activities serve to point out more specifically what it is about the loved one that makes the person worthy of honor as a separate and distinct person. These qualities are independent of the relationship to the lover, and conferring the benefit of such recognition on the loved one is as intrinsic to friendship as is the conferring of affection to romantic love. And in the case of both affection and honor, graciousness is central to the value of the activities from the agent's point of view.

Therefore, whether as welfare activities or as activities of recognition, personally benevolent solitary activities play a crucial and irreplaceable role in integrity on the thick conception. But what of impartially benevolent solitary activities?

5.

It is of first importance to understand the sense in which these solitary activities are impartial and the sense in which they are not. They are not impartial in the sense that agent-neutral activities are. The reason for this is that the agent is dispositionally sensitive to beliefs regarding the identity of the agent of the activity. That is, if you engage in an activity of this sort, you are sensitive to the fact that it is you and not someone else doing it, but you are dispositionally indifferent to beliefs regarding the identity of the independent beneficiary of the activity, as long as the beneficiary falls under a certain description. It is in this latter sense that these activities are impartial. Some persons, for example, take delight in helping other persons who are in need apart from any thought that such assistance is obligatory. Mother Teresa seemed to be an excellent case in point. Crucial to her disposition toward those she served was the belief that they were needy. The belief that a person was significantly needy seemed sufficient to evoke her dedication, subject only to the limitations of time and energy. Yet Mother Teresa's attitude seemed to be that it was not only important that the needy receive help but that it was *she* who played a large role in helping them.

When such activities are truly impartial, personal affection plays no role in their value to the agent. My point here is not that Mother Teresa had no personal affection for those she helped. Rather, it is that insofar as she appreciated persons as in need of help and she valued her activities in this regard, personal affection was an external factor. To the extent that personal affection was not an external factor, her welfare activities on behalf of the needy were personally rather than impartially benevolent. This is because personal affection for another brings with it sensitivity to the identity of the object of affection. Thus unilateral activities of affection are not among impartially benevolent activities. We are left, then, with impartially benevolent welfare activities and impartial honoring activities of the unilateral sort.

For many people impartial welfare activities are a part of their profession or life's work, which they value intrinsically. Dedicated social workers, teachers, lawyers, physicians, and the like are all persons who find intrinsic value in helping others who are in some sense needy. There are, of course, those who enter these professions merely for the external rewards associated with them. This is especially true of those professions that carry with them access to great wealth or prestige. But these are not persons who are *dedicated* professionals or who are dedicated to their work, for to be dedicated in this context is to be dedicated to persons in need. A dedicated social worker is dedicated to those with welfare needs; a dedicated teacher, to students with a need to learn; a dedicated lawyer, to clients in need of legal remedy; and a dedicated physician, to those in need of medical attention. Yet in a very important sense, to be dedicated in this context is to be dedicated to helping with the needs of strangers.

That there are those who are dedicated to the needs of strangers in a way that renders their activities a ground project suitably called their life's work is certain. That there are those who could not find life worth living without such work is also certain. Thus there are those for whom the loss of their work as a ground project would be inconsolable. Also, it is doubtful that most of these people feel that their taking on such a project as their life's work is obligatory, though some of them might. Those who do not, see their activities as not only beneficial to the needy but also as intrinsically rewarding work that is not obligatory, which raises the issue of the role of the aesthetic in an account of these goods. When these nondeontic activities have categorical value to an agent, can their value be adequately understood in nonaesthetic terms? I will argue that they cannot.

It should not be overlooked in this regard that these activities are not agent-neutral activities. Rather, they are agent-centered goods that are not, for these persons, replaceable by impartial concerns as consoling interests, should these goods be lost to them. In fact, some of these agents simply could not survive in a world free of needy people. What does this say about the kind of value at stake for these agents?

One kind of person who might seem to fit the description is the person who excessively "needs to be needed." For some, being needed is at the center of their lives because they have a fragile sense of self. Often, such people are very possessive of those under their care, for without these needy dependents these people have no secure sense of their place in the world. In this sense, these people are more dependent on those in need than the needy are on them. Clearly, when the value of activities involving others is accounted for in this way, neither aesthetic nor moral value seems to be the most prominent.

There are others, however, for whom activities of the sort in question seem to be categorical without this kind of pathological dimension. Instead of being pathological in this sense, the vulnerability to the loss of these activities in their lives seems to reflect a curious blend of what we think are healthy values. On the one hand are the values of respect and sympathy for others, and on the other is finding working with people interesting, fascinating, and captivating, even challenging. To reduce the value of these activities to the social values of respect and sympathy is to distort them, as is to reduce their value to the fascination they bring to the agent.

A certain (mistaken) way of reading Nietzsche derides any notion of "service to humanity." Students sometimes take this tack, espousing the belief that most of humanity is simply contemptible and unworthy of being helped or "served." Failure to recognize this is, on their view, a failure of both judgment and character. Of course, if they are right that strangers are worthy only of contempt, then it does seem rather perverse of people to dedicate their life's work to them. But surely it would be odd that only members of one's communal circle were minimally respectable or estimable in a way that allows sympathy for their needs. These beliefs about the R-qualities and E-qualities of strangers that smother sympathetic response are often just false. The failure to see that they are false is brought about by the absence of the dispositions of respect and esteem in the first place. Since a communal being does have these dispositions and is capable of recognizing the R-qualities and E-qualities of others, the false beliefs are probably not attributable to communal commitments. Rather, they are likely attributable to dispositions that are antithetical not only to impartial sympathy but to communal love as well. After all, it is one thing to be indifferent to strangers about whom one knows nothing; it is another to be averse to helping them because they are held in contempt. To do the latter, one has to know something about them and that something must reveal that they are beneath sympathy. But to be unsympathetic *in general* to the plight of strangers and to find burdensome all activities intended to benefit them is decidedly not required by empirical evidence. This is especially true of a communal being who is a person of integrity. For this is someone who realizes the importance of being considered a separate and distinct person whose sense of self-worth should be considered on the evidence of character. So it is easy enough to see why a respectful and sympathetic person would take an interest in activities that benefit respectable but needy people.

It is, however, one thing to take an interest in these activities and to pursue them and quite another to find the activities interesting, fascinating, captivating, and intrinsically challenging. For most people who have these activities as a central part of their life's work, this aesthetic dimension is almost always a central part of their value. Were it utterly dull and uninteresting to do this work, it is entirely implausible that the activities could play the role they do within the person's psychology. To be sure, finding it fascinating and interesting to help others is to care about others, but there is an aesthetic dimension to this caring that is lost if we are not careful to pay attention to the fact that these are nondeontic activities. Overly moralized conceptual schemes ride roughshod over these phenomenological distinctions. That they do leads to distortions of practical reason, as we will see. For now, we need to note the difference between taking delight in the fact that the needy have their needs met and taking delight in the activities of meeting these needs. Though delight of the second sort expresses respect and sympathy for others, it also reveals another dimension of value, one that is aesthetic. It says something about the kind of aesthetic experience for which people of a certain character have the capacity.

It is easy enough to see that the activity involved in solving a mathematical problem could have an aesthetic dimension independent of its payoff. In fact, those who are incapable of finding mathematics alluring in this sense tend to dread math. But mathematicians—those whose life's work is very much centered on doing math—tend to be those people who experience the aesthetic allure of mathematics. Not only do they find it interesting and fascinating; they are captivated by it. I am claiming that the same thing is true of many of those who make working with the needy the center of their life's work. Thus a full understanding of the value of such work includes both a social and an aesthetic dimension. For people of this sort, their capacity for boredom is underwritten both by their impartial social capacities and by their aesthetic capacities for finding their social work interesting, fascinating, and captivating.

Of course, not all people organize their lives around these kinds of work activities, but the structural significance of a general lack of aesthetic delight in unilateral welfare activities for strangers is gauged by what is both · present and absent in the lives of those who are characterized as lacking it. In a world like ours, much of life is spent dealing with strangers. If it were largely spent with contemptible strangers, this would itself be a serious threat to a healthy integration of personality. Of course, this does not mean that one can fabricate beliefs about the character of others in order to survive. But it does mean that those with integrity are disposed to maintain some hope for the intrinsic value in others, rather than to extinguish it by some general belief about strangers. On the other hand, a general resentment of strangers reveals a disposition aversive to the elements of integrity in others. To be filled with such resentment is an evil to be avoided, and if of sufficient magnitude it can be a categorical evil. So much then for what will be present for the person who has a general attitude of contempt toward strangers to a degree to smother all sympathy for them.

Absent will be a sense of graciousness toward strangers. This is a great loss measured by the resentment that rushes to fill the void. Not all of us feel the call to dedicate our work to the needs of strangers. But it is hard to imagine someone with communal sensibilities who would not also find the complete loss of graciousness to strangers affective of his or her identifying thoughts. Indeed, it seems more plausible that the resentment is a response to a loss than that the value of graciousness is the remedy for resentment. If this is true, then impartial welfare activities of the sort in question are intrinsic human goods structurally crucial to the integrity of any fully developed social being. This is true because severe resentment of strangers is not only a form of alienation from others but also a form of self-alienation for a social being.

Nowhere is this alienation more evident than where impartial honoring activities are viewed with resentment. When a person resents rather than takes delight, both aesthetic and moral, in the legitimate accomplishments of others, there is deep self-alienation as well as alienation from others. A person of integrity in the thick sense is not given to such resentment. The reason is not that the person of integrity is indifferent to the E-qualities of strangers. Rather, it is because the person of integrity in the thick sense is very sensitive to such qualities and takes delight in them. It is only the person with a strong sense of self coupled with a positive disposition toward others who can experience such delight. Those burdened with resentment in these matters lack a very important human good, perhaps one that cannot be replaced by any other. To lack the capacity for graciousness in this regard, then, is to lack a capacity that not only wards off resentment but boredom as well.

6.

We have seen, I believe, that solitary activities of various sorts have distinct places in the psychological structure of the agent of integrity in the thick sense. This is true across the spectrum of these activities, from individual to personally benevolent to impartially benevolent ones, all of which have aesthetic dimensions crucial to their value. What we have not seen is the solution to the integration and the priorities problems regarding these goods. After I address the issue of the general features of shared activities and their categorical value, I will turn to these problems of integration.

It is time now to turn to the topic of shared activities.

17. Shared Activities

Two people share an activity just in case their doing it together is an intrinsic good for both of them. Thus, insofar as two people share an activity, neither is an independent beneficiary of the activity. Rather, to the extent to which engaging in such activities is a good for a person, the value of the activity is dependent on its value for another person, and vice versa. Here, then, is a kind of good such that it is impossible to specify its value to one person independent of its value to another person. We can refer to the participants as the mutual intrinsic beneficiaries of such activities.

To pursue a mutual intrinsic good is to pursue one's own good, which is identical to pursuing the good of another. I hope to show how predominant such goods are to human agency and to the survival of human integrity. I will suggest that the threshold level of such goods in the life of most people must be quite high to maintain the elements of integrity and reasons for living. If I am right, life, for most humans, is worth living only if the greater part of their activities is shared. Also, if I am right, some level of mutuality is more important to most people than their individual autonomy. For if finding one's own good in the good of another is crucial to having a sense of self, then there is no sense of self worth retaining that has an entirely autonomous identity. Moreover, I hope to show that there is an important aesthetic dimension to these mutual intrinsic goods.

1.

Divisions among shared activities can be made in terms of partners and beneficiaries. Shared activities always include partners who are mutual intrinsic beneficiaries, but the relationship between the partners can be either personal or impersonal. Personally shared activities are those activities in which the partners are personally related, and impersonally shared activities are those in which they are not. Think of the difference between sharing a game of bridge with friends versus sharing a game of bridge with a group of strangers who are merely bridge enthusiasts.

As to beneficiaries, there are activities that involve independent beneficiaries and those that do not. Those that do not involve independent beneficiaries are exclusive shared activities. They are exclusive because their value as shared activities excludes the value of any intended benefit to anyone other than the participants in the activities themselves. Other activities involve independent beneficiaries. They are benevolent shared activities because their value as shared activities includes the value of intended benefits to others who are not participants in the activities themselves. In this regard, think of the distinction between the normal value of kissing and the normal value to loving parents of jointly planning their child's surprise birthday party.

Still a third important division is among benevolent shared activities in which the independent beneficiary is specially related to at least one of the mutual beneficiaries and those in which this is not the case. The independent beneficiaries of the first group are intimate and those of the second are nonintimate beneficiaries.

Finally, there are shared activities that include an instrumental benefit to the mutual beneficiaries and those that do not. That this is true is so obvious that it hardly needs discussing. I mention it here only to remind the reader that the presence of instrumental concerns does not in itself vitiate the intrinsic value of a good. Having given due notice, then, I will not in what follows give any great attention to the fact of this distinction.

Though the set of distinctions here is complex, I hope to show that it provides us with a body of data for an understanding of practical reason in human agents that is much richer than one that ignores these distinctions. To compromise on the complexity of the phenomenological data here is to compromise the depth of our understanding of practical reason in human beings. I include the following chart to assist the reader in tracking the relevant phenomena.

I. Personally shared activities
   A. Exclusively shared activities (mutual intrinsic beneficiaries without independent beneficiaries, e.g., playing tennis with a friend who loves the game)
   B. Shared benevolent activities (mutual intrinsic as well as independent beneficiaries)

1. Intimate independent beneficiaries (e.g., parents planning a birthday party for their child together)
2. Nonintimate independent beneficiaries (e.g., husband and wife participating in building houses for Habitat for Humanity)

II. Impersonally shared activities
  A. Exclusively shared activities (mutual intrinsic beneficiaries without independent beneficiaries, e.g., playing tennis with a stranger who loves the game)
  B. Shared benevolent activities (mutual intrinsic as well as independent beneficiaries)
    1. Intimate independent beneficiaries (e.g., parent and a teacher working together to educate the parent's child)
    2. Nonintimate independent beneficiaries (e.g., building houses for Habitat for Humanity with like-minded strangers)

With these divisions in place, the discussion that follows focuses first on personally shared activities and then on those that are impersonally shared. I begin in each case with an analysis of exclusive shared activities, followed by an analysis of shared activities that have intimate independent beneficiaries. I close with an analysis of shared activities that have nonintimate independent beneficiaries. Since the concern is with an analysis of the relationship between the agent-centered goods of an agent's life and the agent's impartial concerns, I discuss only a representative sample of these activities sufficient for the purposes of the present inquiry.

2.

Probably the most representative of exclusive, personally shared activities are those that express affection. They differ from affectionate solitary activities in which the loved one benefits from but does not participate in the activity. The gift received, the compliment accepted, the affection requited—all are benefits of the actions of others. With exclusive shared activities of affection, the loved one is a participant in the activity in just the same way as the lover, for the loved one is also a lover in these activities. Accordingly, lover and loved one are mutual intrinsic beneficiaries, and the activities are exclusive because they do not include intended benefits to those not involved in the activities themselves.

Perhaps the clearest example involves the sexual activities of romantic lovers. A distortion of Victorian mores was that female participation in sexual activity, as love activity, was something done *for* the male lover. As such, the activity from the perspective of the female lover was at most a solitary expression of affection intended for the benefit of the male lover as an independent beneficiary. Not only was this distorting in the sense that the female lover was excluded from the intrinsic beneficiaries of the physical pleasure involved in sexual activities, but also both lovers were deprived of the good of a shared activity. A further distortion is to think that the major flaw with this view was that it cut off access to an important human good to women, namely, the physical pleasure of sex, although this was clearly one of its flaws. To assume this is to assume that the most important benefit of sexual activity is physical pleasure as an individual good. But surely this is false, at least regarding romantic *lovers*. The central value of sexual activity for romantic lovers regarding physical pleasure is that they share the pleasure.

The Victorian view fosters a Don Juan view of romance in which the female lover is a sexual conquest for the sake of the male lover. Criticisms of this view that focus only on how it restricts access to the physical pleasure of sex to women merely revises the male romantic lover; it does nothing to transform him. He now sees himself as an independent benefactor, arrogantly, or humbly, or (worst of all) altruistically providing a good long missing from the lives of women. The woman, however, has been transformed from a passive servant to an effusive female counterpart to the male Don Juan of the revised view. This, I take it, is an adolescent interpretation of the sexual revolution prevalent in erotic magazines.

But surely in assessing the history of sexuality, it is difficult not to view the legacy of the Don Juan lover with either extreme sadness or utter contempt. The sadness is for those restricted by views of romance in which sexual activity as what amounts to a kind of solitary activity. They have lost the good of shared sexual pleasure. The contempt is for the Don Juan lover as willing to sacrifice the goods of shared activity for an individual hedonic good. I suspect that historically a great many psychological ills involving self-contempt have had more than a little of their source in highly individualistic views of sexual activity.

Another distorting view of the good of sexual activity as an expression of affection is a conception of sexuality requiring lovers to justify their engaging in sex as a benevolent rather than as an exclusive shared activity or as also having some instrumental benefit to the lovers. Think of the chilling effects on one's romantic dispositions on being told by one's lover while in the middle of having sex, "This is really good for our health, otherwise we shouldn't be doing it." Or, "This is really pleasant, but it wouldn't be right if we weren't trying for a baby." The value of sex is by no means to be found in the value of physical exercise. And though sexual activity for procreation *can* be very romantic and affectionate, it is neither when accompanied with the necessity of this sense of justification.

That shared activities of this sort (though not necessarily in their romantic exemplification) are categorical goods for many is evidenced by further considerations regarding the level of intimacy crucial to avoiding the debilitating effects of loneliness and isolation mentioned in an earlier chapter. Solitary activities of affection have an entirely different place in human agency than those of shared activities. Both involve intimacy, but the latter in a different way than the former. For the intimacy is shared in the activities themselves in the latter where it is not in the former. Also, solitary activities, as we have seen, put an emphasis on the separateness of the beloved to a degree not found in shared activities. Solitary activities of affection are widespread categorical goods because they uniquely afford the agent the opportunity to express the graciousness of love to the loved one as a separate and distinct person. Exclusive shared activities of affection are widespread categorical goods because they uniquely afford the agent the opportunity to share the loved one intimately through the very activities themselves. The crucial point is that intimacy is achieved in shared activities by virtue of the fact that the lovers share *themselves* in the activities. Thus the good of shared activities is not reducible to some threshold level of solitary goods of affection, for the former includes a greater level of intimacy. Perhaps, then, it is true that it is better to have loved and lost than never to have loved at all. But where the love has never achieved the intimacy of shared mutual affection it is not good enough. For the life of unrequited affection is one kind of hell, just as the life confined to reciprocal but solitary expressions of affection is one kind of unrequited affection. Furthermore, a life that does not include at least the hope of requited affection is difficult if not impossible to survive for anyone for whom romantic love is a categorical good.

That these activities are marked by their delightfulness few would deny, but it might not be clear that this delight has any aesthetic dimension. A little reflection, however, reveals that these activities, when truly shared, are among the most aesthetically charged activities humans engage in. Among the kinds of activities that are most successful in preventing boredom are shared sexual activities, and among the activities that are most devastating to romantic relations are boring sexual activities. It is important, then, not only that shared activities express affection but also that they be delightful in the aesthetic sense, that is, that they be interesting, fascinating, and captivating. Indeed, it seems to be a sign that your romantic love for another has died when the activities shared with her lose their aesthetic appeal, when they are marked with tedium. This fact, I believe, shows that our loving capacities and our aesthetic capacities not only underwrite each other in important ways but also jointly underwrite our capacity for boredom. If this is true, then it is a phenomenological fact about these activities that they sometimes appear within our deliberative field not only as goods of love but as aesthetic goods as well. When they do, it is a distortion of their value to construe them in deontic terms.

This point is even more obvious as it applies to friendship. The long-term relationships of friendship require not only respect, esteem, and love between the friends but shared activities as well. Friends take delight in doing things together, and similar aesthetic sensibilities are crucial for this. Perhaps more than anything else, the common love of the same kinds of activities binds people together in friendship. If two people have no common *tastes* in the kinds of activities they can share, it is impossible for them to be friends over time. Try to imagine what it would be like to maintain the *feelings* of friendship without some substantial common aesthetic *tastes* with the other person. You like the opera and hate polkas; he likes polkas and hates the opera. You like the ballet and hate football; he likes football and hates the ballet. You love poetry and philosophy, and he is bored by them. In short, *everything* you find interesting, fascinating, captivating, and aesthetically delightful, he finds tedious and boring. Friendship would be out of the question, even if you shared a common moral character and had equal esteem for each other. That there could be substantial differences between you over some tastes and still be close friends is beyond doubt, but there must also be substantially shared tastes as well. Overly moralized views of friendship that place the sole emphasis on moral character, then, are to be rejected. Friendship in the central case is not a bonding of mere feeling alone. Nor is it a bonding of feeling plus moral character. It is rather a bonding of feeling, character, and taste, a bonding of emotion, moral sentiment, and aesthetic taste. This fact about friendship is often overlooked, and it is one that is crucial to the normative thoughts of friendship. For friendship to endure, friends must share to a substantial degree a way of life. How could this be possible in terms of moral character alone?

The same question, of course, applies to neighborly love. To think that communities can be bonded together in any substantive way through a system of rights that ensure diversity without a fairly significant set of shared tastes is implausible, to say the least. A normative conceptual scheme limited to the concerns of respect alone virtually ignores the concept of community, not only because it leaves out love but also because it leaves out taste. Just as there is no friendship without shared tastes, there is no community without shared tastes. A group of people who do not share some of the same capacities that underwrite the capacity for boredom will never be a community. Why? Because they will find each other's presence excruciatingly tedious. We need a conceptual scheme that brings this thought to bear on political philosophy. If the political question is taken to be what is the best life *we* can live, then we will conceptualize the goods of that life as including shared aesthetic tastes as much as anything else. To my mind, much of the problem with much political philosophy is that it is overly moralized. Thinking about the good in a way that includes the aesthetic good goes a long way in remedying this.

Whether, then, it is love between friends, family, or neighbors, exclusive shared activities are in the very fabric of all varieties of personal love, as is the aesthetic dimension of these activities. Sufficient argument has already been given for thinking that personal love in at least some of its varieties is a categorical good for most of us. Moreover, even if personal love is not a universal categorical human good, its loss is still not consolable in impartial terms. All this testifies to the inadequacies of a view of human agency that imposes some lexical ordering of priorities across deliberative contexts for human concerns. For the loving person who is also a respectful person will sometimes find that these activities must be secondary to impartial concerns. Later we will see how this plays out regarding the integration and priorities problems.

A similar analysis also applies to exclusive personally shared activities other than those of affection, especially to creative work and play activities, as well as the honoring activities of this sort. But I cannot discuss these here, although a thorough analysis of these activities would, I believe, serve to strengthen the view I am trying to defend. What I must do now, however, is turn to an analysis of benevolent personally shared activities.

3.

Among the most representative examples of personally shared activities with intimate independent beneficiaries are parenting activities, activities shared by parents who love each other, who have a mutual shared interest in parenting, and who love their child. That the parents love each other makes these activities personal rather than impersonal; that the parents are mutual intrinsic beneficiaries makes them shared activities; and that the parents have personal love for their child makes the child an intimate beneficiary who is independent to the extent to which he or she is not a participant in the activities themselves.

Shared procreational interests are sometimes—in fact, quite often—among the interests of romantic lovers who care for each other in ways that naturally lead them to want to share sexual activity for purposes of procreation. In such cases, sexual activity is not only shared affection through physical pleasure, it is shared affection through procreational activity. Later this intimacy is achieved through the shared interest in parenthood, the interest in caring for another together. Through caring for another with whom they are intimately connected and for whom they are personally responsible, they achieve a kind of intimacy, the intimacy of shared concern and responsibility for another, not found in exclusive shared activities. Viewed in this way, shared parenting activities of this sort include the elements of activities of affection and arguably are among the most intimate of such activities. For many, the progression from the intimacy of exclusive shared activities to that of benevolent shared activities is both natural and psychologically necessary for their development as persons. It is as natural and necessary a progression for them as the move for lovers from solitary activities of affection to the intimacy of those exclusively shared between them. That is, moving from loving each other to loving their children together is as natural for them as moving from a compliment to an embrace.

That such activities are common categorical goods seems undeniable. Consider what might happen to couples who lose the opportunity to share parenting activities. One way in which this might happen is through the death of the child. On some such occasions, parents might not only feel grief regarding the child; they might also experience a loss of intimacy *with each other,* a loss not necessarily due to mutual fault finding but to a loss of the opportunity to engage in an activity that was central to their affection for each other.[1]

Another way in which this might happen is when children move out on their own. Sexual activity might not remain the primary medium for sharing affection throughout a couple's relationship, especially if the relationship spans a significant part of their lives. Caring for their children together is often a primary constituent of sharing their affection for each other. Thus when children move out on their own, there is often a need for a period of

---

1. See Ronald Knapp, *Beyond Endurance: When a Child Dies* (New York: Schocken Books, 1986), 142–47.

adjustment. This might be the result of the fact that sexual activity is not as central as at an earlier stage and because parenting activities cannot now function as primary mediums of sharing affection. The struggle that follows need not be a sign that the couple stayed together only for the children. Instead, it might be a sign that a significant good has been lost to them. In this case, it is the loss of a good that brings with it in these contexts the threat of alienation from one's loved one who is valued categorically.[2]

In other contexts, alienation of the parents from each other brings with it the loss of the good of such activities. How could one become a parent with someone, in part to share such intimacy, and experience the loss of these goods without it affecting one's identifying thoughts? Imagine the devastating results on your identifying thoughts on discovering betrayal in this regard by your perceived lover. Imagine that your perceived lover really had no shared parental feelings at all but merely feigned them for purposes of sexual manipulation. That such a discovery could be permanently devastating for some is undeniable, especially for those we admire for the intensity of their capacities for parenting relationships. Accompanying the devastation is often a loss of self-respect for having been susceptible to such manipulation, leaving a sense of isolation and loneliness due to the loss of anticipated or imagined intimacy. In any event, the loss of these goods where once present is not one for which agents can find consolation in their impartial interests.

None of these observations, of course, show that parenting activities are universal categorical goods. They are not. For not everyone, not even every member of a romantic couple, wants to be a parent. Yet we must remember that parenting activities involve nurturing activities, and, to some extent, all forms of personal love include a nurturing interest in a loved one. Therefore, any communal unit that includes more than two members will include potential intimate independent beneficiaries. Two friends caring for a third is certainly among the most intimate of the activities of friendship. This is not only true in cases of caring for the needs of the mutual friend, it is also true for shared honoring activities regarding the friend. Nor, of course, could sense be made of neighborly love without the disposition to take delight in sharing these activities with some of one's neighbors regard-

---

2. I am not familiar with scientific studies on this particular point, but there are studies that address loneliness in old age and in marriage where couples have lost common projects. See Letitia Anne Peplau et al., "Being Old and Living Alone," in *Loneliness: A Sourcebook of Current Theory, Research and Therapy*, ed. Letitia Anne Peplau and Daniel Perlman, 327–47.

ing other neighbors who stand in need of help or deserve special recognition. Thus to the extent to which personal love includes these elements and is a categorical good, so are these activities.

As to the aesthetic dimension of these activities, analogous things can be said here that were said about solitary parenting activities in the previous chapter. Suppose you take both loving and aesthetic delight in some nurturing activities regarding your child. This might show that you love your child, but it would not show that you love your spouse. And though you might love your spouse and not love your children, it seems quite unlikely that you could love your spouse and your children and find it utterly tedious to share nurturing activities regarding the child whom you both love. It is difficult, then, to see how the fact that you would not find some level of these shared activities interesting, fascinating, or captivating as irrelevant to the kind of relationship you have either with your spouse or your children, or both. Nor does it seem that there is anything to prevent a similar analysis from extending to other forms of personal love and the benevolent shared activities associated with them. If this is true, then these goods of activity often appear within our deliberative field as both goods of love and aesthetic goods. And when they do, they appear as nondeontic goods. It is the task of practical reason to integrate them into a meaningful life as the kind of goods they are, not as distorted deontic activities.

4.

The final kind of personally shared activity involves shared activities with nonintimate independent beneficiaries. Here the case that such activities are universally categorical is implausible, although they are increasingly common in our society.

Perhaps the most representative are work activities of this sort. Imagine a couple, both of whom are physicians, operating a clinic for the benefit of the financially disadvantaged. Both have an impartial concern for the health of the disadvantaged, and each intrinsically values the activities as nondeontic activities. But what they value most is that they share the work. The work provides the basis of their sharing their lives together, and they find their intimacy most in sharing these activities. This is not difficult to imagine. History is full of such cases, involving not only physicians but also teachers, social workers, missionaries, scientists, and the like.

Often sustained intimacy for a long-term relationship between two people is not possible, not because they do not love each other but because their commitments to their work prevent it. Of course, sometimes this reflects misplaced priorities, but this is not always true. Sometimes people who love each other have categorical commitments to different kinds of work that are both noble and admirable. In these cases, the demands of work often prevent them from sharing affection and sustaining intimacy. In other cases, people who love each other have categorical commitments to the same kind of work, yet circumstances prevent them from sharing the work. Given the importance of their work and its demands in these contexts, sustained intimacy is often simply impossible. The result in either case is always a sacrifice of something central to their identifying thoughts. This is true, that is, when those involved truly love each other and have categorical commitments to their work. Sometimes the sacrifice is simply so incomprehensible to those involved from the perspective of their deliberations that psychological collapse of one form or another is the inevitable response.

The solution for these people, of course, is to be smiled on by fate so that they can share work to which they have a common commitment. For these individuals, however rare or common they might be, this is the only solution that will preserve their continuing as agents with comprehensible identifying thoughts. It is the only solution because it is the only option that will allow them both to have the intimacy necessary for their survival and the activity that provides meaning to their lives in terms of aesthetically meaningful activity. Moreover, some of those driven to psychological collapse because of such commitments and bad fate are among the most admirable of persons. What we would change regarding these individuals is not their commitments but their external circumstances. In recognizing this, we are recognizing that for most a minimally meaningful life must include not only loving dimensions but aesthetic dimensions as well.

I conclude, then, that all three types of personally shared activities are often of categorical value to human agents. When they are, it is not rational for an agent to give lexical priority across deliberative contexts to impartial norms. Furthermore, since a substantial degree of intimacy is basic to psychological survival, there must be a high threshold of such goods in the lives of most to preserve the basic elements of integrity and reasons for living.

5.

Impersonally shared activities are those shared between persons, A and B, say, who are not specially related. Here it is important to keep two phenomena distinct. The first is the nature of A's dispositional sensitivity to beliefs regarding B's identity. The second is A's sensitivity to B's attitude toward the shared good, in this case, A and B's sharing an activity. In the first case, A is dispositionally indifferent to beliefs regarding B's identity. What is important to A is that B has a certain attitude toward and level of competence at engaging in the activity in question. Anyone with the appropriate attitude toward and level of competence at engaging in that activity is the focus of A's concern. In the second case, the appropriate attitude is that B desires to share the activity as an intrinsic good with someone also wishing to share the activity as an intrinsic good. Thus impersonally shared activities also involve mutual intrinsic beneficiaries.

Yet A's being a mutual beneficiary with B does not mean that A is intimately related to B as in shared activities of the personal sort. Imagine a person who desires a good game of chess. In one case, the desire might find satisfaction in playing against a computer. But this would not be a shared activity, however valuable the activity might be to the person. In another case, the desire might find satisfaction only if the activity is shared with a particular cherished individual. This would be a shared activity of the personal sort. Finally, the desire might be for sharing a good game of chess with *anyone* with a similar attitude toward playing partners and with similar skills as the agent. It is the last for which playing chess is an impersonally shared activity.

As one final preliminary comment, it is also important that these activities are impersonal only in a limited sense. The agent, in desiring a good game of chess, is clearly sensitive to the identity of who is to share the game with the prospective partner, namely, the agent. In this sense, these activities are clearly personal goods. It is only in terms of the relationship to the partners that these activities are impersonal.

One might argue that these activities are rarely, if ever, of categorical value to an agent. Their loss, it seems, is almost completely consolable in terms of personally shared activities. This is because personally shared activities include some value intrinsic to the activity itself, plus the value of sharing this value intimately with a loved one. For instance, playing chess with a friend has the value of sharing a good game of chess with someone who loves chess, but it has the value of friendly intimacy as well. Similarly, one can share the pleasure of sexual activity either with a loved one or with anyone who desires to share that activity merely for mutual sexual satisfaction. But one might argue that personally shared activity includes everything the corresponding impersonal activity does and more. Thus, on this argument, nothing essential to anyone's psychology requires impersonally shared activities.

Initially, this argument presents a plausible line of thought. Reflection reveals, however, that it overlooks an important possibility. There might be an essential place in the lives of normal, minimally healthy agents for activities that are neither individual goods nor intimately shared with loved ones yet they can be intimately shared with those the agent does not love. What is needed, on the one hand, is a way of specifying the kind of activity shared between agents — for example, play activity, sexual activity, or work activity. On the other hand, distinctions are needed regarding whether the activity is shared intimately or, if so, whether the intimacy is personal. If A shared a game of chess with B, we would not assume that it was played with any intimacy, even if they enjoyed the game. That the game involved intimacy, then, would need pointing out as a special feature of the situation. But if A and B shared sexual activity, the normal assumption is that the activity involved some level of intimacy. Yet it would not necessarily involve the intimacy of personally shared activities. The issue then is this: Are there kinds of shared activities that for many healthy human beings require either a lack of intimacy or the lack of the kind of intimacy found in personal love? If there are, a related issue is this: Is there a threshold level of such goods that is essential to the elements of integrity for many of us, and what, if anything, is the aesthetic dimension of such goods?

First consider exclusive shared activities.

6.

It is not an altogether unreliable thought that impersonality might be a desired feature of shared sexual activity in some contexts and at some stages of sexual development. An adolescent who thinks that no sexual activity is to be enjoyed with another outside love is bound to put enormous strains on the relationships he or she enters. The thought that one should trust any physical lover should not be confused with the thought that one should love any physical lover. Moreover, the importance of shared physical pleasure comes long before the importance of adopting a long-term relationship with another. Of course, one does tend to trust those one loves, but trust can certainly come independent of love. The sad thing is that an adolescent can easily conclude that trust plus physical attraction comes to personal love. It does not. What cannot be denied is that, especially for a normal adolescent, sex is fascinating, and it is fascinating before it is love. Recognizing the difference between the fascination of sex as one kind of good and sex as an expression of love as another is therefore crucial to emotional development. And part of that development involves finding ways of enjoying the former without confusing it with the latter, which, of course, need not include intercourse.

The sexual fantasies of most adults probably reveal a desire at some level for activities of the sort in question, that is, for impersonally shared exclusive activities of sexual play.[3] The function of such fantasizing to our identifying thoughts is probably much greater than we might admit in polite company. It might be a real human need for some threshold level of shared sexual activity unaccompanied by the intimacy of personal love. This threshold might be achieved for many through fantasy rather than actual contact with others. Certainly the history of the priesthood suggests that celibacy and the lack of shared sexual activity are ideals of integrity impossible for most people to maintain with psychological health. Perhaps this is reason for thinking that such ideals are undesirable as well. The history of marriage in contexts that required strict premarital chastity is also revealing. It suggests that there is a human good of some significant importance to be found in shared sexual activity not tightly connected with the intimacy of love. It is, after all, true that many people who have extramarital affairs do so not as a result of a loss of love for the spouse or out of love for the extramarital lover. Quite often, such persons feel driven to such affairs against their ideals of themselves.[4] Perhaps this means that we do not yet understand just how important the lack of intimacy of a certain kind is to human development regarding some shared activities. That nature would have designed us to be fascinated with sex in these ways should come as no surprise.

In this regard, it would not be surprising to discover a relationship between the desire for adventure in general and testosterone. That the con-

3. Donald Symons argues that the desire for sexual variety is adaptive in the evolutionary sense for males in a way and to a degree that it is not for females. This could show itself in differences in the kinds of fantasies that recur among females and among males. Apparently, variety of sexual partners is more prominent among males than females. Symons also suggests that the "Coolidge Effect" (male rearousal by a new female) present among the males in many mammal species extends to humans to a significant degree. If this is true, then impersonal sexual activities of this sort might be more important to men than to women. Whether this is true or not I do not know, but the issue should be settled by patient and nonideological inquiry rather than by a priori "moral" principles of either a feminist or a patriarchal sort. See Donald Symons, *The Evolution of Human Sexuality* (New York: Oxford University Press, 1979), 206–52.

4. Symons reports studies that show significant numbers of people, especially men, who do not see their "affairs" as resulting from dissatisfaction with their marriages. See Symons, *The Evolution of Human Sexuality*, 226–46.

nection should sometimes display itself specifically in the desire for sexual adventure would be equally unsurprising. Though sexual adventure does not require the notion of conquest (contrary to some stereotypical understandings of impersonal sex), it does require exploring the unknown. For some, this adventure of discovery might not be possible with a loved one due to familiarity. Of course, that sexual adventure is less frequent does not mean that sexual affection is less abundant. Nor does it mean that adventure is more important than affection. Still, to ignore the need for sexual adventure is to flirt with deep self-deception. Perhaps in no other area of human concern has there been more of a tendency to overly moralize the conception of a human good as in the case of sexual fantasy.

Yet, be this as it may, there are life contexts in which the opportunity for exclusive shared activities is limited, solely or significantly, to those to whom one is not specially related. These may be sexual or nonsexual contexts. In these life contexts, the importance of these impersonal goods becomes far more central to the identifying thoughts of a human agent. Think, for example, of the history of sexual activity of soldiers in wartime with members of the indigenous population in a foreign land. Some such activity is of the personal sort, but surely much is not. But it would be more than a little naive to think that *all* the portion that is not personal is relatively meaningless and manipulative sex. Thus even if exclusive shared activities that are impersonal are not widespread, they may still be categorical goods in some important life contexts. For it is absurd to think that there are any impartial concerns that could provide the intimacy these goods provide, even if this is not the highest form of intimacy.

Perhaps the most important contexts in which impersonally shared activities are categorical are those in which individuals are moving from the relationship of strangers sharing nothing to some form of personal relationship. For such transitions, the goods of impersonally shared activities are indispensable. That they can be transitional goods should be no reason for thinking that when they are they are merely instrumental. Consider sharing an activity—playing tennis, say—with another person. Suppose it is someone you know only as someone with a strong interest in playing a good game of tennis. This is just the sort of thing that often leads subsequently to one's identity beliefs regarding another to function in one's own identifying thoughts. It is the necessity of such transitions in human life that gives these goods their greatest claim to being both categorical and extremely widespread. Imagine a context in which you are not specially related to anyone. Perhaps you have recently changed locations, say, from graduate school to a teaching job someplace where you do not personally know anyone. Unless you are to live the most impoverished life, you will need to make the transition from impersonal to personal relationships with some of the people in your new location. But imagine how difficult it would be to make the transition if you found all the activities available to you with others in your new environment utterly tedious. Suppose that despite your efforts at connecting with others through shared activities you simply cannot find, say, bowling, frog gigging, and endlessly listening to oldies but goodies the least bit interesting. By what psychological mechanism are you to move to more intimate relations? It would seem that without some shared tastes, whatever emotional intimacy you might achieve would be, at best, the psychological equivalent of a one-night stand. Viewed in this way, it is easy to see that impersonal goods of this sort, goods that are both non-deontic and aesthetic, are categorical goods for most of us in their transition function.

7.

But what of benevolent shared activities of the impersonal sort? Are there activities of this sort in which there is a significant place for a lack of intimacy of the personal sort between the mutual beneficiaries? And if so, how important are such activities to the integrity of a human agent?

It is difficult to think of many clear and pure cases of a shared activity that has an intimate independent beneficiary where the mutual beneficiaries are not specially related. One possibility is where the mutual beneficiaries are both specially related to the intimate beneficiary but are not specially related to each other. Another is where only one of the mutual beneficiaries is specially related to the intimate beneficiary. The latter case would be impure in the sense that the mutual beneficiaries would not be sharing the same kind of activity. For the independent beneficiary would not be intimately related to one of the mutual beneficiaries, and this would mark a difference in kind in the activity for this person. An example might be thought to be where A is the parent of C, where B is the teacher of C, and where A and B share the activities of educating the child. Or another is where B is a child psychiatrist and A and B share the activities of bringing a disturbed child to mental health. Often these activities are not truly shared in the sense intended here but are solitary activities from the points of view of A and B. Yet this need not be true. Where it is not, these activities can be central to the lives of the professionals who have a role in these activities as well as to the lives of the nonprofessionals. This is true even if the activities do not have the same kind of value to the nonprofessionals as to the professionals.

Of greater importance no doubt to most people are the activities we share with those who love the ones we love. These are the activities of the first sort referred to above. Yet it is not always possible or best that we try to love all the persons who love the ones we love. That it is important that we like, even if we do not love, some of these people and enjoy sharing with them activities independently benefiting our loved ones should be clear. It should be clear from reflecting on the alienation we would experience on attempting to share our lives with our loved ones but not liking any of the persons they love. In any complex social environment, the alienation that would result from the absence of personal delight of this sort would be intolerable. It is also difficult to see how A and B could love C and not have a strong desire to share at least some threshold level of activities of the sort in question. What must be imagined is a case in which A loves C but is either dispositionally aversive or indifferent to shared activities with some of the people whom C loves. In the latter case, it is difficult to make sense of A's truly loving C. Such indifference to something so important to a loved one is simply incompatible with loving dispositions. In the former case, it is hard to imagine that A would not experience the lack of people with whom to share these activities as anything other than extremely alienating. Or if the aversion is due to jealousy, it is hard to see how the alienation could be anything other than an integrity-distorting emotion.

The value of such activities is not that they are the means to the end of smooth relations with one's loved ones. Rather, they are a part of, not a means to, a relationship with ones loved ones, an essential part in any complex social context. In such contexts, they may very well be categorical goods, losses of which might be inconsolable in anything other than personal terms.

8.

Finally, we must consider impersonally shared activities that have nonintimate independent beneficiaries. Perhaps the most representative are work activities. I am not convinced that there are any forms of shared work in which it is important that the workers do not share any form of personal intimacy. At least, this seems true where the work shared is intrinsically meaningful to the workers. One would think that neighborly love among the community of workers could only enhance the meaning of such activity. Still it might be important in some life contexts that soldiers, for instance, do not become too intimately connected with each other. The reason might be that psychological survival in battle requires a kind of distancing from others. This may be especially true of military leaders. But it is difficult to make out the view that such activities are intrinsically valued nondeontic activities. With shared work activities of intrinsic value as nondeontic activities, it hardly seems plausible that neighborly love could threaten their worth to the agent. If the intimacy of neighborly love is a threat, it seems best to describe the value as the value of solitary activity. Thus an argument that such activities are categorical goods that serve a unique role in human agency is not forthcoming, at least on the grounds that these activities require a unique distance from any form of personal intimacy.

Nonetheless, there are two points regarding the relationships between these activities and intimacy worth noting. The first concedes that the intimacy of neighborly love may not be a threat to the value of shared activities of the sort in question. Yet it observes that the intimacy of other forms of personal love might very well be such a threat, especially for certain individuals. It may be very important—even psychologically vital— to the mental health of a particular physician that the physician not experience romantic love for someone in the medical profession. To do so might threaten both the relationship and the value of the person's work to that person. The reason for this is that the work becomes too pervasive in the person's life and as such is not intrinsically valuable to that person. Here the kind of personal intimacy is such that it threatens to make too pervasive what is already pervasive to the threshold level. No doubt there are many professional philosophers who are grateful that they are romantically loved by nonphilosophers for this very reason.

The second point is that we cannot always expect to feel even neighborly love for those with whom we share work activities of the sort in question. In such contexts, it is nonetheless important that we can participate without being forced into thinking of these activities as solitary activities. Again the reason for this is the debilitating effects of alienation. One prevalent form of alienation in the modern workplace is to be forced into a position of engaging in an activity that one finds intrinsically rewarding but one's fellow workers do not. Imagine, for example, what life would be like to be employed as a philosopher who loved philosophical dialogue but one's colleagues all wished they had gone into another profession. Love of the local philosophical community is the best replacement for this state of affairs. But even where this is not possible, mutual love of the activity itself will go a long way in terms of consolation, especially where there are other good things present in a philosopher's life. I cannot see that this is any different regarding nonphilosophers who are dedicated to their work.

In today's world, then, any realistic assessment of the importance of these goods will assign them an important, even categorical, role to play in a nonalienating form of life for many agents. They may not be universal categorical goods, but they are nonetheless goods that are inconsolable in terms of impartial norms for any agent for whom they are categorical. This, of course, does not mean that their value precludes significant impartial commitment to others by the agent for whom these activities have categorical value. For the agent of integrity will have such concerns. We will see how this is true when we address the priorities problem.

9.

The independent goods of activity—whether of the individual, solitary, or shared variety—are extremely important to the identifying thoughts of many of us, especially to the agent of integrity in the thick sense. To this degree these activities are categorical goods and hold a unique place in human integrity; they represent the indispensable place of the aesthetic in our lives. Our deliberative field, if we are agents of integrity in the thick sense, will include not only goods of respect and goods of love but the aesthetic goods of activity as well. Thus any view of human agency that denies them this place for large portions of humanity is unacceptable. One such view is one that requires a lexical ordering of these goods across deliberative contexts where they are never the overriding consideration in competition with impartial norms. This brings us to the priorities problem to which we must now turn.

18. Normative Thoughts and the Goods of Activity

The integration problem as it relates to the thick conception of integrity is now at its peak level of complexity. All the major goods associated with that conception are before us to be integrated into one conception of agency. The final task, then, is to address the priorities problem as it relates to the goods of activity and the other goods—the goods of respect and esteem and the various goods of personal love. That task, however, is far too complex to address here in anything like a complete way. Consequently, I will address only two kinds of general problems: the first is a problem regarding the concept of permissibility and its place in the normative life, and the second is a problem about the concept of excellence. I will frame both problems within the context of Marcia Baron's recent work on Kant and will argue for another way of seeing things, a way, I believe, that is both closer to Aristotle and to the phenomenology of our reflective experience. In the context of this discussion, I will address issues involving the priorities problem.

1.

One thing to keep in mind is that the goods of activity as we are considering them do not generate thoughts of obligation, but they must be integrated with goods that do. The central question, then, is this: What is the relationship between an agent's deontic beliefs and the goods that generate them and the goods of activity? My primary purpose in this section is to argue against one answer to this question. I will call it the standard view, of which I take Baron's view to be an instance.

The standard view has it that there are three basic deontic categories under which an agent's doing x might be classified. Doing x might be obligatory, merely permissible (but not obligatory), or wrong. The second category, on this way of thinking, is the part of life that is left open apart from one's obligations. The idea is somewhat like a certain version of the work ethic: Play comes only after all the work has been done; similarly, anything that is merely permissible comes only after one has dispatched all of one's obligations. This way of thinking tends to see morality as a kind of side constraint on an agent's pursuit of his or her own good, or, in the case of Kantian internalism, a constraint on the other, nonmoral goods of one's life.

Whether the constraints of morality are minimal or substantial is one of the issues debated among advocates of the standard view. Some of those who think that morality does not take up most of the space in a person's life believe that within the category of the merely permissible is a subcategory of actions that are supererogatory, a class of actions that are not obligatory—not required by duty—but are due special moral praise. Baron is concerned to argue that supererogatory acts "do not form an ethically useful or theoretically interesting kind."[1] On her view, then, the category of acts that are merely permissible does not include a subclass of acts that are supererogatory. What remains are the categories of the obligatory, the wrong, and the merely permissible. Since the merely permissible is that set of acts available to an agent once the demands of morality are met, her view is a clear instance of the standard view.

Baron rejects the category of the supererogatory because she believes that once we understand the role of imperfect duties in Kant's conception of morality we will have no philosophical motive for endorsing the notion of supererogation. There are two very important features of imperfect duties to which Baron calls our attention. The first is that imperfect duties allow for latitude in what is actually required of an agent in a way that imperfect duties do not. The second feature is that imperfect duties require us to take two things as obligatory ends, namely, our own perfection, on the one hand, and the happiness of others, on the other. It is the combination of these features that, on her view, leads to the rejection of supererogation. My interest in her argument is not so much about her rejection of supererogation as it is about how her argument is revealing of her own conceptual scheme and how she understands the general category of the merely permissible.

For our purposes, we can see Baron as trying to carve out a position between two Kantian extremes, a sternly rigorous view that does not allow for the merely permissible at all and a promiscuously latitudinarian view

---

1. Marcia Baron, *Kantian Ethics Almost Without Apology* (Ithaca: Cornell University Press, 1995), 26.

that reflects a minimalist morality. The sternly rigorous view might have it that we always stand either under a perfect duty or under an imperfect duty. If we stand under an imperfect duty, we have either a duty to perfect ourselves, which can take the form of a duty either to develop our moral character or to develop our natural talents, or a duty regarding the happiness of others. On this view, we can neglect some of these duties only if it is impossible to fulfill them all, with the understanding that we can never neglect a perfect duty. The promiscuously latitudinarian view would be one that construed the burdens of perfect duties minimally and allowed latitude not only in *what* we are required to do in regard to the obligatory ends of self-perfection and the happiness of others but also in *how much* we do in these regards. Given that the promiscuously latitudinarian view imposes minimal requirements in terms of both perfect and imperfect duties, there seems to be a good bit of space for the merely permissible, within which there is room for the supererogatory.

Baron's considered view is closer to the stern rigorist view than the promiscuous latitudinarian one. According to Baron, the duty to perfect ourselves morally is a stronger duty than the duty either to develop our talents or to be concerned with the happiness of others. To be sure, these duties can often be fulfilled within a single act or kind of activity: Playing chess with a friend can be conducive to a greater understanding of others and hence develop our character, but it can also hone our skills and talents and promote the happiness of others (the friend). But when all three cannot be done, the duty to develop our character is second in importance only to perfect duties, the duty to respect others. In fact, after perfect duties, according to Baron, we have the duty to do as much as is possible to develop our character. This means, though Baron does not note it, that if developing our talents or promoting the happiness of others conflicts in some contexts with perfecting our character, then it is not permissible for us, in those contexts, to either develop our talents or promote the happiness of others.

With this understanding of Baron in mind, we can raise the issue of just how much moral latitude there is in a person's life regarding the imperfect duty to perfect oneself morally and the merely permissible. And it does not seem that there would be much room at all, certainly no room for the notion of supererogation. The merely permissible seems to be limited, if we use Baron's own examples, to choices between whether or not to eat fish or poultry, or drink wine or beer with a meal, or, perhaps, to choices regarding the nature of one's attire. If the demands of perfect duties and the imperfect duty to perfect oneself morally do not take up most of one's life—

which, I believe, would require some rather inflated views about how close one already is to moral perfection—there will certainly be little room left for the merely permissible once the duties to develop our talents and promote the happiness of others have exhausted their claims, even where the latter claims are construed modestly. The problem Baron has for allowing very much in the way of the merely permissible is this: Any conduct that flows from the commitment to the obligatory ends of perfecting our character, developing our talents, and promoting the happiness of others has moral worth; thus no conduct flowing from the commitment to these obligatory ends could be merely permissible without being supererogatory. Since she denies that such conduct is supererogatory, she has to deny that any of it is merely permissible. And it is for these reasons that merely permissible acts or conduct has to be construed as involving fairly trivial decisions. As a representative of the standard view, then, Baron leaves some place for the merely permissible, but once the demands of morality have made their claims on us that room is small indeed, hardly enough to accommodate the furnishings of supererogation. None of the kinds of acts that fall in the category of the merely permissible seem likely candidates for special moral praise. But I will argue shortly that not only is supererogation left out of her conceptual scheme, but her scheme will not accommodate the nondeontic goods of activity to the threshold level that they plausibly have as categorical goods for most human agents. Moreover, I will argue that to the degree to which she allows the goods of activity within an agent's life she distorts how they appear within an agent's deliberative field by trying to press them too tightly into the category of obligation, even where the concept of obligation is understood in terms of wide imperfect duties.

Not surprisingly, I find the standard view, including Baron's version of it, distorted. But before turning to a more positive account, consider an opposite approach to the relationship between the merely permissible and the obligatory. The view I have in mind is one that has it that the categories of the obligatory and the wrong are those areas where the category of the permissible leaves off. On this view, we might say that work begins only after all the play is finished. For want of a better term, call this the standard denial view. It too, I think, is distorted, but it does serve to bring back onto the scene an aspect of life relegated to obscurity on most contemporary schemes, especially Baron's. An agent's most central reasons for living are seldom best expressed in deontic terms or as afterthoughts. If this is true, then some categorical norms do not generate thoughts of obligation. From this perspective, then, the obligatory is the point where the permissible leaves off.

The distorting feature of both views is that they misconstrue the nature of the integration problem as faced by the agent. They assume in opposite ways that there are two separate integration problems that can be solved independently and then a third that is solved by the function of an asymmetrical regulative norm of practical reason. The standard view assumes some complex solution to the integration problem regarding the goods that generate deontic activities and a separate complex solution to the integration problem regarding the goods of activity and then requires that when there are conflicts the former goods always have priority over the latter regardless of the deliberative context. Somewhat more concretely: The priorities of respect, esteem, and personal love are worked out without reference to the goods of activity; the priorities among the goods of activity are worked out without reference to the goods of respect, esteem, and love; and then it is required that the obligations of the one always take priority over the interests in the other regardless of the deliberative context. The standard denial view, on the other hand, reverses the priorities. Like the standard view, it assumes separate and independent solutions to the integration problems regarding deontic and nondeontic goods. But then it requires that the latter goods always take priority over the former regardless of the deliberative context. Both assume asymmetrical regulative norms: the standard view usually employing an asymmetrical impartial norm; and the standard denial view, asymmetrical partial norms. My criticism of both views is that neither could possibly present a solution to the problem the agent actually faces. Consider first the distorting factor in the standard denial view, the view that is implausible on its face. This view is incompatible with the commitments of both simple respect and any form of personal love. For it entails that there are some things that are permissible from the point of view of an agent of integrity in the thick sense no matter what the consequences to those worthy of simple respect or to loved ones. Favoring one's work no matter what the consequences to strangers or to friends might be an example. It is enough to refute this view that we have shown that in catastrophic contexts an agent either suffers some form of agent breakdown or has reasons for dying. This is true both for simple respect and for personal love in its variety. It is no less true for the goods of activity. We might find a way of thinking that Gauguin was a loving husband and father under some descriptions of what he was willing to allow his wife and children to suffer for his artistic projects. But we will have abandoned any way at all of making sense of the concept of love as applied to him if we say that he was willing to pursue his art regardless of the possible consequences to his family. For either a respectful or a loving agent, there is no activity, absolutely no activity, that is always permissible regardless of the deliberative context. Kissing my wife, finishing this paragraph, attending a graduation ceremony, changing a diaper, registering to vote, donating a kidney—all these and any other activity might take the time crucial to preventing a catastrophe.

The distorting factor, then, of the standard denial view is that it construes the concept of permissibility in a way that fails to recognize something essential about the nature of the integration problem. The integration problem must be understood to recognize the categorical aversions embedded within the commitments of any respectful and loving agent. Therefore, there cannot be an independent solution to the integration problem among the various goods of activity, as is assumed by the standard denial view.

It does not follow from this, however, that the priorities of respect and love can be set independent of considerations of the goods of activity. This is the mistake of the standard view, and it is the source of its distortion.

If we were to say that the permissible is that aspect of life left over after thoughts of obligation and prohibition, we would miss the point—the very crucial point—that a sense of obligation is restricted by the fact that some things make life worth living and are valued accordingly. The facts about our capacity for boredom and the capacities that underwrite that capacity establish this. Human beings cannot long find life minimally meaningful if all its activities are utterly tedious. Reflections on the role of pain in practical reason and the prospects of an eternity of tedium are revealing.

Consider first the role of pain in practical reason. Peter Unger has given powerful arguments to the effect that reflections on pain are revealing regarding our concept of personal identity, and he thinks that his arguments support a physical rather than a memory (or some other psychological) criterion for personal identity over time.[2] (Here I am not so much concerned about the personal identity debate as I am about the role of pain in practical reason.) Unger's argument can be understood in terms of a distinction between a person's core psychology and a person's distinctive psychology. A person's core psychology is composed of those capacities that make a distinctive psychology possible. A person's distinctive psychology, for ex-

2. See Peter Unger, *Identity, Consciousness, and Value* (New York: Oxford University Press, 1990).

ample, might be composed of memories of actual events and episodes in his or her life, along with particular tastes and dispositions. A core psychology is composed of those capacities that make it possible for one to have particular memories, tastes, and commitments. Without the core capacity for having memories, I could not have the particular memory of my daughters' births; without the core capacity for making commitments, I could not have the particular commitments of respect and love that I have; and without the core capacity for boredom and the capacities that underwrite that capacity, I could not have the specific capacity for being fascinated by philosophical inquiry.

Now suppose that we have an account of some plausible set of basic core capacities, a set that anyone must have to be recognizable as a person. Surely among this set of core capacities would be the capacity for pain, the capacity for memory, and the capacities for forming and pursuing ground projects. On a psychological criterion, personal identity is based on one's distinctive psychology, one's connectedness through memory and other psychological continuities. On this view, if you strip away all my distinctive psychological continuities and the physical bases for them, you destroy me, only my body (the rest of it) remains. Hence no distinctive psychological continuity, no personal identity over time. Unger, however, would have us consider whether we can project thoughts of ourselves into the future without our distinctive psychologies. If we can, then our distinctive psychologies are not essential to our personal identities. That we can do this, Unger claims, is revealed by what he calls the Avoidance of Future Great Pain Test. Imagine being faced with a choice in which you can only avoid the most excruciating pain imaginable by having the physical bases for your distinctive psychology surgically removed. All your distinctive memories and along with them all the distinctive psychological attachments you have will be removed. Remaining will be the core capacities, including the capacity to form new distinctive memories and commitments, and their physical bases. If it is possible for you to imagine the intensity and duration of the prospective pain giving you a reason for having the surgery, then you are projecting thoughts of yourself into the future without your distinctive psychology. And this is possible. Indeed, one of the uglier facts about practical reason is that the avoidance of pain at some point can eclipse all our other commitments. Not to recognize this is to take refuge in fantasy. At some point in your sojourn in the fiery lake of eternal hell you would gladly consent to the surgery and a completely new start. The anticipation of pain, then, is very central to our psychology and plays a major role in practical reason for the simple reason that all of us have some threshold level of tolerance for pain below which we have a categorical aversion to any way of life that contains it.

Now to consider the pain of tedium. In *Problems of the Self*, Bernard Williams, in a piece called "The Makropulos Case: Reflections on the Tedium of Immortality," argues that the fact that we eventually die is a good thing.[3] It is a good thing, according to Williams, because there is no description of immortality that would make eternal life worthwhile. Why? Because no matter what you might do in eternity it would eventually become so tedious as to make life unbearable. So the argument looks something like this:

1. If life's activities become tedious to a certain degree, they and the life they constitute will become unbearable.
2. In eternity every kind of activity would eventually become tedious to that degree.
3. Therefore, eternal life would be unbearably tedious no matter what activities it might include.

Of course, one might (mistakenly, I believe) attempt to deny the truth of the second premise, but what seems undeniable is the first premise. If this is true and if Unger is right, then one kind of pain that could make it rational to sacrifice one's distinctive psychology would be the pain of tedium. Actually, if the second premise is also true and Unger is right, then a rather startling conclusion would follow. Imagine that if I were to snap my fingers you would live forever; that is, the snapping of my fingers would have the consequence of making you immortal. If the above argument is sound and if Unger is right, then it would be rational for you to end your life before I could snap my fingers. Moreover, this seems to follow no matter how well your life is now going. As startling as this conclusion is, it is one that we will have to accept if we accept the soundness of the arguments of both Williams and Unger. I believe they are both sound, but one need not agree with the first premise of Williams's argument to get the result that if life were utterly tedious it would be unbearable.

The significance of this is that life has to be minimally interesting to be worth living, but "being interesting" is an aesthetic category, not a

3. See Bernard Williams, *Problems of the Self* (Cambridge: Cambridge University Press, 1973), 82–100.

moral one. If this is true, then for creatures like us a significant place within our conceptual scheme must be given to activities that we find interesting, fascinating, captivating, and the like. I can see only three responses Baron might make that have any initial plausibility. First, she might maintain that the threshold level of nondeontic activities necessary to ward off tedium can be contained within the category of the merely permissible as she conceives it. Second, she might maintain that the deontic activities involved in imperfect duties themselves provide enough in the way of interesting, fascinating, captivating activities to go beyond any threshold of aesthetic goods needed to relieve tedium. And third, she might say that the combination of the activities allowed within her conception of the merely permissible and the aesthetic dimension of deontic activities would more than suffice to prevent devastating tedium.

Now consider each of these in turn. The first, I believe, is easily discharged. If the aesthetic appeal of life's activities is put at a significant threshold level, then the area left on Baron's account for the merely permissible will not suffice to account for the place of these goods in a plausibly meaningful life for most anyone. And surely the threshold must be quite high. If the only activities you could find interesting were choices between items on your meal menu or what apparel to wear for the day, then you would either spend a lot more time doing these things or you would find life unbearable. Though one might object that this is not a very generous reading of the place of the merely permissible in Baron's scheme, I would simply ask the objector to think of how generous we would have to be to Baron, consistent with what she says about imperfect duties, in order to make plausible that she could account for the goods of activity in this way. Refection, I believe, will surely lead us to consider the other alternatives.

The second alternative recognizes that the merely permissible is inadequate to account for the role the aesthetic plays in a minimally meaningful life. In fact, the second alternative seems to be motivated by the thought that the merely permissible is woefully inadequate to accommodate the goods of activity and that the bulk of what is interesting, fascinating, or captivating for a moral agent is to be found in morality itself. Baron suggests this herself:

> Moral excellence on Kant's view is not monotonic; perhaps an assumption that it is monotonic motivates the views that a moral requirement that we become more virtuous would be excessive. Finally, on Kant's view, the practice of living morally, of striving to improve oneself . . . is not just a burden to be endured because of the results of people acting morally; rather, it is meaningful in itself and expressive of one's

moral agency. This view may not be shared by Kant's critics and seems not to be held by supererogationists.[4]

The passage strongly suggests that those disagreeing with Baron's view are lacking in *taste:* Were we (those of us with a different view) more moral we would find the moral life more interesting, fascinating, and captivating.

How plausible is this? We should first note that the rhetorical value of the above passage from Baron loses its homiletic effect when we note the difference between the commitment to improving our character and the commitment to doing *as much as possible* to improve our character. That a life with a commitment to improving one's character would not necessarily be monotonic seems perfectly clear. What seems equally clear is that a life with a commitment to improving one's character as much as possible would be monotonic, not to mention narcissistic, and perhaps the former because of the latter. I do not see that the commitment to improving one's character as much as possible is more important to a good person than either developing one's talents or the happiness of others. Perhaps I am more committed to improving my character than I am to the happiness of others, but I am not more committed to improving my character as much as possible than I am to the happiness of others. If this is a flaw, it is not one that I intend to correct. Nor do I believe that the value of my rational agency is such that it places my self-improvement on such an exalted plane. At any rate, I do not think that the activities of moral self-improvement, though perhaps interesting, are in themselves minimally interesting enough to make life worth living for a person of even average intelligence. Moreover, it is difficult for me to understand anyone for whom they would be sufficiently interesting to carry a life as being anything other than morally narcissistic.

But Baron has other concepts at her disposal. She does not have to put all the weight on the activities of moral self-improvement; she can also point to the activities of bringing happiness to others and to the activities of developing our talents. These surely will include enough for any person to find life meaningful. Indeed, if we bring these activities under the rubric of morality we will find most of what makes life interesting, fascinating, and captivating. However, as plausible as this might sound, there are deep problems with it.[5]

The major problem has to do with the possibility of motivationally over-

4. Baron, *Kantian Ethics Almost Without Apology,* 107.
5. Just how plausible it is must be considered, however, in the light of Baron's view that we have the imperfect duty to do as much as possible to improve our character.

determined actions. Baron's view is that there are no motivationally over-determined actions that have moral worth, and this limits rather severely her access to the above line of thought. To find an activity interesting is to be drawn to doing it for itself. The same can be said of finding something fascinating, captivating, and the like. In short, the aesthetic goods of activity are what they are in virtue of the kind of motivational pull they have. Without this motivational pull, activities of work, of play, of routine, and of creative contribution and achievement are not aesthetic goods of activity. In order for the second alternative to work, the goods of activity would have to be both deontic and aesthetic, which would require that they would have to be motivationally overdetermined. And herein lies Baron's problem.

Baron presents an insightful and interestingly new way of seeing Kant's concern with moral worth. According to Baron, Kant was not nearly as concerned with the moral worth of individual actions as he has been taken to be. Rather, he was concerned with the moral worth of patterns of conduct that reveal character. Only the sense of duty can confer moral worth on individual actions, which is why the moral worth of individual actions cannot be motivationally overdetermined. Perfect duties and the sense of duty associated with them can generate individual deontic acts that have moral worth. Because of the latitude involved in imperfect duties and the role they allow for inclination, the individual actions that satisfy these duties are motivationally overdetermined, and hence, as individual acts, lack moral worth. But viewed not as individual actions but as elements within a pattern of conduct, they reveal a commitment to the obligatory ends of morality and hence have moral worth as deontic conduct, not as deontic acts. Since these duties constitute a great deal of the moral life, Kant's conceptual scheme reveals a greater concern with the sense of duty as a regulative norm than as a determinate norm.

Even nondeontic activities can be seen as having moral worth on Baron's view, not when viewed as individual actions but as patterns of conduct regulated by the sense of duty to have obligatory ends. Even the merely permissible act of having beer rather than wine with my meal has moral worth as a pattern of conduct, if I would be willing to forgo the beer for the wine should duty require it in the context. But deontic acts, involving narrow duties, have moral worth only if the sense of duty is the determinate rather than the regulative motive. Deontic acts cannot be, on her view, motivationally overdetermined: Either the sense of duty is the determinate motive, in which case the action has moral worth, or some nonmoral motive is determinate, in which case the action has no moral worth. Hence if we are to incorporate the development of our talents and the promotion of the happiness of others into morality it cannot be as deontic acts but as deontic conduct. Baron, then, could have us view some individual activities and their worth to us as nondeontic activities, but at the same time she could have us view these same activities more widely as patterns of conduct and hence as deontic conduct. So where is the problem?

The problem is that the aesthetic allure of these activities must be epiphenomenal on her view where they cannot be, namely, at the point of our commitment to them. On Baron's view, any particular engagement in an aesthetic activity can have as its determinate motive an inclination of an aesthetic sort. This allows the inclination a role that is not epiphenomenal but motivationally active in the agent's behavior. But, as an individual act influenced by aesthetic motivation the activity can have no moral worth. It is only when viewed as a pattern of conduct that moral worth can be assigned to such an activity. The behavior can count as moral conduct, however, only if the commitment to obligatory ends is motivated only by the sense of duty, and for this to be true, the aesthetic allure of these activities has to be epiphenomenal to our commitment to incorporating them into our conduct in the first place. In fact, insofar as we think of these activities as conduct that fulfills our duties, we must be willing to do them no matter how dull they might be. Otherwise, our commitment to the obligatory ends of morality is not from the sense of duty. Thus the kind of counterfactual that Kant requires as a test for whether an individual act has moral worth applies to whether a pattern of conduct has moral worth, namely, even where inclination is present it must be the case that the agent would have acted or made the commitment anyway (even against contrary inclination). Baron is therefore forced by the second alternative and her rejection of the moral overdetermination of actions to treat the fact that these activities are interesting, fascinating, and captivating to the agent as the *result* of these activities, not as providing the agent with any motivational pull for being committed to them as patterns of conduct that fulfill the commitment to the obligatory ends of morality. In short, she is forced to treat the aesthetic dimension of these activities as epiphenomenal to our commitment to them.

The grain of truth in Baron's view is that we do respect persons for pursuing what is interesting, fascinating, and captivating to them only if they show sensitivity in their pursuits to respect and sympathy for others and love for their loved ones. But, as I will show, the Aristotelian scheme can not only accommodate these thoughts; it also requires them. Morever, the

Aristotelian scheme is not committed to the motivational inefficacy of the aesthetic dimensions of the kinds of activity we are concerned to accommodate. The real problem with Baron's view, if she takes either the second or third alternative above by assimilating the value of the goods of activity to the value of deontic conduct, is that she forfeits an essential feature of the goods in question. It is essential to the goods of activity that they appear as ends of a certain sort within the agent's deliberative field, namely, goods that are interesting, fascinating, captivating, and the like. Unless they do, the agent is left in a state of boredom and is without a reason for being committed to the activities as the kind of activities we take them to be. Thus it is essential to the capacities that underwrite the capacity for boredom that they are not motivationally inert or epiphenomenal. The attempt to find something interesting *as a means* to relieving boredom is futile, if as a matter of fact there are no activities available to us that have the right kind of motivational pull. Nor is it anything but futile to attempt to find something interesting as a means to fulfilling our duties, even if we believe that we have a duty to develop our talents. It is crucial, then, to these activities having a place in our commitments that they appear within our deliberative field as interesting, fascinating, captivating, and the like, and that as such they have their motivational pull. The psychological *results* of engaging in these activities is possible only when we see them as activities to be pursued for their own sakes. They allure us with the kind of appearance they make as ends within our deliberative field, and it is crucial to this allure that thoughts about relieving boredom, pleasing God, fulfilling our duties are motivationally inert as determinate motives, though they can be present as regulative motives. Just as we cannot relieve our boredom by thinking of what we are doing as means to relieving our boredom, we cannot relieve our boredom by thinking of what we are doing as the fulfillment of duty. The only way to relieve boredom is to lose oneself in some intrinsically meaningful activity, that is, by becoming interested in the doing of something for its own sake and becoming fascinated, captivated, even lost in that activity. This cannot happen as long as the aesthetic dimensions of activities are motivationally inert. Thus it cannot be true that one is engaged in an activity of the sort in question and the aesthetic dimensions of that activity be epiphenomenal. Nor can it be true that we can be committed to them for the activities they are for indirect reasons and bypass their motivational pull in a way that renders epiphenomenal their aesthetic allure. For this reason, Baron cannot accommodate the goods of activity by assimilating them or some substantial portion of them to morality as deontic goods by taking either the second or third alternative above. By trying to force the value of these activities into the category of the deontic, even under the category of wide imperfect duties, she distorts the facts about their phenomenology and has to deny the more plausible naturalistic explanation for why these goods appear within our deliberative field in the first place and give us a basis for our commitments. When we find it interesting and captivating to spend time with others or to engage in the activities that develop our talents, we are moved by our sentiments and tastes, not a sense of obligation. The need to deny this seems motivated more by an almost obsessive sense of responsibility and an exclusive emphasis on the value of rational agency than anything required by an adequate phenomenology of value.[6]

If we are, then, to make a place for these goods in a way that is consistent with their phenomenology, we will have to reject Baron's version of the standard view. Might there be some other version of the standard view that will do the desired work? I do not think so, because any view that does so will have to make rather unrealistic claims about the place of these goods in our lives. They will have to deny that they operate as restrictions on what can be required of us from the moral or any other point of view. For this reason, it is time to consider how the Aristotelian view would accommodate these goods in a way that allows them to have their regulative effect on the other norms of a person's life without generating a sense of obligation. To see this, we need to consider the priorities problem.

2.

Before I proceed, then, to the subject of excellence, I want to address the issue of whether there is anything to fear in the rejection of the standard view. This will allow me to say something very general about the solution to the priorities problem as we now face it. The issue is whether allowing the permissible to function as a restriction on the obligatory is a threat to substantial commitments of impartial obligation. For purposes of illustra-

---

6. This same kind of difficulty faces those like Herman, Sherman, and Wood who want to give an account of friendship and other loving relations within the framework of imperfect duties. The love in parental commitments, in the commitments of friendship, and in the commitments of neighborly love must be epiphenomenal in the agent's commitment to these obligatory ends. But surely this distorts how these commitments enter our lives and how our loved ones appear within our deliberative field.

tion, I remain with activities involving aesthetic appreciation as they might conflict with the interests of persons held in simple respect.

If what I have said thus far is correct, then the agent will have some threshold level of interest in goods of aesthetic activity that is categorical. This will limit but not exclude the emergence of deontic beliefs from other sources within the agent's life. But these other commitments, given that they are categorical, will limit but not exclude the place of aesthetic experience in the agent's life as well. Can we say anything about the boundaries of these limits? I believe we can.

By now, one limit should be clear. The agent of integrity in the thick sense will feel obligated to give priority to the interests of those held in simple respect when their interests are categorical and the interest in aesthetic activity is not at the categorical threshold level for the agent. This is because the reverse priorities would not make sufficient place within the agent's life for those he or she holds in simple respect: the criterion of self-sufficiency would be violated. A similar norm will emerge in contexts in which the frustration of the agent's aesthetic interests would be minor and the benefits to others in terms of their flourishing significant. No respectful agent employing the criterion of self-sufficiency would order his or her life on these priorities because they do no make sufficient place for the goods of respect. Finally, there are those catastrophic contexts in which even if the cost to the agent is categorical in terms of aesthetic experience the agent will clearly feel the obligation to make a categorical sacrifice. These contexts reveal that a respectful agent with a categorical interest in the goods of activity cannot see some lives that preserve the goods of activity but sacrifice the goods of respect as satisfying the criterion of finality. Such a life would not be worthy of choice from the agent's own point of view. In all these contexts, the obligatory limits the permissible. Without these priorities, we are unable to understand the agent as being a respectful person, and we can understand them perfectly clearly from the Aristotelian perspective.

But we are equally unable to understand the agent as having a categorical interest in the goods of aesthetic activity if we do not include a set of priorities according to which the permissible limits the obligatory. Some of these contexts are those in which the interests of others are noncategorical and the agent's interests in aesthetic activity have reached the categorical threshold. But surely this is not too much for the agent to expect. True, it reflects the expectation of others that they make important sacrifices for the sake of the agent's aesthetic interests. But this is no less than the agent is willing to do for others. Here the thought that doing x is permissible for him not only leads to the thought that some things are obligatory for others but also leads to the thought that activities inconsistent with doing x are not obligatory for him. That others must make such a sacrifice does not make this sort of life with its priorities unworthy of choice, and the opposite set of priorities renders the way of life those priorities would structure neither self-sufficient nor final. So, once again, the Aristotelian view is confirmed.

Still other contexts are those in which the interests of others as well as the agent's are at the threshold level. In this regard, it may not be true as Faulkner said that *"Ode on a Grecian Urn* is worth any number of old ladies."[7] But from the viewpoint of most people's experience, some degree of beauty in one's life is worth *some* number of human casualties. To deny this, it seems, is to engage in hypocrisy of the worst sort. If one doubts this, simply reflect on the costs of one's books. I believe that Oxfam can guarantee the saving of many lives for donations less than the cost of paperback copies of *The Limits of Morality*, *The Case for Animal Rights*, and an offprint of "Famine, Affluence, and Morality."[8] For the costs of producing these and other writings thousands of lives could be saved. Wherefore, then, the objection to a copy of Keats and the aesthetic activity of reading fine literature?[9] Those who are apt to read a philosophy book are unlikely not to reason in a way that sets their priorities to ensure that life is full to a certain extent of intellectually interesting, fascinating, and captivating activities. To think that such a life does not cost others is extremely naive, to say the least. To choose such a life in the face of such costs is to endorse the priorities that structure it from the criterion of finality. And to reject the

---

7. See Joseph Blotner, *Faulkner: A Biography* (New York: Vintage Books, 1991), 619.

8. Shelly Kagan, *The Limits of Morality* (Oxford: Clarendon Press, 1989); Tom Regan, *The Case for Animal Rights* (Berkeley: University of California Press, 1982); Peter Singer, "Famine, Affluence, and Morality," *Philosophy and Public Affairs* 1, no. 3 (Spring 1972): 229–43.

9. There is, of course, the possibility of the now-ubiquitous response of the indirect consequentialist here: The real justification for the permissibility of our book purchases is to be found in indirect appeals to utility or some other impersonal end. For this response to work, it must generalize to provide an account for the place of aesthetic considerations within the meaning of our lives. But if I am right that some threshold level of aesthetic concerns is a categorical value for us, the indirect deliberative route to the desired conclusion seems puzzling. From what set of values is one deliberating when one is deliberating about what one's categorical values are going to be?

way of life that would save the lives but would come at the cost of intellectual tedium is to say that the rejected way of life is not self-sufficient. What could better illustrate the fact that our conceptual scheme and our lives confirm that the obligatory is regulated by this aspect of the merely permissible and that the moral is regulated by the aesthetic, as well as being regulated by it. Here again the latitude we expect in the practical life is not consistent with a view of human dignity that is absolute, nonscalar, nonadditive, and immune to trade-offs. This should put to rest the prospects of accounting for these priorities in terms of imperfect duties on the substantive interpretation of the CI procedure and the Formula of Humanity.

Finally, not to be overlooked are those contexts in which the agent finds himself or herself facing a deliberative impasse suspended between stultifying choices. On the one hand is the most aesthetically dreary life and categorical benefits to more than a marginal number of respectable people. On the other hand is a life with at least a bearable level of aesthetic appreciation but with more than a marginal number of respectable people suffering a categorical loss. Here the numbers are not such that they resolve the issue from the point of view of the agent. Awareness of them neither allows the agent to proceed with the activity nor allows him to make the sacrifice.

It is difficult to conceive of someone so aesthetically dense as not to understand the possibility of such contexts after reflection. But it is of the nature of such contexts that normative thoughts—both about the obligatory and about the merely permissible—have found their limit. Instead, there is irresolvable normative confusion, and it is a terrible mistake to think that a person crushed by such a situation lacks significant respect and concern for others. No. Such a person is merely a creature with an aesthetic dimension at the core of life. For most of us in this regard, not only is a life devoid of personal love but with every other good thing one version of hell, but a life with every other good thing yet totally lacking beauty and aesthetic interest is another. These contexts reveal that the agent cannot make a choice because there is no way the agent can order his or her priorities in a way that structures a way of life that accommodates goods that are minimally self-sufficient to make a way of life worthy of choice.

These contexts, therefore, along with the others, serve to indicate the priorities of the agent of integrity regarding the goods of activity. Not only are these priorities dictated by the nature of the integration problem, but I cannot see anything to criticize in the agent who has them. For this reason, I cannot see anything to fear in the rejection of the standard view. Moreover, the Aristotelian view, with its emphasis on the criteria of finality and self-sufficiency and the symmetrical feature of its regulative norms, accommodates these thoughts perfectly.

I turn now to the subject of excellence.

3.

It is one of the positive features of Baron's Kant that he insists on a commitment to excellence, something about which most of contemporary ethics is deplorably silent. Nevertheless, I will argue that Baron's scheme is inadequate to account for the commitment to excellence in an acceptable way.

Within Baron's interpretation of Kant's conceptual scheme, there are two basic ways of accounting for the commitment to excellence: one is indirectly a function of duties to others and the other is a direct function of our imperfect duty to improve ourselves, both of which are functions of our duty to respect rational nature in ourselves and others. I will argue that for the agent of integrity in the thick sense the commitment to excellence is not to be accounted for in these terms.

Certainly, one way in which thoughts of excellence enter the life of the agent of integrity is through the thought that the fates of others depend on one's competence, on one's doing what one does well. Mediocre efforts at doing well at those activities on which others depend indicate a lack of respect, esteem, sympathy, and love for others. They are contrary to the normative thoughts of such sentiments. Unimpassioned affection, tepid congratulations, and halfhearted or neglectful nurturing are all antithetical to the categorical commitments expressed in activities associated with personal love. Lukewarm devotion and inattention to competence are also incompatible with simple respect, esteem, and sympathy for others. Caring and wanting to make one's contributions in the contexts of such caring are simply unrecognizable apart from the commitment to excellence. Also, mediocre results, even when they are from conscientious efforts, are a source of tremendous disappointment to a caring person when those cared for are left wanting in important ways. That the agent of integrity is committed to excellence in this sense, then, is beyond dispute.

Moreover, it is true, as the Kantians claim, that a good person's culpable failure in excellence in the activities that serve the respect for others evokes a sense of self-reproach in such a person. This fact, however, does not confirm the Kantian view. For, as we have already seen, respect, love, and sympathy are symmetrical in their regulative functions; thus it is not simply respect for rational nature that is the foundational value for these commitments. Hence respect for rational nature as an asymmetrical regulative norm is not the foundational value for the commitment to excellence in these regards. Still, it remains true that an important dimension of the commitment to excellence is to be accounted for in terms of our commitments to others.

What might not be so clear is that the agent of integrity is categorically committed to excellence in another sense. At least, it must not be clear if neglect of the topic is a sign of its not being thought sufficiently important to warrant discussion. What I have in mind is the commitment to doing well at activities that are not tightly connected with the fates of others, or at least, need not be.

Perhaps the best way to describe the kind of commitment I have in mind can be put in terms of a musician's concern regarding the performance of a piece of music. Imagine a quartet getting together to play for themselves. They have no concern to play for the public, only for themselves. Having played through the piece, they decide to play it again. One reason they could have for repeating the piece is that they simply enjoyed playing it the first time and would enjoy playing it again. But suppose this is not the case, what other reason might they have? Perhaps they think they did not play it well enough the first time; thus the insistence on playing it again. Any decent musician, or anyone with the slightest understanding of what drives a good musician, will understand this impulse to play it again. The origin of the impulse is not simply the dissatisfaction with the prior performance, though this is an element. Rather, there is a vision of how the piece could be played, and it is this that generates the dissatisfaction with the prior performance. It is the musician's vision of how things could be done that is the foundation for his or her commitment to excellence. A vision of how the piece could be played appears as intrinsically good within the agent's deliberative field, and it is this that grounds the commitment to it.

Now consider two interpretations of the musician's experience constructed from the Stoics and Kant. In *De Finibus* (bk. 3, vi, 22), there appears the following passage from Cicero:

> It will be an error to infer that this [the Stoic] view implies two Ultimate Goods. For though if a man were to make it his purpose to take a true aim with a spear or arrow at some mark, his ultimate end, corresponding to the ultimate good as we pronounce it, would be to do all he could to aim straight: the man in this illustration would have to do everything to aim straight, and yet, although he did everything to attain his purpose, his "ultimate End," so to speak, would be what corresponded to what we call the Chief Good in the conduct of life,

whereas the actual hitting of the mark would be in our phrase "to be chosen" but not "to be desired." [10]

If we apply this passage to the musician, the Stoic musician must be understood on the analogy with the Stoic archer: The role of the target is to provide an opportunity to aim straight. Only in this way is it chosen; otherwise, it is not to be desired. Similarly, the vision of how the music could be played merely provides a target, an opportunity to exercise and develop one's talents; otherwise, it too is an object not to be desired. On this view, then, the vision of how the piece could be played appears within the agent's deliberative field as an instrumental good, one that functions as a way of focusing on something else, namely, on one's talents.

A thought related to this view is found in Kant's view that the good will is good independent of its consequences. Kant argues that we can distinguish between the person who merely wishes for the right thing and the person who truly wills it, and he also argues that we can distinguish between the person who wills the right thing and achieves it and the person who wills the right thing but fails to achieve it. According to Kant, there is a clear moral difference between the person who truly wills the right thing and the person who merely wishes it, but there is no moral difference between the person who wills and achieves and the person who wills and fails, as long as both are truly willing. How do these thoughts apply to the imperfect duty to develop our talents and to our musician? If you are a Kantian musician, your musical ability appears within your deliberative field in a certain way: It appears there as one among possibly several ways of developing your talents and respecting the value of your rational agency. Suppose that within the latitude allowed by the imperfect duty to develop your talents, you decide to fulfill this duty by developing your musical talents as opposed to other talents you might have. You are now gathered with the other members of your quartet, finding yourself with the impulse to play the piece again. What reason might you have for doing this?

Whatever reason it is it cannot be one that makes the extra practice supererogatory as a case of going beyond duty to develop your talents. Nor does it seem that the replaying can be merely permissible, since this occasion is one on which you can develop your talents. In some sense, then, it is a dutiful activity. It is a case of developing your talents as an expression of your respect for your rational nature. You enjoy the activity, but your

10. Cicero, *Di Finibus* (*Cicero XVII*), trans. H. Hackman, Loeb Classical Library (Cambridge, Mass.: Harvard University Press, 1914), 241.

enjoyment is epiphenomenal as a reason for playing. But why, from the point of view of respect for your rational nature, would you play the piece again? Perhaps your playing revealed such mediocrity that you have doubts that you had the target in view. So you play again, concentrating on the vision of how the piece could be played. But, again, you are disappointed. This time you have doubts that you truly willed to play the piece according to the way envisioned. That is, you had the target in view but failed to try hard enough to aim straight; your playing was somewhere between merely wishful playing and truly willful playing. So you play the piece again. On many different occasions and after many attempts, all of which come up clearly short of the vision, you conclude that you and your quartet can approximate the vision only so closely. You tell yourself that you have not failed as a result of merely wishing but of truly willing. In other words, you gave it your best shot, and this thought leaves your conscience clear regarding your dutiful commitment to excellence. The relationship between your sense of self and your pursuit of the vision can be described as the motive to engage in the activity in a way that afterward there cannot be any sense of self-reproach should mediocrity be the result.

There is a difference, though a small one, between the Stoic musician and you as a Kantian musician in your respective commitments to excellence. The Stoic musician is not disappointed at mediocrity when mediocre playing is the result of true effort. Excellent playing is the target, but it is chosen, not desired. Like the archer for whom the target is irrelevant after the release of the arrow, the actual quality of the music is irrelevant after the best effort has been made to play it well. To be sure, the best effort must have been given. Nevertheless, since the happy life is the life of virtue, mediocre music is nothing to the Stoic musician who has given his best effort to play according to the vision.[11] The value of excellence, then, is in the effort, and it is in this that the agent finds his or her well-being. As a Kantian musician, however, you are allowed some degree of disappointment at the fact that the natural lottery prevented you and your quartet from playing in a way that matched the vision. I say some, but not a great deal, for as a Kantian musician you have other duties, especially to perfect your character as much as possible. Of course, if you never had any inclination to develop your talent in the first place, only the sense of duty to do so,

---

11. Lawrence Becker's contemporary version of Stoicism deserves a separate response, one that I cannot attempt here. See Lawrence C. Becker, *A New Stoicism* (Princeton: Princeton University Press, 1998).

there will be no disappointment at all, only the thought that you gave it your best shot.

Now how might an Aristotelian musician contrast with the Stoic and the Kantian in the commitment to excellence? First, it seems plausible that any acceptable view will insist, as does both the Stoic and the Kantian views, that it is important to one's sense of self-respect that one does the best one can, that one puts one's best effort forward. Moreover, what seems right about both views is that if mediocrity is the result of one's best efforts, then there is no room for blame. What reason is there for thinking, then, that there is anything missing from these accounts of the commitment to excellence?

That there is something missing from both accounts is revealed, I believe, in reflections on how important externals are to a caring agent. In this regard, let me draw a parallel between parental love and the commitment to excellence of the sort in question. We cannot, I believe, give a plausible account of a normative conception of love that renders the loving parent invulnerable to some degree of agent breakdown should tragedy befall his or her children. This is because loving a child involves a categorical interest, an interest in an external. As the Stoics knew all too well, it is the commitment to externals that renders one vulnerable to a troubled life. If it is an untroubled life you want, do not become a parent, for nothing generates anxiety as much as the concern over whether something bad is going to happen to your children. Now suppose something bad does happen to your children, and you have the thought analogous to the thought of the musician, "I wish I could raise my children all over again." What might motivate such a thought?

You might worry that you did not have a target the first time around, that you simply failed to give enough thought to what a good parent should try to provide for his or her children. Surely, sometimes this is the form of parental self-reproach. But assume that this is not the case, that though you had the right target in mind you simply did not put forth your best effort at being a good parent, that your parenting was somewhere between merely wishful parenting and truly willful parenting. This thought could certainly motivate the desire to raise your children all over again. But assume that neither of these motivates the desire to raise your children again, that you had the right target in view and that you made your most conscientious efforts at hitting it; yet the desire to raise your children again persists with some intensity. If we take the Stoic archer analogy seriously, a good outcome to your children of your best efforts to secure their well-being will be chosen but not desired. Thus a bad outcome will not redound negatively on your happiness; it will leave you untroubled, in a state of ataraxia. Since acting virtuously is all that matters to happiness and you have acted virtuously in doing the best you can to secure a good outcome for your children, the bad outcome will not matter. But, of course, parental love in those we respect the most is not like this at all. Loving children in a way that involves the kind of commitment we respect renders a person extremely vulnerable to bad outcomes. Imagine someone telling bereaved parents that they had done their best to prevent tragedy coming to their children. In the absence of some indication by the parents that they thought the tragedy due to their negligence, such comments would be nothing short of inhumanely insensitive. Grief need not include self-blame, but its presence is natural to those sentiments connected to externals, as parental love most surely is. In this context, the desire to raise one's children all over again is simply a function of the desire to have better luck next time, a desire that expresses our vulnerability. Thus there is an essential connection between the commitment to excellence we expect in loving parents and a kind of vulnerability that is at the heart of a loving parent's psychology. Nowhere else is it more obvious that hitting the target means so much, even when missing is not something we see as our fault.

Something similar is true of the musician, or the poet, writer, scientist, athlete, or philosopher who is committed to excellence at his or her activities. To be committed to excellence at these activities is to be committed to the value of an external, and this fact is not captured either by the Stoic or the Kantian account. The Stoic account fails because it cannot account for the fact that missing the target no matter what the effort is a source of tremendous stress to the musician committed to excellence. The actual quality of one's music is part of the meaning of one's life at its core to a person for whom being a musician is a categorical commitment. Thus committing yourself to excellence at music is to render yourself vulnerable to bad outcomes. The only way to avoid this is to avoid the commitment to excellence at music. Nor will it be consoling that the bad outcome, the mediocrity of your music, is not due to lack of effort on your part. Failure in this regard might leave your *moral* integrity in place but utterly shatter you as a person. For this reason, the Kantian analysis of the commitment to excellence in terms of respect for your rational agency is woefully inadequate. No self-respecting musician, poet, athlete, or philosopher could find an epitaph that read "She gave it her best shot" anything other than patronizing.

It is also difficult to know in advance whether one is going to be good enough at these activities to hit the target. In fact, it seems to me that those we esteem a great deal, perhaps the most, are those who take the chance of investing their lives in these activities when the odds are that they will not hit the target at which they aim. The odds against even the brightest graduate students going on to make a significant contribution to their fields is surely quite high. Do we encourage them, then, to aim only at respectability? If we do, have we encouraged a commitment to excellence? The truth is that the commitment to excellence has an ineliminably brutal element to it. This is not because of competition with others, but because there is a vision of how things could be done and one might simply fail in one's efforts to realize that vision. Do we think people have an obligation to take on such a commitment? I do not think so, yet among those we esteem most are people who are committed to excellence in just this way. Is their commitment to excellence supererogatory? Again, this seems to miss the value of excellence from the agent's point of view. Rather, the best way to describe such a commitment is in terms of the nonmoral regulating the moral, the aesthetic regulating the deontic.

On the Aristotelian model, the vision of how things could be done appears within our deliberative field as good. And against this vision we measure ourselves and invest a good bit of the meaning of our lives in approximating that vision. When we fall too far short of that vision, such failure diminishes the meaning of our lives from our own point of view. A life of mediocrity is neither self-sufficient nor final, even when one has given one's best efforts at avoiding it, for the person for whom the commitment to excellence is at the core of life. Of course, for the agent of integrity in the thick sense, the commitment to excellence is regulated by other commitments. The dedicated musician we admire must integrate the concern for excellent music into a life that expresses due concern for the other goods within the deliberative field. But this does not change the fact that just as these other commitments involve the commitment to externals and thus to devastating vulnerability, so does the commitment to excellence. Thus any attempt by the Kantian to relegate the commitment to excellence at these activities to a marginal place in life is doomed to distortion, which shows, I believe, that the commitment to excellence also regulates these other commitments. I cannot see, then, that the imperfect duty to develop our talents, and the role it has on Baron's view as an expression of our respect for our rational agency, captures the phenomenology of excellence in those whom we esteem most for their commitments. The complexities of the integration problem for the agent who is respectful and sympathetic to others, who is personally loving as a parent, a friend, and a neighbor, and who is committed to excellence make it impossible for any regulative norm to function asymmetrically. The problem for such a norm is that it cannot order the agent's priorities in a way that makes life both self-sufficient and final in terms of the goods that appear within the agent's deliberative field.

4.

I want now to say why I think these points about excellence are both neglected and significant. Almost no one talks about excellence anymore, especially moral philosophers. True, there are commercial advertisements that bandy about some rhetoric in this regard, but no one takes it for anything other than manipulative discourse. The concept of excellence is increasingly less mentioned in faculty meetings. Discussions of the curriculum mention any number of things, some of which are very important in their own right. Most prominent these days are expansion issues involving diversity, and there is the increasing dominance of talk about student interest. But seldom mentioned is excellence. One might say that excellence is not a concern for the curriculum but a presupposition of it. But if this is true, why is the modern university more and more concerned with student interest as a source of demand for classes? Surely at the core of the university of the past was not only a commitment to being good at what was offered in the curriculum but also a judgment about a core of things that it is good to be good at. No longer. Now the contemporary university merely serves either the market demands of student interests[12] or the demands of social justice as it sees them. Excellence at intrinsically valuable activities is less and less a part of its mission. Moral philosophers do nothing to alter this by neglecting the importance of a dedication to excellence in a life well lived.

There is certainly a danger to emphasizing excellence, and I am not thinking of the political dangers. The most fundamental is that having encouraged a categorical commitment one will facilitate emotional collapse in

12. Think here of how, at least in the United States, teaching performance is evaluated in universities. It is done almost exclusively by students, and their evaluations are given great weight. If ever there was a practice that encouraged excellence at personal politics and mediocrity in teaching, this is it. True, some will be excellent teachers despite the practice, but the institution of teaching will not itself be excellent. Indeed, it will be replaced by a form of entertainment, with teachers acting as celebrities and students becoming more and more passive in the pursuit of learning.

those who fail for lack of talent. While there are ways to minimize such results—careful and reasonable assessment of possibilities—there is no way to ensure that it will not happen. It will. But what is the option? Much of our sense of self is predicated on both our efforts and our abilities at achieving excellence. Even if we eliminated this aspect of the human good, there would still be the concern for excellence relating to the welfare of others. But I find it difficult to believe that the concern for excellence at non-deontic activities can be eliminated without severe harms to human life and character.

It seems that there are three major options. First, we can attempt to eliminate the danger just mentioned by denying that there is anything intrinsically important about excellence in these activities. That is, we can say that such excellence is unimportant. Having said this, though, we will have said that people should find their sense of self in other activities or in idleness. I must admit that if the reader does not find this ludicrous, then I have nothing else in the way of argument. Second, we can attempt to eliminate the danger by changing the name of mediocrity to excellence and hope that self-deception ensures the success of the project. But this comes not only at the cost of our integrity; it also brings the danger of a spreading disease: Once self-deception about nondeontic activities has set in, our sense of obligation will not long find immunity. This is too much to pay, and it is too great a danger. Finally, we can recognize that there is no fail-safe environment for humans, and that the earning of one's own self-esteem is, in part, measured in terms of these activities. There is no categorical good without the possibility of categorical loss. Take precautions and sin bravely, then, is the final and only option for the agent of integrity.

Failure to pursue excellence and to encourage it is a failure in courage, and no badly formulated egalitarian thesis can change this fact. The failure of modern universities is to be found largely in the lack of courage to demand excellence in things that are not externally or instrumentally justified. The hypocrisy is that it is done in the name of equality and humanity. When we have solved all our issues of justice, the danger of failure in the activities that mean most to us will remain. We must be mindful, however, that mediocrity then will be a failure in courage rather than in talent or resource. For our universities, this seems true by and large now.

It is, I believe, one of the tragedies of our time that the concept of excellence has become at best an afterthought in our conceptual scheme. Indeed, I believe it is a source of a great deal of self-alienation among modern persons, something we cannot long endure and remain agents of integrity. In adopting a way of thinking that attempts to eliminate the possibility of our own failure, we have cut ourselves off from the possibility of our own success. Having done both, we are left to construct our sense of self-approval out of raw feelings. In adopting a sense of equality that runs scared of the possibility of the failure of others, we have cut ourselves off from the possibility of their success. And again, having done both, we are left to construct our social relations out of raw feelings. This cannot be done; the project fails, and so does the way of thinking that leads to the project. The lesson is that we cannot succeed with a thin, value-neutral conception of integrity. It must be thick. It must allow not only for the commitments of simple respect, esteem, and sympathy but also for those of friendship, familial and neighborly love, and to excellence at what one does, including intrinsically meaningful work. It must wed an agent's normative thoughts to a robust meaningful life. This is best achieved, I believe, in the Aristotelian conception of integrity I have tried to defend here.

Bibliography

Ackrill, J. L. "Aristotle on Eudaimonia." In *Essays on Aristotle's Ethics*, edited by Amelie Oksenberg Rorty, 7–33. Berkeley: University of California Press, 1980.

Allison, Henry E. *Kant's Theory of Freedom*. Cambridge: Cambridge University Press, 1990.

Anderson, Arnold E. *Practical Comprehensive Treatment of Anorexia Nervosa and Bulimia*. Baltimore: Johns Hopkins University Press, 1985.

Annas, Julia. "Personal Love and Kantian Ethics in Effi Briest." *Philosophy and Literature* 8 (April 1984): 15–31.

Aristotle. *Eudemian Ethics: Books I, II, and VIII*. 2d ed. Translated by Michael Woods. Clarendon Aristotle Series. Oxford: Oxford University Press, 1992.

———. *Nicomachean Ethics*. Translated by Martin Ostwald. Indianapolis: Library of Liberal Arts, Bobbs-Merrill, 1962.

———. *The Politics*. Edited by Stephen Everson and translated by Benjamin Jowett. Cambridge Texts in the History of Political Thought. Cambridge: Cambridge University Press, 1988.

Aristotle: A Collection of Critical Essays. Edited by J. M. E. Moravcsik. Garden City, N.Y.: Anchor Books, 1967.

Aristotle, Kant, and the Stoics. Edited by Stephen Engstrom and Jennifer Whiting. Cambridge: Cambridge University Press, 1996.

Baier, Annette C. *Moral Prejudices*. Cambridge, Mass.: Harvard University Press, 1995.

Baron, Marcia. "The Alleged Repugnance of Acting from Duty." *Journal of Philosophy* 81 (April 1984): 197–220.

———. *Kantian Ethics Almost Without Apology*. Ithaca: Cornell University Press, 1995.

———. "Was Effi Briest a Victim of Kantian Morality?" In *Friendship: A Philosophical Reader*, edited by Neera Kapur Badhwar, 192–210. Ithaca: Cornell University Press, 1993.

Becker, Lawrence C. *A New Stoicism.* Princeton: Princeton University Press, 1998.

―――. *Reciprocity.* London: Routledge and Kegan Paul, 1986.

Bednar, Richard L., M. Gawain Wells, and Scott R. Peterson. *Self-Esteem: Paradoxes and Innovations in Clinical Theory and Practice.* Washington, D.C.: American Psychological Association, 1989.

Berlin, Isaiah. *The Crooked Timber of Humanity.* Princeton: Princeton University Press, 1990.

Blotner, Joseph. *Faulkner: A Biography.* New York: Vintage Books, 1991.

Blum, Lawrence. *Friendship, Altruism, and Morality.* London: Routledge and Kegan Paul, 1980.

Bond, E. J. *Reason and Value.* Cambridge: Cambridge University Press, 1983.

Bosanquet, Mary. *The Life and Death of Dietrich Bonhoeffer.* New York: Harper and Row, 1968.

Brandt, Richard. *A Theory of the Good and the Right.* New York: Oxford University Press, 1979.

Brennan, Tim. "Loneliness at Adolescence." In *Loneliness: A Sourcebook of Current Theory, Research and Therapy,* edited by Letitia Anne Peplau and Daniel Perlman, 269–91. New York: John Wiley, 1982.

Broadie, Sarah. *Ethics with Aristotle.* London: Oxford University Press, 1991.

Brown, Robert. *Analyzing Love.* Cambridge: Cambridge University Press, 1987.

Camus, Albert. *The Myth of Sisyphus and Other Essays.* Translated by Justin O'Brien. New York: Vintage Books, 1991.

Cheek, Jonathan M., and Stephen R. Briggs. "Shyness as a Personality Trait." In *Shyness and Embarrassment: Perspectives from Social Psychology,* edited by W. Ray Crozier, 315–55. Cambridge: Cambridge University Press, 1990.

Cicero. *Di Finibus (Cicero XVII).* Translated by H. Hackman. Loeb Classical Library. Cambridge, Mass.: Harvard University Press, 1914.

Costa-Gavras, Constantin. *The Music Box.* Tri Star, 1989.

Cottingham, John. "Ethics and Impartiality." *Philosophical Studies* 43 (1983): 83–99.

―――. "Partiality, Favouritism and Morality." *Philosophical Quarterly* 36 (July 1984): 357–73.

Cummiskey, David. *Kantian Consequentialism.* New York: Oxford University Press, 1996.

Cutrona, Carolyn E. "Transition to College: Loneliness and the Process of Social Adjustment." In *Loneliness: A Sourcebook of Current Theory, Research and Therapy,* edited by Letitia Anne Peplau and Daniel Perlman, 291–309. New York: John Wiley, 1982.

Daniels, Norman. "Reflective Equilibrium and Archimedean Points." *Canadian Journal of Philosophy* 10, no. 1 (March 1980): 83–103.

―――. "Wide Reflective Equilibrium and Theory Acceptance in Ethics." *Journal of Philosophy* 76 (1979): 256–82.

Dante. *The Inferno.* Translated by John Ciardi. New York: New American Library, 1954.

Darwall, Stephen L. *Impartial Reason.* Ithaca: Cornell University Press, 1983.

Davidson, Donald. "Deception and Division." In *The Multiple Self,* edited by Jon Elster, 79–92. Cambridge: Cambridge University Press, 1985.

de la Pena, Augustin M. *The Psychobiology of Cancer: Automation and Boredom in Health and Disease.* New York: Praeger, 1983.

Donagan, Alan. *The Theory of Morality.* Chicago: University of Chicago Press, 1977.

Dworkin, Ronald. *Taking Rights Seriously.* Cambridge, Mass.: Harvard University Press, 1977.

Ellis, M. J. *Why People Play.* Englewood Cliffs, N.J.: Prentice Hall, 1973.

Essays in Ancient Greek Philosophy. Edited by John P. Anton and Anthony Preus. Albany: State University of New York Press, 1983.

Essays on Aristotle's Ethics. Edited by Amelie Oksenberg Rorty. Berkeley: University of California Press, 1980.

Flanagan, Owen. *Varieties of Moral Personality.* Cambridge, Mass.: Harvard University Press, 1991.

Frankfurt, Harry G. *The Importance of What We Care About.* Cambridge:University Press, 1988.

Fried, Charles. *An Anatomy of Values.* Cambridge, Mass.: Harvard University Press, 1970.

Friendship: A Philosophical Reader. Edited by Neera Kapur Badhwar. Ithaca: Cornell University Press, 1993.

Fromm-Reichmann, F. "Loneliness." *Psychiatry* 22 (1959): 1–15.

Galston, William. *Liberal Purposes: Goods, Virtues, and Diversity in the Liberal State.* New York: Cambridge University Press, 1991.

Gewirth, Alan. *Reason and Morality.* Chicago: University of Chicago Press, 1978.

Gomberg, Paul. "Patriotism Is Like Racism." *Ethics* (October 1990): 144–50.

Hallie, Philip. *Lest Innocent Blood Be Shed.* New York: Harper and Row, 1979.

Hardie, W. F. R. "The Final Good in Aristotle's Ethics." In *Aristotle: A Collection of Critical Essays,* edited by J. M. E. Moravcsik, 297–322. Garden City, N.Y.: Anchor Books, 1967.

Harris, George W. "Aristotelian Ethics, Contemporary." In *Encyclopedia of Ethics,* vol. 1, 2d ed., edited by Charlotte Becker and Lawrence Becker. New York: Garland, 1999.

———. *Dignity and Vulnerability: Strength and Quality of Character.* Berkeley: University of California Press, 1997.

———. "Frankena and the Unity of Practical Reason." *Monist* (July 1981): 406–17.

———. "A Paradoxical Departure from Consequentialism." *Journal of Philosophy* 86, no. 2 (February 1989): 90–102.

Harsanyi, John. "Morality and the Theory of Rational Behavior." In *Utilitari-*

anism and Beyond, edited by Amartya Sen and Bernard Williams, 39–62. Cambridge: Cambridge University Press, 1982.

Hartman, Lorne M., and Patricia A. Cleland. "Social Anxiety, Personality, and the Self." In *Shyness and Embarrassment: Perspectives from Social Psychology,* edited by W. Ray Crozier, 315–55. Cambridge: Cambridge University Press, 1990.

Harwood, Ronald. *The Dresser.* New York: S. French, 1982.

Having Children: Philosophical and Legal Reflections on Parenthood. Edited by Onora O'Neill and William Ruddick. New York: Oxford University Press, 1979.

Herman, Barbara. "Making Room for Character." In *Aristotle, Kant, and the Stoics,* edited by Stephen Engstrom and Jennifer Whiting, 33–62. New York: Cambridge University Press, 1996.

————. "On the Value of Acting from the Motive of Duty." *Philosophical Review* 66, no. 2 (July 1981): 233–50.

————. *The Practice of Moral Judgment.* Cambridge, Mass.: Harvard University Press, 1993.

Hill, Thomas. *Dignity and Practical Reason in Kant's Moral Theory.* Ithaca: Cornell University Press, 1992.

————. "Servility and Self-Respect." *Monist* 57, no. 1 (1973): 87–104.

Hurka, Thomas. *Perfectionism.* New York: Oxford University Press, 1993.

Jones, Warren H. "Loneliness and Social Behavior." In *Loneliness: A Sourcebook of Current Theory, Research, and Therapy,* edited by Letitia Anne Peplau and Daniel Perlman, 238–52. New York: John Wiley, 1982.

Kagan, Shelly. *The Limits of Morality.* Oxford: Clarendon Press, 1989.

Kant, Immanuel. *Critique of Practical Reason.* Translated by Lewis White Beck. Indianapolis: Bobbs-Merrill, 1956.

————. *Groundwork of the Metaphysic of Morals.* Translated by H. J. Paton. New York: Harper Torchbooks, 1964.

————. *Lectures on Ethics.* Translated by Louis Infield. Indianapolis: Hackett, 1963.

————. *The Metaphysics of Morals.* Edited and translated by Mary Gregor. Cambridge Texts in the History of Philosophy. Cambridge: Cambridge University Press, 1996.

Kekes, John. "Constancy and Purity." *Mind,* no. 92 (1983): 499–518.

Kenny, Anthony. *The Aristotelian Ethics.* London: Oxford University Press, 1978.

————. *Aristotle on the Perfect Life.* London: Oxford University Press, 1992.

Keyt, David. "Intellectualism in Aristotle." In *Essays in Ancient Greek Philosophy,* edited by John P. Anton and Anthony Preus, 364–87. Albany: State University of New York Press, 1983.

Kierkegaard, Søren. *Fear and Trembling.* Translated by Walter Lowrie. New York: Anchor Books, 1954.

Knapp, Ronald J. *Beyond Endurance: When a Child Dies.* New York: Schocken Books, 1986.

Korsgaard, Christine M. *Creating the Kingdom of Ends.* Cambridge: Cambridge University Press, 1996.

———. "From Duty and for the Sake of the Noble." In *Aristotle, Kant, and the Stoics: Rethinking Happiness and Duty,* edited by Stephen Engstrom and Jennifer Whiting, 203–36. New York: Cambridge University Press, 1996.

———. "Skepticism about Practical Reason." *Journal of Philosophy* 83, no. 1 (January 1986): 5–25.

———. *The Sources of Normativity.* Cambridge: Cambridge University Press, 1996.

Kraut, Richard. *Aristotle on the Human Good.* Princeton: Princeton University Press, 1989.

Kymlicka, Will. *Liberalism, Community and Culture.* Oxford: Clarendon Press, 1989.

———. *Multicultural Citizenship: A Liberal Theory of Minority Rights.* Oxford: Oxford University Press, 1995.

Lemos, Noah. *Intrinsic Value: Concept and Warrant.* New York: Cambridge University Press, 1994.

Loneliness: A Sourcebook of Current Theory, Research and Therapy. Edited by Letitia Anne Peplau and Daniel Perlman. New York: John Wiley, 1982.

McAdams, Dan P. *Intimacy: The Need to Be Close.* New York: Doubleday, 1989.

McDowell, John. "Deliberation and Moral Development in Aristotle's Ethics." In *Aristotle, Kant, and the Stoics,* edited by Stephen Engstrom and Jennifer Whiting, 19–35. New York: Cambridge University Press, 1996.

———. "Might There Be External Reasons." In *Mind, World, and Ethics,* edited by J. E. J. Altham and Ross Harrison, 68–85. Cambridge: Cambridge University Press, 1995.

McFall, Lynne. "Integrity." *Ethics* 98 (October 1987): 5–20.

The Marx-Engels Reader. Edited by Robert C. Tucker. New York: W. W. Norton, 1972.

Mead, George Herbert. *Mind, Self, and Society.* Edited by Charles W. Morris. Chicago: University of Chicago Press, 1962.

Menges, Chris. *A World Apart.* Atlantic Entertainment and British Screen, 1988.

Mill, John Stuart. *Utilitarianism.* Indianapolis: Bobbs-Merrill, 1957.

The Multiple Self. Edited by Jon Elster. Cambridge: Cambridge University Press, 1985.

Nagel, Thomas. "Aristotle on Eudaimonia." In *Essays on Aristotle's Ethics,* edited by Amelie Oksenberg Rorty, 7–14. Berkeley: University of California Press, 1980.

Nisbet, Robert. *Prejudices: A Philosophical Dictionary.* Cambridge, Mass.: Harvard University Press, 1982.

Nozick, Robert. *Anarchy, State, and Utopia.* New York: Basic Books, 1974.

Nussbaum, Martha. "Aristotle on Human Nature and the Foundations of Ethics." In *World, Mind, and Ethics: Essays on the Ethical Philosophy of Bernard Williams, edited by J. E. J. Altham and Ross Harrison, 86–131. Cambridge: Cambridge University Press, 1995.

———. The Fragility of Goodness. Cambridge: Cambridge University Press, 1986.

Oates, Stephen B. Let the Trumpet Sound: The Life of Martin Luther King, Jr. New York: Mentor, 1985.

Overload and Boredom: Essays on the Quality of Life in the Information Society. Edited by Orrin E. Klapp. New York: Greenwood Press, 1986.

O'Neill, Onora. "Begetting, Bearing, and Rearing." In Having Children: Philosophical and Legal Reflections on Parenthood, edited by Onora O'Neill and William Ruddick, 25–38. New York: Oxford University Press, 1979.

———. Constructions of Reason: Explorations of Kant's Practical Philosophy. Cambridge: Cambridge University Press, 1989.

———. Towards Justice and Virtue: A Constructive Account of Practical Reason. Cambridge: Cambridge University Press, 1996.

Parfit, Derek. Reasons and Persons. London: Clarendon Press, 1984.

Parkes, Colin Murray. Bereavement: Studies of Grief in Adult Life. New York: International Studies Press, 1972.

Payne, Robert. The Life and Death of Mahatma Gandhi. New York: E. P. Dutton, 1969.

Pears, David. "The Goals and Strategies of Self-Deception." In The Multiple Self, edited by Jon Elster, 59–78. Cambridge: Cambridge University Press, 1985.

———. Motivated Irrationality. Oxford: Clarendon Press, 1984.

Peirce, Charles Sanders. "The Fixation of Belief." In Philosophical Writings of Peirce, edited by Justus Buchler, 5–22. New York: Dover Publications, 1955.

Peplau, Letitia Anne, Tora K. Bikson, Karen S. Rook, and Jacqueline D. Goodchilds. "Being Old and Living Alone." In Loneliness: A Sourcebook of Current Theory, Research and Therapy, edited by Letitia Anne Peplau and Daniel Perlman, 327–47. New York: John Wiley, 1982.

Play: In Animals and Humans. Edited by Peter K. Smith. Oxford: Basil Blackwell, 1984.

Posner, Gerald. Hitler's Children. New York: Random House, 1991.

Railton, Peter. "Alienation, Consequentialism, and the Demands of Morality." In Friendship: A Philosophical Reader, edited by Neera Kapur Badhwar, 211–44. Ithaca: Cornell University Press, 1993.

Rawls, John. "The Independence of Moral Theory." In Proceedings of the American Philosophical Association, 5–22. New York: American Philosophical Association, 1974.

———. "A Kantian Conception of Equality." In Readings in Social and Political Philosophy, edited by Robert M. Stewart, 187–95. New York: Oxford University Press, 1986.

———. Political Liberalism. New York: Columbia University Press, 1993.

———. A Theory of Justice. Cambridge, Mass.: Harvard University Press, 1971.

Raz, Joseph. *The Morality of Freedom.* Oxford: Clarendon Press, 1986.

Regan, Tom. *The Case for Animal Rights.* Berkeley: University of California Press, 1982.

Richards, David A. J. *A Theory of Reasons for Action.* Oxford: Clarendon Press, 1971.

Richardson, Henry S. *Practical Reasoning about Final Ends.* Cambridge: Cambridge University Press, 1994.

Rook, Karen S., and Letitia Anne Peplau. "Perspectives on Helping the Lonely." In *Loneliness: A Sourcebook of Current Theory, Research and Therapy,* edited by Letitia Anne Peplau and Daniel Perlman, 351–78. New York: John Wiley, 1982.

Sachs, David. "How to Distinguish Self-Respect from Self-Esteem." *Philosophy and Public Affairs* 10 (1981): 346–60.

Sacks, Oliver. *Seeing Voices: A Journey into the World of the Deaf.* New York: Harper Perennial, 1990.

Sandel, Michael. *Liberalism and the Limits of Justice.* Cambridge: Cambridge University Press, 1982.

Scheffler, Samuel. *The Rejection of Consequentialism.* Oxford: Oxford University Press, 1982.

Schopenhauer, Arthur. *The Will to Live: Selected Writings.* Edited by Richard Taylor. New York: F. Ungar, 1967.

———. *The World as Will and Representation.* Translated by E. F. G. Payne. Indian Hills, Colo.: Falcon's Wing Press, 1958.

Scott, Derek. "Sex Differences Within Anorexia Nervosa." In *Anorexia Nervosa,* edited by Derek Scott, 59–73. New York: New York University Press, 1988.

Seligman, Martin E. P. *Helplessness: On Depression, Development, and Death.* San Fransisco: W. H. Freeman, 1975.

Sells, Michael A. *The Bridge Betrayed: Religion and Genocide in Bosnia.* Berkeley: University of California Press, 1996.

Sher, George. *Beyond Neutrality: Perfectionism and Politics.* Cambridge: Cambridge University Press, 1997.

Sherman, Nancy. *Making a Necessity of Virtue: Aristotle and Kant on Virtue.* Cambridge: Cambridge University Press, 1997.

Shirer, William. *Love and Hatred: The Troubled Marriage of Leo and Sonya Tolstoy.* New York: Simon and Schuster, 1994.

Sichrovsky, Peter. *Born Guilty.* New York: Basic Books, 1988.

Singer, Peter. "Famine, Affluence, and Morality." *Philosophy and Public Affairs* 1, no. 3 (Spring 1972): 229–43.

Slote, Michael. *Goods and Virtues.* Oxford: Clarendon Press, 1983.

Stocker, Michael. *Plural and Conflicting Values.* Oxford: Clarendon Press, 1990.

———. "The Schizophrenia of Modern Ethical Theories." In *The Virtues: Contemporary Essays on Moral Character,* edited by Robert B. Kruschwitz and Robert C. Roberts, 36–45. Belmont, Calif.: Wadsworth, 1986.

Stroebe, Wolfgang, and Margaret S. Stroebe. *Bereavement and Health: The Psychological and Physical Consequences of Partner Loss*. Cambridge: Cambridge University Press, 1987.

Styron, William. *Sophie's Choice*. New York: Random House, 1976.

Suedfield, Peter. "Aloneness as a Healing Experience." In *Loneliness: A Sourcebook of Current Theory, Research and Therapy*, edited by Letitia Anne Peplau and Daniel Perlman, 54–70. New York: John Wiley, 1982.

Symons, Donald. *The Evolution of Human Sexuality*. New York: Oxford University Press, 1979.

Tamir, Yamir. *Liberal Nationalism*. Princeton: Princeton University Press, 1993.

Taylor, Charles. "A Most Peculiar Institution." In *World, Mind, and Ethics*, edited by J. E. J. Altham and Ross Harrison, 132–55. Cambridge: Cambridge University Press, 1995.

Taylor, Gabriele. *Pride, Shame, and Guilt: Emotions of Self-Assessment*. Oxford: Clarendon Press, 1985.

Troyat, Henri. *Tolstoy*. New York: Dell Publishing, 1967.

Unger, Peter. *Identity, Consciousness, and Value*. New York: Oxford University Press, 1990.

The Virtues: Contemporary Essays on Moral Character. Edited by Robert Kruschwitz and Robert C. Roberts. Belmont, Calif.: Wadsworth, 1986.

Weiss, Robert S. *Loneliness: The Experience of Emotional and Social Isolation*. Cambridge, Mass.: MIT Press, 1973.

Wenz, F. V. "Seasonal Suicide Attempts and Forms of Loneliness." *Psychological Reports* 40 (1977): 807–10.

Williams, Bernard. *Ethics and the Limits of Philosophy*. Cambridge, Mass.: Harvard University Press, 1985.

———. *Moral Luck*. Cambridge: Cambridge University Press, 1981.

———. *Problems of the Self*. Cambridge: Cambridge University Press, 1973.

———. "Replies." In *World, Mind, and Ethics*, edited by J. E. J. Altham and Ross Harrison, 186–94. Cambridge: Cambridge University Press, 1995.

Williams, Bernard, and J. J. C. Smart. *Utilitarianism: For and Against*. Cambridge: Cambridge University Press, 1973.

Wolf, Susan. "Moral Saints." In *The Virtues: Contemporary Essays on Moral Character*, edited by Robert B. Kruschwitz and Robert C. Roberts, 137–52. Belmont, Calif.: Wadsworth, 1986.

Wood, Allen. "The Final Form of Kant's Practical Philosophy." In *Kant's "Metaphysics of Morals,"* edited by Nelson Potter and Mark Timmons. Spindel Conference 1997. *Southern Journal of Philosophy* 36, supplement (1988): 1–20.

World, Mind, and Ethics: Essays on The Ethical Philosophy of Bernard Williams. Edited by J. E. J. Altham and Ross Harrison. Cambridge: Cambridge University Press, 1995.

Index

Text: 10/13 Aldus
Display: Aldus
Composition: G & S Typesetters, Inc.
Printing and binding: Haddon Craftsmen